THE REGIONAL LAW OF REFUGEE PROTECTION IN AFRICA

The Regional Law of Refugee Protection in Africa

MARINA SHARPE

OXFORD
UNIVERSITY PRESS

OXFORD
UNIVERSITY PRESS

Great Clarendon Street, Oxford, OX2 6DP,
United Kingdom

Oxford University Press is a department of the University of Oxford.
It furthers the University's objective of excellence in research, scholarship,
and education by publishing worldwide. Oxford is a registered trade mark of
Oxford University Press in the UK and in certain other countries

First Edition published in 2018

Published in the United States of America by Oxford University Press
198 Madison Avenue, New York, NY 10016, United States of America

British Library Cataloguing in Publication Data
Data available

Library of Congress Control Number: 2018936568

ISBN 978–0–19–882622–4

For my mother Naomi Sharpe, for everything.
And to the memory of Barbara Harrell-Bond.

Foreword

I became a refugee in 1965, at the age of 12. My father represented Malawi at the United Nations. He resigned this post due to the cabinet crisis and we sought safety in Zambia. Threats forced us to flee again, this time to Tanzania. My father worked there as a teacher and I continued my secondary education and went on to study law at the University of Dar es Salaam. In 1988 I returned to Malawi, where I worked for the government as a lawyer, diplomat, High Court judge, and ombudsman. Additionally, gratitude for my family's treatment in Tanzania motivated me to work for Save the Children and the United Nations High Commissioner for Refugees. Today, I am back in Tanzania, as a judge of the African Court on Human and Peoples' Rights.

My family's experience in Tanzania is a testament to the welcome refugees in Africa enjoyed during the sixties. I see it reflected in the 1969 Convention Governing the Specific Aspects of Refugee Problems in Africa, which the Organization of African Unity was drafting during the early years of my family's time in exile. The Convention's preamble begins by noting states' desire to provide refugees 'with a better life and future'. Due to this generous approach, my family's refugee experience did not derail my father's career or my dreams of becoming a diplomat and a lawyer.

If I had been born in 2003 instead of 1953, I fear my experience would have been very different. Today, there are refugee children all over Africa who are not in school. Their parents are often not permitted to work. Families are regularly confined to refugee camps in circumstances of enforced dependency, their most fundamental human rights violated. In this contemporary context, *The Regional Law of Refugee Protection in Africa* is critical.

It is the first treatise on the legal and institutional framework for refugee protection on the continent. We have needed this book for decades. With the fiftieth anniversary of the 1969 Convention's adoption coming up in 2019 and refugee numbers on the rise, *The Regional Law of Refugee Protection in Africa* has been published not a moment too soon.

Drawing on both regional refugee and human rights law, it cogently analyses the rights to which refugees are entitled and articulates the African Union institutional architecture for their implementation. It will equip officials—including me and my colleagues on the bench—with background essential to ensuring that laws, policies, and decisions relating to refugees reflect their rights. It will also assist professors in educating the next generation of refugee advocates and serve as a foundation for further academic work on African refugee law.

The welcome we received in Tanzania ensured that my parents never had to choose between our family's safety and their children's future. *The Regional Law of Refugee Protection in Africa* will contribute to the urgent work we must now do to prevent those who are forced to flee today from facing this terrible choice. I urge all stakeholders to read it and commend Dr Sharpe for writing it.

The Honourable Justice Tujilane R Chizumila
Judge of the African Court on Human and Peoples' Rights
Arusha
March 2018

Acknowledgements

This book is based on my DPhil thesis, which I submitted to the University of Oxford's Faculty of Law in 2016. It would not exist without the generous doctoral scholarship I received from the Pierre Elliott Trudeau Foundation. I am enormously grateful to the Trudeau Foundation's founders, funders, board, and staff, especially Élise Comtois, Jennifer Petrela, Elizabeth Rivera, Morris Rosenberg, and Josée St-Martin. I am also very grateful to my doctoral supervisor, Guy S Goodwin-Gill, for his support and guidance.

My long-time mentor, Barbara Harrell-Bond, undertook the path-breaking work that introduced me (and so many others) to refugee issues and she afforded me several opportunities in the field, to which Alice Edwards and David Cantor have added. Laura Davis, Lee Anne de la Hunt, Carla Ferstman, Elena Fiddian-Qasmiyeh, Karisia Gichuke, Marika Giles-Samson, Emily Lecker, Francesco Messineo, Violeta Moreno-Lax, David Nachfolger, Siobhan O'Connor, Jason Pobjoy, Peter Sahlas, Amy Schwartz, Matthew Scott, Simon Sharpe, Sarah Singer, Tamara Wood, and Ruvi Ziegler were wonderful sounding boards for matters academic, legal, and beyond. Among colleagues, I am especially grateful to Jean-François Durieux, who has been both a collaborator and a mentor.

My interim doctoral examiners, Dapo Akande, Vaughn Lowe, and Stefan Talmon, provided valuable feedback on draft thesis chapters that have become part of this book. I am indebted to my DPhil examiners, Cathryn Costello and Guglielmo Verdirame, whose thorough and perceptive feedback was invaluable as I transformed my thesis into this book. I am also grateful to Erika de Wet, Johnstone Oketch, and the anonymous Oxford University Press referees who provided helpful reviews of my manuscript, and to the Honourable Justice Tujilane Chizumila for writing the foreword. Merel Alstein, Natasha Flemming, Kimberly Marsh, and Jack McNichol of OUP, and OUP's production team, did a wonderful job shepherding this book from proposal through to finished product.

The work of transforming my thesis into this book was mostly undertaken as a Steinberg Post-Doctoral Fellow in International Migration Law and Policy at the Centre for Human Rights and Legal Pluralism, Faculty of Law, McGill University. This was made possible by the late Arnold and the late Blema Steinberg, who created the Fellowship; by François Crépeau, who supervised my work; and by Nandini Ramanujam, who runs the centre. I am also grateful for support from Robert Greenhill, who gave me time to finalize my manuscript alongside our work together.

I am grateful for financial support from Linacre College, Oxford, in the form of the David Daube Scholarship and a travel grant, and from Oxford's Faculty of Law for a travel grant. UNHCR's Policy Development and Evaluation Service funded my archival research in Geneva, which would not have been possible without UNHCR's archivists. UNHCR's Protection Policy and Legal Advice section, Kees Wouters in particular, afforded me several opportunities to participate in policy dialogue and development, which made important intellectual contributions to this book.

This work was informed by years spent working with and for refugees in Africa, as a legal adviser with Africa Middle East Refugee Assistance (AMERA) in Cairo and with the Refugee Law Project (RLP) in Kampala, as legal officer of the International Refugee Rights Initiative in Kampala and as a member of the board of Asylum Access. I am grateful for these experiences and for my colleagues, especially Emily Arnold-Fernandez, Olivia Bueno, Deirdre Clancy, Soo-Ryun Kwon, and Salima Namusobya, from whom I learned a great deal. The book was also enriched by the many people who agreed to be interviewed for my research, including Olabisi Dare, George Okoth-Obbo, and Maya Sahli-Fadel. (Of course, any errors or omissions are solely my own.)

I am indebted to my wonderful husband, William Sillery, for so much, not least the many ways in which he supported me while I completed my doctorate and then this book. I am also very grateful to my late maternal grandparents, Beatrice and Alex Shtull, for enabling several stages of my seemingly unending education.

The path that led to this book was inspired by my late father, Colin Robertson Sharpe, a medical doctor who went on to complete pioneering doctoral and post-doctoral research in cancer epidemiology. I hope my work will one day inspire my daughter, the immaculate Lila River Sillery, as he inspired me.

This book is dedicated to my mother, Naomi Sharpe, for the limitless support she has provided at every stage of my life. I was able to write this book, above all, because of her.

The experiences of my refugee clients at AMERA and RLP motivated this work. I hope it might contribute to assisting those among them who remain in exile and to improving the circumstances of the too many others similarly situated.

Marina Sharpe
Montreal
April 2018

Note on Previous Publication

Parts of Chapters 3 and 4 draw on 'The 1969 African Refugee Convention: Innovations, Misconceptions, and Omissions' (Marina Sharpe (2012) 58 McGill LJ 95). Parts of Chapters 2 and 6 draw on 'Organization of African Unity and African Union Engagement with Refugee Protection: 1963–2011' (Marina Sharpe (2013) 21 Afr J Intl & Comp L 50). Section B in Chapter 4 draws on 'The 1969 OAU Refugee Convention in the Context of Individual Refugee Status Determination' (Marina Sharpe, in Volker Türk, Alice Edwards, and Cornelis Wouters (eds), *In Flight from Conflict and Violence: UNHCR's Consultations on Refugee Status and Other Forms of International Protection* (CUP 2017)).

Summary Table of Contents

II. THE INSTITUTIONAL ARCHITECTURE

Table of Contents

Table of Cases

INTERNATIONAL AND REGIONAL CASES

African Commission on Human and Peoples' Rights

African Court on Human and Peoples' Rights

European Court of Human Rights

International Court of Justice

United Nations Human Rights Committee

NATIONAL CASES

Australia

Egypt

Kenya

Malawi

South Africa

Uganda

United Kingdom

Table of Treaties

Table of Statutes

RWANDA

SENEGAL

SIERRA LEONE

SOMALIA

SOUTH AFRICA

SOUTH SUDAN

SWAZILAND

TANZANIA

TOGO

TUNISIA

UGANDA

ZAMBIA

ZIMBABWE

Acronyms and Abbreviations

1951 Convention	Convention relating to the Status of Refugees
1967 Protocol	Protocol relating to the Status of Refugees
1969 Convention	Convention Governing the Specific Aspects of Refugee Problems in Africa
1969 Event(s)	External aggression, occupation, foreign domination or events seriously disturbing public order
Abuja Treaty	Treaty Establishing the African Economic Community
AEC	African Economic Community
African Charter	African Charter on Human and Peoples' Rights
African Commission	African Commission on Human and Peoples' Rights
African Court	African Court on Human and Peoples' Rights
African Court Protocol	Protocol to the African Charter on Human and Peoples' Rights on the Establishment of the African Court on Human and Peoples' Rights
Arab Convention	Arab Convention on Regulating Status of Refugees in the Arab Countries
Assembly	(AU) Assembly of Heads of State and Government
AU	African Union
Aznar Protocol	Protocol on Asylum for Nationals of Member States of the European Union
BPEAR	(OAU) Bureau for the Placement and Education of African Refugees
CAP	Common African Position on Humanitarian Effectiveness
CAT	Convention against Torture and Other Cruel, Inhuman or Degrading Treatment or Punishment
CCAPRRI	(AU) Coordinating Committee on Assistance and Protection to Refugees, Returnees and Internally Displaced Persons
CCAR	(OAU) Coordinating Committee on Assistance to Refugees
CCFDHA	(AU) Coordinating Committee on Forced Displacement and Humanitarian Action
Children's Charter	African Charter on the Rights and Welfare of the Child
CIDT	Cruel, inhuman or degrading punishment and treatment, within the meaning of article 5 of the African Charter
Commission	(OAU) Commission of Ten/Fifteen/Twenty/the Whole on Refugee Problems in Africa
Committee of Legal Experts	1969 Convention drafting committee
CRRF	Comprehensive Refugee Response Framework
CSSDCA	(AU) Conference on Security, Stability, Development and Cooperation in Africa
DHA	(South Africa's) Department of Home Affairs
DRC	Democratic Republic of the Congo
EAC	East African Community

ECA	(UN) Economic Commission for Africa
ECHR	European Convention for the Protection of Human Rights and Fundamental Freedoms
ECOSOC	(UN) Economic and Social Council
ECOWAS	Economic Community of West African States
ExCom	Executive Committee of the United Nations High Commissioner for Refugees' Programme
EU	European Union
Free Movement Protocol	Protocol to the Treaty Establishing the African Economic Community Relating to Free Movement of Persons, Right of Residence and Right of Establishment
HARDP	AU Commission Department of Political Affairs' Division of Humanitarian Affairs, Refugees and Displaced Persons
HPF	(AU) Humanitarian Policy Framework
HRC	(UN) Human Rights Committee
ICARA	International Conference on Assistance to Refugees in Africa
ICC	International Criminal Court
ICCPR	International Covenant on Civil and Political Rights
ICESCR	International Covenant on Economic, Social and Cultural Rights
ICJ	International Court of Justice
IDP	internally displaced person
IFA	internal flight alternative
IHL	international humanitarian law
ILC	International Law Commission
Kampala Convention	Convention for the Protection and Assistance of Internally Displaced Persons in Africa
Malabo Protocol	Protocol on Amendments to the Protocol on the Statute of the African Court of Justice and Human Rights
Merged Court Protocol	Protocol on the Statute of the African Court of Justice and Human Rights
MPF	(EU) Migration Partnership Framework
Nationality Protocol	Draft Protocol to the African Charter on Human and Peoples' Rights on the Right to a Nationality in Africa
New Merged Court	African Court of Justice and Human and Peoples' Rights
NGO	non-governmental organization
OAHG	(OAU) Assembly of Heads of State and Government
OAU	Organization of African Unity
OAU Charter	Charter of the Organization of African Unity
OCM	(OAU) Council of Ministers
PRC	(AU) Permanent Representatives' Committee
PRC Sub-Committee	(AU) Permanent Representatives' Committee Sub-Committee on Refugees, Returnees and Internally Displaced Persons in Africa
PSC	(AU) Peace and Security Council
PSC Protocol	Protocol Relating to the Establishment of the Peace and Security Council of the African Union
REC	regional economic community
Rome Statute	Rome Statue of the International Criminal Court
RSD	refugee status determination

SADR	Saharawi Arab Democratic Republic
SARRED	International Conference on the Plight of Refugees, Returnees and Displaced Persons in Southern Africa
Special Rapporteur	African Commission Special Rapporteur on Refugees, Asylum Seekers, Internally Displaced Persons and Migrants in Africa
STC	(AU) Specialized Technical Committee
STC on Migration, Refugees and IDPs	Specialized Technical Committee on Migration, Refugees and Internally Displaced Persons
UDHR	Universal Declaration of Human Rights
UN	United Nations
UN Charter	Charter of the United Nations
UNGA	General Assembly of the United Nations
UNHCR	Office of the United Nations High Commissioner for Refugees
UNSC	United Nations Security Council
VCLT	Vienna Convention on the Law of Treaties
WHS	World Humanitarian Summit
Women's Protocol	Protocol to the African Charter on Human and Peoples' Rights on the Rights of Women in Africa

1

Introduction

There are just two legally binding regional refugee protection regimes in the world: in Africa and in Europe. The European Union (EU) began developing its common asylum system in 1999.[1] At the end of 2016, the EU was hosting about eleven per cent of the global refugee[2] population of 17,183,525.[3] European refugee law has been analysed extensively.[4] The Organization of African Unity (OAU, now African Union (AU)) regional regime began developing in 1964. At the end of 2016 AU member states were hosting about thirty-two per cent of the world's refugees, or 5,531,005 individuals.[5] Yet there is little recent academic work on African regional refugee law. The law of refugee protection in Africa has not received scholarly attention commensurate with the scale of displacement on the continent.[6]

This book responds to the gap. Part I construes the regional refugee protection regime as a normative network comprised of international and regional refugee law, and international and regional human rights law. It considers relevant treaties and the relationships between them: between international and regional refugee law, and between regional refugee law and regional human rights law. The regional

[1] European Council, 'Tampere European Council 15 and 16 October 1999: Presidency Conclusions' (15–16 October 1999) <http://www.europarl.europa.eu/summits/tam_en.htm> accessed 3 January 2018.

[2] For the purposes of figures derived from UNHCR Population Statistics Database, 'refugee' includes individuals in a refugee-like situation (individuals granted complementary protection or enjoying temporary protection) and excludes asylum seekers.

[3] In 2016 there were 1,887,348 refugees in the EU (derived from UNHCR's Population Statistics Database <http://popstats.unhcr.org> on 23 November 2017).

[4] See, for example, Olga Ferguson, *The Common European Asylum System: Background, Current State of Affairs, Future Direction* (TMC Asser 2007); Guy S Goodwin-Gill and Hélène Lambert (eds), *The Limits of Transnational Law: Refugee Law, Policy Harmonization and Judicial Dialogue in the European Union* (CUP 2010); Elspeth Guild, *The First Decade of European Union Migration and Asylum Law* (Martinus Nijhoff 2012); Hélène Lambert, Jane McAdam, and Maryellen Fullerton (eds), *The Global Reach of European Refugee Law* (CUP 2013); Violeta Moreno-Lax, *Accessing Asylum in Europe: Extraterritorial Border Controls and Refugee Rights under EU Law* (OUP 2017).

[5] Derived from UNHCR's Population Statistics Database <http://popstats.unhcr.org> on 23 November 2017.

[6] The works describing this displacement situation include Robin Ramcharan, 'The African Refugee Crisis: Contemporary Challenges to the Protection of Refugees and Displaced Persons in Africa' (2000) 8 Afr YB Intl L 119; Bonaventure Rutinwa, 'The End of Asylum? The Changing Nature of Refugee Policies in Africa' (2002) 21 RSQ 12; Jeff Crisp, 'No Solution in Sight: The Problem of Protracted Refugee Situations in Africa' in Itaru Ohta and Yntiso D Gebre (eds), *Displacement Risks in Africa: Refugees, Resettlers and Their Host Population* (Kyoto University Press 2005); and Guglielmo Verdirame and Barbara Harrell-Bond, *Rights in Exile: Janus Faced Humanitarianism* (Berghahn Books 2005).

institutions supportive of this treaty regime are addressed in Part II. This consideration of the regional refugee and human rights law regime, the relationships between these legal instruments, and the institutional architecture supportive of this treaty framework represents the first complete articulation of the regional legal framework for refugee protection in Africa.

This introductory chapter begins by presenting the book's structure in more detail. Section B then delineates the limits of this otherwise broad work. Section C provides context, with a contemporary overview of the state of refugee protection in Africa and in each of its principal geographic sub-regions: East Africa (including the Horn of Africa), Central Africa and the Great Lakes, West Africa, Southern Africa, and North Africa.[7] Section D then concludes with an outline of the theoretical approach to regime relationships employed here, which is detailed in this introduction because it underpins analysis in both Chapters 4 and 5.

A. Structure

Part I, on the regional treaty framework for refugee protection in Africa, contains four chapters. Chapter 2 details the history of the regional refugee instrument: the OAU Convention Governing the Specific Aspects of Refugee Problems in Africa[8] (1969 Convention).[9] It provides brief overviews of the 1969 Convention and of the OAU, the continental organization responsible for its adoption. The 1969 Convention has no official *travaux préparatoires*. Informed by archival research, Chapter 2 sketches a drafting history of the 1969 Convention. Chapter 3 builds upon this basic and historical foundation by analysing key provisions of the 1969 Convention in depth, especially the article I(2) refugee definition, which includes a discussion of prima facie refugee status determination (RSD). Chapter 3 also analyses the extent of an individual's right to asylum under the 1969 Convention; non-refoulment; responsibility sharing, temporary protection, and voluntary repatriation; and the article III prohibition of subversive activities.

Chapter 4 addresses the relationship between the 1969 Convention and its international counterpart, the Convention relating to the Status of Refugees (1951 Convention).[10] This includes both the overall systemic relationship between the two instruments, as well as discrete relationships of interpretation and relationships of conflict between them. Relationships of interpretation are those in which one norm

[7] The sub-regions used here are those employed by UNHCR. East Africa is comprised of Chad, Djibouti, Eritrea, Ethiopia, Kenya, Somalia, Sudan, South Sudan, and Uganda. Central Africa and the Great Lakes is comprised of Burundi, Cameroon, the Central African Republic, the Democratic Republic of the Congo, the Republic of the Congo, Rwanda, and Tanzania. West Africa is comprised of Burkina Faso, Côte d'Ivoire, Ghana, Guinea, Liberia, Mali, Niger, and Senegal. Southern Africa is comprised of Angola, Botswana, Malawi, Mozambique, Namibia, South Africa, Zambia, and Zimbabwe. North Africa is comprised of Algeria, Egypt, Libya, Mauritania, Morocco, Tunisia, and the Saharawi Arab Democratic Republic (SADR) (SADR's statehood is not recognized internationally, but SADR is a member of the AU).

[8] Organization of African Unity Convention Governing the Specific Aspects of Refugee Problems in Africa (adopted 10 September 1969, entered into force 20 June 1974) 1001 UNTS 45.

[9] This treaty is often referred to as the OAU Convention. The AU refers to it officially as the '1969 OAU Convention'. For the sake of brevity, '1969 Convention' is used here.

[10] (Adopted 28 July 1951, entered into force 22 April 1954) 189 UNTS 137.

assists in the interpretation of another.[11] In relationships of conflict, by contrast, two applicable norms point to incompatible conclusions.[12] Chapter 4 analyses the systemic relationship between the 1951 and 1969 Conventions in terms of RSD as well as in relation to refugee rights, and isolated relationships of interpretation and relationships of conflict between the treaties.

Part I concludes in Chapter 5 with a discussion of the role of regional human rights law in refugee protection in Africa. This includes a general discussion of human rights in refugee protection, a more specific discussion of the role of the core African human rights instruments—principally the African Charter on Human and Peoples' Rights[13] (African Charter)—and, finally, analysis of several relationships of interpretation and relationships of conflict between the African Charter and the 1969 Convention. Together, Chapters 2 to 5 portray the regional treaty framework for refugee protection in Africa.

Part II turns to the institutional architecture supportive of this treaty framework. A refugee, by definition, lacks the protection of his or her state of nationality or—in the case of a stateless refugee—former habitual residence, and the duty of protection falls to the host state. In discharging this duty, host states are supported by the Office of the United Nations High Commissioner for Refugees (UNHCR), the mandate of which includes assisting governments in 'seeking permanent solutions for the problem of refugees'[14] and supervising the application of the 1951 Convention.[15]

At the regional level, the AU plays a role similar—though not analogous—to that of UNHCR. The involvement of the AU's predecessor, the OAU, in refugee issues is clearly contemplated by article VII of the 1969 Convention,[16] and the AU, as well as the OAU before it, have engaged consistently with refugee issues.[17] Moreover, considering the AU as part of the institutional architecture for refugee protection in Africa is responsive to Heyns and Viljoen's call for a 'holistic view of human rights protection in Africa', which includes human rights roles for AU structures beyond just the African Commission on Human and Peoples' Rights (African Commission) and the African Court on Human and Peoples' Rights (African Court).[18] Just as no treatment of refugee protection on the international plane would be complete without discussing UNHCR, this discussion of refugee protection in Africa necessarily addresses the OAU and the AU. It does so across two chapters, which together form Part II of this book.

[11] International Law Commission, 'Conclusions of the Work of the Study Group on the Fragmentation of International Law: Difficulties Arising from the Diversification and Expansion of International Law' (2006) 2 UNYBILC 175 175 (ILC) para 2.

[12] ibid. [13] (Adopted 27 June 1981, entered into force 21 October 1986) 21 ILM 58.

[14] UNGA Res 428 (V) (14 December 1950) Annex, para 1.

[15] 1951 Convention (n 10) art 35.

[16] Under article VII, states parties are required to provide the OAU with 'information and statistical data' to enable the OAU's Administrative Secretary-General to 'make reports' to competent OAU organs.

[17] See Chapter 6.

[18] Christof Heyns and Frans Viljoen, 'An Overview of International Human Rights Protection in Africa' (1999) 15 S Afr J Hum Rts 421, 433.

The first chapter in Part II, Chapter 6, addresses the historical role of the OAU, and the contemporary role of the AU, in refugee issues in Africa. Chapter 7 then covers the refugee roles of AU judicial bodies with human rights mandates. These are the African Commission, as well as the current and contemplated African human rights courts: the operational African Court and the theoretical African Court of Justice and Human Rights and African Court of Justice and Human and Peoples' Rights.

Chapter 8 completes the book with a summary of its main assertions and some concluding reflections. This book reflects legal and factual information available as of 1 January 2018.

B. Contours

The contours of this book are delineated in four respects. Firstly, while refugees in Africa are, of course, entitled to the protection of international human rights law—regional human rights law applies alongside, and in addition to, cognate legal frameworks on the international plane—the explicit treatment of human rights law is limited here to the regional legal framework. The role of international human rights law in refugee protection has been addressed elsewhere,[19] indeed with a call for others to 'build upon this basic analysis to define the entitlements of sub-groups of the refugee population entitled to claim additional protections'.[20]

Secondly, several sub-regional arrangements in Africa, including regional economic communities—such as the East African Community and the Economic Community of West African States—include human rights protection[21] or otherwise affect refugees,[22] especially insofar as they allow sub-regional freedom of movement.[23] Such sub-regional arrangements are beyond the scope of this work, which focuses exclusively on the regional plane, but their role in and impact upon refugee protection in Africa constitutes an important avenue for further research.

Thirdly, UNHCR's role in Africa is not addressed. The focus here is on the regional regime. This is supported by, but strictly speaking does not include, international organizations such as UNHCR. Furthermore, UNHCR's work in Africa was recently covered elsewhere.[24]

[19] James C Hathaway, *The Rights of Refugees Under International Law* (CUP 2005).

[20] ibid 8.

[21] See Frans Viljoen, 'The Realization of Human Rights in Africa Through Sub-regional Institutions' (1999) 7 Afr YB Intl L 186; Frans Viljoen, *International Human Rights Law in Africa* (2nd edn, OUP 2012) chap 11.

[22] See, for example, Jeremy Levitt, 'Conflict Prevention, Management, and Resolution: Africa–Regional Strategies for the Prevention of Displacement and Protection of Displaced Persons: The Cases of the OAU, ECOWAS, SADC and IGAD' (2001) 11 Duke J Comp & Intl L 39; 'Regional Governance, Migration, and Social Protection in Africa and Europe: a Special Issue of Regions & Cohesion' (2014) 3 Regs & Cohesion.

[23] In this regard, see, for example, Aderanti Adepoju, Alistair Boulton, and Mariah Levin, 'Promoting Integration Through Mobility: Free Movement under ECOWAS' (2010) 10 RSQ 120.

[24] Cristiano D'Orsi, *Asylum-Seeker and Refugee Protection in Sub-Saharan Africa: The Peregrination of a Persecuted Human Being in Search of a Safe Haven* (Routledge 2015) chap 5.

Finally, this book is about the law of refugee protection in Africa, not about the practical dimensions of refugee issues there, nor about policy solutions to such challenges. While the law, of course, has a critical role to play in resolving refugee problems, in that all action in favour of refugees must be guided by the legal framework, this work is focused on articulating that legal framework as such, rather than on describing forced displacement in Africa or on prescribing policy to respond to related challenges.

C. Refugees in Africa

While this work is about the law of refugee protection in Africa and not about the practical state or the policy of refugee protection there, the law must be situated within the context in which it applies. It is, however, difficult to generalize about the state of refugee protection on the continent. While Africa is subject to a uniform regional legal regime (save for variations due to states' individual treaty ratifications and reservations), displacement and protection trends vary from one country to the next and from one sub-region to the other. This section nevertheless attempts to summarize the contemporary state of refugee protection in Africa and in each of its sub-regions, and to situate the current context in some historical perspective.

Africa's approach to refugees was for decades described as exemplarily hospitable. UNHCR, for example, characterized the 'generosity of hosting countries in Africa' as 'outstanding',[25] while others have referred to the sixties, seventies, and eighties as a 'golden age' of asylum in Africa.[26] Crisp describes this period as follows:

> Governments allowed large numbers of refugees to enter and remain on their territory. Many refugees enjoyed reasonably secure living conditions and were able to benefit from a range of legal, social, and economic rights. Considerable numbers of refugees were provided with land and encouraged to become self-sufficient. In some States, refugees were allowed to settle permanently and to become naturalised citizens. While the deportation and expulsion of refugees was not unknown, the principle of voluntary repatriation was broadly respected.[27]

This generosity can be attributed to the conditions in the decades of and following decolonization. Refugees were relatively few and were mostly a product of independence struggles and wars of national liberation. As a result, they were welcomed by newly independent states in the spirit of pan-Africanism and anti-colonialism prevailing at the time. Furthermore, African states were more prosperous than they are today, and their support of refugees was recognized in international assistance packages.[28]

[25] UNHCR, 'UNHCR Global Appeal 2015 Update' <http://www.unhcr.org/ga15/index.xml> accessed 24 September 2015, 108.

[26] See, for example, Jeff Crisp, 'Forced Displacement in Africa: Dimensions, Difficulties, and Policy Directions' (2010) 29 RSQ 1, 3.

[27] ibid. [28] ibid 4.

These conditions and the generosity they engendered no longer prevail.[29] While African states still produce and host refugees, 'the ideological and material underpinnings of Africa's tradition of hospitality towards refugees' have, since the nineties, been 'progressively dismantled'.[30] The decline in the quality of refugee protection in Africa has occurred because of the effect of significant increases in the number of people displaced on the continent combined with several internal and external factors.

Displacement generally no longer stems from anti-colonial struggles, but from internal conflict and sub-regional crises that have forced unprecedented numbers of people from their homes. Today, such situations include the Lake Chad basin (Cameroon, Chad, Niger, and Nigeria) health and nutrition crisis, conflict in the Central African Republic, near-famine conditions in the Horn of Africa, ongoing internal strife in Somalia, and the conflict in South Sudan.

The international community has not done its part to respond to the rising displacement generated by these crises and other such situations. Industrialized states have since the eighties introduced a range of measures, such as visa regimes and carrier sanctions, to prevent refugee arrivals. In addition, financial responsibility sharing in the form of rich states sharing the cost of refugee hosting with African countries is on the wane. The financial squeeze is exacerbated by low rates of economic growth in some African states.

Internally, African states increasingly view refugees as a threat to political security and social stability, especially in the context of relief efforts that sometimes privilege refugees over their local hosts, which has contributed to xenophobia and anti-refugee sentiment. Additionally, African states now sometimes view refugees as threats to national security and diplomatic relations.

The declining quality of refugee protection in Africa has led to several practical protection problems, including

> cases of refoulement and/or denial of access to asylum; weak national legal and institutional mechanisms in the protection of refugees; non-enjoyment by refugees of basic rights such as freedom of movement and right to work, [and a lack of] access to basic services including health and education; SGBV [sexual and gender-based violence]; inability to attain self-sufficiency and build livelihoods; [and] difficulty to ensure the sustainability of return and reintegration.[31]

Certain protection issues have risen to the level of becoming significant continental displacement trends. Many refugee situations in Africa are now protracted, meaning they involve a refugee population numbering over 25,000 and have persisted for five or more years.[32] For example, in 2015 there were about half a million Somali refugees in Kenya's Dadaab camp complex, some of whom had been there since the

[29] Rutinwa (n 6); Crisp (n 26); Jacob van Garderen and Julie Ebenstein, 'Regional Developments: Africa' in Andreas Zimmermann (ed), *The 1951 Convention Relating to the Status of Refugees and its 1967 Protocol* (OUP 2011).

[30] Crisp (n 26) 5; see, also, Rutinwa (n 6) 12.

[31] UNHCR (n 25) 114.

[32] Crisp (n 26) 13.

facility was established in 1991.[33] The challenge of hosting large refugee populations over many years has led states in Africa to increasingly settle refugees in camps. They are a very visible reminder to donors of how some of the world's poorest states are hosting the greatest number of refugees, and camps also create pressure aimed at inducing refugees to repatriate. Four of the largest refugee camps in the world—Ethiopia's Dollo Ado, Kenya's Dadaab and Kakuma and Uganda's Bidi Bidi—are in Africa.

The trends of protracted refugee situations and widespread encampment are nowhere more pronounced than in East Africa, the sub-region with the continent's largest refugee population. At the end of 2016, there were 3,290,324 refugees in East Africa,[34] mainly from the Democratic Republic of the Congo (DRC), Somalia, and South Sudan.[35] As with the continent as a whole, refugee movements in East Africa were historically linked to independence struggles.[36] Today, forced displacement within and to East Africa is largely a result of conflict, principally in Somalia (in 2016, nearly one million of East Africa's refugees were from Somalia),[37] South Sudan (at the end of 2016, there were 1.4 million South Sudanese refugees),[38] Sudan (at the end of 2016, there were 650,000 refugees from Sudan),[39] and Yemen (95,000 Yemenis have fled to Djibouti, Ethiopia, Somalia, and Sudan since 2015).[40]

A significant portion of East Africa's Somali refugee population resides in Kenya's Dadaab complex, which had 238,617 registered inhabitants as of October 2017.[41] This encamped population accounts for more than half of Kenya's total refugee population, which at the end of 2016 was 451,099.[42] Kenya's refugee population is the third largest in East Africa after Uganda, which at end-2016 was hosting 940,835 refugees[43] (including 640,000 from South Sudan),[44] and Ethiopia, which at end-2016 had 791,631 refugees.[45]

Midway through 2015 the major refugee protection challenges in East Africa were food insecurity, a shortage of land, limits on humanitarian access, and restrictions on

[33] Ben Rawlence, 'The Other Refugee Crisis' *The New York Times* (9 October 2015) <https://www.nytimes.com/2015/10/10/opinion/the-other-refugee-crisis.html> accessed 25 April 2017.

[34] Derived from UNHCR's Population Statistics Database <http://popstats.unhcr.org> on 24 November 2017.

[35] UNGA, 'Assistance to Refugees, Returnees and Displaced Persons in Africa, Report of the Secretary General' (22 August 2017) UN Doc A/72/354, para 6.

[36] Gaim Kibreab, 'Forced Migration in the Great Lakes and Horn of Africa' in Elena Fiddian-Qasmiyeh and others (eds), *The Oxford Handbook of Refugee and Forced Migration Studies* (OUP 2014) 573.

[37] UNGA (n 35) para 7; in this connection, in 2013, UNHCR launched the Global Initiative on Somali Refugees.

[38] ibid para 8. [39] ibid para 10. [40] ibid para 6.

[41] UNHCR, 'Dadaab Refugee Complex' <http://www.unhcr.org/ke/dadaab-refugee-complex> accessed 23 November 2017.

[42] UNHCR, 'Global Focus: Kenya' <http://reporting.unhcr.org/node/2537> accessed 23 November 2017.

[43] UNHCR, 'Global Focus: Uganda' <http://reporting.unhcr.org/node/5129> accessed 23 November 2017.

[44] UNGA (n 35) para 8.

[45] UNHCR, 'Global Focus: Ethiopia' <http://reporting.unhcr.org/node/5738> accessed 23 November 2017.

refugees' freedom of movement.[46] The latter is a particularly significant challenge. While East African governments have always been hostile to refugee freedom of movement and residence, from the sixties until the mid-eighties, they nevertheless allowed refugees to self-settle.[47] However, halfway through the eighties, governments in the sub-region began to enforce encampment. This policy reached its high point in the aftermath of the Rwandan genocide and continues to this day.

East Africa is the first (and currently the only) sub-regional site for the roll out of the global Comprehensive Refugee Response Framework (CRRF). The CRRF emerged from the New York Declaration for Refugees and Migrants,[48] which was the result of a high-level summit on refugee and migration issues convened by the UN General Assembly in September 2016 with a view to improving international responses to large-scale movements of refugees and migrants. The CRRF will be developed by UNHCR further to initial elements relating to reception and admission; support for immediate and ongoing needs; support for host countries and communities; and durable solutions.[49] Programming around these initial elements is currently being rolled out in Djibouti, Ethiopia, and Uganda, as well as in relation to the Somali situation (Tanzania announced its withdrawl from the CRRF in February 2018). Among CRRF activities, in June 2017 Uganda, together with UNHCR, hosted the Solidarity Summit on Refugees, where high-level delegates pledged political, technical, and financial support to assist Uganda in refugee protection.[50] The next phase of the African CRRF roll-out will encompass Malawi, Rwanda, and Zambia, with a view to eventually covering the entire continent.

At the end of 2016 there were 1,380,901 refugees in the Central Africa and Great Lakes sub-region,[51] the majority of whom fled conflict or unrest in Burundi, the Central African Republic and the eastern DRC.[52] Since political violence erupted in Burundi in April 2015, over 417,000 people have fled the country for the DRC, Rwanda, Tanzania, and Uganda.[53] The Burundi situation was dwarfed, however, by the conflict in the Central African Republic, which as of mid-2016 had produced about 481,000 refugees, who fled to Cameroon, Chad, the Congo, and the DRC.[54] By the end of 2016 ongoing conflict in the DRC, particularly in the Kasai region, had displaced nearly 570,000 Congolese.[55]

At the end of 2016 there were 267,973 refugees in West Africa.[56] The principal causes of displacement in the region include human rights violations; intercommunal clashes, including between pastoral and sedentary farmers over land; near-famine

[46] UNGA, 'Assistance to Refugees, Returnees and Displaced Persons in Africa, Report of the Secretary General' (20 August 2016) UN Doc A/70/337, para 4.

[47] Kibreab (n 36) 579.

[48] UNGA Res 71/1 (16 September 2019) UN Doc A/RES/71/1. [49] ibid Annex I.

[50] For more information on the CRRF and its activities, see the CRRF Global Digital Portal at <http://crrf.unhcr.org/en/>.

[51] Derived from UNHCR's Population Statistics Database <http://popstats.unhcr.org> on 24 November 2017.

[52] UNGA (n 46) paras 10–15. [53] UNGA (n 35) para 11. [54] ibid para 13.

[55] ibid para 15.

[56] Derived from UNHCR's Population Statistics Database <http://popstats.unhcr.org> on 24 November 2017.

conditions in the Lake Chad basin; and a volatile security situation in central and northern Mali.[57] More generally, Fresia identifies conflict, expulsion caused by economic crises, and the trafficking of minors as key causes of displacement in the West Africa sub-region.[58] Most recently, the Boko Haram crisis and EU efforts to externalize migration control, particularly in Niger, have contributed to displacement dynamics in West Africa.

At the end of 2016 there were 161,127 refugees in Southern Africa.[59] Historically, refugees in this sub-region fled civil wars—resulting predominantly from white minority rule—within Southern Africa. Over the past twenty years, however, there has been a steady increase in arrivals from further afield on the continent,[60] with refugees heading mainly for South Africa. Protection activities in the sub-region focus on reducing xenophobia and statelessness, strengthening national asylum systems, promoting refugees' self-reliance,[61] and addressing mixed migration.[62]

At the end of 2016 there were 396,511 refugees in North Africa.[63] As a result of instability, relative proximity to Europe, and the presence of smugglers, states in North Africa—Libya in particular—have historically been transit, rather than final, destinations. However, recent EU and Italian efforts to prevent refugees from reaching Europe via the Mediterranean mean that states in North Africa are increasingly hosting refugees and other migrants, sometimes in horrific conditions. The situation in Libya is particularly dire. In 2017 reports emerged of refugees and other migrants in Libya being auctioned in underground slave markets.[64] In response to this and other severe abuses, in November 2017 Rwanda offered to resettle up to 30,000 African refugees and migrants from Libya, constituting a rare example of intra-African resettlement. Additionally, the AU and EU agreed at their Côte d'Ivoire summit to an urgent evacuation of refugees and migrants from Libyan detention camps, with UNHCR and the International Organization for Migration effectuating the evacuation missions.[65]

In addition to the population in Libya, North Africa's refugee population also includes a sizeable population of individuals from Eritrea, Ethiopia, Somalia, South Sudan, and Sudan in Egypt;[66] about 46,000 Malian refugees in Mbera camp in Mauritania; and about 165,000 Saharawi refugees living in five camps near Tindouf,

57 UNGA (n 35) paras 14–16.

58 Marion Fresia, 'Forced Migration in West Africa' in Elena Fiddian-Qasmiyeh and others (eds), *The Oxford Handbook of Refugee and Forced Migration Studies* (OUP 2014) 543.

59 Derived from UNHCR's Population Statistics Database <http://popstats.unhcr.org> on 24 November 2017.

60 Jonathan Crush and Abel Chikanda, 'Forced Migration in Southern Africa' in Elena Fiddian-Qasmiyeh and others (eds), *The Oxford Handbook of Refugee and Forced Migration Studies* (OUP 2014) 560.

61 UNGA (n 46) para 18.

62 UNGA (n 35) para 18.

63 Derived from UNHCR's Population Statistics Database <http://popstats.unhcr.org> on 24 November 2017.

64 See, for example, Nima Elbagir, Raja Razek, Alex Platt, and Bryony Jones, 'People for Sale: Where Lives are Auctioned for $400' *CNN* (no date) <http://edition.cnn.com/2017/11/14/africa/libya-migrant-auctions/index.html> accessed 23 November 2017.

65 BBC, 'Libya Migrants: Emergency Evacuations Operation Agreed' (30 November 2017) <http://www.bbc.com/news/world-africa-42179434> accessed 27 December 2017.

66 See Neil Brown, Sean Riordan, and Marina Sharpe, 'The Insecurity of Eritreans and Ethiopians in Cairo' (2004) 16 IJRL 661.

Algeria. The Western Sahara refugee situation is among the most protracted in the world.[67]

D. Approach to Regime Relationships

The concurrent applicability of regional refugee and human rights law to refugees in Africa results in both apparent and genuine norm conflicts, as is demonstrated in Chapters 4 and 5. Chapter 4 treats the relationship between the 1951 and 1969 Conventions and raises several conflicts between the two refugee instruments. The Chapter 5 discussion of regional human rights law in refugee protection raises several conflicts between the African Charter and the 1969 Convention.

The approach to conflicts adopted here is that postulated by the International Law Commission (ILC) in its Fragmentation Report.[68] The Report was produced in response to concerns 'that specialized law-making and institution-building tends to take place with relative ignorance of legislative and institutional activities in the adjoining fields and of the general principles and practices of international law. The result is conflicts between rules or rule-systems, deviating institutional practices and, possibly, the loss of an overall perspective on the law'.[69] In addressing such concerns, the Fragmentation Report seeks to answer three questions: 'What is the nature of specialized rule-systems? How should their relations inter se be conceived? Which rules should govern their conflicts?'.[70] The Report's responses to questions two and three govern the resolution of the apparent and genuine norm conflicts that arise in Chapters 4 and 5. Because such conflicts arise across two chapters, the ILC's approach to norm conflicts is outlined at the outset in this introduction.

The Fragmentation Report 'adopts a wide notion of conflict as a situation where two rules or principles suggest different ways of dealing with a problem'.[71] The same conception is employed here. This broad notion of conflict must, however, be understood in the context of the strong presumption in international law against normative conflict.[72] As a result of this presumption, the ILC's starting point for resolving norm conflicts is to seek to harmonize apparently conflicting standards through interpretation.[73] In this regard, determining the relationship of two or more norms to each other is essentially a process of treaty interpretation, conducted in accordance with the Vienna Convention on the Law of Treaties'[74] (VCLT) articles 31 to 33[75]—in particular the principle of systemic integration enshrined at article 31(3)(c)—and bearing in mind any conflict clauses in the treaties under interpretation.[76]

[67] Sari Hanafi, 'Forced Migration in the Middle East and North Africa' in Elena Fiddian-Qasmiyeh and others (eds), *The Oxford Handbook of Refugee and Forced Migration Studies* (OUP 2014) 589.

[68] ILC, 'Fragmentation of International Law: Difficulties Arising From the Diversification and Expansion of International Law—Report of the Study Group of the International Law Commission' (13 April 2006) A/CN4/L682 (Fragmentation Report).

[69] ibid para 8. [70] ibid para 483. [71] ibid para 25. [72] ibid para 37.

[73] ibid para 24.

[74] (Adopted 23 May 1969, entered into force 27 January 1980) 1155 UNTS 331.

[75] ILC (n 11) para 3. [76] ibid para 30.

According to the principle of systemic integration, a treaty does not operate 'in a vacuum', but rather 'in the context of a wider framework of legal rules of which it forms only a part'.[77] In other words, a treaty must be interpreted so as to cohere with the broader normative context in which it applies.

The ILC's focus on harmonization through systemic integration has been affirmed by subsequent scholarship, which has for the most part sought to 'dispel persisting myths surrounding the fragmentation debate';[78] one scholar has even suggested that 'it is time to bury the f-word'.[79] Indeed, in the current thinking, 'convergence and unity are becoming more of a dominating feature of international law discourse than the claims to autonomy and specificity of different regimes'.[80] That said, there is a limit to harmonization, which can resolve apparent norm conflicts but not genuine ones.[81] An apparent conflict gives way to a genuine norm conflict when interpretation cannot harmonize the apparent conflict away. In such circumstances, the ILC approach requires that definite relationships of priority be established.

Relationships of priority are established by applying one of three interpretive maxims: *lex specialis*, which prioritizes specificity; *lex posterior*, which prioritizes more recent norms; and *lex superior*, which prioritizes hierarchically superior norms.[82] According to *lex specialis*, if 'two or more norms deal with the same subject matter, priority should be given to the norm that is more specific'.[83] *Lex posterior* expresses the rule found in article 30 of the VCLT, which provides that when the parties to a treaty are also party to an earlier treaty concerned with the same matter and the earlier treaty has not been suspended or terminated, then the earlier treaty applies only to the extent that it is compatible with the later treaty.[84] *Lex superior* relates to status. As there is no general hierarchy of sources in international law, *lex superior* is only relevant regarding conflicts between or among *jus cogens*, obligations *erga omnes* and/or article 103 of the Charter of the United Nations,[85] which are hierarchical in the order mentioned.

Neither *lex specialis* nor *lex posterior* 'can be regarded as of absolute validity. There are a number of principles which must be weighed and reconciled in the light of the circumstances of the particular case'.[86] Among these principles are that, as

[77] *Interpretation of the Agreement of 25 March 1951 between the WHO and Egypt* (Advisory Opinion) ICJ Rep 1980, 73, para 10.

[78] Violeta Moreno-Lax, 'Systematising Systemic Integration: "War Refugees", Regime Relations, and a Proposal for a Cumulative Approach to International Commitments' (2014) 12 J Intl Crim Justice 907, 907.

[79] Anne Peters, 'The Refinement of International Law: From Fragmentation to Regime Interaction and Politicization' (2016) Max Planck Institute for Comparative Public Law & International Law Research Paper No 2016-19 <https://papers.ssrn.com/sol3/papers.cfm?abstract_id=2823512> accessed 20 December 2016, 1.

[80] Mads Andenas and Eirik Bjorge, 'Introduction: From Fragmentation to Convergence in International Law' in Mads Andenas and Eirik Bjorge (eds), *A Farewell to Fragmentation* (CUP 2015) 2.

[81] Christopher J Borgen, 'Resolving Treaty Conflicts' (2005) 37 Geo Wash Intl LR 573, 605–06.

[82] Fragmentation Report (n 68) para 412.

[83] ILC (n 11) para 5.

[84] ibid para 24.

[85] Charter of the United Nations (adopted 26 June 1945, entered into force 24 October 1945) 1 UNTS XVI.

[86] CW Jenks, 'The Conflict of Law-Making Treaties' (1953) 30 B YB Intl L 401, 407.

mentioned earlier in this section, *lex posterior* does not usually apply unless the parties to the treaties under consideration are the same,[87] and it may not apply when the treaties under consideration do not form part of the same regime.[88] The most generally applicable interpretive maxim is therefore *lex specialis*. It may not, however, be applied if the nature of the more general law or party intent suggests that it would not be appropriate for the more specialist norm to prevail, if the application of the more specialist law would frustrate the purpose of the general law, or if third-party beneficiaries or the balance of rights and obligations established by the more general law would be negatively affected by the application of *lex specialis*.[89] When *lex specialis* is invoked, the more general law is not extinguished. Rather, it continues to operate 'in the background, continuing to influence the interpretation and application of the norm to which priority has been given'.[90]

Further to this ILC-sanctioned approach, the relationships of interpretation identified here will be articulated using traditional modes of treaty interpretation. Relationships of conflict will be resolved through harmonization or, failing that, using the relevant interpretive maxim. Before turning to these relationships, however, the focus is on elucidating the instrument at the core of the legal regime for refugee protection in Africa: the 1969 Convention. Chapter 2 provides an overview of the 1969 Convention and the organization responsible for its adoption, and situates it in new historical perspective; Chapter 3 then analyses the 1969 Convention in depth.

[87] ILC (n 11) para 25. [88] ibid para 26. [89] ibid para 10.
[90] Fragmentation Report (n 68) para 411.

PART I

THE TREATY FRAMEWORK

2

The Drafting of the 1969 Convention

A. Introduction

Analyses of the Organization of African Unity Convention Governing the Specific Aspects of Refugee Problems in Africa[1] (1969 Convention) have been constrained by the lack of *travaux préparatoires*. The absence of any official account of the Convention's elaboration has led to speculation about the factors that prompted the Organization of African Unity (OAU) to embark upon the project of adopting a regional refugee instrument. One myth has dominated the discourse: that the OAU's interest in a regional refugee instrument was a result of the inability of the persecution-based Convention relating to the Status of Refugees (1951 Convention)[2] refugee definition to respond to African realities.[3] Relying on the resolutions of OAU bodies, material in the archives of the Office of the United Nations High Commissioner for Refugees (UNHCR),[4] and the three secondary sources that have considered the 1969 Convention's drafting in depth[5]—the most valuable of which is largely overlooked in the literature[6]—this chapter corrects this misconception and provides a more complete legal history of the 1969 Convention. In addition to its contribution to the historical record, this chapter provides a foundation for understanding the 1969 Convention, which is discussed in more detail in Chapter 3, the relationship between the 1951 and 1969 Conventions, which is the subject of Chapter 4, and the

[1] (Adopted 10 September 1969, entered into force 20 June 1974) 1001 UNTS 45.

[2] (Adopted 28 July 1951, entered into force 22 April 1954) 189 UNTS 137.

[3] George Okoth-Obbo, 'Thirty Years On: A Legal Review of the 1969 OAU Convention Governing the Specific Aspects of Refugee Problems in Africa' (2001) 20 RSQ 79, 109; see, for example, Ousmane Goundiam, 'African Refugee Convention' [1970] Migr News 3, 8; Jennifer Hyndman and Bo Victor Nylund, 'UNHCR and the Status of Prima Facie Refugees in Kenya' (1998) 10 IJRL 21, 34–35; Jamil Ddamulira Mujuzi, 'The African Commission on Human and Peoples' Rights and the Promotion and Protection of Refugees' Rights' (2009) 9 Afr Hum Rts LJ 160, 163; Rachel Murray, 'Refugees and Internally Displaced Persons and Human Rights: the African System' (2005) 24 RSQ 56, 57; Jennifer L Turner, 'Liberian Refugees: a Test of the 1969 OAU Convention Governing the Specific Aspects of Refugee Problems in Africa' (1994) 8 Geo Immigr LJ 281, 286.

[4] Archival research was conducted in June 2011 at UNHCR headquarters in Geneva.

[5] Louise W Holborn, *Refugees: A Problem of our Time—The Work of the United Nations High Commissioner for Refugees, 1951–1972*, vol I and II (Scarecrow Press 1974); Ivor C Jackson, *The Refugee Concept in Group Situations* (Martinus Nijhoff 1999); Okoth-Obbo (n 3).

[6] This is Holborn (n 5).

roles of the OAU and African Union (AU) in refugee issues on the continent, which is addressed in Chapter 6.

The chapter begins with overviews of the OAU and the 1969 Convention. The majority of the chapter is then devoted to sketching a drafting history of the 1969 Convention. This reveals that the initial impetus for a regional refugee instrument was to render international refugee law applicable in Africa and to address the issue of subversion. When the former was achieved in 1967 with the adoption of the Protocol relating to the Status of Refugees[7] (1967 Protocol), addressing refugee issues particular to Africa became the focus of the drafting initiative.

B. The OAU

The OAU was established on 25 May 1963 with the adoption of its Charter (OAU Charter), to promote regional cooperation among newly independent African states. The organization's specific purposes were to promote the unity and solidarity of African states; coordination and cooperation among them to improve the lives of African peoples; defence of their sovereignty, territorial integrity, and independence; the eradication of all forms of colonialism; and the promotion of international cooperation.[8] Added to these goals were those relating to economic integration articulated in the Treaty Establishing the African Economic Community,[9] which from 1994 constituted a second legal basis of OAU operations.

The OAU was not a legislative body. Rather, the OAU was to achieve the abovementioned objectives primarily through the harmonization of member state policies.[10] This occurred through the Assembly of Heads of State and Government (OAHG), the OAU's 'supreme organ', the role of which was to 'discuss matters of common concern to Africa with a view to coordinating and harmonizing the general policy of the Organization'.[11] The work of the OAHG was operationalized by the Council of Ministers (OCM or the Council), composed of member states' foreign or other ministers and charged with implementing OAHG decisions and coordinating inter-African cooperation in accordance with OAHG instructions.[12] In addition to the OAHG and the OCM, the OAU was also composed of an Addis Ababa-based General Secretariat and a Commission of Mediation, Conciliation and Arbitration.[13] The latter body was, however, never operationalized. Rather, it 'remained dormant from the first day of its establishment because member states have shown a strong preference for political process of conflict resolution rather than for judicial means of settlement'.[14] Other bodies followed later in the organization's

[7] (Adopted 31 January 1967, entered into force 4 October 1967) 606 UNTS 267.

[8] Charter of the Organization of African Unity (25 May 1963) 479 UNTS 39, art II(1).

[9] (Adopted 3 June 1991, entered into force 12 May 1994) 30 ILM 1241.

[10] Tiyanjana Maluwa, 'International Law Making in the Organization of African Unity: An Overview' (2000) 12 Afr J Intl Comp L 201, 201.

[11] OAU Charter (n 8) art VIII. [12] ibid art XIII. [13] ibid art VII.

[14] International Panel of Eminent Personalities, 'Rwanda: The Preventable Genocide' (OAU 2000) para 11.4.

development. For example, in 1993 the Mechanism of Conflict Prevention, Management and Resolution was established to prevent and address conflict.[15]

The OAU eventually came to be viewed as ineffective. Zard explains that its rigorous adherence to the principle of non-interference in the internal affairs of member states,[16] its subordination to state interest, and its persistent financial difficulties often precluded it from 'asserting any form of moral authority or leadership in tackling some of Africa's chronic problems'.[17] This was especially the case in light of modern challenges facing the continent. Having focused on decolonization and liberation from minority rule and firmly committed to non-interference, the OAU was not equipped to deal effectively with contemporary issues such as conflict and economic growth.

The first major move to revitalize the regional organization came in 1999 with the Sirte Declaration, which set out plans to establish what would become the AU.[18] This new body was born—superseding the OAU and incorporating the African Economic Community—on 26 May 2001, with the entry into force of its Constitutive Act.[19] At this time, all assets and liabilities of, and all matters relating to, the OAU devolved to the new AU.[20]

C. Overview of the 1969 Convention

The 1969 Convention is the regional legal instrument governing refugee protection in Africa. It was adopted on 10 September 1969 at the 6th Ordinary Session of the OAHG, when it was signed by forty-one heads of state or government. It entered into force on 20 June 1974 after ratification by one-third of OAU member states.[21] It has since been ratified by forty-six of the AU's fifty-five member states,[22] making it one of Africa's most widely ratified regional instruments; only the AU's Constitutive Act and the African Charter on Human and Peoples' Rights have more ratifications.

The 1969 Convention contains a preamble and fifteen articles. Article I provides two refugee definitions. The first[23] replicates the 1951 Convention refugee definition[24] as amended by the 1967 Protocol, while the second is unique to the 1969

[15] OAU, 'Declaration of the Assembly of Heads of State and Government on the Establishment Within the OAU of a Mechanism for Conflict Prevention, Management and Resolution' (1994) 13 RSQ 174; see Chris J Bakwesegha, 'The Role of the Organization of African Unity in Conflict Prevention, Management and Resolution' (Special Issue 1995) 7 IJRL 207.

[16] OAU Charter (n 8) art III(2), which lists 'Non-interference in the internal affairs of States' as a principle of the Union.

[17] Monette Zard, 'African Union' in Matthew Gibney and Randall Hansen (eds), *Immigration and Asylum From 1900 to the Present* (ABC-CLIO 2005) 6–7.

[18] OAU (OAHG), 'Sirte Declaration' (OAU Sirte 9 Sept 1999) AHG/Draft/Decl (IV) Rev 1.

[19] Constitutive Act of the African Union (adopted 11 July 2000, entered into force 26 May 2001) 2158 UNTS 3 (AU Constitutive Act). The AU is discussed in Chapter 6.

[20] OAHG, 'Decision on the Interim Period' (AU Durban 9–10 July 2002) ASS/AU/Dec.1-8(I) para 2.

[21] 1969 Convention (n 1) art XI.

[22] For ratification information, see section D.5 of this chapter.

[23] 1969 Convention (n 1) art I(1).

[24] 1951 Convention (n 2) art 1A(2).

Convention. It provides that the 'term "refugee" shall also apply to every person who, owing to external aggression, occupation, foreign domination or events seriously disturbing public order in either part or the whole of his country of origin or nationality, is compelled to leave his place of habitual residence in order to seek refuge in another place outside his country of origin or nationality'.[25] This definition is addressed in depth in Chapter 3.

The third paragraph of article I, like the 1951 Convention, prevents a person with more than one nationality from being recognized as a refugee if he or she has not availed him or herself of the protection of each such state of nationality, unless he or she has a valid reason based on well-founded fear. This is accomplished by defining 'a country of which he is a national',[26] though the precise language of article I(2) is 'country of ... nationality'. This incongruence is an isolated instance of poor drafting in what is otherwise a well-written legal instrument.

Article I also covers cessation[27] and exclusion.[28] These two paragraphs largely mirror the 1951 Convention,[29] with some additions and omissions. Two additional cessation clauses provide that the 1969 Convention shall cease to apply to any refugee who has 'committed a serious non-political crime outside his country of refuge after his admission to that country as a refugee'[30] or has 'seriously infringed' the 1969 Convention's purposes and objectives.[31] Two further points of distinction regarding cessation are that the 1969 Convention does not include the 1951 Convention clause that mitigates the cessation of an individual's refugee status if he or she can 'invoke compelling reasons arising out of previous persecution for refusing to avail himself of the protection of the country of nationality'.[32] Nor does the 1969 Convention provide for the cessation of a stateless person's refugee status if

[25] 1969 Convention (n 1) art I(2).

[26] Article I(3) of the 1969 Convention provides: 'In the case of a person who has several nationalities, the term "a country of which he is a national" shall mean each of the countries of which he is a national, and a person shall not be deemed to be lacking the protection of the country of which he is a national if, without any valid reason based on well-founded fear, he has not availed himself of the protection of one of the countries of which he is a national'.

[27] 1969 Convention (n 1) art I(4). [28] ibid art I(5).

[29] The 1951 Convention's article 1C cessation clauses provide that the 1951 Convention shall cease to apply to any person who would otherwise qualify as a refugee if he or she has: (1) voluntarily re-availed him or herself of the protection of his or her country of nationality; (2) voluntarily re-acquired his or her former nationality; (3) acquired a new nationality and enjoys protection from that country; or (4) has voluntarily re-established him or herself in the country in which he or she feared persecution. It further provides that the 1951 Convention shall cease to apply if (5) the circumstances in connection with which the person was recognized as a refugee have ceased to exist.

[30] 1969 Convention (n 1) art I(4)(f). A similar provision appears as an exclusion clause in the 1951 Convention, in which context the 'serious non-political crime' must obviously have been committed *prior to* admission to the country of asylum.

[31] ibid art I(4)(g).

[32] 1951 Convention (n 2) art 1C(5); under the language of this provision, the exemption from cessation applies only to article 1A(1) refugees, however, 'Application of the "compelling reasons" exception is interpreted to extend beyond the actual words of the provision to apply to Article 1A(2) refugees' (UNHCR, 'Guidelines on International Protection: Cessation of Refugee Status under Article 1C(5) and (6) of the 1951 Convention relating to the Status of Refugees (the "Ceased Circumstances" Clauses)' (10 February 2003) para 21). The absence of the exemption from cessation from the 1969 Convention is addressed in Chapter 4, section D.1.a.

the circumstances in the country of former habitual residence on which such status was based cease to exist.[33]

An additional exclusion clause[34] adds 'acts contrary to the purposes and principles of' the OAU.[35] A further difference is that the 1969 Convention does not include a provision like the 1951 Convention's article 1E, which prevents the 1951 Convention from applying to 'a person who is recognized by the competent authorities of the country in which he has taken residence as having the rights and obligations which are attached to the possession of the nationality of that country'. The article 1E exclusion clause was included in the 1951 Convention to cover ethnic Germans who fled to the Federal Republic of Germany, where the constitution recognized them as possessing the rights and obligations attached to German nationality.[36] They were therefore seen as not in need of international protection. Because no analogous situation existed in Africa when the 1969 Convention was drafted, it would not have made sense for the 1969 Convention to include an article 1E-like provision.

Finally, the sixth paragraph of article I mandates the 'Contracting State of Asylum' to determine refugee status. This allocation of responsibility for RSD is remarkable because it is without parallel in the 1951 Convention. Article I(6) is strikingly relevant in the current global context, in which states often try to shirk or shift responsibility for determining refugee status.

Article II of the 1969 Convention relates to asylum, including innovative paragraphs on the nature of asylum[37] and states parties' responsibilities in relation to it,[38] non-refoulement,[39] responsibility sharing,[40] and temporary protection;[41] each of these is addressed in detail in Chapter 3. Article II also requires that, 'For reasons of security', contracting states shall 'as far as possible, settle refugees at a reasonable distance from the frontier of their country of origin'; this is analysed in Chapter 5.[42]

Article III, titled the 'Prohibition of Subversive Activities', articulates refugees' duty to respect the laws and regulations of the host state,[43] repeating article 2 of the 1951 Convention,[44] and further prohibits them from engaging in subversive

[33] 1951 Convention (n 2) art 1C(6).

[34] The 1951 Convention's article 1F exclusion clauses provide that the 1951 Convention shall not apply to 'any person with respect to whom there are serious reasons for considering that: (a) he has committed a crime against peace, a war crime, or a crime against humanity . . . (b) he has committed a serious non-political crime outside the country of refuge prior to his admission to that country as a refugee; (c) he has been guilty of acts contrary to the purposes and principles of the United Nations'.

[35] 1969 Convention (n 1) art I(5)(c).

[36] Guy S Goodwin-Gill and Jane McAdam, *The Refugee in International Law* (3rd edn, OUP 2007) 161. In the modern context, UNHCR explains that 'This exclusion clause may only apply if the applicant has taken up regular or permanent residence in a country, and if the status given to him or her by that country means that he or she effectively enjoys the rights and obligations of its own nationals', and that it is 'of crucial importance that the status provides protection against *refoulement* as well as the right to return, re-enter, and remain in the country where the person concerned has taken residence' (UNHCR, 'Self-Study Module on Refugee Status Determination' (UNHCR 2005) 73).

[37] 1969 Convention (n 1) art II(2).

[38] ibid art II(1).

[39] ibid art II(3).

[40] ibid art II(4).

[41] ibid art II(5).

[42] ibid art II(6); see section D.2.b.

[43] ibid art III(1).

[44] This provides: 'Every refugee has duties to the country in which he finds himself, which require in particular that he conform to its laws and regulations as well as to measures taken for the maintenance of public order'.

activities against any OAU member state.[45] States parties to the 1969 Convention undertake to support this by prohibiting refugees 'residing in their respective territories from attacking any State Member of the OAU, by any activity likely to cause tension between Member States, and in particular by use of arms, through the press, or by radio';[46] this is without parallel in the 1951 Convention. The 1969 Convention's emphasis on prohibiting subversive activities is clearly the reason behind the additional cessation clause mentioned earlier in this section, through which the 1969 Convention will cease to apply to any refugee who has 'seriously infringed' the Convention's 'purposes and objectives'.[47] In other words, the article I(4)(g) cessation clause operationalizes or enforces the prohibition of subversive activities. The prohibition of subversive activities is addressed at length in Chapter 3,[48] as well as in Chapter 5.[49]

Article IV on non-discrimination in the application of the 1969 Convention follows article 3 of the 1951 Convention;[50] however, discrimination is prohibited on the additional grounds of nationality, membership of a particular social group, and political opinion. Article V relates to voluntary repatriation, which is addressed in detail in Chapter 3.[51]

Article VI(1) reflects article 28(1) of the 1951 Convention, which mandates contracting states to provide refugees with travel documents; however, it is 'Subject to Article III'[52] prohibiting subversive activities. This implies that a state would not be required by the 1969 Convention to issue a travel document to a refugee who had engaged in subversion.[53] In view of article II(5) on temporary protection, article VI(2) provides, 'Where an African country of second asylum accepts a refugee from a country of first asylum, the country of first asylum may be dispensed from issuing a document with a return clause'.[54] Article VI(3), like article 28(2) of the 1951 Convention, provides that travel documents issued under previous treaties shall be recognized as if they had been issued pursuant to the 1969 Convention.

Articles VII and VIII relate to state cooperation with the OAU and UNHCR respectively (collaboration between the OAU and UNHCR is called for in preambular paragraph 11). Article VII mandates states parties to provide the OAU with information on the condition of refugees, the implementation of the 1969 Convention and any national laws, regulations or decrees relating to refugees. Article VIII(1) requires states to cooperate with UNHCR. Article VIII(2) provides

45 1969 Convention (n 1) art III(1).

46 ibid art III(2).

47 ibid art I(4)(g); see Joan Fitzpatrick, 'Current Issues in Cessation of Protection Under Article 1C of the 1951 Refugee Convention and Article I.4 of the 1969 OAU Convention' (2001) UNHCR <http://www.refworld.org/docid/3bf925ef4.html> accessed 13 January 2015, 13.

48 See section C.4.

49 See section D.2.a.

50 The 1951 Convention prohibits discrimination on the grounds of race, religion and country of origin ((n 2) art 3).

51 See section C.3.

52 1969 Convention (n 1) art VI(1).

53 Article I(4)(g) of the 1969 Convention—providing that the Convention shall cease to apply to any person who has seriously infringed the instrument's purposes and objectives (which clearly include the prohibition of subversive activities)—is of even greater effect: the 1969 Convention ceases to apply to any refugee who has committed subversive activities, therefore such individuals have no right to a travel document or any other benefit of the Convention.

54 1969 Convention (n 1) art VI(2).

that the 1969 Convention 'shall be the effective regional complement in Africa' of the 1951 Convention. This clause is analysed in detail in Chapter 4 on the relationship between the 1951 and 1969 Conventions.[55]

Article IX on the settlement of disputes provides that any dispute between contracting states relating to the 1969 Convention's interpretation or application shall be referred to the OAU's Commission for Mediation, Conciliation and Arbitration. As mentioned in section B, this Commission was never operationalized and, in any case, it ceased to exist even on paper in 2001 when the OAU was supplanted by the AU. The 1969 Convention itself therefore no longer addresses dispute settlement in any relevant way, but jurisdiction in this regard can be located within the AU's broader legal framework. This unambiguously assigns jurisdiction relating to 'the interpretation, application or validity of... Union treaties and all subsidiary legal instruments adopted within the framework of the' AU or the OAU to the African Court of Justice and Human and Peoples' Rights (New Merged Court).[56] This court has, however, yet to be created.[57] Until or unless the New Merged Court is established, authority over disputes relating to the 1969 Convention rests logically with the African Court on Human and Peoples' Rights (African Court),[58] based on its jurisdiction over 'all cases and disputes submitted to it concerning the interpretation and application of the [African] Charter, this Protocol and any other relevant Human Rights instrument ratified by the States concerned'.[59] While this provision is less clearly worded than that relating to the New Merged Court, an eminent scholar has found it sufficient to currently vest the African Court with jurisdiction over the 1969 Convention.[60]

The final six articles of the 1969 Convention are technical provisions, relating to signature and ratification (article X), entry into force (article XI), amendment (article XII), denunciation (article XIII), registration with the United Nations (UN) (article XIV), and notifications (article XV).

The aspects of the 1969 Convention discussed summarily in this section are for the most part those that mirror or vary only slightly from the 1951 Convention. Such repetition was required to operationalize certain aspects of the 1951 Convention in relation to the broader class of individuals who qualify for refugee status under the regional instrument. For example, for the 1951 Convention's exclusion clauses to apply to article I(2) refugees, such clauses needed to be reproduced within the 1969 Convention itself. However, most of the 1969 Convention's nine substantive provisions represent significant departures from the international refugee instrument; these novel aspects are discussed in Chapter 3.

[55] See section C.

[56] Protocol on the Statute of the African Court of Justice and Human Rights (adopted 1 July 2008) AU Doc Assembly/AU/Dec 196 (XI), art 28(b).

[57] See Chapter 7, section D.

[58] Notwithstanding one primary source and several secondary sources that assert, without any legal basis, that the African Commission has supervisory jurisdiction over the 1969 Convention; see Chapter 7, section B.3.a.

[59] Protocol to the African Charter on Human and Peoples' Rights on the Establishment of an African Court on Human and Peoples' Rights (adopted 10 June 1998, entered into force 25 January 2004) OAU Doc OAU/LEG/EXP/AFCHPR/PROT, art 3(1).

[60] Frans Viljoen, *International Human Rights Law in Africa* (2nd edn, OUP 2012) 435–36.

Such unique provisions reflect the 1969 Convention's objective, as announced by the treaty's title: to address aspects of the refugee problem specific to Africa. Indeed, Rwelamira explains that the final text of the 1969 Convention 'settled for only the specific aspects of the African refugee [problem] which were not adequately catered for under the 1951 Convention'.[61] This was not, however, the objective at the outset of the drafting process. The impetus for a regional refugee instrument and how this initial objective transformed during the drafting process is the subject of the balance of this chapter.

D. Drafting History

Work on the issue of refugee protection in Africa began very soon after the OAU's formation, as evidenced by a 1964 resolution of the OCM's 2nd Ordinary Session. The resolution established an ad hoc commission consisting of representatives to the OAU from Burundi, Cameroon, Congo-Léopoldville (now the Democratic Republic of the Congo (DRC)), Ghana, Nigeria, Rwanda, Senegal, Sudan, Tanganyika (now Tanzania), and Uganda (Commission)[62] to examine '(a) the refugee problem in Africa and make recommendations to the Council of Ministers on how it can be solved; [and] (b) ways and means of maintaining refugees in their country of asylum'.[63]

The drafting process to which this resolution ultimately gave rise is the subject of varied and conflicting accounts, in part because of the lack of *travaux préparatoires*. These accounts can essentially be divided into two categories. On the one hand are the majority of commentators, who address the 1969 Convention's drafting history only briefly and without reference to primary sources such as OAU resolutions and archival material. They tend to view the OAU's interest in a regional instrument as resulting from the failure of the 1951 Convention refugee definition to qualitatively reflect the causes of forced displacement in Africa.[64] On the other hand are the three writers who have addressed the 1969 Convention's drafting in some depth.[65] These accounts correctly attribute the motivations behind the 1969 Convention to two factors: the dateline contained in article 1A(2) of the 1951 Convention and the issue of subversion.

Both factors were related to the circumstances prevailing in Africa during the sixties, which Nyanduga describes:

> The 1969 OAU Convention was adopted by African States at a time in history when the continent was gripped by the struggle for liberation, following the independence of many

[61] Medard RK Rwelamira, 'Some Reflections on the OAU Convention on Refugees: Some Pending Issues' (1983) 16 Comp & Intl LJ S Afr 155, 167.

[62] The Commission later became known as the Commission of Ten on Refugee Problems in Africa; it is discussed further in Chapter 6, section B.1.a.

[63] OAU (OCM), 'Resolution on the Problem of Refugees in Africa' (OAU Lagos 24–29 February 1964) CM/Res 19 (II).

[64] See n 3.

[65] Holborn (n 5) 183–88; Jackson (n 5) 177–96; Okoth-Obbo (n 3) 109–12.

African States in the late 1950s and the 1960s. A considerable number of African States continued to be under colonial and foreign domination. Most of southern Africa was ruled by white racist regimes.... The struggle for independence and liberation in Africa prior to and after the creation of the OAU had forced the outflow of people from their territories escaping colonial oppression and foreign domination. While in exile, many of these people organized movements for the freedom and liberation of their countries. Freedom was won peacefully in many cases, while several African States won their independence through armed struggle.[66]

According to Rutinwa, these circumstances led to three distinct causes of displacement in Africa in the sixties: the disputed reconfiguration of certain colonial boundaries during the years leading up to independence; violent decolonization campaigns, especially in southern Africa; and the civil wars that plagued some newly independent states, particularly Burundi, Zaire (now the DRC) and Rwanda.[67] (Indeed, the OCM resolution establishing the Commission took particular note of Rwandan refugees and the related 'very heavy charge on the countries adjacent to Rwanda'.[68]) Individuals fleeing for these reasons were not, however, covered by the 1951 Convention, because before 1967 it did not apply to events occurring after 1 January 1951.[69]

The subversion issue gave rise to two separate concerns. Firstly, that refugees from newly independent states might use countries of asylum as bases from which to overthrow the regimes from which they had fled, thereby compromising both the stability of newly self-governing countries as well as friendly relations among OAU member states.[70] The second concern related to subversion, which arose slightly later in the drafting process, was that freedom fighters combating persistent colonialism or minority rule deserved refugee protection, but were not covered by the 1951 Convention refugee definition.[71] Essentially, states wanted to guard against destabilizing subversion while also being able to afford protection to individuals fomenting subversion aimed at liberation. The dateline issue mentioned earlier in this section and these two concerns related to subversion had distinct influences on the final form of the 1969 Convention, as will become clear from the account of drafting that follows.

The Commission's first report was drawn up in Addis Ababa, Ethiopia, in 1964. It contained principles that were ultimately reflected in the 1969 Convention and ended up guiding much of the OAU's action in favour of refugees.[72] These principles,

66 Bahame Tom Mukirya Nyanduga, 'Refugee Protection Under the 1969 OAU Convention Governing the Specific Aspects of Refugee Problems in Africa' (2004) 47 German YB Intl L 85, 86.

67 Bonaventure Rutinwa, 'Relationship Between the 1951 Refugee Convention and the 1969 OAU Convention on Refugees' in Volker Türk, Alice Edwards, and Cornelis Wouters (eds), *In Flight from Conflict and Violence: UNHCR's Consultations on Refugee Status and Other Forms of International Protection* (CUP 2017) 97.

68 OAU (OCM) (n 63) para 2.

69 1951 Convention (n 2) art 1A(2).

70 UNHCR, *The State of the World's Refugees 2000: Fifty Years of Humanitarian Action* (OUP 2000) 54; see, also, OAU (OAHG), 'Declaration on the Problem of Subversion' (OAU Accra 21–25 October 1965) AHG/Res 27 (II).

71 Okoth-Obbo (n 3) 111.

72 EM Ngung, 'The Role of Regional and Sub-Regional Organizations in Situations of Conflict and Displacement' (1999) 18 RSQ 97, 97.

in particular principles 2, 4, and 5, reflected serious concern about subversion. The principles included:

1. Refugees who wish to return to their countries of origin must be helped to do so under the most peaceful and normal of conditions with a view to their complete integration.
2. In the countries of refuge, refugees must be settled, as far as possible, a long way from the frontiers of their countries of origin, for obvious security reasons, as much for the sake of the refugees themselves as for the countries of origin and of refuge.
3. The term 'refugee' will be limited to citizens of countries, the political, social, racial, or religious conditions of which have brought about a need for expatriation through fear or oppression, imprisonment or other similar difficulties.
4. Countries of refuge must in no case allow refugees to attack their country of origin. In the same way the countries of origin must not consider the harbouring of refugees as an unfriendly gesture, and must desist from any attack on the countries of refuge through the media or press or radio or by resorting to arms.
5. Countries which have a refugee problem must begin or continue bilateral negotiations, with a view to solving all the difficulties likely to arise by peaceful means and in accordance with the principles and objectives of the Organization of African Unity [including] the principle of the settlement of refugees away from the border.[73]

In addition, and most importantly, the Commission's report recommended that the OAU 'draft a special convention on the status of African refugees'.[74]

1. The first/Kampala draft convention

At its 3rd Ordinary Session, held in Cairo, Egypt, in July 1964, the OCM took note of the Commission's report and, further to it, invited the Commission to 'draw up a draft Convention covering all aspects of the problem of refugees in Africa'.[75] The OCM requested that the draft, once complete, be circulated by the OAU's Administrative Secretary-General to member states, with a view to considering the draft and comments thereon at its 4th Ordinary Session. The OCM also recommended that the Commission become a permanent OAU body.[76] Thus began work on the first draft of the 1969 Convention, known as the Kampala draft after the Commission's 1964 drafting session in the Ugandan capital.

The Kampala draft was largely concerned with making international refugee law applicable in Africa. Thus it 'employed the form and much of the working of the 1951 Refugee Convention, although it eliminated the dateline contained therein'.[77] Furthermore, while the draft was similar to the 1951 Convention, it was in many respects far less protective.[78] This posed a significant problem for UNHCR. Eberhard

[73] Cited in Holborn (n 5) 851–52. [74] Holborn (n 5) 185.

[75] OAU (OCM), 'Resolution on the Commission on the Problem of Refugees in Africa' (OAU Cairo 13–17 July 1964) CM/Res 36 (III) para 6.

[76] Rachel Murray, *Human Rights in Africa: From the OAU to the African Union* (CUP 2004) 196.

[77] Philip E Chartrand, 'The Organization of African Unity and African Refugees: A Progress Report' (1975) 137 World Aff 265, 270.

[78] Holborn (n 5) 186.

Jahn, then Deputy Director of UNHCR's legal division, summarized his office's concerns: 'there are omissions which, from the point of view of the international protection of refugees, are undesirable. The Draft does not contain any provision on such elementary rights as wage-earning employment, elementary education, public relief, labour legislation and social security. It does not stipulate freedom of movement and it makes the issuance of travel documents merely optional and gives less protection against expulsion'.[79] Similarly, in a July 1965 letter, then Deputy High Commissioner Prince Sadruddin Aga Kahn wrote, 'We are concerned at possibility of African Regional Convention which departs from universal 1951 Convention and provides substantially lesser standard of treament for African refugees as for example on wage earning employment and expulsion.... Moreover believe present draft would seriously jeopardise protocol or other instrument to extend effects 1951 Convention to post dateline refugees'.[80]

Most concerning was perhaps draft article 31, which provided that the African refugee convention would supersede all preceding bilateral and multilateral agreements relating to refugees.[81] Holborn explains that 'the emergence of an instrument which in any sense superseded or competed with the 1951 Convention would seriously impair the universal character of the Convention which the UNHCR had spent years fostering'.[82] This concern is reflected in a 1965 letter from UNHCR's representative in Tanzania to Deputy High Commissioner Aga Kahn, which warns that 'if the 1951 Convention was denounced by the African states, a refugee from an African state would have more rights in a European country than in an African brother country, which could hardly be the intention of the OAU'.[83]

UNHCR shared its misgivings about the Kampala draft with OAU officials—notably Assistant Secretary-General Mohamed Sahnoun—and with member states, encouraging them to transmit comments reflecting UNHCR's concerns.[84] UNHCR also moved to make an all-encompassing regional instrument unnecessary. Indeed, 'The High Commissioner's interest in seeking the rapid adoption of the [1967] Protocol was partly stimulated by the efforts of the [OAU] member states ... to draft their own regional convention on refugees'.[85] Thus while the OAU was working on an African refugee convention, UNHCR convened the Bellagio Colloquium, the work of which led to the adoption of the 1967 Protocol.[86]

The Kampala draft was presented to the OCM at its 4th Ordinary Session, held in Nairobi, Kenya, in February and March 1965. Likely prompted by the

[79] Eberhard Jahn, 'Development in Refugee Law in the Framework of Regional Organizations Outside Europe' (1966) 4 Association for the Study of the World Refugee Problem Bulletin 77, 82.

[80] Letter dated 14 July 1965, UNHCR archives, fonds 1/5/11/1.

[81] UNHCR memo dated 29 April 1965, UNHCR archives, fonds 1/5/11/1.

[82] Holborn (n 5) 185.

[83] Letter dated 5 July 1965, UNHCR archives, fonds 1/5/11/1.

[84] UNHCR memo dated 21 May 1965, UNHCR archives, fonds 1/5/11/1.

[85] UNHCR (n 70) 56.

[86] Holborn (n 5) 185–86.

member state comments UNHCR had encouraged, the Council ultimately shared UNHCR's view that the Kampala draft suffered serious shortcomings. Accordingly, it established a committee of legal experts (Committee of Legal Experts) to revise the Kampala draft.[87] The experts were nominated by the ten states represented on the Commission and were instructed to meet prior to 30 July 1965, in order to have a revised draft convention ready for consideration at the OCM's 5th Ordinary Session.

2. The second/Léo draft convention

OAU Assistant Secretary-General Sahnoun suggested that UNHCR provide the Committee of Legal Experts with a draft convention on which to base their work. A memorandum by UNHCR's Jahn, titled 'Action to be taken by the Legal Division in connection with the Draft Convention relating to the Status of Refugees in Africa', explains:

> Ambassador Sahnoun thought that since the Draft Convention relating to the Status of Refugees in Africa as it now stands [the Kampala draft], appears neither to meet the aims for which such an instrument was first envisaged by the OAU, nor to be in full harmony with the world-wide 1951 Convention, it would be preferable that the Committee of Legal Experts, when it meets in July 1965, does not adopt this Draft Convention. He rather had in mind a legal instrument much more concise and much more specifically relevant to Africa; he described a 'Protocole d'Accord' which should regulate relations between Member States with regard to refugee problems in Africa; it should inter alia deal with asylum (not a hostile act), with the obligations of refugees and of asylum countries, with the problem of voluntary repatriation, with the possibility of settling problems between Member States in conformity with Article XIX of the OAU Charter.[88] ... Ambassador Sahnoun said he would be very pleased if, on a very confidential basis, we could prepare for him a draft of such a Protocol which, after careful study by the Secretariat, could be proposed to the Committee of Legal Experts and to the Member States as a OAU Secretariat paper.[89]

Assistant Secretary-General Sahnoun's proposal is the first suggestion that the African refugee convention should not duplicate its international counterpart, but rather should address refugee issues particular to Africa. Sahnoun's proposed document was produced by UNHCR and annexed to a 'Note Submitted by the United Nations High Commissioner for Refugees on Measures Being Examined Within the Framework of the Organization of African Unity for Regulating Refugee Problems Between Member States'.[90] However, according to UNHCR's representative in Léopoldville (now Kinshasa)—where the Committee of Legal Experts met in July 1965—'under the prevailing circumstances, it was completely impossible' to have

[87] OAU (OCM), 'Resolution on the Problem of Refugees' (OAU Nairobi 26 February to 9 March 1965) CM/Res 52 (IV) para 3.

[88] This provides for the establishment of a Commission of Mediation, Conciliation and Arbitration, which member states pledge to use 'to settle all disputes among themselves by peaceful means'.

[89] Memo dated 15 May 1965, UNHCR archives, fonds 1/5/11/1.

[90] Dated June 1965, UNHCR archives, fonds 1/5/11/1.

the UNHCR draft adopted.[91] Indeed, the draft that emerged from the Léopoldville meeting, known as the Léo draft, was far from the Protocole d'Accord that Sahnoun had suggested and UNHCR had provided.

Rather, the Léo draft 'largely followed ... the 1951 United Nations Refugee Convention, although the various standards of treatment provided for were not the same'.[92] Specifically, it contained a refugee definition, which reproduced the 1951 Convention definition without the dateline (article 1), and provisions concerning: the general obligations of refugees (article 2); the prohibition of subversive activities (article 3); non-discrimination (article 4); religion (article 5); rights granted apart from the Convention (article 6); the term 'in the same circumstances' (article 7); exemption from reciprocity (article 8); exemption from exceptional measures (article 9); provisional measures (article 10); residence prior to the Convention (article 11); refugee seamen (article 12); personal status (article 13); moveable and immovable property (article 14); artistic rights and industrial property (article 15); right of association (article 16); access to courts (article 17); wage-earning employment and self-employment (article 18); liberal professions (article 19); identity papers (article 20); travel documents (article 21); fiscal charges (article 22); transfer of assets (article 23); refugees unlawfully in the country of refuge (article 24); expulsion (article 25); prohibition of expulsion or return (article 26); naturalization (article 27); and executory and transitory provisions (articles 28–38).[93]

With these provisions, the Léo draft came closer to the wording of the 1951 Convention but it still failed to win OAU approval because, in the eyes of many OAU members, on the one hand, it overlapped with the 1951 Convention and, on the other, was still far less protective than the international instrument.[94] In the words of Assistant Secretary-General Sahnoun, '*l'impression qui se dégage ici de plus en plus, est qu'en fait la convention adoptee à Léopoldville est encore moins libérale que la convention générale*'.[95] Similarly, UNHCR's view of the Léo draft—like its opinion of the earlier Kampala draft—was that it would 'dangerously impair the universal value of the principles of the 1951 Convention, and would hinder efforts currently being undertaken to extend the Convention's scope'.[96]

With the OAU secretariat, many OAU member states, and UNHCR in agreement about the Léo draft's shortcomings, the two organizations worked together to advance the drafting process. The OAU's Administrative Secretary-General prepared a report for the 2nd Ordinary Session of the OAHG in Accra, Ghana, in October 1965, highlighting the concerns his organization and UNHCR shared. With the benefit of the OAU report, the OAHG rejected the Léo draft and requested that the Commission 'provide legal experts at the highest level possible to re-examine the draft OAU convention on the status of refugees having regard to the views expressed

[91] Memo dated 21 July 1965, UNHCR archives, fonds 1/5/11/1.

[92] Jackson (n 5) 180.

[93] Léo draft, UNHCR archives, fonds 1/5/11/1.

[94] Chartrand (n 77) 270.

[95] Author's translation: the impression increasingly coming out of this is that, in fact, the convention adopted in Léopoldville is even less liberal than the general convention (Letter dated 27 July 1965, UNHCR archives, fonds 1/5/11/1).

[96] Jackson (n 5) 181.

by the Assembly at its present session and to report back to the Assembly'.[97] Such views included the OAHG's desire 'to give all possible assistance to refugees from any Member State on a humanitarian and fraternal basis' as well as concerns about subversion and that refugee protection should not undermine inter-state relations.[98]

The OAHG also requested that OAU member states that had not already done so 'ratify the United Nations Convention relating to the Status of Refugees and . . . apply meanwhile the provisions of the said Convention to refugees in Africa'.[99] According to Jackson, this 'can be taken as the first clear indication that the African refugee convention should not cover the same ground as the 1951 Convention, the overriding character of which was implicitly recognised'.[100] Similarly, the High Commissioner explained in his October 1965 statement to his Executive Committee (ExCom) that most delegations in Accra had agreed that instead of creating a convention 'covering all aspects of the problem of refugees in Africa', the OAU should 'recognise the universal principles of the 1951 Convention and supplement the latter with a view to regulating certain aspects of the refugee problems peculiar to the region in particular in so far as they concern relations between member states'.[101] Thus Assistant Secretary-General Sahnoun's view that the regional instrument should not duplicate its international counterpart, but rather should address refugee problems particular to Africa, was gaining ground.

3. The third/Addis Ababa draft convention

Despite the consensus that emerged in Accra, the third draft convention, known as the Addis Ababa draft after the Committee of Legal Experts' September 1966 meeting in Ethiopia, 'still tended to cover the same ground as the 1951 Convention, though its provisions were more liberal than those of the preceding drafts and it contained new articles felt to be essential for dealing with the refugee situations in Africa'.[102]

Jackson describes the Addis Ababa draft as being shorter than its predecessor because a number of the Léo draft's provisions corresponding to articles in the 1951 Convention were removed.[103] Such provisions were no longer necessary because the Addis Ababa draft contained a preliminary conflict clause:

> (1) In all matters relating to the status, condition and treatment of refugees Member States shall, save as hereinafter provided, apply the provisions of the convention relating to the status of Refugees signed in Geneva on 28 July 1951, irrespective of the dateline and of any geographical limitation.

[97] OAU (OAHG), 'Resolution on the Problem of Refugees in Africa' (OAU Accra 21–25 October 1965) AHG/Res 26 (II) para 6.

[98] ibid paras 1–3.

[99] ibid; this call was reiterated several times, next in OAU (OCM), 'Resolution on the Problem of Refugees in Africa' (OAU Kinshasa 4–10 September 1967) CM/Res 104 (IX) para 1.

[100] Jackson (n 5) 182.

[101] UNHCR, 'Statement by the High Commissioner to the 15th Session of the Executive Committee of the High Commissioner's Programme' (29 October 1965) A/AC.96/310, 1.

[102] Holborn (n 5) 187.

[103] Jackson (n 5) 182.

(2) Should the provisions of this Convention conflict with any of those of the Convention of 28 July 1951, the provisions of this Convention shall prevail.[104]

The Addis Ababa draft went on to provide a refugee definition replicating that of the 1951 Convention and including a second clause outlining factors to consider in determining whether the African convention would apply prima facie to groups of refugees.[105] Other provisions related to asylum (article III); general obligations (article IV); the prohibition of subversive activities (article V); extradition (article VI); rights granted apart from the Convention (article VII); repatriation (article VIII); wage-earning and self-employment (article IX); liberal professions (article X); identity papers (article XI); travel documents (article XII); cooperation of the national authorities with the OAU and UNHCR (article XIII); and the settlement of disputes (article XIV). Like the Kampala and Léo drafts before it, the Addis Ababa draft failed to win OCM support.[106]

4. The fourth/OAU Secretariat draft convention

At its 7th Ordinary Session, held in October and November 1966 in Addis Ababa, the Council handed the job of drafting the African refugee convention over to the OAU Secretariat.[107] It also expressed in no uncertain terms the consensus that had begun to emerge in Accra, noting its desire 'that the African instrument should govern the specifically African aspects of the refugee problem and that it should come to be the effective regional complement of the 1951 … Convention'.[108]

This approach was inspired in large part by the fact that by the time of the OCM's 7th Ordinary Session in 1966, the 1967 Protocol was well on its way to adoption, meaning the 1951 Convention would soon apply in Africa.[109] Indeed, the OCM noted in Addis Ababa its appreciation for 'the efforts of the … [UNHCR] to ensure the … [1951] Convention's universality'.[110] Holborn describes the Council's 7th Ordinary Session as 'a turning point in the drafting of the OAU Convention; from then on drafts almost totally omitted any reference to matters already covered in the 1951 Convention and concentrated instead on matters particularly affecting refugees in Africa'.[111] According to Rutinwa, 'the drafters of the OAU Convention did not have misgivings about the substantive provisions of the 1951 Convention. Their only problem was the [optional] geographical and [mandatory] temporal limitations in it. This is why, when they became aware that these limitations would soon go, they decided to focus on the peculiar problems of refugee flows in Africa, which were not covered by the 1951 Convention'.[112]

[104] Cited in Jackson (n 5) 183.
[105] See Chapter 3, section B.4.b.
[106] Holborn (n 5) 187.
[107] OAU (OCM), 'Resolution on the Adoption of a Draft Convention on the Status of Refugees in Africa' (OAU Addis Ababa 31 October to 4 November 1966) CM/Res 88 (VII) para 2.
[108] ibid preambular para 6 (emphasis added).
[109] Okoth-Obbo (n 3) 110.
[110] OAU (OCM) (n 107) para 5.
[111] Holborn (n 5) 187.
[112] Rutinwa (n 67) 101.

The OAU Secretariat presented its draft convention, now the fourth to come before the OCM, to the body's 9th Ordinary Session in Kinshasa in September 1967. By this time, the 1967 Protocol had received three of the six accessions it needed to enter into force.[113] The imminent applicability of the 1951 Convention in Africa did not, however, obviate the need for a regional instrument. OAU member states agreed in Kinshasa that the regional convention remained necessary in order to address refugee situations specific to Africa.[114] Furthermore, certain African states—notably Nigeria and Uganda—were critical of the 1967 Protocol because, while it removed the 1951 Convention's dateline, it failed to address refugee protection concerns particular to their region.[115] Thus African efforts 'were channelled into the adoption of a complementary regional instrument'.[116] Yet while it was agreed that an African refugee convention remained necessary, the Council did not in Kinshasa accept the OAU Secretariat's draft, and the Committee of Legal Experts was sent back to work on what would be the fifth, and final, draft of the regional refugee convention.

5. The fifth/final draft convention

An important source of inspiration for the Committee of Legal Experts in its final push on the convention, especially regarding the refugee definition, was the October 1967 Conference on the Legal, Economic and Social Aspects of African Refugee Problems,[117] convened in Addis Ababa by the Dag Hammarskjöld Foundation, the OAU, the UN Economic Commission for Africa and UNHCR. The conference report[118] contained thirteen official recommendations, five of which 'were directed at legal aspects of African refugee problems and were to have an important effect upon the shaping of the OAU Refugee Convention during the final stage of its drafting'.[119]

One of the conference's thirteen recommendations 'was the first occasion on which the view was officially expressed that the 1951 Convention definition—while universally applicable—might not be sufficient to cover all refugee situations in Africa'.[120] The word 'officially' is important, because Egypt had made this point unofficially earlier, at a 1964 Cairo meeting of the Asian-African Legal Consultative Committee. There, Egypt expressed reservations about the inability of the 1951 Convention's refugee definition to cover those fleeing their country for generalized

[113] Holborn (n 5) 188. [114] ibid.

[115] Sara E Davies, 'Redundant or Essential? How Politics Shaped the Outcome of the 1967 Protocol' (2007) 19 IJRL 703, 724–5.

[116] Viljoen (n 60) 242.

[117] Lars-Gunnar Eriksson, Goran Melander, and Peter Nobel, *An Analysing Account of the Conference on the African Refugee Problem, Arusha, May 1979* (Scandinavian Institute of African Studies 1981) 11; Richard Greenfield, 'The OAU and Africa's Refugees' in Yassin El-Ayouty and I William Zartman (eds), *The OAU After Twenty Years* (Praeger 1984) 222.

[118] United Nations Economic Commission for Africa and others, 'Final Report of the Conference on the Legal, Economic and Social Aspects of the African Refugee Problems' December 1968 (on file with the author).

[119] Chartrand (n 77) 276. [120] Jackson (n 5) 187.

reasons.[121] The Egyptian delegation to the 1967 conference, supported by several others, followed up on its 1964 position, specifically requesting that the refugee definition apply to individuals obliged to flee from their country due to aggression or external subversion.[122]

The Egyptian request resulted in recommendation II of the 1967 conference, which advised African countries that a new definition should be found for the term 'refugee', taking into account the specific aspects of the refugee situation in Africa.[123] Such 'specific aspects' were largely the result of persistent colonial domination and minority rule on the continent:

> the question of whether the African Convention extends protection to persons engaged in military struggle remains a controversial one. This issue was discussed at length at the Conference on the Legal, Economic and Social Aspects of African Refugee Problem held in Addis Ababa in 1967. General consensus existed that the question of freedom fighters was intricately linked to the question of subversion. While support of freedom fighters intent on overthrowing a government of an independent African state could not conceivably be condoned in any way, it was accepted unreservedly that in a spirit of African solidarity it was the duty of every African country to assist freedom fighters who were fighting for the liberation of the African continent from colonial or racial domination. Such persons had no duty to abstain from activities aimed at overthrowing the internal structures in these colonial or minority-regime dominated countries. At any rate, African solidarity and the principles of the OAU as expressed in its Charter, clearly state that in seeking freedom for the African Continent, it is legitimate, indeed imperative to assist liberation movements. It was against this background that Article 1(2) was added to the general refugee definition taken from the 1951 Convention.[124]

At its 10th Ordinary Session, held in Addis Ababa in February 1968, the OCM took note of the 1967 conference report and drew the attention of member states and the OAU's Administrative Secretary-General to its recommendations.[125]

The Committee of Legal Experts met in Addis Ababa in June 1968 to produce the fifth draft convention. The OAU Secretariat provided a report including a second Secretariat-produced draft to inform the Committee's work.[126] Considering the 1967 conference's recommendation II and the OCM's endorsement of it, this Secretariat draft included the 1951 Convention refugee definition plus a second part in which 'external aggression and occupation, foreign domination or internal subversion' were grounds for refugee status.[127] The Secretariat draft also included

[121] ibid 186; the Asian-African Legal Consultative Committee's refugee work is described in Eberhard Jahn, 'The Work of the Asian-African Legal Consultative Committee on the Legal Status of Refugees' (1967) 27 Heidelberg J Intl L 122.

[122] Jackson (n 5) 189. [123] ibid. [124] Rwelamira (n 61) 169.

[125] OAU (OCM), 'Resolution on the Problem on Refugees in Africa' (OAU Addis Ababa 20–24 February 1968) CM/Res 141 (X) para 2.

[126] 'Report of the Administrative Secretary-General for the Meeting of the OAU Commission on Refugees Held in Addis Ababa from 17th to 23rd June 1968', UNHCR archives, fonds 1/5/11/1.

[127] ibid; the Secretariat's draft definition provided: 'The term "refugee" shall also apply to every person who, owing to external aggression and occupation, foreign domination or internal subversion on a part of or the whole of his country of origin or nationality, is compelled to leave his place of habitual residence whether inside or outside his country of nationality in order to seek refuge in another place within or outside his country of origin or nationality'.

a clause governing the regional instrument's relationship to the 1951 Convention. It provided that, 'In accordance with Resolution OAHG/Res.26, Member States shall, save as herein provided, apply the provisions of the U.N. Convention of 28 July 1951 relating to the status of refugees, irrespective of the dateline and of any geographical limitation as provided in the Protocol on the Status of Refugees of 31 January 1967'.[128]

The Committee of Legal Experts maintained the Secretariat's draft with only minor revisions, including to the second part of its refugee definition. The Committee replaced the word 'subversion' with 'disorder', considering 'subversion' to be ambiguous.[129] It also discarded an illogical idea contained in the Secretariat's draft: that someone could become a refugee within his or her country of origin.[130] The clause concerning the relationship between the regional instrument and its global counterpart was also amended to read, 'Member States shall apply the provisions of the United Nations Convention of 28 July 1951 relating to the Status of Refugees, as modified by the Protocol on the Status of Refugees of 31 January 1967',[131] thereby eliminating the words 'save as herein provided', which would have made the regional instrument supreme in specified instances.[132]

At its 11th Ordinary Session, held in Algiers, Algeria, in September 1968, the OCM requested that 'Member States, who have not yet done so, ... communicate to the General Secretariat before 15 December 1968 their comments on the OAU draft Convention on the Problem of Refugees'.[133] In February 1969, once such comments had been received, the Committee of Legal Experts presented its final draft to the OCM, for what was by then the Council's fifth consideration of the draft African refugee convention. This time, however, the document won the OCM's

[128] (n 126) art IX(2). OAHG resolution 26, adopted in 1965, reaffirms the OAHG's desire 'to give all possible assistance to refugees from any Member State on a humanitarian and fraternal basis'; recalls the principles that give rise to the 1969 Convention article III prohibition of subversive activities; 'Requests all Member States never to allow the refugee question to become a source of dispute among them'; notes UNHCR assistance to African states; requests African UN Economic and Social Council members increase African representation on UNHCR's ExCom; asks the 1969 Convention drafting committee to continue its work; and requests that OAU member states 'ratify the ... [1951 Convention] and to apply meanwhile the provisions of the said Convention to refugees in Africa'.

[129] Jackson (n 5) 190; presumably 'disorder' somehow became article I(2)'s 'events seriously disturbing public order', though no information was found about this.

[130] See n 127. The draft definition adopted by the Committee of Legal Experts provided, 'The term 'refugee' shall also apply to every person who, owing to external aggression, occupation, foreign domination or internal disorder affecting either part or the whole of his country of origin or nationality, is compelled to leave his place of habitual residence in order to seek refuge in another place outside his country of origin or nationality' ('Draft OAU Convention Governing the Specific Aspects of the Problem of Refugees in Africa', UNHCR archives, fonds 1/5/11/1).

[131] 'Draft OAU Convention Governing the Specific Aspects of the Problem of Refugees in Africa', UNHCR archives, fonds 1/5/11/1, art VIII(2).

[132] No clause explicitly specifying that the 1951 Convention should be applied ultimately made its way into the version of the regional instrument that was adopted in 1969. Instead, the 1969 Convention recognizes the 1951 Convention as 'the basic and universal instrument relating to the status of refugees' (preambular para 9) and calls on OAU member states to acceded to it and the 1967 Protocol and to 'meanwhile apply their provisions to refugees in Africa' (preambular para 10).

[133] OAU (OCM), 'Resolution on the Problem of Refugees in Africa' (OAU Algiers 4–12 September 1968) CM/Res 149 (XI) para 1.

unanimous support, and was signed by forty-one African states on 10 September 1969.[134] It entered into force upon ratification by one-third of OAU member states on 20 June 1974, a day that has since been celebrated as Africa Refugee Day[135] and was subsequently also recognized as World Refugee Day.

To date, the 1969 Convention has been ratified by forty-six of the AU's fifty-five member states. The Sahrawi Arab Democratic Republic (SADR) has neither signed nor ratified the 1969 Convention. Djibouti, Eritrea, Madagascar, Mauritius, Namibia, São Tomé and Príncipe, and Somalia have signed but not ratified the 1969 Convention. The 1951 Convention is even more widely supported in Africa. Only the Comoros, Eritrea, Libya, and Mauritius have neither signed nor ratified the 1951 Convention or its 1967 Protocol. Madagascar is a party to the 1951 Convention but not the 1967 Protocol, and it and the Republic of the Congo continue to recognize the 1951 Convention's European geographical limitation.[136] Cape Verde is party to the 1967 Protocol but not the 1951 Convention.

E. Conclusions

The most important aspect of this legal history for contemporary understanding of the 1969 Convention is certainly its elucidation of the various objectives that underpinned the Convention. The project to draft a regional refugee instrument was initially aimed at making international refugee law applicable in Africa and addressing the issue of subversion. Particularly persuasive in respect of the former is that early drafts of the 1969 Convention included only the 1951 Convention refugee definition (without the dateline); dissatisfaction with the international refugee definition was simply not an initial factor motivating the adoption of a regional instrument. Once the 1967 Protocol was adopted, the principal objective of the regional Convention became addressing refugee issues particular to Africa, chiefly subversion.

This explains why the Convention emerged as it did: as a very succinct instrument, addressing refugee issues particular to Africa and only refugee issues particular to Africa. This feature is relevant to understanding the 1969 Convention, to which the next chapter is devoted, and it is *critical* to understanding the relationship between the 1951 and 1969 Conventions, which is the subject of Chapter 4.

[134] Chartrand (n 77) 271.

[135] OAU (OCM), 'Resolution on Africa Refugee Day' (OAU Addis Ababa 13–21 February 1975) CM/Res 398 (XXIV).

[136] Articles 1B(1) and 1B(2) of the 1951 Convention allow states to opt out of its geographical limitation upon signature, ratification, or accession, or subsequently by notifying the UN Secretary General.

3
The 1969 Convention

A. Introduction

Africa hosts almost one-third of the world's refugees amid falling standards of refugee protection,[1] yet the Organization of African Unity Convention Governing the Specific Aspects of Refugee Problems in Africa (1969 Convention) remains incompletely understood or misunderstood in scholarly literature.[2] In the wake of its adoption, analysis understandably focused on highlighting the Convention's remarkable legal innovations, without delving into them in any depth.[3] Almost fifty years later, however, the discussion has scarcely moved on. When it receives attention—usually around significant anniversaries[4]—the 1969 Convention is either uncritically praised[5] or analysis focuses on the regional refugee definition,[6] at the expense of critical inquiry into other aspects of the treaty.[7] In this context, this chapter attempts to provide a more complete account of the novel provisions in the 1969 Convention.

It starts in section B with the Convention's regional refugee definition, beginning with a description of article I(2)'s international influence. Section B then goes on to

[1] See Chapter 1, section C.

[2] (Adopted 10 September 1969, entered into force 20 June 1974) 1001 UNTS 45.

[3] See Ousmane Goundiam, 'African Refugee Convention' [1970] Migr News 3; Paul Weis, 'The Convention of the Organization of African Unity Governing the Specific Aspects of Refugee Problems in Africa' (1970) 3 Rev des droits de l'homme 449.

[4] See, for example, George Okoth-Obbo, 'Thirty Years On: A Legal Review of the 1969 OAU Convention Governing the Specific Aspects of Refugee Problems in Africa' (2001) 20 RSQ 79; Joe Oloka-Onyango, 'Human Rights, the OAU Convention and the Refugee Crisis in Africa: Forty Years After Geneva' (1991) 3 IJRL 453; Micah Bond Rankin, 'Extending the Limits or Narrowing the Scope? Deconstructing the OAU Refugee Definition Thirty Years On' (2005) 21 S Afr J Hum Rts 406; MR Rwelamira, 'Two Decades of the 1969 OAU Convention Governing the Specific Aspects of the Refugee Problem in Africa' (1989) 1 IJRL 557; Ray Wilkinson, 'Thirty Years After . . . The OAU Refugee Convention was a Model of Generosity, but Times Have Changed' [1999] Refugees 4.

[5] Rankin (n 4) 410. See, for example, Jennifer L Turner, 'Liberian Refugees: a Test of the 1969 OAU Convention Governing the Specific Aspects of Refugee Problems in Africa' (1994) 8 Geo Immigr LJ 281.

[6] See, for example, Chris J Bakwesegha, 'The OAU and African Refugees' in Yassin El-Ayouty (ed), *The Organization of African Unity after Thirty Years* (Greenwood Publishing Group 1994); Rainer Hofmann, 'Refugee Law in the African Context' (1992) 52 Heidelberg J Intl L 318.

[7] Pieces by Okoth-Obbo (n 4), Edwards (Alice Edwards, 'Refugee Status Determination in Africa' (2006) 14 Afr J Intl Comp L 204) and Rankin (n 4) are notable exceptions.

interpret the definition using orthodox methods. These and the overall context and object and purpose of the 1969 Convention are discussed, followed by analysis of the 'every person' and the 'external aggression, occupation, foreign domination or events seriously disturbing public order' (1969 Events) elements. This is followed by an analysis of the test for refugee status under article I(2), as well as a discussion of certain discrete issues (internal flight alternative (IFA), ongoing risk, and sur place claims) that arise within this test. Section B then addresses how article I(2) has been invoked in practice, specifically in South Africa and Kenya. The final sub-section in section B addresses prima facie refugee status determination (RSD). Section C covers four further key features of the 1969 Convention: its progressive development of an individual right to asylum; non-refoulement under the 1969 Convention; the formalization of responsibility sharing, a type of temporary protection, and voluntary repatriation; and the Convention's prohibition of subversive activities. Section D concludes.

B. The Regional Refugee Definition

The most celebrated feature of the 1969 Convention is certainly its article I(2) refugee definition. Okoth-Obbo notes that it has 'generated a reputation which borders on the mythical'.[8] The Convention relating to the Status of Refugees (1951 Convention) defines a refugee as someone with a well-founded fear of being persecuted for his or her race, religion, nationality, membership of a particular social group, or political opinion.[9] As discussed in Chapter 2, the 1969 Convention includes this definition at article I(1) and provides at article I(2), 'The term "refugee" shall also apply to every person who, owing to external aggression, occupation, foreign domination or events seriously disturbing public order in either part or the whole of his country of origin or nationality, is compelled to leave his place of habitual residence in order to seek refuge in another place outside his country of origin or nationality'.

Domestic refugee legislation in Africa generally incorporates both the 1951 Convention article 1A(2)/1969 Convention article I(1) refugee definition, as well as this regional definition.[10] For example, article I(2) is reflected in the national

[8] Okoth-Obbo (n 4) 109.

[9] (Adopted 28 July 1951, entered into force 22 April 1954) 189 UNTS 137, art 1A(2), which, as amended by the 1967 Protocol, provides that the term 'refugee' shall apply to any person who 'owing to well-founded fear of being persecuted for reasons of race, religion, nationality, membership of a particular social group or political opinion, is outside the country of his nationality and is unable or, owing to such fear, is unwilling to avail himself of the protection of that country; or who, not having a nationality and being outside the country of his former habitual residence, is unable or, owing to such fear, is unwilling to return to it'.

[10] The refugee acts of Algeria (Décret no 1963-274 du 1963 fixant les modalités d'application de la Convention de Genève du 28 juillet 1951 relative au statut des Réfugiés), Botswana (Refugees (Recognition and Control) Act of 1968), Morocco (Décret no 2-57-1256 du 2 safar 1377 (29 août 1957) fixant les modalités d'application de la convention relative au statut des réfugiés signée à Genève le 28 juillet 1951), and Swaziland (The Refugees Control Order, 1978) do not reflect the 1951 Convention

refugee laws of Angola, Benin, Burkina Faso, Burundi, Central African Republic, Gabon, Ghana, Lesotho, Liberia, Malawi, Mozambique, Nigeria, the Republic of the Congo, Rwanda, Senegal, Somalia, South Africa, Sudan, Tanzania, Uganda, and Zimbabwe.[11] Incorporation is generally accomplished by reproducing both refugee definitions in full. Less often, the definitions are incorporated by reference, such as in the acts of Benin, Gabon, Ghana, and Senegal.[12]

Article I(2) is generally viewed in the literature as having expanded refugee protection on the continent, at law if not in practice. Based on her review of this literature, Wood articulates four ways in which article I(2) is seen as having broadened refugee protection in Africa.[13] First and foremost, the definition focuses on general conditions in the country of origin, rather than on the refugee's individual fear of persecution. Secondly, this focus on general conditions supports the protection of individuals fleeing events that cause widespread or indiscriminate harm, such as violence and war. Thirdly, that the relevant event need only have occurred 'in either part or the whole of' the country of origin has been interpreted as disabusing article I(2) of the so-called IFA.[14] Finally, largely as a result of the foregoing, article I(2) is often viewed as particularly well suited to so-called group RSD and protection in mass influx.[15] The balance of this chapter is devoted to unpacking these claims about, and other aspects of, article I(2), as well as to other salient features of the 1969 Convention, beginning with its international influence.

1. Global influence

Article I(2) has been globally influential in four significant respects. Firstly, it informed how refugees are defined in Latin America. The region's 1984 Cartagena Declaration cites 'the precedent of the OAU [Organization of African Unity] Convention (article 1, paragraph 2)' and goes on to recommend that the 1951 Convention refugee definition be expanded in Latin America to also include 'persons who have fled their country because their lives, safety or freedom have been threatened by generalized violence, foreign aggression, internal conflicts, massive violation of human rights or other circumstances which have seriously disturbed public order'.[16] Additionally, Belize's refugee

and/or the 1969 Convention, either because the national law pre-dates the 1969 Convention, or because the state has not brought its refugee law into conformity with its international obligations.

[11] Jamil Ddamulira Mujuzi, 'The African Commission on Human and Peoples' Rights and the Promotion and Protection of Refugees' Rights' (2009) 9 Afr Hum Rts LJ 160, 166.

[12] Marina Sharpe, 'The 1969 OAU Refugee Convention in the Context of Individual Refugee Status Determination' in Volker Türk, Alice Edwards, and Cornelis Wouters (eds), *In Flight from Conflict and Violence: UNHCR's Consultations on Refugee Status and Other Forms of International Protection* (CUP 2017) 124.

[13] Tamara Wood, 'Expanding Protection in Africa? Case Studies of the Implementation of the 1969 African Refugee Convention's Expanded Refugee Definition' (2015) 26 IJRL 555, 559.

[14] See section B.2.e of this chapter.

[15] See section B.4 of this chapter.

[16] Cartagena Declaration on Refugees (22 November 1984) in 'Annual Report of the Inter-American Commission on Human Rights' OAS Doc OEA/Ser.L/V/II.66/doc.10, rev.1, 190–93 (1984–1985) section III.3.

law defines a refugee in terms almost identical to the 1969 Convention's article I(2).[17]

Secondly, the influence of article I(2) is also apparent in the League of Arab States' Arab Convention on Regulating Status of Refugees in the Arab Countries (Arab Convention). This instrument includes a refugee definition similar to the 1951 Convention's article 1A(2) and also defines a refugee as 'Any person who unwillingly takes refuge in a country other than his country of origin or his habitual place of residence because of sustained aggression against, occupation and foreign domination of such country or because of the occurrence of natural disasters or grave events resulting in major disruption of public order in the whole country or any part thereof'.[18] The Arab Convention also has several further provisions that echo aspects of the 1969 Convention, including the prohibition of subversive activities and temporary protection. The Arab Convention was adopted by the League of Arab States in 1994 but has yet to enter into force; the League is currently working towards the adoption of a new regional instrument. Several Arab League states are also African Union (AU) member states and/or are party to the 1969 Convention.[19]

Thirdly, article I(2) influenced the mandate of the Office of the United Nations High Commissioner for Refugees (UNHCR). The agency's Executive Committee (ExCom) recommended in 1981 that the 1951 Convention refugee definition be broadened to take account of mass displacement, and in so doing used—without attribution—the wording of the 1969 Convention's article I(2).[20] According to the High Commissioner's report to the General Assembly of the United Nations (UNGA), ExCom had recommended that 'the measures of protection ... should extend both to persons who are refugees within the traditional refugee definition as well as to persons meeting "wider" criteria, i.e., persons who are compelled to seek refuge outside their country of origin because of external aggression, occupation, foreign domination or events seriously disturbing public order in either part or the whole of that country'.[21]

While this did not lead to any amendment of the 1951 Convention, article I(2) did influence the High Commissioner's competence. Successive UNGA and Economic and Social Council resolutions have extended UNHCR's mandate beyond the individuals covered by the 1951 Convention refugee definition and UNHCR's statute.[22] Former High Commissioner Sadako Ogata acknowledged in

[17] Refugees Act 2000 (Belize) s 4(1)(c), cited in Wood (n 13) 560.

[18] (Adopted 1994) <http://www.refworld.org/publisher,LAS,,,4dd5123f2,0.html> accessed 18 April 2017, art 1.

[19] The following League of Arab States members are also AU member states: Algeria, Comoros, Djibouti, Egypt, Libya, Mauritania, Morocco, Somalia, Sudan, and Tunisia.

[20] Richard Greenfield, 'The OAU and Africa's Refugees' in Yassin El-Ayouty and I William Zartman (eds), *The OAU After Twenty Years* (Praeger 1984) 224. See Chapter 4, section C.1 on ExCom Conclusion 22, which also uses the language of the 1969 Convention's article I(2), but in the context of minimum standards of treatment in mass influx.

[21] UNGA, 'Report of the United Nations High Commissioner for Refugees' (18 August 1982) 37th Session (1982) UN Doc Supp No 12 (A/37/12) para 13.

[22] See, for example, UNGA Res 48/118 (20 December 1993); UNGA Res 3143 (XXVIII) (14 December 1973); ECOSOC Res 2011 (LXI) (2 August 1976).

1994 that this iterative process meant that 'the terminology employed for refugees who may not come within the terms of the 1951 Convention definition (and that in the UNHCR Statute) is neither consistent nor clear'.[23] To clarify the scope of her mandate, the High Commissioner explained that her office had, 'in recent years adopted the usage of regional instruments such as the OAU Refugee Convention and the Cartagena Declaration, using the term "refugee" in the broader sense, to denote persons outside their countries who are in need of international protection because of a serious threat to their life, liberty or security of person in their country of origin as a result of persecution or armed conflict, or serious public disorder'.[24] Today, when UNHCR conducts RSD pursuant to its mandate, in addition to the 1951 Convention definition, it also considers as refugees 'persons outside their country and unable to return owing to serious and indiscriminate threats to life, physical integrity or freedom resulting from generalised violence or events seriously disturbing public order'.[25]

Finally, the African refugee definition influenced the development of complementary protection,[26] which arose to address individuals who do not meet the 1951 Convention refugee definition but who nevertheless require international protection. Thus on the whole, article I(2) has influenced how refugees are defined beyond Africa and who qualifies for international protection. Indeed, according to Hathaway, save for the 1951 Convention's article 1A(2), the African refugee definition is 'the most influential conceptual standard of refugee status'.[27]

2. Interpreting article I(2)

Interpreting the article I(2) regional refugee definition involves determining the meaning of its key terms: 'every person'; 'owing to'; the 1969 Events; 'in either part or the whole of'; 'compelled'; and 'place of habitual residence'. 'Every person' and each of the 1969 Events are addressed first, followed by 'owing to' and the final three clauses, which are analysed together in terms of the test for refugee status under article I(2). These terms' meanings are determined in accordance with the Vienna Convention on the Law of Treaties (VCLT),[28] which provides an authoritative set of rules governing treaty interpretation. An overview of these rules follows, to background the interpretive exercise.

[23] UNHCR, 'Note on International Protection (submitted by the High Commissioner)' (7 September 1994) A/AC.96/830, para 32.

[24] ibid. [25] UNHCR, 'Protection Induction Programme' (2006) 89.

[26] Edwards (n 7) 210; Gino J Naldi and Cristiano D'Orsi, 'The Multi-faceted Aspects of Asylum-Law Applicable to Africa: Analysis for Reflection' (2014) 36 Loy LA Int'l & Comp L Rev 115, 128.

[27] James C Hathaway, *The Law of Refugee Status* (Butterworths 1991) 19.

[28] Vienna Convention on the Law of Treaties (adopted 23 May 1969, entered into force 27 January 1980) 1155 UNTS 331.

(a) *The Vienna rules*

The interpretive rules articulated by the VCLT also constitute customary international law. This is important for two reasons. Firstly, the Vienna rules' customary status renders them binding on all states, regardless of whether the state in question has ratified the VCLT.[29] Secondly, the Vienna rules apply regardless of whether the treaty under interpretation pre-dates the VCLT, which, like all treaties, does not apply retroactively.[30] (The 1969 Convention was adopted a few months after the VCLT but entered into force several years before it.)

The VCLT's article 31 'General Rule of Interpretation' is particularly relevant. Article 31(1) provides that a 'treaty shall be interpreted in good faith in accordance with the ordinary meaning to be given to the terms of the treaty in their context and in the light of its object and purpose'.[31] According to Sinclair, the ordering of these elements is important: 'the initial search is for the "ordinary meaning" to be given to the terms of the treaty in their "context"; it *is in light of* the object and purpose of the treaty that the initial and preliminary conclusion must be tested and either confirmed or modified'.[32] The context largely relates to the text of a treaty, including its preamble and any annexes;[33] the object and purpose of a treaty is similarly derived from its text.[34]

Article 31(3)(b) provides that there 'shall be taken into account, together with the context: ... Any subsequent practice in the application of the treaty which establishes the agreement of the parties regarding its interpretation'.[35] Such subsequent practice includes judicial decisions,[36] which are relied upon in the interpretation that follows. In this context, it must be noted that African states for the most part do not report their RSD decisions.[37] A limited number of otherwise unreported RSD decisions were, however, obtained through UNHCR's RefWorld, personal contacts, and secondary sources; these contributed greatly to the analysis.

Some commentary on the VCLT maintains that the subsequent practice referred to by article 31(3)(b) must be common to all,[38] or at least a reasonable number of,[39] the parties to the treaty being interpreted for it to have authoritative bearing on the interpretation. The paucity of reported refugee jurisprudence in Africa makes even the lower of these standards impossible to reach. Jurisprudence is considered

[29] *Territorial Dispute (Libyan Arab Jamahiriya v Chad)* (Judgment) [1994] ICJ Rep 6, 21.

[30] VCLT (n 28) art 4.

[31] ibid art 31(1).

[32] Ian Sinclair, *The Vienna Convention on the Law of Treaties* (2nd edn, Manchester University Press 1984) 130.

[33] VCLT (n 28) art 31(2).

[34] Richard Gardiner, *Treaty Interpretation* (2nd edn, OUP 2010) 196–97.

[35] VCLT (n 28) art 31(3)(b).

[36] Gardiner (n 34) 229.

[37] This includes even South Africa, the continent's best-resourced jurisdiction. At first instance, applicants in South Africa only receive written reasons for negative determinations, and these reasons are not reported. Appellate decisions are reasoned, but again these are not reported. Decisions in cases that proceed to judicial review are sometimes reported or otherwise published, but these are not usually decisions on the merits. For a time, Benin's refugee jurisprudence was reported at <www.cnarbenin.bj>, however the cases are no longer online and the website has not been updated since 2015.

[38] See, for example, Sinclair (n 32) 138.

[39] Gardiner (n 34) 236.

regardless; while the necessarily limited number of decisions cited are not conclusive, they are certainly—and at the very least—instructive.

Article 31(3)(c) also mandates the consideration of any 'relevant rules of international law applicable in the relations between the parties'.[40] This reflects the principle of systemic integration, pursuant to which treaties, as incarnations of international law, are 'limited in scope and ... predicated for their existence and operation on being part of the international law system'.[41] Therefore, they must be invoked and interpreted against the background of other principles of international law, with the result that 'every treaty provision must be read not only in its own context, but in the wider context of general international law'.[42] The International Law Commission explains article 31(3)(c) as simply requiring that a sense of 'coherence and meaningfulness' be integrated into the process of treaty interpretation.[43]

Article 31(3)(c) is, however, far from clear. It raises three questions: the meaning of 'rules of international law', which rules are 'relevant', and who 'the parties' are. The first of these questions has a straightforward answer: the 'rules of international law' are those articulated in the Statute of the International Court of Justice (ICJ), which lists the sources of international law as treaties, international custom, and general principles of law, and as subsidiary sources, judicial decisions and academic commentary.[44]

The second question, relating to relevance, raises two sub-issues. The first is that of inter-temporality: are the relevant rules those that existed in 1969 when the Convention was adopted, or are they those in force at the time of interpretation? Gardiner's authoritative view affirms contemporaneity but allows subsequent legal developments to be considered when the treaty under interpretation was intended to be interpretive evolutively.[45] Given the 1969 Convention's object and purpose of refugee protection and the necessity of an evolutionary approach in giving effect to this, it is justified to interpret the 1969 Convention evolutively.[46] Thus rules of international law adopted after 1969 are relevant in the interpretation. The second sub-issue is substantive: which rules of international law are relevant to the interpretation of the 1969 Convention? The answer to this question lies in the ordinary meaning of 'relevant'. Thus, an investment treaty is irrelevant to the interpretation

[40] On the use of international law in the interpretation of the 1969 Convention, see Tamara Wood, 'The African War Refugee: Using IHL to Interpret the 1969 African Refugee Convention's Expanded Refugee Definition' in David James Cantor and Jean-Francois Durieux (eds), *Refuge from Inhumanity? Refugee Protection and the Laws of War* (Martinus Nijhoff 2014) 185–89.

[41] Campbell McLachlan, 'The Principle of Systemic Integration and Article 31(3)(c) of the Vienna Convention' (2005) 54 Intl & Comp LQ 279, 280.

[42] Sinclair (n 32) 139.

[43] International Law Commission, 'Fragmentation of International Law: Difficulties Arising From the Diversification and Expansion of International Law – Report of the Study Group of the International Law Commission' (13 April 2006) A/CN4/L682, para 419.

[44] Statute of the International Court of Justice (adopted 18 April 1946) UKTS 67 (1946) art 38(1).

[45] Gardiner (n 34) 278.

[46] In relation to the 1951 Convention, Hathaway has argued that 'the obligation to interpret the text of a treaty in the light of its object and purpose should be conceived as incorporating the overarching duty to interpret a treaty in a way that ensures its effectiveness' (James C Hathaway, *The Rights of Refugees Under International Law* (CUP 2005) 62).

of the 1969 Convention, however the 1951 Convention and human rights treaties are clearly relevant.

The final question relates to the meaning of 'the parties', which is a reference not to the parties in an interpretive dispute, but rather to all the parties to the treaty being interpreted.[47] This raises the question of whether 'it is necessary that all of the parties to the treaty being interpreted are also party to the second treaty being relied upon as a "rule of international law"?'.[48] This question has yet to be definitely answered,[49] though Pobjoy has outlined the three dominant approaches, which range from a narrow affirmative answer to a broader negative one.[50] The latter approach is adopted here. It is explained by Pauwelyn as requiring the taking into account of rules that 'can be said to be at least implicitly accepted or tolerated . . . in the sense that [the rule] can reasonably be considered to express the common intentions or understandings of all members as to the meaning of the . . . term concerned'.[51]

(b) Context and object and purpose

The context of the 1969 Convention and its object and purpose are addressed here, at the outset of the interpretive exercise, because they are relevant to the whole analysis. As discussed in Chapter 2, during drafting, the process of independent state-building, coupled with ongoing minority rule in Southern Africa, brought two concerns to the fore. States wanted to deal humanely with people fleeing the anti-colonial struggle and with freedom fighters combating persistent colonialism. However, they did not want international relations to be undermined by individuals intent on subverting newly independent countries of origin. These twin concerns are apparent in several Convention provisions.

The humanitarian concern is apparent in preambular paragraphs 1 and 2. The former notes 'with concern the constantly increasing numbers of refugees in Africa' and indicates states' desire to find 'ways and means of alleviating their misery and suffering as well as providing them with a better life and future'. The latter recognizes 'the need for an essentially humanitarian approach towards solving the problem of refugees'. The preamble goes on in paragraph 3 to recognize the concern with international relations in Africa: 'refugee problems are a source of friction among many Member States' and states are 'desirous of eliminating the source of such discord'. Preambular paragraph 4 speaks directly to the balance states were trying to strike, noting that they were 'Anxious to make a distinction between a refugee who seeks a peaceful and normal life and a person fleeing his country for the sole purpose of fomenting subversion from outside'. In respect of the latter, preambular paragraph 5 notes that the activities of 'subversive elements should be discouraged'.

[47] Gardiner (n 34) 269.
[48] Jason Pobjoy, *The Child in International Refugee Law* (CUP 2017) 41.
[49] Gardiner (n 34) 269.
[50] Pobjoy (n 48) 42–43.
[51] Joost Pauwelyn, 'The Role of Public International Law in the WTO: How Far Can We Go?' (2001) 95 AJIL 535, 576, cited in Pobjoy (n 48) 42.

Thus states agreed, at article II(2), that the 'grant of asylum to refugees is a peaceful and humanitarian act and shall not be regarded as an unfriendly act by any Member State' and also undertook, at article III(2), 'to prohibit refugees residing in their respective territories from attacking any State Member of the OAU'. Furthermore, states depoliticized refugee protection by devising a definition that would allow them to 'acknowledge that a foreigner is a refugee without implicitly accusing another government of being persecutory'.[52]

While colonialism and minority rule no longer prevail in Africa and the OAU's preoccupation with non-interference has largely given way to the AU principle of non-indifference,[53] the 1969 Convention's post-colonial context and object and purpose of dealing humanitarianly with refugees while also safeguarding international relations must be borne in mind throughout the interpretation of article I(2). This begins with the 'every person' clause.

(c) 'Every person'

Article I(2) begins by stating that the 'term "refugee" shall also apply to every person who'; it then goes on to the descriptive portion of the definition. The 'every person' element communicates the scope of the definition's applicability. Its ordinary meaning is abundantly clear: article I(2) provides refugee status to each and every individual who meets its substantive criteria. Rankin, however, addresses whether the 1969 Convention applies to 'every person' or only to 'every African', because 'some states', which he does not name, 'take the view that it only applies to African refugees'.[54] The idea that the 1969 Convention does not apply to individuals from outside Africa was similarly implied in the Kenyan case of an Iraqi asylum seeker.[55]

Ultimately, Rankin finds that the 1969 Convention's field of application is not limited to African refugees. He bases his conclusion on the ordinary meaning of 'every person', the 1969 Convention's humanitarian object and purpose, and the universal applicability of the 1951 Convention's refugee definition, which is replicated at article I(1) of the 1969 Convention, as well as on some other more tangential arguments.[56]

Rankin's conclusion is certainly correct, and reflects state practice in South Africa at least. The chairperson of that country's Refugee Appeal Board stated that it would apply article I(2) 'to anyone from any part of the world and not only Africans. The reasons here fore is that when the OAU Convention was incorporated into the Refugees Act, it did not specify that it would only apply to the African continent

[52] Michael Kagan, 'Legal Refugee Recognition in the Urban South: Formal v. De Facto Refugee Status' (2007) 24 Refuge 11, 16.

[53] Ben Kioko, 'The Right of Intervention Under the African Union's Constitutive Act: From Non-interference to Non-intervention' (2003) 85 IRRC 807.

[54] Rankin (n 4) 420.

[55] *Adel Mohamed Abdulkader Al-Dahas v The Attorney General, The Principal Immigration Officer, the Minister for State for Provincial Administration & Internal Security and UNHCR*, Miscellaneous Civil Application 1546 of 2004, High Court of Kenya (1 March 2007) para 35.

[56] Rankin (n 4) 420–21.

but was left open'.[57] The view that article I(2) can apply to all refugees in Africa also reflects recent UNHCR guidance.[58]

(d) The 1969 Events

The context and object and purpose of the 1969 Convention, discussed earlier in this section, and the drafting history elucidated in Chapter 2,[59] suggest that the first three 1969 Events were included in article I(2) with colonialism and white minority rule in mind. It is not, however, sufficient to merely determine that the 1969 Events refer to this historical context. Now that colonialism and minority rule no longer prevail in Africa, the 1969 Events must be interpreted in contemporary terms. 'Aggression' (as well as 'occupation') has an autonomous legal meaning, to which the interpretation now turns.

(i) External aggression

The international crime of aggression was not defined until recently, despite the Charter of the United Nations' (UN Charter) mention of 'the suppression of acts of aggression' as among the world body's purposes and member states' related commitment to 'refrain in their international relations from the threat or use of force against the territorial integrity or political independence of any state'.[60] Echoing this prohibition, in 1974, a special committee of the UNGA defined aggression as 'the use of armed force by a State against the sovereignty, territorial integrity or political independence of another State, or in any other manner inconsistent with' the UN Charter.[61]

When the AU adopted its Non-Aggression and Common Defence Pact in 2005, it used and expanded upon this UN notion of aggression, defining it as 'the use, intentionally and knowingly, of armed force or any other hostile act by a State, a group of States, an organization of States or non-State actor(s) or by any foreign or external entity, against the sovereignty, political independence, territorial integrity and human security of the population of a State Party to this Pact, which are incompatible with the Charter of the ... UN or the [AU] Constitutive Act'.[62] The AU thus specified the required intent and, given the prevalence of rebel groups in Africa, broadened aggression to cover the acts of non-state entities. The Protocol on Amendments to the Protocol on the Statute of the African Court of Justice and Human Rights, which endowed the unestablished African Court of Justice and

[57] Cited in Tal Hanna Schreier, 'An Evaluation of South Africa's Application of the OAU Refugee Definition' (2008) 25 Refuge 53, 56.

[58] UNHCR, 'Guidelines on International Protection No. 12: Claims for refugee status related to situations of armed conflict and violence under Article 1A(2) of the 1951 Convention and/or 1967 Protocol relating to the Status of Refugees and the regional refugee definitions' (2 December 2016) HCR/GIP/16/12, para 47.

[59] See section D.

[60] Charter of the United Nations (adopted 26 June 1945, entered into force 24 October 1965) 1 UNTS XVI, arts 1(1) and 2(4).

[61] UNGA Res 3314 (XXIX) (14 December 1974) art 1.

[62] (Adopted 31 January 2005, entered into force 18 December 2009) art 1(c).

Human Rights with international criminal jurisdiction,[63] returned to a formulation closer to the UN notion, including among its list of acts constituting aggression the 'use of armed forces against the sovereignty, territorial integrity and political independence of any state, or any other act inconsistent with the provisions of the Constitutive Act of the ... [AU] and the Charter of the' UN.[64]

Despite the existence of these international definitions, when drafting the Rome Statute of the International Criminal Court (ICC), states were unable to agree on a definition for the crime of aggression; the Rome Statute entered into force in 2002 without one. Aggression was subsequently defined at the 2010 Rome Statute Review Conference in exactly the terms the UN special committee had used.[65] In late 2017 the ICC's Assembly of States Parties adopted a resolution deciding to activate the Court's jurisdiction over aggression as of 17 July 2018.[66] The definition of aggression is thus now settled international law, possibly with an African regional variant in line with the AU Non-Aggression and Common Defence Pact.

With this settled international definition largely mirroring the UN Charter understanding of aggression, which prevailed during the 1969 Convention's drafting and which the drafters thus likely had in mind, 'external aggression' can be interpreted in line with the Rome Statute's usage. Indeed, UNHCR's Guidelines on International Protection No 12 define 'external aggression' as used in the 1969 Convention in exactly these terms: 'the use of armed force by a state against the sovereignty, territorial integrity or political independence of another state, or in any other manner inconsistent with the [UN] Charter'.[67]

Clearly this definition encompasses the colonialism and minority rule about which the drafters were concerned in the sixties, but the definition is sufficiently broad to also encompass modern situations. According to Edwards, 'in order to secure its modern relevance, ... [external aggression] must be interpreted in its widest sense to apply also to events fuelled or supported from outside'.[68] Thus 'external aggression' covers 'international conflict or foreign invasion' and 'due to its lack of specificity, it also arguably encompasses not only wars of aggression but also acts of aggression short of war, although perhaps not mere frontier incidents'.[69] In short, beyond situations squarely captured by the Rome Statute definition of aggression, 'external aggression' also covers disruptive events in the country of origin caused by a foreign power or with an international dimension. For example, in 1985 the UN Security Council characterized South Africa's armed attack of the Angolan province of Cabinda as an act of aggression.[70]

[63] See Chapter 7, section D.

[64] Protocol on Amendments to the Protocol on the Statute of the African Court of Justice and Human Rights (adopted 27 June 2014) Annex, art 28M(B)(a). It is interesting that both AU definitions use 'and' in the enumeration of the interests threatened by aggression, whereas the UN used 'or'.

[65] Rome Statue of the International Criminal Court (adopted 17 July 1998, entered into force 1 July 2002) 2187 UNTS 3, art 8*bis*(2).

[66] ICC Assembly of States Parties, 'Draft Resolution Proposed by the Vice-Presidents of the Assembly: Activation of the Jurisdiction of the Court over the Crime of Aggression' (14 December 2017) ICC-ASP/16/L.10, para 1.

[67] UNHCR (n 58) para 54.

[68] Edwards (n 7) 214.

[69] ibid 213.

[70] UNSC Res 567 (20 June 1985).

(ii) Occupation

'Occupation' has been defined in international humanitarian law (IHL) for some time. According to the annex to the Hague Convention (IV) respecting the Laws and Customs of War on Land, territory is occupied when 'it is actually placed under the authority of the hostile army'. The provision goes on to specify that the 'occupation extends only to the territory where such authority has been established and can be exercised'.[71] On its face and because of the Hague Convention's scope, occupation in this sense can only arise in situations of international armed conflict, and not in non-international armed conflict. The war in the Democratic Republic of the Congo (DRC), in which Uganda,[72] as well as Burundi and Rwanda,[73] were held to be occupying powers, provides a recent African example of this form of occupation.

The fourth Geneva Convention definition of occupation, however, recognizes that international occupation may occur even in the absence of armed resistance,[74] and hence even in the absence of formal war. According to Rankin, this Geneva Convention understanding of occupation is 'more germane to refugee problems in Africa because it focuses on de facto control of territory', regardless of whether occupation is complete and even if war is not formally declared.[75]

UNHCR's understanding of 'occupation' extends beyond these IHL versions of the concept. In discussing situations that might give rise to protection under article I(2) of the 1969 Convention, UNHCR's guidelines mention 'situations not classified as "occupation" within the meaning of IHL, where armed group(s) from either within or outside the country exercise control over territory'.[76] In support of this understanding, UNHCR cites the African Commission on Human and Peoples Rights' statement on Mali, which identified the activities of terrorist groups in northern Mali as occupation.[77] Given the 1969 Convention's humanitarian object and purpose, coupled with Wood's incisive critique of the narrow use of IHL to interpret article I(2),[78] 'occupation' should be understood beyond its narrow IHL meaning. Thus 'occupation' within the meaning of article I(2) covers situations of international armed conflict in which all or a portion of state territory is under the exercised authority of a hostile army, whether or not war has been formally declared, as well as situations in which all or a portion of state territory is actually controlled by domestic or foreign armed groups.

[71] Convention (IV) respecting the Laws and Customs of War on Land and its annex: Regulations concerning the Laws and Customs of War on Land (18 October 1907) 205 CTS 277, art 42.

[72] *Armed Activities in the Territory of the Congo* (*Democratic Republic of the Congo v Uganda*) (Judgment) [2005] ICJ Rep 2005 168, 227–31.

[73] *Democratic Republic of Congo v Burundi, Rwanda and Uganda* comm no 277/99, 12th Annual Activity Report of the Af Cm HPR (2006).

[74] Convention (IV) relative to the Protection of Civilian Persons in Time of War (21 October 1950) 75 UNTS 287, art 2.

[75] Rankin (n 4) 422–23.

[76] UNHCR (n 58) para 55, emphasis added.

[77] African Commission, 'Statement by the African Commission on the Present Human Rights Situation in Mali' (18 January 2013) <http://www.achpr.org/press/2013/01/d140/> accessed 11 January 2017.

[78] See Wood (n 40), especially 193–95.

(iii) Foreign domination

'Foreign domination' has no autonomous legal meaning. Its ordinary meaning of international control clearly captures colonialism. Indeed, according to Rankin, the term has been used in international law beyond the 1969 Convention to refer to colonialism, and may even have been included in the 1969 Convention to ensure that article I(2) would cover refugees from colonialism.[79] He explains that colonialism was not 'initially analysed as an infringement on the conquered state's sovereignty', because in a colonial state, sovereignty rests with the metropolitan power.[80] Strictly speaking, aggression and occupation are predicated on the interaction of two sovereigns. They may not, therefore, have been sufficient to capture individuals fleeing colonialism as originally understood. This, according to Rankin, may have led the drafters to 'include the broader concept of foreign domination'.[81] Edwards, too, views 'foreign domination' as broader than 'occupation'.[82]

Thus 'foreign domination' certainly captures forms of foreign control beyond simply colonialism. The term's ordinary meaning does not, however, convey just how far 'foreign domination' should extend. Edwards wonders whether 'foreign domination' covers the degree of control exercised by multilateral lenders and foreign donors, UN sanctions or puppet governments.[83] The 1969 Convention's eighth preambular paragraph states that African problems 'must be solved in the spirit' of the OAU Charter, which Edwards points out lists 'the fight against neo-colonialism in all its forms' as among its aims,[84] leading her to conclude that 'foreign domination' may be interpreted expansively.[85] The African Charter on Human and Peoples' Rights (African Charter) construes foreign domination in a similarly broad manner, noting that it may be 'political, economic or cultural'.[86] UNHCR's recent assessment supports these views. The agency defines 'foreign domination' within the meaning of the 1969 Convention as 'the political, economic or cultural control of a state by (agents of) one or more other states, association of states, or state-governed international organizations'.[87] This is broad enough to cover both colonialism and contemporary forms of foreign domination, so constitutes a sensible definition of the term.

(iv) Events seriously disturbing public order

The end of colonialism and minority rule diminished the significance of the three 1969 Events discussed earlier in this section.[88] Okoth-Obbo even finds that article

[79] Rankin (n 4) 423.

[80] Jenik Radon, 'Balance of Power: Redefining Sovereignty in Contemporary International Law' (2004) 40 Stanford J Intl L 195, 199 in Rankin (n 4) 423.

[81] ibid. [82] Edwards (n 7) 216. [83] ibid.

[84] Charter of the Organization of African Unity (25 May 1963) 479 UNTS 39, preambular para 6 (emphasis added).

[85] Edwards (n 7) 216.

[86] African Charter on Human and Peoples' Rights (adopted 27 June 1981, entered into force 21 October 1986) 21 ILM 58, art 20(3).

[87] UNHCR (n 58) para 55.

[88] Edwards (n 7) 216; Bahame Tom Mukirya Nyanduga, 'Refugee Protection Under the 1969 OAU Convention Governing the Specific Aspects of Refugee Problems in Africa' (2004) 47 German YB Intl L 85, 92; Okoth-Obbo (n 4) 115–16.

I(2) 'should be upgraded to more properly reflect the actual situations which today cause people to flee as refugees in Africa'.[89] With 'external aggression', 'occupation', and 'foreign domination' being less common causes of refugee flight today,[90] 'events seriously disturbing public order' is particularly significant. Indeed, it is currently the cause of flight most frequently employed in the adjudication of refugee status under article I(2).[91] Interpreting 'events seriously disturbing public order' raises issues of both meaning and threshold, as well as the discrete questions of whether the term protects so-called environmental refugees and whether it covers events of a non-international character.

No international requirement

The latter question was raised by Edwards further to the interpretive maxim *noscitur a sociis*,[92] which mandates that words be interpreted in line with the language surrounding them. Since 'external aggression', 'occupation', and 'foreign domination' each involve an international element, it is plausible that 'events seriously disturbing public order' should be interpreted as involving the same. However, Edwards concludes that 'events seriously disturbing public order' may be domestic, because *noscitur a sociis* may equally be 'applied to cover events that share the fact that there is a serious disruption to society that threatens the lives and freedoms of human beings (rather than the international character of the events)'.[93] Furthermore, Edwards notes that 'there is no explicit language in Article 1(2) to suggest that the disruption needs to arise from outside the territory, in addition to which the term "public order" is most commonly applied in terms of internal security or stability of society'.[94] This latter argument is so convincing that Edwards need not have raised *noscitur a sociis*. Treaty terms are first and foremost to be construed in accordance with their ordinary meaning; interpretive maxims are only relevant when such meaning is unclear. The ordinary meaning of 'events seriously disturbing public order' does not exclude purely domestic disturbances.

State practice affirms this conclusion. For example, in 2010 and 2011, each of Ghana, Guinea, Liberia, and Togo recognized prima facie the refugee status of individuals fleeing the purely domestic post-election violence in Côte d'Ivoire.[95] A 2013 DRC declaration of prima facie status offered protection under article I(2)'s 'events

[89] Okoth-Obbo (n 4) 116; contra: Ruma Mandal, 'Protection Mechanisms Outside the 1951 Convention ("Complementary Protection")' (2005) UNHCR Legal and Protection Policy Research Series <http://www.unhcr.org/435df0aa2.pdf> accessed 8 December 2010, 14.

[90] See, however, Wood (n 40) 189–91 for a discussion of the contemporary relevance of 'external aggression', 'occupation', and 'foreign domination'.

[91] Sharpe (n 12) 133. [92] Edwards (n 7) 217. [93] ibid. [94] ibid.

[95] Ghana, 'Declaration of Refugee Status' (no date) (on file with the author); Guinea, Ministère de l'administration du territoire et de la decentralisation, letter to the UNHCR Representative in Guinea (10 January 2011) (on file with the author); Liberia Refugee Repatriation and Resettlement Commission, 'LRRRC Gazette' (15 December 2010) (on file with the author); Togo, Ministère de la sécurité et de la protection civile, letter to the UNHCR Representative in Togo (20 October 2011) (on file with the author). It should be noted that none of these declarations specified the instrument or provision pursuant to which status was being recognized. However, it was likely to be article I(2), as Côte d'Ivoire's post-election violence was clearly neither external aggression, occupation, nor foreign domination.

seriously disturbing public order' clause to individuals who had fled the Central African Republic in 2010 and 2012, during which years the country was experiencing civil war.[96] In 2014 Kenya issued a declaration of prima facie status in respect of individuals who had fled events seriously disturbing public order in South Sudan, which was then—and remains—gripped by civil war.[97] Additionally, events deemed by the Beninese, Chadian, and South African jurisprudence to constitute 'events seriously disturbing public order' were for the most part non-international: again, the 2010 post-election violence in Côte d'Ivoire; the conflict between the forces of General Laurent Nkunda and the national army in the Kivu region of the DRC; the 2002 civil war in Côte d'Ivoire; the Angolan civil war; the Rwandan genocide;[98] the 1993–2006 Burundian civil war; clan fighting in Kismayo and Mogadishu, Somalia;[99] and generalized insecurity in the eastern part of the DRC.[100] Indeed, Edwards herself notes that states have 'shown a willingness to protect persons fleeing internal, as well as external, disturbances'.[101] Moreover, UNHCR's understanding of 'events seriously disturbing public order' encompasses both international and internal events.[102]

Public order

Having established that 'events seriously disturbing public order' may be non-international, the next logical step is to determine the meaning of 'public order', which though a technical legal term, does not have one consistent legal meaning. 'Public order' is used elsewhere in international law, including three times in the 1951 Convention. Both Edwards and Rankin take this as their starting point, in Rankin's case because the 1969 Convention's status as the regional complement of the 1951 instrument suggests that terms used in both treaties should be understood analogously.[103] Article 2 of the 1951 Convention requires that refugees conform to 'measures taken for the maintenance of public order'. Article 28 directs states to issue refugees with travel documents 'unless compelling reasons of national security or public order otherwise require'. Finally, article 32 prohibits expulsion 'save on grounds of national security or public order'. Rankin argues sensibly that this article 32 use of 'public order' is most closely aligned with article I(2)'s use of the term.[104] Grahl-Madsen's analysis of the *travaux préparatoires* indicates that 'public order' in article 32 was a reference to acts that would undermine 'the preservation of peace and tranquillity in the society at large'.[105]

[96] DRC, 'Arrête ministeriel no 25/CAB/MININTERSEDAC/050/2012 du 11 Fev 2013 portant reconnaissance du statut de refugie "prima facie" ' (11 February 2013) (on file with the author).

[97] Kenya, Gazette Notice No 5274 (1 August 2014) <https://perma.cc/ZQR4-NLHB> accessed 23 March 2017.

[98] Unreported cases, on file with the author.

[99] Schreier (n 57) 57 and 59.

[100] *Felix Onasisi Mubala v The Chairperson of the Standing Committee for Refugee Affairs and Others*, Western Cape High Court 10971/2013 (8 November 2013) <http://www.refworld.org/cases,ZAF_HC,539aad4e4.html> accessed 13 April 2017.

[101] Edwards (n 7) 218.

[102] UNHCR (n 58) para 56.

[103] Rankin (n 4) 425.

[104] ibid.

[105] Atle Grahl-Madsen, 'Commentary on the Refugee Convention 1951: Articles 2–11, 13–37' (1997) UNHCR <http://www.refworld.org/pdfid/4785ee9d2.pdf> accessed 13 January 2017, 129.

Other instances of 'public order' in international law include elsewhere within the 1969 Convention,[106] as well as in the Cartagena Declaration[107] and in the International Covenant on Civil and Political Rights (ICCPR).[108] The latter's use of public order is most helpful. The ICCPR uses the term in the context of permissible limitations on certain rights. For example, freedom of movement and residence 'shall not be subject to any restrictions except those which are provided by law, are necessary to protect national security, public order (ordre public), public health or morals or the rights and freedoms of others'.[109] The use of French refers to public order's origins in France's Napoleonic Code. This concept of 'ordre public' is broad, not unlike the common law's 'public policy'.[110] Additionally, the use of 'public order' alongside 'national security' in the ICCPR, as well as in articles 28 and 32 of the 1951 Convention, suggests that the term involves issues which, while serious, are less grave than those implicated by 'national security'. Anything so serious as to threaten national security, such as terrorism, would of course also threaten public order, but certain disturbances, such as protests, might threaten public order without implicating national security. In Edwards's words, while 'national security and public order are often invoked simultaneously, "public order" also relates to localised insecurity or chaos'.[111]

Rankin's analysis concludes by noting that 'public order' 'is a concept that looks to the basic standards governing the state in its relation to the community and its members'.[112] Edwards sums up by suggesting the meaning of 'public order' will depend on the context, and each of administrative, social, political, and moral order may be involved.[113] Certainly, on its ordinary meaning alone, 'public order' is a very general term. It may be that it was included for precisely this reason, and its related ability to function as a 'basket clause capturing a generic set of refugee producing situations'.[114] Understanding the term in this expansive manner is certainly in line with the 1969 Convention's humanitarian object and purpose.

Environmental events

An additional question is whether 'events seriously disturbing public order' must be generated by human activity; in other words, whether the clause permits refugees from environmental disasters, such as desertification, drought, earthquakes, and floods. This question is particularly salient given the drought and related famine currently plaguing the Horn of Africa. The term 'events' is certainly broad enough to encompass such occurrences. Scholarly and policy opinion is, however, divided. Edwards,[115] Hathaway,[116] and Mandal[117] are of the view that 'events seriously

[106] 'Public order' is used in the article III prohibition of subversive activities and in the article VI provision on travel documents.

[107] 'Public order' is used in the section III(3) refugee definition.

[108] Articles 12, 14, 19, 21, and 22 mention public order.

[109] (Adopted 16 December 1966, entered into force 23 March 1976) 999 UNTS 171, art 12(3).

[110] WA Bewes, 'Public Order (Ordre Public)' (1921) 37 LQR 315, 315.

[111] (n 7) 219.

[112] (n 4) 425.

[113] (n 7) 220.

[114] Rankin (n 4) 423; contra: Edwards (n 7) 217–18.

[115] (n 7) 225–27.

[116] (n 27) 16–17.

[117] (n 89) 14.

disturbing public order' must be solely human-made, while Naldi,[118] Rwelamira,[119] Viljoen,[120] a UNHCR working group,[121] and Wood[122] find that the 1969 Convention can provide refugee status to individuals fleeing environmental events.

State practice on whether 'events seriously disturbing public order' covers environmental disruption is equally divided. For example, Kenya recognized Somalis fleeing the 2011 drought prima facie, under article I(2).[123] By contrast, Uganda was of the view that people fleeing the 2002 eruption of Mount Nyiragongo in the DRC were not refugees, and offered them only temporary protection.[124] Similarly, a 1998 South African White Paper, prepared in connection with the drafting of that country's Refugees Act, states that the 'government … does not agree that it is appropriate to consider as refugees, persons fleeing their countries of origin solely for reasons of poverty or other social, economic or environmental hardships'.[125]

The Nansen Initiative recently sought to advance thinking on this controversial issue. In her technical paper for the project, Wood finds that 'events seriously disturbing public order' should be interpreted to include environmental disasters. She bases this conclusion on three arguments.[126] Firstly, the ordinary meaning of 'events seriously disturbing public order' does not exclude natural hazards; rather, the language emphasizes the effects of the events and is neutral as to their cause. Secondly, disturbances or disasters rarely, if ever, have solely environmental causes; socio-political factors almost always play a role.[127] Finally, in addition to 'ordinary meaning', two further principles of treaty interpretation equally do not support distinguishing between natural and human-made events. First among these is the context in which 'events seriously disturbing public order' appears: alongside 'external aggression, occupation and foreign domination', each of which involves a serious disruption that threatens lives. This shared feature demands that 'it is the effect of the risk, not its origins or internal characteristics, which is paramount'.[128] Furthermore, the 1969 Convention's object and purpose of refugee protection

[118] Gino Naldi, *The Organization of African Unity: An Analysis of its Role* (2nd edn, Mansell 1999) 83.

[119] (n 4) 558; note, however, that Rwelamira is internally inconsistent on this point, noting on the same page that events seriously disturbing public order must be 'man-made'.

[120] Frans Viljoen, *International Human Rights Law in Africa* (2nd edn, OUP 2012) 243.

[121] UNHCR, 'Persons Covered by the OAU Convention Governing the Specific Aspects of Refugee Problems in Africa and by the Cartagena Declaration on Refugees (Submitted by the African Group and the Latin American Group)' (1992) UNHCR EC/1992/SCP/CRP6 <http://www.refworld.org/topic,50ffbce51b1,50ffbce51ba,3ae68cd214,0,,SESSIONALREPORT,.html> accessed 25 January 2017, para 7.

[122] Tamara Wood, 'Protection and Disasters in the Horn of Africa: Norms and Practice for Addressing Cross-Border Displacement in Disaster Contexts' (2015) The Nansen Initiative <http://www.nanseninitiative.org/wp-content/uploads/2015/03/190215_Technical_Paper_Tamara_Wood.pdf> accessed 23 January 2017.

[123] Vikram Kolmannskog, '"We Are in Between": Case Studies of the Protection of Somalis Displaced to Kenya and Egypt During the 2011 and 2012 Drought' (2014) 2 Intl J Soc Sci Stud 83, 85–86.

[124] Wood (n 122) 25.

[125] South Africa, 'Draft Refugee White Paper' (1998) Gazette General Notice 1122, 7, cited in Wood (n 124) 25.

[126] Wood (n 122) 26.

[127] See, generally, Amartya Sen, *Poverty and Famines: An Essay on Entitlement and Deprivation* (OUP 1981).

[128] Wood (n 122) 26.

mitigate against interpreting 'events seriously disturbing public order' as excluding environmental occurrences.

Wood's view that 'events seriously disturbing public order' may include environmental disasters is sound. Her view is bolstered by three further considerations, the first two of which take aim at potential arguments against Wood's interpretation. Firstly, according to the ICJ, an evolutionary interpretive approach is only warranted if the parties to the treaty in question intended it.[129] The drafting history discussed in Chapter 2 revealed no such specific intention. It is thus important to highlight that the view of article I(2) as capable of protecting individuals displaced by environmental events does not depend on an evolutive interpretation. Rather, the 1969 Convention will protect individuals in flight from an environmental event if such event is sufficiently severe that it seriously disturbs public order. In other words, the interpretation is based on ordinary meaning, rather than on any evolutive approach. Secondly, because the 1969 Convention is the 'regional complement' to the 1951 Convention,[130] the latter is the most relevant rule 'of international law applicable in the relations between the parties' to which the article 31(3)(c) principle of systemic interpretation speaks. The 1969 Convention must therefore be interpreted in line with its global counterpart. The 1951 Convention does not extend refugee status to individuals in flight from environmental events, which raises the possibility of viewing Wood's approach to article I(2) as an impermissible departure from the 1951 Convention's article 1A(2). However, the divergence between environmental refugees under article 1A(2) and such refugees under article I(2) is permissible because the 1969 Convention addresses refugee issues particular to Africa;[131] this is precisely the sense in which it is the 1951 Convention's 'regional complement'.

Thirdly, in 1990, states in Africa adopted the African Charter on the Rights and Welfare of the Child (Children's Charter).[132] Its article 25 covers family unity, with paragraph 2(b) focusing on separation from parents during displacement. This provision mentions 'separation ... caused by internal and external displacement arising from armed conflicts or natural disasters'. While this provision does not describe children externally displaced by natural disasters as 'refugees', it does mention natural disasters alongside armed conflict, which clearly does produce refugees. Article 25(2)(b) of the Children's Charter therefore lends a measure of support to the inclusion of natural disasters within the meaning of 'events seriously disturbing public order'.

Until there is a critical mass of state practice and/or jurisprudence on this issue, whether article I(2) permits refugees from environmental disasters will remain somewhat unsettled. In the meantime, construing article I(2) as affording refugee protection to individuals in flight from major environmental events is in line with the ordinary meaning of 'events seriously disturbing public order' and is supported

[129] Sondre Torp Helmersen, 'Evolutive Treaty Interpretation: Legality, Semantics and Distinctions' (2013) 6 European J Leg Stud 127.

[130] See Chapter 4. [131] See Chapter 2, sections D.4–5.

[132] (Adopted 11 July 1990, entered into force 29 November 1999) OAU Doc CAB/LEG/24.9/49(1990).

somewhat by other regional law, and arguments that might mitigate this expansive interpretation are ultimately unpersuasive.

The 'serious' threshold

Having ascertained the broad meaning of 'public order', the next step in interpreting 'events seriously disturbing public order' relates to the threshold of disturbance necessary to ground a claim for refugee status. The use of the plural 'events' rather than the singular 'event' suggests that a one-time occurrence that does not itself lead to further disruption would not qualify as 'serious'. According to recent UNHCR guidance, the 'threshold of "serious" refers to public disorder events likely to disrupt the normal functioning of the institutions of the state and affect internal and external security and stability of the state and society'.[133] This explanation is reasonable, except the meaning of the reference to the '*external* security and stability of the state and society' is not clear. Additionally, it would have been preferable to refer to 'the state *or* society', since state structures can be propped up through illegitimate means, such as the unlawful use of force.

In practice

Given the difficulty of interpreting 'events seriously disturbing public order' precisely based on the term's ordinary meaning alone, authoritative sources that provide examples of 'events seriously disturbing public order', such as case law and UNHCR guidance, are particularly important. UNHCR's Guidelines on International Protection No 12 list the following examples of 'events seriously disturbing public order': international and non-international armed conflict within the meaning of IHL; violence by or between different societal groups or between the state and non-state actors;[134] and situations of generalized violence, meaning 'violence that is widespread, affecting large groups of persons or entire populations, serious and/or massive human rights violations, or events characterised by the loss of government control and its inability of unwillingness to protect its populations—including situations characterized by repressive and coercive social controls by non-state actors, often pursued through intimidation, harassment and violence'.[135] Widespread human rights violations should have been included in this list, in particular because scholars who have addressed whether massive human rights violations constitute 'events seriously disturbing public order' have answered this question affirmatively.[136]

UNHCR's guidance also lists the following factual indicators of the presence of 'events seriously disturbing public order':

> a declared state of emergency; violations of IHL including war crimes; acts of terrorism; a significant number of people killed, injured or displaced; the closure of schools; a lack of food, medical services and supplies, and other vital services such as water, electricity and sanitation; a change in, or collapse of, government institutions and services, political systems or the

[133] UNHCR (n 58) para 56. [134] ibid. [135] ibid para 58.

[136] Edwards (n 7) 222–25; Tal Schreier, 'The Expanded Refugee Definition' in Fatima Khan and Tal Schreier (eds), *Refugee Law in South Africa* (Juta 2014) 83–85.

police and justice system; the imposition of parallel or informal justice and administrative systems; and/or non-state actors controlling state territory.[137]

Interestingly, the last indicator is also suggestive of occupation within the meaning of article I(2), indicating that 'events seriously disturbing public order' may overlap to some extent with other 1969 Events. Several among these indicators describe violations of rights guaranteed under international human rights law, further suggesting that widespread rights violations may constitute 'events seriously disturbing public order'.

A review of available case law reveals conflict as the most common situation found to constitute an event 'seriously disturbing public order'. This was evident in unreported decisions from Benin, Chad, and South Africa.[138] These decisions did not distinguish between conflicts among clans or rebels and conflict between the government on the one hand and clans or rebels on the other. Examples of the conflicts deemed by the Beninese, Chadian, and South African jurisprudence to constitute 'events seriously disturbing public order' were mentioned earlier in this section.[139] Available declarations of prima facie status relate exclusively to conflict. As mentioned earlier in this section,[140] refugees have been recognized on a prima facie basis due to the post election violence in Côte d'Ivoire and civil wars in the Central African Republic and South Sudan.

Two South African Refugee Appeal Board cases reviewed by Schreier further qualify the meaning of 'events seriously disturbing public order'. In the first, concerning religious violence in Nigeria, the board found that the term implies the government's loss of control. The board recognized the existence of violence between Christians and Muslims but did not characterize this as 'events seriously disturbing public order' because such events imply 'that the government is no longer in control ... [which] is not the case in Nigeria at all, [since] the government is firmly in control'.[141] The second case expanded upon this notion, holding that where

> law and order has broken [down] and the government is unwilling or unable to protect its citizens, it can be said that there are events seriously disturbing public order. To determine when a disturbance had taken place involves weighing the degree and intensity of the conduct complained of against the degree and nature of the peace which can be expected to prevail in a given place at a given time. The test should be objective.[142]

A 2009 South African Refugee Appeal Board case concerning an applicant from the Kivu region of the eastern DRC reached a similar conclusion: 'Where law and order has broken down and the government is unwilling or unable to protect its citizens it can be said that there are events seriously disturbing public order'.[143] Thus according to these cases, it is not only the loss of government control that is salient; such loss of control must also threaten civilian protection.

[137] UNHCR (n 58) para 59.
[138] On file with the author.
[139] See text attached to n 98.
[140] See text attached to n 95 and ff.
[141] South African Refugee Appeal Board Decision 1433/06, para 22, cited in Schreier (n 57) 60.
[142] South African Refugee Appeal Board Decision 729/06, para 13, cited in Schreier (n 57) 61.
[143] Cited in Wood (n 13) 565.

Nigerian case law appears to consistently absorb generalized violence within article I(2) of the 1969 Convention. All Nigerian decisions available—of which there were four, three relating to applicants from the DRC and one from Somalia—noted only that 'The applicant is outside of her country of nationality or habitual residence and is unable to return there owing to serious and indiscriminate threats to life, physical integrity or freedom resulting from generalized violence or events seriously disturbing public order'.[144] This language mirror's UNHCR's broader refugee definition, which it applies when conducting RSD under its mandate.[145] In applying the 1969 Convention, the Nigerian decisions make the existence of 'serious and indiscriminate threats to life, physical integrity or freedom' the threshold consideration for recognition under article I(2), whether such threats stemmed from generalized violence or events seriously disturbing public order. It is unclear why Nigerian practice operationalizes article I(2) via UNHCR's broadened refugee definition; this seems an incorrect conflation of what are two similar but distinct legal criteria for refugee status.

This Nigerian error aside, in summary, 'events seriously disturbing public order', as understood in jurisprudence from Benin, Chad, and South Africa, implies conflict—whether international or non-international and whether among non-state actors or between non-state actors and the government—leading to loss of governmental control that threatens the civilian population, and the unwillingness or inability of the government to regain such control.

Taken together, the foregoing suggests that disturbances to public order include international and non-international armed conflict, environmental disasters, generalized violence, and widespread human rights violations. Such events may ground a claim for refugee protection under article I(2) when they disrupt the normal functioning of the institutions of the state and affect the security and stability of the state or society.

(e) The test for refugee status

Having interpreted article I(2)'s scope and the meaning of each of the 1969 Events, three clauses still require elaboration: 'in either part of the whole of', 'compelled', and 'place of habitual residence'. Each of these contributes to the test for refugee status under article I(2). It is important to examine this test, because there is an erroneous interpretive consensus around article I(2) characterized by the almost universal propensity to view the provision as remarkably 'inclusive',[146] 'expansive',[147] 'extensive',[148] 'wide',[149] or 'broad'.[150] This somewhat

[144] Nigerian decisions in April 2010 report of the Nigerian Eligibility Committee, on file with the author.

[145] See section B.1 of this chapter.

[146] Jeff Crisp, 'Forced Displacement in Africa: Dimensions, Difficulties, and Policy Directions' (2010) 29 RSQ 1, 3.

[147] Nierum S Okogbule, 'The Legal Dimensions of the Refugee Problem in Africa' (2004) 10 E Afr J Peace & Hum Rts 176, 183; Hofmann (n 6) 323; Turner (n 5) 286.

[148] Ivor C Jackson, *The Refugee Concept in Group Situations* (Martinus Nijhoff 1999) 177.

[149] Naldi and D'Orsi (n 26) 128; Emmanuel Opoku Awuku, 'Refugee Movements in Africa and the OAU Convention on Refugees' (1995) 39 J Afr L 79, 82; Okoth-Obbo (n 4) 112.

[150] Eduardo Arboleda, 'Refugee Definition in Africa and Latin America: The Lessons of Pragmatism' (1991) 3 IJRL 185, 194; Naldi and D'Orsi (n 26) 127.

flawed consensus flows from the view that article I(2) is susceptible to a completely objective application in RSD.[151] The test for refugee status under article I(2) is not, however, entirely objective.

In moving away from the 1951 Convention's emphasis on individualized persecution linked to enumerated grounds in favour of a focus on the disruptive conditions in the country of origin, and in requiring 'neither the elements of deliberateness nor discrimination inherent in the 1951 Convention definition',[152] the article I(2) refugee definition certainly stresses objective considerations. According to Hathaway, it 'acknowledges the reality that fundamental forms of abuse may occur not only as a result of the calculated acts of the government . . . but also as a result of that government's loss of authority'.[153] But the view that this outward orientation means that the article I(2) refugee definition is 'based solely on objective criteria'[154] and therefore mandates an entirely objective test of refugee status is overstated, overlooking elements of the regional refugee definition that mandate an assessment of the connection between the relevant 1969 Event and flight.

Commentary on the 1969 Convention rarely addresses this nexus or indeed the test for refugee status under article I(2). Rather, there seems to be an implicit or unarticulated assumption that an individual would not flee a 1969 Event but for a nexus between the event and a risk of harm. In what represents an uncommon consideration of this issue, Hathaway finds that the 1969 Convention article I(2)

> definition . . . leaves open the possibility that the basis or rationale for the harm may be indeterminate. So long as a person 'is compelled' to seek refuge because of some anticipated serious disruption of public order, she need not be in a position to demonstrate any linkage between her personal status (or that of some collectivity of which she is a member) and the impending harm. Because the African standard emphasizes assessment of the gravity of the disruption of public order rather than motives for flight, individuals are largely able to decide for themselves when harm is sufficiently proximate to warrant flight.[155]

Hathaway's view is thus that in the determination of refugee status, flight itself provides sufficient evidence of the threat of harm. While in most cases such will indeed be the case, this approach obfuscates the importance of two textual elements of article I(2), which suggest that the nexus between the 1969 Event and flight ought to be more than merely assumed.

(i) Nexus requirement

The first textual element is 'compelled'. Refugee status under article I(2) depends on the individual having been 'compelled to leave' because of a 1969 Event. On its

[151] See, for example, Arboleda (n 150) 195; Okoth-Obbo (n 4) 112; Weis (n 3) 455; WJEM van Hövell tot Westerflier, 'Africa and Refugees: the OAU Refugee Convention in Theory and Practice' (1989) 7 NQHR 172, 175.

[152] Mandal (n 89) 13.

[153] (n 27) 17.

[154] Awuku (n 149) 81.

[155] (n 27) 18.

ordinary meaning alone, the use of 'compelled' strongly suggests that the African refugee definition requires a nexus between the 1969 Event and the individual's flight. The authors who have addressed this issue agree. Edwards argues that

> it would not be unreasonable in status procedures to require a claimant from Kinshasa ... to justify why he or she departed the city on the basis of generalised violence occurring in North Kivu, an area thousands of miles from the capital. In all likelihood, it would be quite difficult for him or her to prove that he or she was 'compelled' to leave as a result of those events if one only considered the objective facts. Importing a subjective analysis does not mean that an individual needs to prove that flight was the only alternative available, but it does introduce a causal connection or nexus between the flight and the event in question.[156]

In Wood's view, 'compelled' should be read with the 1969 Convention's article II(3) non-refoulement provision, which 'only prevents the return of a person "where his life, physical integrity or liberty would be threatened"'.[157] Rankin approaches the nature of 'compelled' with some ambivalence, though he too concedes that it may mandate an assessment of the link between the 1969 Event and the individual: 'Is the mere existence of an OAU event enough to demonstrate that someone has been compelled? Or is it necessary to show linkages between an asylum seeker and a particular event? Until these questions are answered compelled remains ambiguous'.[158] Thus there seems to be a consensus among those who have considered the issue that the import of 'compelled' has been overlooked, and that it brings a consideration of the nexus between the 1969 Event and the individual into the determination of refugee status under article I(2). While the term 'compelled' is on its own insufficient to illuminate the nature of the nexus required—this issue is addressed later in this section—what is clear is that the mere existence of a 1969 Event somewhere in the country of origin or nationality is not sufficient to ground a claim for refugee status under article I(2).

The second textual element suggesting that the nexus between the 1969 Event and flight ought to be more than merely presumptive is 'owing to'. The ordinary meaning of 'owing to' is analogous to 'as a result of', 'due to', or 'because of'. Under the article I(2) definition, a refugee is someone who, as a result of, due to or because of a 1969 Event, flees his or her place of habitual residence. Put this way, it becomes clear that flight must be connected to a risk of harm to the individual stemming from a 1969 Event.

Additionally, a mere assumption that flight was the result of threatened harm does not reflect the targeted nature of the 1969 Convention and the nature of refugee protection more generally. It is axiomatic that the 1969 Convention extends refugee protection only where such protection is necessary to safeguard an individual from a 1969 Event, and refugee law in general provides international protection only where the protective relationship between the individual and his or her country of origin has broken down. That the 1969 Convention and refugee law more generally do not extend international protection indiscriminately requires that the 1969 Convention's refugee definition not be applied in an indiscriminate manner. Relying

[156] (n 7) 229–30. [157] (n 40) 195. [158] (n 4) 412.

solely on objective criteria to determine refugee status 'could (and does) give rise to situations where asylum is sought by persons who flee for reasons unconnected to the event in question, but who can use that event to claim asylum'.[159] This could not have been intended.

Several unreported South African decisions reviewed by Schreier demonstrate an assessment of the nexus between the 1969 Event and flight, further to the definition's 'compelled' element.[160] Moreover, a recent judicial review of a South African decision found that determining whether an individual qualifies under section 3(b) (South Africa's domestic equivalent of article I(2)) requires

> (i) an assessment by the relevant authority of the existence of objectively ascertainable circumstances in the person's country of origin, and
> (ii) assuming that it is satisfied upon such assessment that such circumstances correspond with any of those stipulated in the definition, a decision whether their effect on the individual concerned has been such as to force him or her to leave the place where he or she ordinarily resided. The qualifying criteria thus posit refugee status in the category concerned being determined with regard to the causative effect of a given situation on an individual. The test is predominantly objective in character, but the required consideration by the relevant authority of the causative effect of the circumstances involved on the person concerned introduces a subjective element that demands that the individual's personal circumstances be taken into account.... where volition rather than compulsion is the predominant factor in the person's decision to leave his or her home, he or she does not qualify as a refugee in terms of s 3(b).[161]

There is thus clear judicial support, from South Africa at least, of the nexus requirement advanced here.

Schreier, however, cautions against an overwrought assessment, citing an unreported case in which the South African Department of Home Affairs challenged refugees' compulsion to flee Somalia because they had already endured nearly twenty years of civil war there.[162] Certainly, article I(2)'s 'compelled' element should not be employed to compound the separate credibility assessment that forms part of RSD in any case, nor does it justify in-depth scrutiny of the reasonableness of a refugee's flight. Rather, on its own, 'compelled' merely requires a nexus between the 1969 Event and flight. The nature of that nexus is elaborated by the 'place of habitual residence' element.

Nature of the nexus

That some nexus between the 1969 Event and flight is required raises the question of the nature of the connection necessary. The regional refugee definition provides that a refugee must have been 'compelled to leave' his or her 'place of habitual residence'. According to Rankin, this latter clause is used to focus 'attention on

[159] Edwards (n 7) 230. [160] (n 57) 57–60.

[161] *Radjabu v The Chairperson of the Standing Committee for Refugee Affairs* [2015] 1 All SA 100 (WCC) (*Radjabu*) (4 September 2014) <http://www.refworld.org/cases,ZAF_HC,540874f94.html> accessed 13 April 2017 para 6.

[162] (n 136) 88.

those who face danger because of the state of their communities', resulting in 'an implied relationship or geographic nexus between an OAU event and a person's place of habitual residence'.[163] Thus the article I(2) definition requires physical proximity between the 1969 Event and the individual's home. A South African Refugee Appeal Board case relating to a man from Kismayo, Somalia—then gripped by clan warfare—demonstrates this. The decision noted that it 'is clear that anyone coming from … southern Somalia, such as Kismayo, whether anything has happened to them or not, fall within the group of asylum seekers needing international protection'.[164]

Three South African Refugee Appeal Board decisions analysed by Schreier demonstrate such an assessment of whether the 1969 Event occurred in the applicant's place of habitual residence. In the first, refugee status was denied to a man from the objectively safe town of Lubumbashi in the DRC, who encountered violence while on vacation in Pweto.[165] The second case concerned a woman from Uvira, a town in the DRC's South Kivu province. She fled fighting in Uvira but spent nine months in Moba before eventually fleeing to South Africa. The Refugee Appeal Board recognized Uvira as the applicant's place of habitual residence and accorded her refugee status on that basis:

> The last location where the appellant 'resided' in the DRC was Moba where she had fled to after leaving Mulonge village in Uvira. The Board has reservations whether Moba can be seen as the appellant's habitual residence and finds that it was not whether or not she was compelled to leave it. The Board finds that Uvira was the appellant's place of habitual residence which she was compelled to leave in order to seek refuge elsewhere. The appellant's evidence indicates that she was compelled to leave her place of habitual residence due to events seriously disturbing or disrupting public order i.e. the fighting taking place in the eastern DRC and specifically Uvira.[166]

In the third case, a man originally from Kinshasa moved to Bukavu and, after four years, fled violence there. The Refugee Appeal Board rejected his application for refugee status, determining that Kinshasa was his place of habitual residence and he could safely return there.[167] This overly restrictive interpretation of 'place of habitual residence' aside, these cases together demonstrate that in South Africa at least, refugee status under article I(2) depends on an assessment of whether the 1969 Event affected the refugee's home.

The requirement that flight must be from the 'place of habitual residence' also explains why the words 'in either part or the whole of his country of origin or nationality' do not expand the refugee definition by as much as might be initially expected. The language makes it at least initially plausible that an individual may be recognized as a refugee if his or her flight is prompted by a 1969 Event taking place anywhere in his or her country of origin or nationality. However, as discussed earlier

[163] (n 4) 432 (emphasis added).
[164] South African Refugee Appeal Board decision no 159/2004, 3, cited in Schreier (n 57) 57.
[165] (n 57) 60.
[166] South African Refugee Appeal Board decision no 378/05, para 21-2, cited in Schreier (n 57) 59.
[167] Schreier (n 136) 90.

in this section, there is 'a necessary link between the asylum seeker and the OAU event ... the nexus is created by the fact that an asylum seeker is compelled to leave his or her place of habitual residence'.[168]

Moreover, for textual reasons the qualification 'in either part or the whole of his country of origin or nationality' likely relates only to the fourth and final 1969 Event, 'events seriously disturbing public order'. The interpretive maxim *ejusdem generis* provides that 'general words following special words are limited to the genus indicated by the special words'.[169] This suggests that because 'events seriously disturbing public order' is not separated from 'in either part or the whole of his country of origin or nationality' by a comma, the former qualifies only the latter. Furthermore, the necessity of specifying 'in either part or the whole of his country of origin or nationality' attaches only to 'events seriously disturbing public order'. External aggression, occupation, and foreign domination, even if only physically prevailing in one part of a state, will by definition affect the country as a whole.[170] The inclusion of 'in either part or the whole of his country of origin or nationality' thus should not be taken to imply that an individual may justifiably flee a 1969 Event not directly connected to him or her.

In summary, the terms 'compelled' and 'owing to', coupled with the 1969 Convention's obvious purpose of offering protection only to those at risk of harm, imply that the regional refugee definition requires a nexus between the 1969 Event and flight. The requirement that an individual has fled his or her 'place of habitual residence' and the limited applicability of 'in either part or the whole of his country of origin or nationality' clarifies that the nature of the nexus required is one of geographic proximity. Thus in principle, refugee status under the 1969 Convention's article I(2) should depend on an assessed, as opposed to an assumed, geographic nexus between the 1969 Event and the individual's flight. This calls into question the sufficiency of determining refugee status on a purely objective basis, which in any case would often be little more than an exercise of determining nationality.[171]

However, it should be noted that in situations in which the 1969 Event affects the whole of the country of origin or nationality, the existence of such a nexus may, as a purely procedural matter, be presumed. Any other approach would belabour the obvious and, particularly in large-scale influxes, risks overwhelming already strained RSD processes. This approach finds support in the 1969 Convention's humanitarian object and purpose. Furthermore, the presumption of a nexus between a widespread 1969 Event and flight is clearly the basis on which prima facie RSD—a common practice in Africa—rests,[172] and this has been the approach in individual claims in South Africa at least.[173] There, decision makers have relied on 'implicit

[168] Rankin (n 4) 434; see, also, Jacob van Garderen and Julie Ebenstein, 'Regional Developments: Africa' in Andreas Zimmermann (ed), *The 1951 Convention Relating to the Status of Refugees and its 1967 Protocol* (OUP 2011) 191.

[169] Sinclair (n 32) 153. [170] Edwards (n 7) 227. [171] ibid.

[172] See section B.4 of this chapter.

[173] Schreier (n 57) 55; Anais Tuepker, 'On the Threshold of Africa: OAU and UN Definitions in South African Asylum Practice' (2002) 15 JRS 409, 418.

"white lists" of refugee producing countries'[174] and focused on 'merely confirming the nationality of an asylum seeker'.[175] Most importantly, the nexus requirement should not be taken to diminish the scope and humanitarian orientation of the article I(2) refugee definition. Rutinwa expresses this well when he notes that the 'value and positive contribution of the extended definition were not the introduction of a new and wider definition of a refugee. Its qualities lie in defining a "refugee" in such terms as would make it easier to make a determination that a person seeking asylum indeed did qualify as a refugee'.[176]

(ii) Internal flight alternative, ongoing risk, and sur place claims

Three further issues of note regarding the test for refugee status under article I(2) are IFA, ongoing risk, and sur place claims. IFA is often invoked in RSD under the 1951 Convention, with the effect of requiring a person to seek protection within his or her country of origin before it can be granted abroad. Scholars have argued that article I(2)'s explicit contemplation of the disruption of public order being in only part of the country of origin precludes the consideration of IFA in RSD under article I(2).[177] Indeed, a 2006 Benin case raised internal flight but held that this was not required.[178] In a subsequent case, Benin's eligibility board made a principled decision not to consider whether protection might have been found within the country of origin.[179] A 2012 South African High Court case found that the IFA 'does not apply when a claim is made in terms of section 3(b) of the Act'.[180] This decision was recently affirmed by the same South African High Court in *Armand*.[181] A subsequent High Court case raised the possibility that the South African Refugee Appeal Board might hold a different view of IFA under section 3(b), though the decision did not

[174] Observers have raised concerns about the 'white list' approach (Lee Anne de la Hunt, 'Refugee Law in South Africa: Making the Road of the Refugee Longer' in Legal Resources Foundation, *A Reference Guide to Refugee Law and Issues in Southern Africa* (Legal Resources Foundation, 2002) 34; Schreier (n 57) 55; Tuepker (n 173) 418), in particular because they may be unduly circumscribed. Schreier, for example, notes that the South African practice 'may include generalized and hence incorrect assumptions about what constitutes an OAU . . . event and a lack of appropriate consideration of the other elements of the definition' ((n 57) 61). A related problem is that applicants who are not from listed countries may find it comparatively difficult to have their refugee status recognized. Tuepker explains, 'What is troubling is the frequent link to a converse practice of rejecting applicants on the basis of nationality' ((n 173) 418). It seems that 'white lists'—and the use of presumptions more generally—constitute an efficient mode of determining refugee status in certain contexts, as long as they and presumptions are not construed restrictively and do not lead to scepticism about the claims of individuals not from listed countries or from countries other than those in respect of which a presumption has been invoked.

[175] Schreier (n 57) 55; see, also, de la Hunt (n 174) 34.

[176] Bonaventure Rutinwa, 'Relationship Between the 1951 Refugee Convention and the 1969 OAU Convention on Refugees' in Volker Türk, Alice Edwards, and Cornelis Wouters (eds), *In Flight from Conflict and Violence: UNHCR's Consultations on Refugee Status and Other Forms of International Protection* (CUP 2017) 115.

[177] See, for example, Schreier (n 136) 86.

[178] Unpublished, on file with the author.

[179] Unpublished (2008), on file with the author.

[180] *Katabana v Chairperson of the Standing Committee for Refugee Affairs*, Western Cape High Court 25061/2011 (14 December 2012) <http://www.refworld.org/cases,ZAF_HC,539ab5144.html> accessed 9 April 2017, para 20.

[181] *Armand v Refugee Appeal Board*, Western Cape High Court 19483/2015 (*Armand*) (28 February 2015) <http://www.refworld.org/cases,ZAF_HC,58b7dd714.html> accessed 13 April 2017, paras 76–77.

determine the matter.[182] The checklist that guides decision-makers through RSD in Burkina Faso instructs them not to consider the possibility of internal flight.[183] This approach reflects relevant UNHCR guidance, which asserts that based on a plain reading of article I(2), IFA is not relevant under the 1969 Convention.[184]

The South African cases discussed earlier in this section in the context of 'place of habitual residence' also shed light on IFA.[185] The woman from Uvira in the DRC was recognized as a refugee, despite having spent nine months in the relatively safe town of Moba on her way to South Africa. Rankin terms this a 'continuing compulsion'.[186] This recognition that the compulsion to flee may continue throughout a period of relative safety en route to the host country augurs against IFA. By contrast, the man who encountered violence while on vacation in Pweto was denied refugee protection in South Africa because he could safely return home to Lubumbashi. The man who fled Bukavu was not recognized as a refugee in South Africa because his (former) place of habitual residence, Kinshasa, was safe. While these latter two cases may be taken to suggest that IFA may enter RSD through the back door of 'place of habitual residence', encountering a 1969 Event while away from home and being denied refugee status on that basis is factually quite distinct from the IFA requirement.

Wood contends that the possibility of internal relocation should be considered in RSD under article I(2). She argues that the 1969 Convention 'establishes a system of international protection for persons who [are] unable to secure the protection of their home state. In light of this purpose, it … makes sense that persons who can access meaningful and effective state protection in their country of origin are not entitled to it elsewhere'.[187] Furthermore, she points out that article I(2) protects individuals compelled to leave their 'place of habitual residence in order to seek refuge in another place outside his country of origin', thereby suggesting that if sanctuary can be found within the country of origin, the individual would not have been 'compelled' to seek it abroad.[188] This view was shared by the South African Refugee Appeal Board in 2008 at least, when a representative told Schreier that 'if possible, an asylum seeker needs to have exhausted all internal remedies in his or her country of origin, prior to seeking protection abroad'.[189]

IFA is not, however, a creature of refugee treaties. Rather, the doctrine was created by refugee decision makers applying the 1951 Convention; it did not even exist when the 1969 Convention was being drafted. The 1969 Convention itself must therefore be viewed as neutral as to the possibility of internal relocation. The question of whether RSD under article I(2) should consider IFA is best answered

[182] *Owale Mayemba v Chairperson of the Standing Committee for Refugee Affairs*, Western Cape High Court 19960/2014 (10 June 2015) <http://www.refworld.org/cases,ZAF_HC,55e072904.html> accessed 13 April 2017, paras 46–49.

[183] Unpublished, on file with the author.

[184] UNHCR, 'Guidelines on International Protection No 4: "Internal Flight or Relocation Alternative" within the Context of Article 1A(2) of the 1951 Convention and/or 1967 Protocol Relating to the Status of Refugees' (2003) HCR/GIP/03/04, para 5; UNHCR (n 58) para 60.

[185] See text attached to notes 165–67. [186] (n 4) 433. [187] (n 122) 28–29.

[188] ibid 29. [189] (n 57) 56.

through 'subsequent practice in the application of the treaty',[190] which in this case comes in the form of case law. While there is limited jurisprudence available on this issue, the decisions that explicitly consider it—which were discussed earlier in this section—universally reject the IFA requirement. Thus IFA is not a relevant consideration in RSD under article I(2). Nor may IFA enter RSD through the back door of 'place of habitual residence'; while refugee status has been denied because of the absence of a nexus between the 1969 Event and the place of habitual residence, this is not the same as requiring a refugee to seek safety in the country or origin or nationality before her refugee status may be recognized abroad.

Article I(2) is seemingly drafted in backward-looking terms. In contemplating individuals compelled to flee owing to a 1969 Event, the language of the 1969 Convention suggests that such an event has either already occurred or has at least commenced. This may be taken to suggest a backward-looking (*ex tunc*) test of refugee status. Given this, it is important to highlight that the test for refugee status is, internationally as well as in Africa, always forward-looking (*ex nunc*), because refugee protection does not serve to remedy past harm. Rather, it protects individuals from prospective or future harm. To qualify for refugee status under article I(2), the 1969 Event in question, or the threat thereof, must therefore be ongoing, or stability must have not yet returned to the country of origin or nationality. In other words, the external aggression, occupation, foreign domination, or events seriously disturbing public order, or the threat thereof, that prompted flight must continue to prevail at the time of RSD.

The final issue of note is whether article I(2) permits sur place claims. A 2009 decision from Benin recognized a refugee sur place under article I(2), making no distinction as to whether the applicant was, at the time of the 1969 Event, inside or outside his country of origin.[191] Uganda has in certain cases adopted an analogous approach.[192] Contrary opinion has, however, emerged from South Africa. According to the chairperson of its Refugee Appeal Board, 'the OAU Convention ... cannot apply to a sur place case because of the wording of the definition ... you must be compelled to leave your habitual place of residence'.[193] While in line with the language of article I(2), this restrictive approach contradicts the 1969 Convention's context: the 1969 Convention was adopted in part to protect individuals fighting colonialism and racist regimes from outside their countries of origin. Moreover, a recent South African case recognized the possibility of sur place claims.[194] Finally, the restrictive approach would create a protection gap for individuals visiting the putative host country when conflict erupted. Not surprisingly, therefore, UNHCR guidance sensibly views article I(2) as permitting sur place claims.[195]

190 VCLT (n 28) art 31(3)(b).
191 2009 Benin decision, on file with the author.
192 Sharpe (n 12) 138.
193 Schreier (n 57) 56.
194 *Armand* (n 181) para 11.
195 UNHCR (n 58) para 52.

3. Article I(2) in practice

It is clearly important to interpret the key terms of article I(2) and to understand their import in the test for refugee under the regional definition. In practice, however, article I(2) is rarely employed in this way. Indeed, it is rarely employed at all, as demonstrated by Wood in her important study of protection in practice. It provides the only practical account of article I(2) in refugee protection in Africa. Drawing on fieldwork in Kenya and South Africa, which together received half of all asylum applications in Africa in 2012,[196] Wood analyses whether article I(2) 'actually provides the basis for protection of persons who fall outside' the 1951 Convention refugee definition.[197] Overall, she finds that article I(2) is very poorly implemented in RSD in Kenya and South Africa, and therefore barely expands the scope of refugee protection in each country.

Section 3(b) of South Africa's 1998 Refugees Act defines a refugee in almost the same terms as article I(2) of the 1969 Convention;[198] the minor variations in wording are of no effect in practice.[199] Applications for refugee status are adjudicated in the first instance by officers with South Africa's Department of Home Affairs (DHA), which in 2011 rejected approximately 95 per cent of cases.[200] Applicants are notified by letter of the DHA's decision, but only negative determinations contain reasons; positive decisions include neither reasons nor an identification of the refugee definition employed. Rejected applicants may appeal to the Refugee Appeal Board, an independent statutory body. All Refugee Appeal Board decisions are reasoned, though they are not officially reported or otherwise published. Refugee Appeal Board decisions may be judicially reviewed by courts that do report their jurisprudence, though courts generally remit cases to the Refugee Appeal Board for reconsideration, rather than rendering decisions on the merits.[201] Moreover, since South Africa's Refugees Act entered into force in 2000, refugee cases that have proceeded to judicial review have for the most part concerned only procedural issues, such as access to reception facilities, procedural fairness, detention and deportation, and the right to work.[202]

As a result of this unavailability of first instance, appellate administrative, and judicial jurisprudence, Wood's analysis is based on the limited published studies of South African RSD,[203] interviews, and 250 first instance decision letters she collected. Taken together, these suggest that the section 3(b) refugee definition is very rarely applied in South Africa, leading Wood to conclude that the DHA is 'failing to consider applicants' claims under the expanded refugee definition, even in situations where the claim involves precisely the kinds of generalized harm envisaged by the definition'.[204] In one RSD case that proceeded to judicial review,

[196] Wood (n 13) 556. [197] ibid.

[198] Section 3 provides that 'a person qualifies for refugee status for the purposes of this Act if that person … (b) owing to external aggression, occupation, foreign domination or events seriously disturbing or disrupting public order in either a part or the whole of his or her country of origin or nationality, is compelled to leave his or her place of habitual residence in order to seek refuge elsewhere'.

[199] Wood (n 13) 563. [200] ibid 565. [201] ibid 563. [202] ibid 566.

[203] Including an important study by Roni Amit: 'No Refuge: Flawed Status Determination and the Failures of South Africa's Refuge System to Provide Protection' (2011) 23 IJRL 458.

[204] (n 13) 565.

this failure was called 'a significant error of law'.[205] Pre-2011 Refugee Appeal Board decisions seen by Schreier[206] and Wood employed section 3(b) more frequently than the DHA; however, in 2011 the board underwent a complete staff turnover, and Wood could not obtain decisions from the new cohort of decision makers.[207] Section 3(b) has not been considered judicially in any substantive way, as the few refugee status cases that have been judicially reviewed concern purely procedural issues, the 1951 Convention (section 3(a)) definition,[208] or contain no substantive reasoning regarding refugee status under section 3(b).[209] Overall, Wood finds that 'a large number of asylum seekers who might qualify for protection under the expanded refugee definition are not having their claims considered according to its terms. The expanded protection envisaged by the definition, and reflected in South Africa's Refugees Act, is therefore not being realized in practice'.[210]

The situation in Kenya is similar. There, RSD is conducted by UNHCR, though responsibility for RSD is slowly transitioning to Kenya's Department of Refugee Affairs.[211] In conducting RSD in Kenya, UNHCR applies the 1951 Convention refugee definition as well as its extended mandate definition.[212] Thus at the moment, article I(2) does not even feature in RSD in Kenya. In practice, however, UNHCR's extended mandate definition is very similar to article I(2), and the two are often conflated in practice.[213] When Wood was conducting her fieldwork in Kenya in late 2012, individuals from central and southern Somalia, as well as individuals arriving in Kakuma camp from Darfur, were recognized on a prima facie basis pursuant to the extended mandate/article I(2) definition (Kenya stopped according prima facie status to Somalis in April 2016). This extended definition was not employed at all within individual RSD.[214] On the whole, Wood concludes that

> in South Africa and Kenya, the extent to which the 1969 Convention's expanded refugee definition provides broader protection in practice is, at best, limited. The widespread failure of decision makers in both countries to consider refugee applicants' claims under the definition's terms means that potentially large numbers of persons who fall within the 1969 Convention's expansive refugee regime are being denied the protection to which they are entitled.[215]

Wood posits three reasons for this failure. Firstly, the refugee protection regimes in both Kenya and South Africa are seriously overburdened. In this context, Wood finds it unsurprising that claims do not receive fulsome consideration including article I(2).[216] Secondly, what decisions are available from South Africa are generally

[205] *Hassan Asman Harerimana v The Chairperson of the Refugee Appeal Board and Others*, Western Cape High Court 10972/2013 (*Harerimana*) (11 December 2013) <http://www.refworld.org/cases,ZAF_HC,539ab2d44.html> accessed 13 April 2017, para 39.

[206] (n 57). [207] (n 13) 565–66. [208] ibid 566.

[209] See, for example, *Harerimana* (n 205) para 40. An exception is *Radjabu* (n 161).

[210] (n 13) 566.

[211] See Madeline Garlick, Elspeth Guild, Caitlin Procter, and Machiel Salomons, 'Building on the Foundation: Formative Evaluation of the Refugee Status Determination Transition Process in Kenya' (UNHCR 2015) <http://www.refworld.org/docid/559f9a4a4.html> accessed 13 January 2017.

[212] See text attached to n 25. [213] Wood (n 13) 572–73. [214] ibid 573.

[215] ibid 574. [216] ibid 574–75.

very poorly reasoned. Amit characterizes first instance decision making in South Africa as 'a bureaucracy that mass produces rejection letters without any evidence of a reasoned decision making process'.[217] The quality of UNHCR's decisions in Kenya is also poor.[218] Such reasoning suggests an inability to properly apply article I(2).[219] Indeed, in its Resolution on Assistance to Refugees, Returnees and Displaced Persons in Africa, the UNGA called on UNHCR, the international community, and others to 'intensify their support to African Governments through appropriate capacity-building activities, including training of relevant officers'.[220] Thirdly, Wood speculates that the failure to apply article I(2) may stem from xenophobic and anti-refugee sentiment.[221]

4. Prima facie RSD

While article I(2) is not expanding refugee protection in Kenya and South Africa in individually determined cases, it is contributing to refugee protection in cases adjudicated on a prima facie basis. There are, however, three misconceptions related to prima facie RSD. Firstly, that article I(2) introduced or provides the legal foundation for prima facie RSD.[222] Secondly, prima facie RSD is often conflated with the legally erroneous concept of 'group' RSD. Finally, there is misunderstanding about the nature of the refugee status that results from prima facie RSD. This section addresses each of these misconceptions in turn.

(a) Prima facie RSD and the 1969 Convention

Prima facie RSD is a process whereby an individual's refugee status is recognized on the basis of a presumption of inclusion within RSD. Examples of the attribution of prima facie RSD to article I(2) of the 1969 Convention abound. Nobel notes that the 1969 Convention's regional refugee definition is 'the legal basis for admitting refugee masses upon a group determination of their status'.[223] The Lawyers Committee for Human Rights[224] maintains that the 1969 Convention 'introduced the notion of group determination of refugee status'[225] and suggests that 'the preferable practice of group eligibility ... is provided for under the OAU Convention'.[226] Milner explains that 'by making refugee status contingent on generalized situations in the refugee's country of origin, the 1969 OAU Convention allows states

[217] Roni Amit, 'All Roads Lead to Rejection: Persistent Bias and Incapacity in South African Refugee Status Determination' (2012) African Centre for Migration & Society Research Report <http://www.migration.org.za/publication/all-roads-lead-rejection-persistent-bias-and-incapacity-south-african-refugee-status-det> accessed 27 July 2012, 18.

[218] Wood (n 13) 575. [219] ibid.

[220] UNGA Res 71/173 (19 December 2016) UN Doc A/RES/71/173, para 20.

[221] (n 13) 575–76. [222] Okoth-Obbo (n 4) 118; Rankin (n 4) 416.

[223] Peter Nobel, 'Refugees, Law, and Development in Africa' (1982) 3 Mich YB Intl L Stud 255, 262.

[224] This organization is now known as Human Rights First.

[225] Lawyers Committee for Human Rights, *African Exodus: Refugee Crisis, Human Rights and the 1969 OAU Convention* (Lawyers Committee for Human Rights 1995) 5.

[226] ibid 22.

to recognize entire groups of individuals as refugees on the basis of shared characteristics and common cause of flight'.[227] D'Orsi notes that the 1969 Convention 'is meant to promote the prima facie recognition of groups of refugees'.[228] Most recently, Beyani noted that under the 1969 Convention 'both group and individual eligibility to refugee status determination exists'.[229]

Rather than being based in analysis of the 1969 Convention, these attributions of prima facie RSD to article I(2) arise from the common practice in Africa of determining refugee status on a prima facie basis in situations of mass influx.[230] For example, as mentioned earlier in this section, prima facie recognition was used by Ghana, Guinea, Liberia, and Togo in relation to individuals fleeing post-election violence in Côte d'Ivoire.[231] In late 2012 Kenya recognized refugees from central and southern Somalia, as well as individuals from Sudan's Darfur region arriving in Kakuma camp, on a prima facie basis.[232]

When compared to the 1951 Convention refugee definition, article I(2) certainly includes elements that are easier to apply in mass influx. Rutinwa explains, 'the grounds for which a person could be recognized as a refugee under the extended definition made it easier to accord refugee status to groups of refugees on grounds that could be easily established based on objective circumstances in the country of origin, in contrast with the cognizable grounds under ... the 1951 Convention, which essentially could only be established through an individualized and costly assessment of refugee claims'.[233] Kenya's Refugees Act even describes article I(2) refugees as '*prima facie*' refugees.[234]

Despite this alignment between article I(2) and prima facie RSD, a close reading of the 1969 Convention, as well as the Convention's drafting history, reveals no specific intent to introduce or promote the use of prima facie RSD. As mentioned in Chapter 2,[235] the third/Addis Ababa draft of the 1969 Convention included a clause outlining factors to consider in determining whether the African Convention would apply prima facie to groups of refugees. This draft clause was not, however, retained, and the 'every person' language in articles I(1) and I(2) is in the singular.

Furthermore, despite suggestions to the contrary,[236] the 1969 Convention is not unique in its applicability to situations of mass influx. Durieux and McAdam maintain that the 1951 Convention 'contains nothing to suggest its inapplicability in cases of mass influx'.[237] Nor is article I(2) of the 1969 Convention the only refugee

[227] James Milner, *Refugees, the State and the Politics of Asylum in Africa* (Palgrave Macmillan 2009) 7.

[228] Cristiano D'Orsi, 'Sub-Saharan Africa: Is a New Special Regional Refugee Law Regime Emerging?' (2008) 68 Heidelberg J Intl L 1057, 1065.

[229] Chaloka Beyani, *Protection of the Right to Seek and Obtain Asylum Under the African Human Rights System* (Martinus Nijhoff 2013) 44.

[230] Note, however, that Kenya's implementation of the 1969 Convention does relate prima facie RSD to the regional refugee instrument, by empowering the relevant Minister to declare a specific group to be refugees within the meaning of the 1969 Convention article I(2) refugee definition (Refugees Act, 2006 (Kenya) s 3(3)).

[231] See n 95. [232] Wood (n 13) 571. [233] Rutinwa (n 176) 109.

[234] Refugees Act, 2006 (Kenya) s 3(2); see also n 230. [235] See section D.3.

[236] See, for example, Viljoen (n 120) 243.

[237] Jean-François Durieux and Jane McAdam, 'Non-Refoulement through Time: The Case for a Derogation Clause to the Refugee Convention in Mass Influx Emergencies' (2004) 16 IJRL 4, 9.

definition that permits prima facie RSD. If the objective circumstances that triggered the application of the presumption of eligibility for refugee status 'are those under Article 1A(2) of the 1951 Refugee Convention ... then the persons recognised to be prima facie refugees are refugees within the meaning of' that article.[238] Refugees who fled Hungary for Austria and Yugoslavia following the 1956 Soviet invasion and occupation were recognized on a prima facie basis under the 1951 Convention.[239] Prima facie RSD is not a product of the 1969 Convention, nor is it inherently or exclusively linked to the 1969 Convention. Rather, it arose as a matter of practical necessity in situations of mass influx.[240]

(b) 'Group' RSD

Prima facie RSD must be distinguished from the non-existent 'group' determination of refugee status. The consensus in the literature is that prima facie RSD is a process whereby an individual's refugee status is recognized on the basis of a legal presumption.[241] This understanding was articulated first by Jackson,[242] and was subsequently reiterated by Rutinwa,[243] Durieux and Hurwitz,[244] Durieux and McAdam,[245] Durieux,[246] and Albert.[247]

Recently, however, UNHCR published its Guidelines on International Protection No 11 on the Prima Facie Recognition of Refugee Status. These guidelines describe prima facie RSD as 'the recognition by a State or UNHCR of refugee status on the basis of readily apparent, objective circumstances in the country of origin', which brings individuals fleeing such circumstances 'within the applicable refugee definition'.[248] The guidelines do not construe such recognition as resulting from a presumption. Edwards explained that the agency decided not to mention presumptions for several reasons. Firstly, UNHCR generally avoids the use of legal presumptions

[238] Bonaventure Rutinwa, 'Prima Facie Status and Refugee Protection' (2002) UNHCR New Issues in Refugee Research Working Paper No 69 <http://www.unhcr.org/3db9636c4.pdf> accessed 8 December 2016, 5.

[239] Sara E Davies, 'Redundant or Essential? How Politics Shaped the Outcome of the 1967 Protocol' (2007) 19 IJRL 703, 713.

[240] Matthew Albert, 'Governance and Prima Facie Refugee Status Determination: Clarifying the Boundaries of Temporary Protection, Group Determination, and Mass Influx' (2010) 29 RSQ 61, 66–68.

[241] For a more general discussion of the legal meaning of prima facie, see Georg Nils Herlitz, 'The Meaning of the Term "Prima Facie"' (1994–1995) 55 Louisiana L Rev 391.

[242] Jackson (n 148) 4.

[243] Rutinwa (n 238) 6.

[244] Jean-François Durieux and Agnes Hurwitz, 'How Many Is Too Many? African and European Legal Responses to Mass Influx of Refugees' (2004) 47 German YB Intl L 105, 120.

[245] Durieux and McAdam (n 237) 12.

[246] Jean-François Durieux, 'The Many Faces of "Prima Facie": Group-Based Evidence in Refugee Status Determination' (2008) 25 Refuge 151.

[247] Albert (n 240) 65, although Albert uses the language of 'inference'. Understanding prima facie RSD as these scholars have is not incompatible with the article I(2) nexus requirement discussed in section B.2.e above; a prima facie approach would simply presume the existence of a nexus between the 1969 Event and flight, and recognize an individual's refugee status on that basis.

[248] UNHCR, 'Guidelines on International Protection No. 11: Prima Facie Recognition of Refugee Status' (24 June 2015) HCR/GIP/15/11, para 1.

in its guidelines because the varied approaches to them across legal systems—for example, in some jurisdictions presumptions shift the burden of proof, while in others they change the standard of proof—undermines the consistent approach that UNHCR seeks to promote. Relatedly, in the context of prima facie RSD, UNHCR did not view either of the above-mentioned effects of legal presumptions as appropriate. Finally, the mention of a presumption in the guidelines risked creating confusion between a legal presumption employed within RSD, which is the understanding at the core of the academic consensus about prima facie RSD, and the nature of the refugee status that prima facie RSD confers,[249] which—as discussed later in this section—Okoth-Obbo has mischaracterized as merely presumptive.[250]

This divergence between the scholarship and UNHCR's approach aside, it is at least settled that prima facie RSD involves recognizing refugee status based on readily apparent circumstances in the country of origin. That this practice has been widely used in situations of mass influx,[251] which are characterized by 'the arrival across an international border of persons seeking protection in such numbers and at such a rate as to render individual determination of their asylum claims impracticable',[252] is the source of the erroneous conflation of prima facie RSD with the 'group' determination of refugee status. In fact, there is no such thing as 'group' RSD; it is just an imprecise way of expressing the resort to prima facie RSD in mass influx situations. Under a prima facie process of status determination, 'it is not the refugee quality ... of the entire group that is determined, but that of each individual in the group. Groups do not accrue refugee status, be it prima facie or by any other means. Only individuals do'.[253] Albert puts it similarly when he maintains that prima facie RSD is 'better described as being an expedited form of individual RSD, not "group" RSD'.[254] This view is confirmed by UNHCR's guidance, which explains that 'situations have ... arisen in which entire groups have been under circumstances indicating that members of the group could be considered individually as refugees.... Recourse has therefore been had to *so-called* "group determination" of refugee status, whereby each member of the group is regarded prima facie (i.e. in the absence of evidence to the contrary) as a refugee'.[255] The more recent UNHCR guidelines also make this point: although 'a prima facie approach may be applied within individual refugee status determination procedures ..., it is more often used in group situations, for example where individual status determination is impractical, impossible or unnecessary in large-scale situations'.[256] Furthermore, aspects of the article I(2) refugee definition—such as the requirement that flight be from

[249] Email correspondence with Alice Edwards, Senior Legal Coordinator and Chief, Protection Policy and Legal Advice Section, UNHCR, 10 December 2013.

[250] Okoth-Obbo (n 4) 119.

[251] UNHCR Global Consultations, 'Protection of Refugees in Mass Influx Situations: Overall Protection Framework' UN Doc EC/GC/01/4 (19 February 2001) paras 3–4.

[252] UNHCR, 'Guidelines on the Application in Mass Influx Situations of the Exclusion Clauses of Article 1F of the 1951 Convention relating to the Status of Refugees' (February 2006) para 1.

[253] Durieux and Hurwitz (n 244) 118. [254] Albert (n 240) 83.

[255] UNHCR, *Handbook on Procedures and Criteria for Determining Refugee Status* (UNHCR 1992) para 44 (emphasis added).

[256] UNHCR (n 248) para 2.

one's 'place of habitual residence'—as well as aspects of the 1969 Convention more generally—such as article VI on the provision of travel documents—only make sense when applied to individuals, so the 1969 Convention could not have been intended to apply to groups.[257]

(c) *The nature of refugee status recognized on a prima facie basis*

A final issue relates to the nature of the refugee status that recognition on a prima facie basis confers. There is a view that such recognition creates only a 'presumption of refugeehood and therefore entails an incomplete (or secondary) refugee status',[258] in terms of both its durability and the post-recognition rights that attach. Okoth-Obbo evidences this view when he notes that the 'prima facie concept refers to the provisional consideration of a person or persons as refugees without the requirement to complete refugee status determination formalities to establish definitively the qualification or not of each individual'.[259] This implies that refugees recognized on a prima facie basis receive only temporary protection and do not qualify for the full range of rights conferred under individual processes of recognition. Indeed, according to the Lawyers' Committee for Human Rights, 'the notion of group eligibility under the OAU Convention was based on the premise of legally institutionalized temporary protection'.[260] Refugees recognized on a prima facie basis have also been referred to as 'non-Convention' refugees.[261]

Durieux and Hurwitz,[262] Durieux and McAdam,[263] Jackson,[264] and Rutinwa[265] have each, however, rejected this view of prima facie refugee status as temporary and incomplete, based on the conclusiveness of the presumption of refugeehood employed in their conception of prima facie RSD. While each author accepts that prima facie refugee status is indeed presumptive, the 'operation of the presumption provides full and sufficient evidence'[266] of refugee status, unless the host state subjects it to additional scrutiny.

That the presumption of refugee status within a process of prima facie RSD is conclusive suggests that refugees recognized pursuant to such a process are refugees like any other. Indeed, Rutinwa argues, 'if persons recognised as refugees on a prima facie basis are presumed to be refugees within the definitions found under the relevant instruments, it logically follows that their treatment should be in accordance with the standards stipulated under those instruments'.[267] Similarly, Durieux and McAdam maintain, 'One must conclude that prima facie recognition entails full

257 Tamara Wood, 'The 1969 African Refugee Convention's Expanded Refugee Definition: Scope and Application in Mass Influx Situations' (Refugee Law Initiative 2nd Annual Conference, London, June 2017).

258 Durieux and McAdam (n 237) 12.

259 Okoth-Obbo (n 4) 119.

260 Lawyers Committee for Human Rights (n 225) 30.

261 Jennifer Hyndman and Bo Victor Nylund, 'UNHCR and the Status of Prima Facie Refugees in Kenya' (1998) 10 IJRL 21, 41.

262 Durieux and Hurwitz (n 244) 120.

263 Durieux and McAdam (n 237) 12.

264 Jackson (n 148) 4.

265 Rutinwa (n 238) 14.

266 Durieux and Hurwitz (n 244) 120.

267 Rutinwa (n 238) 14.

refugee status, and beneficiaries of it are entitled, in Contracting States, to the standards of treatment stipulated by the 1951 Convention'.[268] Recent UNHCR guidance supports this view. The organization's Guidelines on International Protection No 11 provide that each

> refugee recognized on a prima facie basis benefits from refugee status in the country where such recognition is made, and enjoys the rights contained in the applicable convention/instrument. Prima facie recognition of refugee status is not to be confused with an interim or provisional status, pending subsequent confirmation. Rather, once refugee status has been determined on a prima facie basis, it remains valid in that country unless the conditions for cessation are met, or their status is otherwise cancelled or revoked.[269]

State practice affirms this conclusion. For example, Ghana's prima facie declaration of refugee status in respect of Ivoirians fleeing the 2010 post-election violence recognized the relevant individuals as refugees 'for the purposes of the Refugee Law 1992'.[270] Section 11 of Ghana's 1992 Refugee Law provides refugees in Ghana with the rights specified in the 1951 and 1969 Conventions and the Protocol relating to the Status of Refugees (1967 Protocol),[271] without distinguishing between refugees recognized on a prima facie basis and those recognized in traditional RSD. Similarly, Uganda's Refugees Act 2006 does not distinguish between refugees recognized on a prima facie basis or via traditional procedures.[272] Even in Kenya, where the Refugees Act 2006 distinguishes between 'statutory' (1951 Convention article 1A(2) definition) and '*prima facie*' (1969 Convention article I(2) definition) refugees,[273] every refugee—whether statutory or prima facie—is 'entitled to the rights ... contained in the international conventions to which Kenya is party'.[274]

Once one understands what prima facie RSD is and how it operates, it becomes clear that it is merely a procedural tool that can have no effect on substantive rights. While this resolves the question of the nature of the status that attaches to refugees recognized on a prima facie basis, it raises the related wider issue of the nature of refugee status that results from recognition—whether on a prima facie basis or otherwise—under article I(2) of the 1969 Convention. This critical issue is addressed in Chapter 4.

C. Other Novel Features

In addition to article I(2), other aspects of the 1969 Convention have made important contributions to refugee protection, including how it has advanced an individual right to asylum.

[268] Durieux and McAdam (n 237) 12.
[269] UNHCR (n 248) para 7 (footnotes omitted).
[270] Ghana (n 95).
[271] (Adopted 31 January 1967, entered into force 4 October 1967) 606 UNTS 267.
[272] The Refugees Act 2006 (Uganda) No 21, s 2.
[273] The Refugees Act 2006 (Kenya) s 3.
[274] ibid s 16.

1. Bolstering an individual right to asylum

The 1951 Convention does not establish any individual right to asylum. The Universal Declaration of Human Rights (UDHR), by contrast, enshrines the right of individuals to 'seek and to enjoy' asylum,[275] but stops short of recognizing any individual right to asylum. The UN Declaration on Territorial Asylum[276]—which is recalled at paragraph 7 of the preamble to the 1969 Convention—is similarly circumscribed. This resolution was followed, ten years after is adoption, by the UN Conference on Territorial Asylum, which also failed to recognize or codify any individual right to asylum.[277] In 1981, however, the African Charter recognized for the first time the right of persecuted individuals to 'seek and obtain asylum in other countries in accordance with the laws of those countries and international conventions'.[278] This is analysed in Chapter 5. It suffices to note here that despite this African Charter provision, the general conclusion remains that the grant of asylum is within the exclusive discretion of states; as states have no obligation to grant asylum, individuals have no right to asylum corresponding to their UDHR right to 'seek and to enjoy' it.[279]

While the 1969 Convention reflects this general conclusion, it nevertheless significantly 'strengthens the institution of asylum'[280] by providing, 'Member States of the OAU shall use their best endeavours consistent with their respective legislations to receive refugees and to secure the settlement of those refugees who, for well-founded reasons, are unable or unwilling to return to their country of origin or nationality'.[281] This urging of states to grant asylum is 'a further inroad into the traditional international law perspective which has tended to regard asylum as an exclusive right of the sovereign state', but it is 'certainly not a right to be enforced by an individual against a state'.[282] The 1969 Convention does not stop there; mirroring part of the preamble to the UN Declaration on Territorial Asylum, it characterizes the grant of asylum as a 'peaceful and humanitarian act' that 'shall not be regarded as an unfriendly act by any Member State'.[283] Article II of the 1969 Convention only, however, requires that states use their 'best endeavours consistent with their respective legislations' to welcome refugees; the language is not mandatory. The Pan-African Conference on the African Refugee Problem, held in Arusha, Tanzania, in May 1979, recognized that 'while on the international level asylum is still a right of

[275] UNGA Res 217A (III) (10 December 1948) art 14(1). See, generally, Alice Edwards, 'Human Rights, Refugees, and the Right "To Enjoy" Asylum' (2005) 17 IJRL 293.

[276] UNGA Res 2312 (XXII) (14 December 1967).

[277] Hathaway (n 27) 13–6; Agnes Hurwitz, *The Collective Responsibility of States to Protect Refugees* (OUP 2009) 21–23.

[278] African Charter (n 86) art 12(3) (emphasis added).

[279] Guy S Goodwin-Gill and Jane McAdam, *The Refugee in International Law* (3rd edn, OUP 2007) 358; Paul Weis, 'The United Nations Declaration on Territorial Asylum' (1969) 7 Can YB Intl L 92, 137–9.

[280] Hofmann (n 6) 324.

[281] 1969 Convention (n 2) art II(1); presumably, 'well-founded reasons' must be read as referring to both the article I(1) and article I(2) refugee definitions, despite that fact that only article I(1) explicitly includes a requirement that the reasons for flight be well-founded.

[282] Rwelamira (n 4) 170.

[283] 1969 Convention (n 2) art II(2).

the State, some progress has been made in the 1969 OAU Refugee Convention in the direction of strengthening the position of the individual in relation to asylum'.[284] Going even further, at its Regional Conference on Assistance to Refugees, Returnees and Displaced Persons in the Great Lakes Region, held in Bujumbura in February 1995, the OAU concluded that 'the granting of asylum should be considered a responsibility and an obligation under international law'.[285] On the whole, the 1969 Convention advances, but does not enshrine, an individual right to asylum.

2. Broadened non-refoulement?

While the 1969 Convention's contribution to the advancement of an individual right to asylum may be characterized as modest, its role regarding non-refoulement is usually characterized as being somewhat more significant. Thorough analysis, however, reveals that the 1969 Convention does not broaden non-refoulement by as much as is often posited.

The general principle of non-refoulement provides that an individual cannot be returned to a state where there is a real chance that he or she will face persecution, other ill-treatment or torture. This is codified in, or has been judicially read into, international refugee[286] and human rights instruments,[287] and case law and most commentators view the norm as customary international law.[288] Some have even suggested that the norm is ripe for recognition as jus cogens.[289] Human rights-based non-refoulement (also known as complementary protection) is discussed in Chapter 5; the focus here is on non-refoulement under refugee law. In this context, the norm, as articulated at article 33(1) of the 1951 Convention, prohibits states

[284] Lars-Gunnar Eriksson, Goran Melander, and Peter Nobel, *An Analysing Account of the Conference on the African Refugee Problem, Arusha, May 1979* (Scandinavian Institute of African Studies 1981) 47.

[285] Naldi and D'Orsi (n 26) 136.

[286] See, for example, 1951 Convention (n 9) art 33; 1969 Convention (n 2) art II(3).

[287] See, for example, Convention against Torture and Other Cruel, Inhuman or Degrading Treatment or Punishment (adopted 10 December 1984, entered into force 26 June 1987) 1465 UNTS 85, art 3(1); International Covenant on Civil and Political Rights (adopted 16 December 1966, entered into force 23 March 1976) 999 UNTS 171, art 7, read with para 12 of HRC, 'General Comment No 31: The Nature of the General Legal Obligation Imposed on States Parties to the Covenant' (29 March 2004), which states, 'the article 2 obligation requiring that States Parties respect and ensure the Covenant rights for all persons in their territory and all persons under their control entails an obligation not to extradite, deport, expel or otherwise remove a person from their territory, where there are substantial grounds for believing that there is a real risk of irreparable harm, such as that contemplated by articles 6 and 7 of the Covenant, either in the country to which removal is to be effected or in any country to which the person may subsequently be removed'.

[288] See, for example, *Attorney General v Kituo Cha Sheria & 7 Others* [2017] eKLR 15; *Kituo Cha Sheria, Abebe Dadi Tully, Ahmed Bashir Mohamed, Eugene Bwimana, Dachassa Galdi Nure, Muhima Sebihendo Joh, Mbuzukongire Nzabona and Said Abdullahi Abukar v the Attorney General*, Petition Nos 19 and 115 of 2013, High Court of Kenya (26 July 2013) para 44; Elihu Lauterpacht and Daniel Bethlehem, 'The Scope and Content of the Principle of Non-refoulement: Opinion' in Erika Feller, Volker Türk and Frances Nicholson (eds), *Refugee Protection in International Law: UNHCR's Global Consultations on International Protection* (CUP 2003) 140; Cathryn Costello and Michelle Foster, 'Non-refoulement as Custom and Jus Cogens? Putting the Prohibition to the Test' (2016) 46 NYIL 2015 273; contra: James C Hathaway, 'Leveraging Asylum' (2009) 45 Texas Intl LJ 503.

[289] Costello and Foster (n 288).

from expelling or returning 'a refugee in any manner whatsoever to the frontiers of territories where his life or freedom would be threatened on account of his race, religion, nationality, membership of a particular social group or political opinion'. The second paragraph of article 33 permits a national security exception.[290]

The 1969 Convention's non-refoulement provision, by contrast, seems an amalgam of the 1951 Convention's article 33(1) and article 3(1) of the UN Declaration on Territorial Asylum.[291] The 1969 Convention provides: 'No person shall be subjected by a Member State to measures such as rejection at the frontier, return or expulsion, which would compel him to return to or remain in a territory where his life, physical integrity or liberty would be threatened for the reasons set out in Article I, paragraphs 1 and 2'.[292] This is indeed broader than the 1951 Convention's non-refoulement provision, in three important respects; however, the 1969 Convention does not expand non-refoulement as greatly as is often suggested.

The first sense in which non-refoulement seems, at least initially, to be broader under the 1969 than under the 1951 Convention is textual, in two respects. Firstly, the 1969 Convention protects from return to situations in which the individual's life, physical integrity or liberty would be threatened, whereas the 1951 Convention lists only life and freedom. While 'liberty' and 'freedom' are presumably analogous, the 1969 Convention's inclusion of 'physical integrity' may broaden protection from refoulement somewhat, assuming that a situation could threaten one's physical integrity but not his or her freedom. Second, the 1969 Convention's non-refoulement provision protects 'persons', while the 1951 Convention's article 33 protects 'refugees'. However, article 33 'also applies to asylum seekers, at least during an initial period and in appropriate circumstances, for otherwise there would be no effective protection'.[293] Thus while the textual ambit of article II(3) may seem significantly wider than article 33, the scope of the protection is actually only slightly broader.

Secondly, the 1969 Convention's non-refoulement provision encompasses rejection at frontiers, while the 1951 Convention makes no such explicit provision. As a result, many commentators view non-refoulement under the 1969 Convention as broader than under the 1951 Convention.[294] State practice, however, has aligned the universal refugee regime with the standard of the 1969 Convention. According to Goodwin-Gill and McAdam, 'By and large, States in their practice and in their recorded views, have recognized that non-refoulement applies to the moment at

[290] This provides, 'The benefit of the present provision may not, however, be claimed by a refugee whom there are reasonable grounds for regarding as a danger to the security of the country in which he is, or who, having been convicted by a final judgment of a particularly serious crime, constitutes a danger to the community of that country'.

[291] This provides, 'No person referred to in article 1, paragraph 1, shall be subjected to measures such as rejection at the frontier or, if he has already entered the territory in which he seeks asylum, expulsion or compulsory return to any State were he may be subjected to persecution' (UNGA Res 2312 (XXII) (14 December 1967).

[292] 1969 Convention (n 2) art II(3).

[293] Goodwin-Gill and McAdam (n 279) 232.

[294] See, for example, Georges Abi-Saab, 'The Admission and Expulsion of Refugees with Special Reference to Africa' (2000) 8 Afr YB Intl L 71, 89; Okogbule (n 147) 184; UNHCR, *The State of the World's Refugees 2000: Fifty Years of Humanitarian Action* (OUP 2000) 57; van Garderen and Ebenstein (n 168) 186.

which asylum seekers present themselves for entry, either within a State or at its border'.[295] Indeed, this was the view of a South African court regarding asylum seekers held in an airside detention facility for deportees in transit. It held that under both the 1951 and 1969 Conventions, the applicants should be allowed to enter South Africa.[296] At present, therefore, the 1969 Convention's conception of non-refoulement is no broader than that of the 1951 Convention as far as applicability at frontiers is concerned.

Finally, the 1969 Convention expands non-refoulement because it does not include a national security exception like the one found in its universal counterpart. However, the 1969 Convention does not render non-refoulement absolute, as many scholars have suggested.[297] Pursuant to articles I(4)(f) and I(4)(g), the application of the 1969 Convention, and hence protection from refoulement, ceases if the individual concerned commits a serious non-political crime outside the country of refuge after admission as a refugee or if he or she seriously infringes the Convention's purposes and objectives. This, according to D'Sa, implies that the 1969 Convention, like the 1951 Convention, allows expulsion—and hence the risk of refoulement—in limited circumstances, 'although the OAU appears to deal with the latter somewhat indirectly'.[298] Of course, an individual whose refugee status has ceased pursuant to article I(4)(f) or I(4)(g) might still be protected from refoulement under another (human rights) instrument.[299]

In practice, in Africa non-refoulement is often honoured in the breach. For example, many refugees from the 1994 Rwandan genocide were prevented from entering Tanzania.[300] In 1996, thousands of refugees fled war ravaged Liberia and elsewhere in West Africa aboard two ships, the Zolotitsa and the Bulk Challenge. The latter, carrying about two thousand refugees, was refused entry to several West African nations, until Ghana capitulated to international pressure and allowed the ship to land. About a month later, the Zolotitsa, carrying 450 refugees from Liberia and elsewhere, was denied entry to ports in Benin, Côte d'Ivoire, Ghana, Nigeria, and Togo. After three weeks at sea, it returned to Monrovia.[301] In 1999 hundreds of refugees from the war in Sierra Leone were refused entry to Guinea.[302] Several years later refugees from the Angolan civil war were turned away from Namibia.[303] In

[295] Goodwin-Gill and McAdam (n 279) 208.

[296] *Abdi and Dhiblawe v The Minister of Home Affairs and Others* [2011] 3 All SA 117 (SCA) (15 February 2011) (*Abdi*) para 22.

[297] See, for example, Abi-Saab (n 294) 90; Beyani (n 229) 49; Mandal (n 89) 15; Rachel Murray, 'Refugees and Internally Displaced Persons and Human Rights: the African System' (2005) 24 RSQ 56, 57.

[298] Rose D'Sa, 'The African Refugee Problem, Relevant International Conventions and Recent Activities of the Organization of African Unity' (1984) 31 NILR 378, 388.

[299] See Chapter 5, section C.2.a.

[300] Sergio Carciotto and Cristiano D'Orsi, 'Access to Socio-Economic Rights for Refugees: A Comparison Across Six African Countries' (March 2017) The Scalabrini Institute for Human Mobility in Africa <http://sihma.org.za/wp-content/uploads/2017/03/Access-to-socio-economic-rights_refugees.pdf> accessed 28 March 2017, 18.

[301] Paul Kuruk, 'Asylum and the Non-Refoulement of Refugees: The Case of the Missing Shipload of Liberian Refugees' (1999) 35 Stanford J Intl L 313.

[302] Carciotto and D'Orsi (n 300) 18. [303] ibid.

2010, UNHCR characterized Kenya's return of Somali refugees as refoulement.[304] The nature of returns to Somalia was called into question again in 2013, after the 21 September terrorist attack on Westgate Mall in Nairobi led the Kenyan government to redouble its efforts to repatriate Somali refugees.[305] Following further terrorist attacks in 2014, Kenya attempted to amend section 14 of its Refugees Act 2006, to limit the number of refugees in the country to 150,000.[306] In April 2016 Kenya revoked the prima facie status of Somali refugees,[307] and Human Rights Watch subsequently found evidence of forced returns to Somalia.[308] In 2010 Uganda forcibly returned 1,700 Rwandans.[309] Rwandans in Tanzania have on several occasions been similarly repatriated.[310] In 2015 Niger returned hundreds of people who had fled militant attacks to northern Nigeria, raising UNHCR's concern.[311] In May 2016 Sudan arrested hundreds of Eritreans in Khartoum and forced them home.[312]

Despite these examples of refoulement, 'on no occasion have any Sub-Saharan African governments clearly denied the binding nature of the principle of non-refoulement in official statements'.[313] Furthermore, in Egypt,[314] Kenya,[315] and

[304] Katy Migiro, 'Kenya Illegally Forcing Refugees back to Somalia: UNHCR' Reuters (Nairobi, 3 November 2010) <http://af.reuters.com/article/topNews/idAFJOE6A20JL20101103> accessed 17 March 2017.

[305] Emmanuel Kisiangani and Hawa Noor, 'Is Kenya Prioritising National Security Concerns Over the Rights of Refugees?' (15 January 2014) <https://issafrica.org/iss-today/the-controversial-repatriation-of-somali-refugees-from-kenya> accessed 10 April 2017.

[306] *Coalition for Reform and Democracy, Kenya National Commission on Human Rights and Samuel Njuguna Ng'ang'a v Republic of Kenya and Attorney General*, Petition No 628 of 2014 consolidated with Petition No 630 of 2015 and Petition No 12 of 2015, High Court of Kenya (23 February 2015) (*CORD*).

[307] *Kenya National Commission on Human Rights and Legal Advice Centre T/A Kituo Cha Sheria v The Hon. Attorney General, The Ministry of Interior & Coordination of National Government, Major General (RTD) Joseph Nkaissery and Dr. (ENG) Karanja Kibicho*, Petition No 227 of 2016, High Court of Kenya (9 February 2017) (*Kenya National Commission on Human Rights*) 3.

[308] Human Rights Watch, 'Kenya: Involuntary Refugee Returns to Somalia' (14 September 2016) <https://www.hrw.org/news/2016/09/14/kenya-involuntary-refugee-returns-somalia> accessed 17 March 2017.

[309] Amnesty International, 'Uganda Forcibly Returns 1,700 Rwandan Asylum-Seekers' (16 July 2010) <https://www.amnesty.org/en/latest/news/2010/07/uganda-forcibly-returns-1700-rwandan-asylum-seekers/> accessed 17 March 2017.

[310] Sreeram Sundar Chaulia, 'The Politics of Refugee Hosting in Tanzania: From Open Door to Unsustainability, Insecurity and Receding Receptivity' (2003) 3 JRS 147.

[311] William Spindler, 'UNHCR Urges Suspension of Returns to Nigeria from Niger' (16 January 2015) <http://www.unhcr.org/news/latest/2015/1/54b8f4019/unhcr-urges-suspension-returns-nigeria-niger.html> accessed 17 March 2017.

[312] Martin Plaut, 'Europe's Crackdown on African Immigration is Hitting Vulnerable Refugees' *The Guardian* (26 January 2017) <https://www.theguardian.com/commentisfree/2017/jan/26/europe-crackdown-africa-immigration-vulnerable-refugees-sudan-eritrea> accessed 24 April 2017.

[313] Cristiano D'Orsi, *Asylum-Seeker and Refugee Protection in Sub-Saharan Africa: The Peregrination of a Persecuted Human Being in Search of a Safe Haven* (Routledge 2015) 59.

[314] *Zahra Soliman Ahmed v Mohamed Hosni Mubarak and Others*, Administrative Court of Justice, First Constituency (5 July 2010) <http://www.refworld.org/cases,EGY_CS,5270dc8a4.html> accessed 13 April 2017.

[315] *Abdulatiff Issaa Bare & Another v Republic* [2016] eKLR; *Ali Ahmed Saleh v Republic* [2016] eKLR; *DMM v Republic* [2016] eKLR; *Mohamed Maalim Abudullah v Republic* [2015] eKLR; *Abdi Kaarshe Mohammed & 4 Others v Republic* [2014] eKLR; *Bivamunda Erick v Republic* [2014] eKLR; *Mohamed Abdi Mohamed v Republic* [2012] eKLR; *Hussein Abdillahi & Another v Republic* [2012] eKLR; and *Rada Haile and Abel Burhamu v Republic* [2012] eKLR.

South Africa[316] at least, courts have halted deportations in view of international and domestic prohibitions against refoulement. Kenya's High Court recently ruled on the government's 2016 decision to repatriate all Somali refugees,[317] quashing the plan in view of international and domestic legal prohibitions against refoulement, as well as discrimination.[318] In a separate case, Kenya's High Court invalidated the Refugees Act amendment that capped the number of refugees allowed in the country at 150,000, finding it would breach the non-refoulement rule.[319] Most recently, Kenya's Court of Appeal affirmed that 'there does exist a firm basis for the argument and conclusion that indeed the principle of non-refoulement is a norm of customary international law'.[320] Thus instances of non-refoulement in Africa should, in line with the approach in *Nicaragua*,[321] be viewed as breaches of the rule, rather than as indications of the emergence of a new regional custom disavowing non-refoulement.

3. Responsibility sharing, temporary protection, and voluntary repatriation

The 1969 Convention formalized versions of three important refugee law concepts: responsibility sharing, temporary protection, and voluntary repatriation. Article II(4) articulates an early notion of responsibility sharing, providing, 'Where a Member State finds difficulty in continuing to grant asylum to refugees, such Member State may appeal directly to other Member States and through the OAU, and such other Member States shall in the spirit of African solidarity and international cooperation take appropriate measures to lighten the burden of the Member State granting asylum'. Such 'appropriate measures' include regional resettlement, financial support and political responsibility sharing.[322] Article II(4) was significantly ahead of its time. The next major regional responsibility-sharing regime did not emerge until 1999, when the EU began developing its common asylum system; the international community did not take any major steps towards global responsibility sharing until the New York Declaration was adopted in 2016.

Prescience aside, responsibility sharing is little used in practice because of the limited resources of African states.[323] For example, between 1997 and 2001, Benin and Burkina Faso received 226 resettled African refugees as part of a pilot project financed by UNHCR's Trust Fund for Enhancing Resettlement Activities. An evaluation of the project found it unsuccessful, due principally to the difficult economic

[316] *Abdi* (n 296); *Kabuika v Minister of Home Affairs* 1997 (4) SA 241 (C).

[317] The decision also addressed plans to close Dadaab and Kakuma camps and shutter the Department of Refugee Affairs.

[318] *Kenya National Commission on Human Rights* (n 307) 34–35.

[319] *CORD* (n 306) para 427.

[320] *Attorney General v Kituo Cha Sheria & 7 Others* [2017] eKLR 15.

[321] *Case Concerning the Military and Paramilitary Activities in and Against Nicaragua (Nicaragua v United States of America)* (Merits) [1986] ICJ Rep, para 98.

[322] Durieux and Hurwitz (n 244) 128–29.

[323] ibid 128.

circumstances in both countries.[324] More recently, in November 2017 Rwanda offered to resettle up to thirty thousand African migrants (many if not most of whom are likely refugees) from abysmal conditions in Libya. Hopefully in time this offer will be seen as the beginning of an era of increased responsibility sharing within the region.

Normatively, article II(4) may ground an argument against restrictions on refugees' rights. Arguably, a host state should appeal to other states to assist it with refugee hosting before it resorts to rights restrictions as a way of mitigating the challenges of refugee hosting in conditions of scarcity.

Temporary protection describes a variety of practices. According to Fitzpatrick, it is 'a magic gift, assuming the desired form of its enthusiasts' policy objectives'.[325] The dual meaning that has been attributed to the notion of temporary protection articulated in the 1969 Convention reflects Fitzpatrick's description. Temporary protection finds expression at article II(5) of the 1969 Convention, which provides, 'Where a refugee has not received the right to reside in any country of asylum, he may be granted temporary residence in any country of asylum in which he first presented himself as a refugee pending arrangement for his re-settlement in accordance with the preceding paragraph', which refers to article II(4) on responsibility sharing. York University's Centre for Refugee Studies interpreted this as implying that the nature of protection granted under the 1969 Convention is of limited duration:

> The debate about temporary versus permanent refugee protection has no real currency in the South, where protection has almost always been assumed to be temporary, even if it lasted for a long time. Protection has usually been provided by neighbouring countries with the clear understanding that the refugees would eventually return home. In fact, in Africa, temporary protection is not only common practice, it is given prominence in the Organisation [sic] of African Unity's 1969 Convention ... Article II(5).[326]

The version of temporary protection posited by the 1969 Convention does not, however, imply limited protection. Rutinwa explains that article II(5)

> applies to persons who have been recognised as refugees but for one reason or another have not been granted the right of residence for any duration at all. It is not intended to determine the duration of residence for all refugees who have been recognised and granted asylum.... [Furthermore,] where a person is resettled from one African country to another on account of the first country not being able to continue to provide him or her asylum, the function of resettlement in this case is not to terminate but to continue the refugee status of that person but in a different country.[327]

[324] Stefan Sperl and Irinel Bradisteanu, 'Refugee Resettlement in Developing Countries: The Experience of Benin and Burkina Faso, 1997–2003' UNHCR Evaluation and Policy Analysis Unit and Resettlement and Special Cases Section (2004) <http://www.refworld.org/docid/546467964.html> accessed 18 April 2017, 1.

[325] Joan Fitzpatrick, 'Temporary Protection of Refugees: Elements of a Formalized Regime' (2000) 94 AJIL 279, 280.

[326] Centre for Refugee Studies Refugee Research Unit, York University, 'The Temporary Protection of Refugees: A Solution-Oriented and Rights Regarding Approach' (1996) Discussion Paper prepared under the auspices of the research project 'Toward the Reformulation of International Refugee Law', 22, cited in Rutinwa (n 238) 16.

[327] (n 238) 16.

Put this way, it becomes clear that the 1969 Convention's article II(5) notion of temporary protection serves to operationalize the article II(4) provision on responsibility sharing and has little in common with later versions of temporary protection designed to limit states' obligations towards refugees. Under the 1969 Convention, it is the sojourn in the first country of asylum, not the protection, that is temporary.[328]

While the notion of temporary protection articulated by the 1969 Convention is a humanitarian one, it is premised on an idea that is fundamentally less so. Article II(5) exists to remedy the situation where a refugee has received asylum but no corresponding right of residence. That a refugee could be recognized as such but could also be lawfully deprived of a right of residence must be queried. A state's realization of its obligations under the 1951 Convention—which applies coextensively with the 1969 Convention[329]—to ensure refugees' rights clearly depends on their presence in the territory of the asylum state.[330] Furthermore, article II(1), in urging states to grant asylum, conceives of such asylum in terms of reception and securing the 'settlement' of refugees.

Article V of the 1969 Convention addresses voluntary repatriation.[331] Its first paragraph articulates the core principle: 'The essentially voluntary character of repatriation shall be respected in all cases and no refugee shall be repatriated against his will'. This principle is an important corollary of article II's provisions on asylum, particularly article II(3) on non-refoulement. The clauses that follow the core principle are premised on the assumption that the conditions for safe return have been met and detail the duties of countries of asylum and origin and refugee-assisting agencies. The sending state, in collaboration with the receiving state, must 'make adequate arrangements for the safe return of refugees who request repatriation',[332] while the country of origin must 'facilitate their resettlement and grant them the full rights and privileges of nationals of the country, and subject them to the same obligations'.[333] The Convention mandates countries of asylum, countries of origin, voluntary agencies, and international and inter-governmental organizations to assist refugees with the process of return.[334] It provides in particular that states of origin should use the news media and the OAU to invite refugees home and should provide assurances regarding the circumstances prevailing there, and that host countries should ensure that such information is received.[335] Article V also provides that, upon return, refugees must not be penalized for having fled.[336]

The 1969 Convention was the first, and remains the only, international legal instrument to formally insist on the voluntariness of refugee repatriation,[337] however previous articulations of the concept appear in the UNHCR statute,[338] an

[328] ibid. [329] See Chapter 4.

[330] See Violeta Moreno-Lax, 'Seeking Asylum in the Mediterranean: Against a Fragmentary Reading of EU Member States' Obligations Accruing at Sea' (2011) 23 IJRL 174, 204–05.

[331] For a detailed analysis of this provision, see D'Orsi (n 313) chap 8.

[332] 1969 Convention (n 2) art V(2). [333] ibid art V(3). [334] ibid art V(5).

[335] ibid art V(4). [336] ibid.

[337] UNHCR, 'Handbook, Voluntary Repatriation: International Protection' (UNHCR 1996) <http://www.unhcr.org/3bfe68d32.pdf> accessed 4 February 2011, Annex 3.

[338] UNGA Res 428 (V) (14 December 1950) Annex, para 1.

early UNGA resolution,[339] and the constitution of the International Refugee Organization,[340] UNHCR's predecessor. Its originality aside, article V(1) is a 'powerful statement of principle'[341] which despite isolated critiques,[342] is hailed as representing an early articulation of a principle that has become a cornerstone of the international regime for refugee protection.[343]

The principle of voluntary repatriation is often misinterpreted in the African context to suggest that repatriation sits atop a hierarchy of solutions.[344] In fact, article V is 'much more about elaborating the principles and the modalities of effecting voluntary repatriation than a prescription of it as the only solution'.[345] Despite this clear articulation of principles and modalities, the corollary of the incidences of refoulement mentioned earlier in this section is that the principle of voluntary repatriation is often violated in Africa. D'Orsi points out that UNHCR has 'admitted that in the last decades a good proportion of repatriations, including the ones in Sub-Saharan Africa, have occurred under "some form of duress" '.[346] Kenya's return of refugees from the Dadaab camp complex to Somalia, further to a November 2013 tripartite agreement between Kenya, Somalia, and UNHCR and in view of the government's desire to close Dadaab—which was recently deemed unconstitutional by the High Court of Kenya[347]—provides a recent example of major repatriation exercise which may not be entirely voluntary. Indeed, Kenya has notably described this repatriation as 'humane', rather than as 'voluntary'.[348]

339 UNGA Res 8(I) (12 February 1946).

340 Constitution of the International Refugee Organization (adopted 15 December 1946, entered into force 20 August 1948) 18 UNTS 3, art 2(1)(a).

341 Durieux and Hurwitz (n 244) 130.

342 Barutciski argues that the standard introduced by article V(1) is incoherent: 'There are at least two ways to read this provision. If the two phrases of this sentence are meant to be read separately, the first phrase ignores the possibility of involuntary repatriation when a person is no longer a refugee according to the cessation clause found in article I(4)(e). The second phrase may suggest, a contrario, that refugees can be voluntarily repatriated, which is clearly not the case given the inclusion of the term "refugee" which applies only to individuals who have reason to fear danger, and who are protected under the OAU Convention's non-refoulement guarantee. If the drafters intended that the two phrases of this sentence be read jointly in order to establish a single standard that relates to persons who satisfy the refugee definition, then the latter inconsistency still applies and a coherent provision would have stated that "no refugee shall be repatriated", regardless of whether it is against his or her will' (Michael Barutciski, 'The Development of Refugee Law and Policy in South Africa: a Commentary on the 1997 Green Paper and 1998 White Paper/Draft Bill' (1998) 10 IJRL 700, 718). Article V(1)'s punctuation suggests that the drafters intended Barutciski's second reading, and in that context 'refugee' should be interpreted to imply an individual who was recognized as a refugee but who, at the time of repatriation, falls into the category of person described at article I(4)(e), whether or not the cessation clause has actually been invoked.

343 Voluntary repatriation is one of UNHCR's trio of 'durable solutions' for refugees; the others are local integration and resettlement; see, generally, Marjoleine Zieck, *UNHCR and Voluntary Repatriation of Refugees: A Legal Analysis* (Martinus Nijhoff 1997).

344 Rutinwa (n 238) 15–16. 345 ibid 16. 346 D'Orsi (n 313) 271.

347 *Kenya National Commission on Human Rights* (n 307).

348 Norwegian Refugee Council, 'A Review of the Legal Framework Relating to the Proposed Closure of the Dadaab Refugee Camp and Repatriation of Somali Refugees' (2017) <https://www.nrc.no/resources/reports/a-review-of-the-legal-framework-relating-to-the-proposed-closure-of-the-dadaab-refugee-camp-and-repatriation-of-somali-refugees/> accessed 19 December 2017, 91.

Nevertheless, the return of peace to Angola, Liberia, Namibia, and Sierra Leone led to large-scale voluntary repatriations of refugees to these countries.[349] Numerous voluntary repatriation exercises have also played out in East Africa. Repatriations are typically operationalized by way of a tripartite agreement between the host state, the country of origin, and UNHCR. For example, a 1997 tripartite agreement regulated the repatriation of refugees to the DRC from Tanzania.[350] Under article 2, Tanzania agreed to uphold the voluntary nature of the repatriation. Pursuant to articles 4 and 16, the repatriation was to be coordinated and funded by UNHCR. Article 17 established the Commission for the Voluntary Repatriation of the Congolese Refugees in Tanzania, on which each contracting party was represented and which was responsible for monitoring the agreement's implementation and the reintegration of returnees.

4. The prohibition of subversive activities

The first paragraph of the 1969 Convention's article III, titled the 'Prohibition of Subversive Activities', requires that refugees 'abstain from any subversive activities against any Member State of the OAU'. 'Subversive activities' is not defined, but the provision goes on, at article III(2), to require that states 'prohibit refugees residing in their respective territories from attacking any State Member of the OAU, by any activity likely to cause tension between Member States, and in particular by use of arms, through the press, or by radio'.

The Lawyers Committee for Human Rights interprets this article III(2) specification as defining 'subversive activities', noting that the meaning of the term 'becomes fairly clear in the second clause by the ominous bracketing of "use of arms" with the use of press and radio'. It goes on to note that the prohibition is 'presumably also intended to limit parties and other political associations among refugees'.[351] However, a plain reading of article III suggests that the activities prohibited by paragraph 2 are mere illustrations of subversion, as opposed to a definition or indication of the concept as a whole. Moreover, other provisions of the 1969 Convention point to how the prohibition of subversive activities should be understood.

The 1969 Convention's preambular paragraph 5 notes that the assembled heads of state and government were 'Determined that the activities of… subversive elements should be discouraged, in accordance with the Declaration on the Problem of Subversion and [the] Resolution on the Problem of Refugees adopted at Accra in 1965'. The relevant portion of the Accra resolution calls on the Commission[352] to 're-examine the draft OAU convention … having regard to the views expressed by the Assembly at its present session'.[353] According to Okoth-Obbo, this is a reference

[349] Naldi and D'Orsi (n 26) 149.

[350] Tripartite Agreement on the Voluntary Repatriation of Congolese Refugees from Tanzania (1997) <http://www.refworld.org/docid/3ee84d5b4.html> accessed 20 April 2017.

[351] Lawyers Committee for Human Rights (n 225) 93.

[352] See Chapter 6, section B.1.a.

[353] OAU (OAHG), 'Resolution on the Problem of Refugees in Africa' (OAU Accra 21–25 October 1965) AHG/Res 26 (II) para 6.

to the 1965 Declaration on the Problem of Subversion,[354] and that Declaration is, as mentioned earlier in this section, recalled in the 1969 Convention's preambular paragraph 5. The Declaration can thus shed light on the meaning of 'subversive activities'.

Rather unhelpfully, the Declaration on the Problem of Subversion does not define 'subversion' or 'subversive activity'. On the whole, however, it expresses OAU member states' concern with fostering friendly relations among themselves and protecting newly independent regimes from internal as well as external threats.[355] Indeed, the Declaration's preamble notes that states were 'Desirous of consolidating the fraternal links that unite us' and the Declaration goes on to refer to article III(5) of the OAU Charter,[356] which unreservedly condemns 'in all its forms . . . subversive activities on the part of neighbouring States or any other States'.

These provisions make clear that the OAU was concerned with the classic international relations notion of subversion. According to this, subversion is the 'overthrow of the legal, political and social order of the state which another state attempts or achieves by propagating its ideology amongst the political forces of the state which is the target of this undertaking. It converts those forces to its ideology by supporting them in their efforts to capture power'.[357] It is interesting to note that this understanding of subversion relates to interstate conduct, while the 1969 Convention's article III is clearly concerned with individual conduct. The AU's Non-Aggression and Common Defence Pact defines 'acts of subversion' as 'any act that incites, aggravates or creates dissention within or among Member States with the intention or purpose to destabilize or overthrow the existing regime or political order by, among other means, fomenting racial, religious, linguistic, ethnic and other differences, in a manner inconsistent with the Constitutive Act, the Charter of the United Nations and the Lomé Declaration'.[358] The Pact was only adopted in 2005, so strictly speaking it cannot shed light on 'subversion' within the meaning of the 1969 Convention; however, its definition and the classical international relations notion of subversion articulated earlier in this section are similar and together go some way towards elucidating 'subversion'.

The specific contours of subversion in the refugee context cannot, however, be determined in isolation from human rights law—specifically the freedoms of expression, association, and assembly—because individual refugees who might be caught by the prohibition of subversive activities still enjoy these freedoms, though perhaps with some limitations. This analysis is conducted in Chapter 5.

Four additional 1969 Convention provisions reinforce the article III prohibition of subversive activities. As mentioned in Chapter 2, the article I(4)(g) cessation clause relating to serious infringements of the 1969 Convention's purposes and

354 (n 4) 130.

355 OAU (OAHG), 'Declaration on the Problem of Subversion' (OAU Accra 21–25 October 1965) AHG/Res 27 (II).

356 ibid para 1.

357 Etienne Mbaya, 'Political Asylum in the Charter of the OAU: Pretensions and Reality' (1987) 35 L & State 63, 74–75.

358 (n 62) art 1(a).

objectives operationalizes the prohibition of subversive activities. The article I(5)(c) exclusion clause prevents the 1969 Convention from applying to individuals 'guilty of acts contrary to the purposes and principles of the' OAU, which include 'Non-interference in the internal affairs of States', 'Respect for the sovereignty and territorial integrity of each State', and 'Unreserved condemnation ... of subversive activities on the part of ... States'.[359] Article II(2) characterizes the granting of asylum as 'a peaceful and humanitarian act', which 'shall not be regarded as an unfriendly act'. Finally, article II(6) directs states to 'settle refugees at a reasonable distance from the frontier of their country of origin', for 'reasons of security'.

The aftermath of the Rwandan genocide provides a cautionary tale of what can happen when these provisions—the exclusion clause in particular—are not applied and illustrates the prohibition of subversive activities' contemporary relevance. According the Adelman, compassion for refugees from Rwanda led officials 'to overlook the fact that this exodus included the genocidal killers among the ... innocent refugees'. As a result, the ex-*Forces armées Rwandaise* 'and their *interahamwe* minions quickly took over control of the camps [in the eastern DRC], began to regroup and make plans for the recapture of Rwanda and, presumably, the completion of the unfinished genocide of the Tutsi'.[360] Events such as this are presumably what the prohibition of subversive activities and its related provisions were aimed at preventing. Indeed, Okoth-Obbo invokes the DRC example in support of the prohibition, which he argues should be duly enforced, albeit with some modifications.[361]

The prohibition of subversive activities has also, however, been heavily criticized. Mbaya views it as 'ensuring that the African refugee is considered as a subhuman species'.[362] Less rhetorically but no less critically, Bakwesega points out that because of the prohibition, a refugee's stay in the host state 'is contingent upon their passivity and silence, even though the motive behind their flight might have been the search for freedom of expression'.[363] Ultimately, these contrasting views can be reconciled by interpreting the prohibition of subversive activities in line with relevant human rights law provisions, which analysis is, as mentioned earlier in this section, undertaken in Chapter 5.

D. Conclusions

This chapter focused on the 1969 Convention, beginning with its article I(2): its international influence, its key terms, and the individual determination of refugee status under it. It then addressed how the definition is (or is not) implemented in status determination, in individual as well as in prima facie procedures. This was

359 OAU Charter (n 84) arts III(2), (3), and(5).

360 Howard Adelman, 'The Use and Abuse of Refugees in Zaire: April 1996 to March 1997' (2001) Stanford University <http://web.stanford.edu/~sstedman/2001.readings/Zaire.htm> accessed 3 February 2015.

361 Okoth-Obbo (n 4) 134–35. 362 Mbaya (n 357) 76.

363 Chris J Bakwesegha, 'Forced Migration in Africa and the OAU Convention' in Howard Adelman and John Sorenson (eds), *African Refugees: Development Aid and Repatriation* (Westview Press 1994) 11.

followed by a discussion of other novel features of the Convention: asylum; non-refoulement; responsibility sharing, temporary protection, and voluntary repatriation; and the prohibition of subversive activities.

Having discussed the 1969 Convention's innovations in this chapter, Chapter 4 is devoted to a critical omission from it: the instrument's silence regarding refugees' civil, political, and socioeconomic rights. What will emerge is that this silence was not an omission as such, but rather an example of what is perhaps the 1969 Convention's most important innovation: the nature of its relationship to the 1951 Convention. The 1969 Convention was not only innovative in, among other things, incrementally expanding the range of individuals who could qualify for refugee status. In drawing on the existing universal instrument for the content of the status of which this broadened class of individuals would benefit, the drafters found a pioneering yet pragmatic way of ensuring that refugees in Africa are guaranteed the same rights as refugees elsewhere, while at the same time ensuring that issues particular to them—which Chapter 2 demonstrated was an important objective of the 1969 Convention—were not neglected. This chapter's focus on the 1969 Convention's innovations was thus only a preview of how innovative the instrument really is.

4

The Relationship between the 1951 and 1969 Conventions

A. Introduction

The relationship between the Convention relating to the Status of Refugees[1] (1951 Convention) and the Organization of African Unity Convention Governing the Specific Aspects of Refugee Problems in Africa[2] (1969 Convention) in states party to both instruments[3] has, remarkably, received almost no attention in the literature on the 1969 Convention.[4] This is surprising given the attention paid in recent years to the relationships between different regimes of international law,[5] and because the relationship between the 1951 and 1969 Conventions has important procedural

[1] (Adopted 28 July 1951, entered into force 22 April 1954) 189 UNTS 137.

[2] (Adopted 10 September 1969, entered into force 20 June 1974) 1001 UNTS 45.

[3] Most states in Africa are party to both the 1951 and 1969 Conventions. Djibouti, Eritrea, Madagascar, Mauritius, Namibia, the Saharawi Arab Democratic Republic, São Tomé and Príncipe, and Somalia are not party to the 1969 Convention. The Comoros, Eritrea, Libya, and Mauritius are not party to the 1951 Convention or its 1967 Protocol; Cape Verde is not party to the 1951 Convention but has ratified the 1967 Protocol. The states that are party to the 1951 Convention and its 1967 Protocol but not the 1969 Convention are Djibouti, Namibia, São Tomé and Príncipe, and Somalia; Madagascar is party to the 1951 Convention only and recognizes its geographical limitation to Europe, while the Republic of the Congo is party to both the 1951 Convention and its 1967 Protocol but recognizes the European geographical limitation. The states that are party to the 1969 Convention but not the 1951 Convention or its 1967 Protocol are the Comoros and Libya.

[4] An exception is an article on which this chapter draws: Marina Sharpe, 'The 1969 African Refugee Convention: Innovations, Misconceptions, and Omissions' (2012) 58 McGill LJ 95.

[5] See, for example, Martti Koskenniemi and Päivi Leino, 'Fragmentation of International Law: Postmodern Anxieties?' (2002) 15 Leiden J of Intl L 553; Seyed Ali Sadat-Akhavi, *Methods of Resolving Conflicts Between Treaties* (Martinus Nijhoff 2003); Andreas Fischer-Lescano and Gunther Teubner, 'Regime-Collisions: The Vain Search for Legal Unity in the Fragmentation of Global Law' (2004) 25 Mich J Intl L 999; International Law Commission, 'Fragmentation of International Law: Difficulties Arising From the Diversification and Expansion of International Law – Report of the Study Group of the International Law Commission' (13 April 2006) A/CN4/L682 (Fragmentation Report); Tamara Wood, 'The African War Refugee: Using IHL to Interpret the 1969 African Refugee Convention's Expanded Refugee Definition' in David James Cantor and Jean-François Durieux (eds), *Refuge from Inhumanity? Refugee Protection and the Laws of War* (Martinus Nijhoff 2014); Mads Andenas and Eirik Bjorge (eds), *A Farewell to Fragmentation: Reassertion and Convergence in International Law* (CUP 2015); Michaela Hailbronner, 'Laws in Conflict: The Relationship Between Human Rights and International Humanitarian Law under the African Charter on Human and Peoples' Rights' (2016) 16 Afr Hum Rts LJ 339.

and substantive implications. Most significant among the procedural implications, states party to both refugee instruments must determine which refugee definition should be considered first in refugee status determination (RSD). Most important among the substantive implications is the rights to which refugees recognized only under the 1969 Convention—whether for procedural reasons or for not meeting the 1951 Convention refugee definition—are entitled, a question raised by the 1969 Convention's silence regarding refugees' civil and political and socioeconomic rights.

This chapter begins with an articulation of the various approaches to RSD in states party to both refugee Conventions. In addition to surveying state practice in relation to this important procedural issue, the section also elucidates how and why a refugee might be recognized only under the 1969 Convention. The implications of such singular recognition in terms of refugee rights are then analysed. After considering Executive Committee (ExCom) Conclusion 22 on protection in large-scale influx, it is argued—based on the law of treaties, general international law, the equality principle, and McAdam's view that the 1951 Convention is the *lex specialis* for all persons in need of international protection—that in states party to both refugee Conventions, refugees recognized only under the 1969 Convention are entitled to the standards of treatment under the 1951 Convention. Finally, other aspects of the relationship between the 1951 and 1969 Conventions are considered. These are analysed within two categories. In the first, the relationships are complementary or interpretive: one instrument addresses an issue on which the other is silent or addresses a common issue more generously. The relationship of interpretation addressed relates to the 1951 Convention's article 1C(5) 'compelling reasons' proviso. The second category addresses inconsistencies between the 1951 and 1969 Conventions. These relationships of conflict relate to the freedoms of movement and association and the provision of travel documents.

In states with municipal refugee law, certain aspects of the relationship between the 1951 and 1969 Conventions may be articulated by such domestic legislation or in related regulations. Uganda's Refugees Act, 2006, for example, includes the 1951 Convention and the regional refugee definitions, and all refugees under the Act are entitled to a range of rights derived from the 1951 Convention.[6] While such state practice can resolve the issues raised here in particular jurisdictions, the focus here is on the international plane. Articulating the relationship between the 1951 and 1969 Conventions on this plane contributes to a complete elucidation of the two treaties, the 1969 Convention in particular, and to understanding the situation for refugees in monist jurisdictions. Legislation and other forms of state practice will, however, be invoked as relevant to the analysis of the relationship between the two instruments on the international plane.

[6] The Refugees Act, 2006 (Uganda) No 21 of 2006.

B. The Refugee Definitions in Status Determination

When African states adjudicate refugee claims pursuant to the international and regional refugee definitions, the decision on refugee status is generally made by an administrative eligibility committee on which a variety of government departments are represented. The Office of the United Nations High Commissioner for Refugees (UNHCR) usually has advisory observer status, as is the case in Benin, Chad, Ethiopia, Gabon, Mozambique, Niger, Tanzania, and Zambia.[7] Eligibility committees approach RSD in three principal ways. The first approach is for the committee itself to interview the refugee, which is the approach in Chad.[8] Under the second approach, another state official conducts the status determination interview and the eligibility committee makes a decision based on notes or a transcript from such interview. This is the approach in Uganda[9] and Tanzania.[10] In the third and final approach, used in Angola, Mozambique, and Zambia, an eligibility official from the government's refugee or immigration department conducts the interview and provides the eligibility committee with a transcript and a reasoned recommendation, on which the committee bases its decision.[11] Some states combine elements from two or more of these approaches.

Appeals are generally, though not always, available. In some cases, such as in Uganda, the same eligibility committee that decided the first instance case—though sometimes featuring new members—hears and decides the appeal.[12] In other countries, such as Malawi and Tanzania, a separate administrative appeals body exists.[13] Rarely is judicial review available, whether at the appellate level or as a third tier of review. It is legally possible in South Africa, Uganda, and Zambia. It has occurred in Uganda[14] but not in Zambia, while in South Africa it has occurred to a limited extent, though this has usually been on procedural rather than substantive grounds.[15]

Three procedural approaches to the instrument pursuant to which refugee status is adjudicated in states party to both the 1951 and 1969 Conventions have been observed.[16] States may employ one of these approaches, or two or three of them in combination. In what may be termed a sequential approach, adjudication begins with article 1A(2) of the 1951 Convention. Article I(2) of the 1969 Convention is considered only if the individual does not qualify for refugee status under the 1951 Convention. This is the approach in Benin and Burkina Faso; in the latter, decisions

[7] Marina Sharpe, 'The 1969 OAU Refugee Convention in the Context of Individual Refugee Status Determination' in Volker Türk, Alice Edwards, and Cornelis Wouters (eds), *In Flight from Conflict and Violence: UNHCR's Consultations on Refugee Status and Other Forms of International Protection* (CUP 2017) 124–25; note that all examples cited in this section B are merely illustrative, not exhaustive.

[8] ibid 125.

[9] Marina Sharpe and Salima Namusobya, 'Refugee Status Determination and the Rights of Recognized Refugees under Uganda's Refugees Act 2006' (2012) 24 IJRL 561, 569.

[10] Sharpe (n 7) 125. [11] ibid. [12] Sharpe and Namusobya (n 9) 570.

[13] Sharpe (n 7) 125–26.

[14] See *Tesfaye Shiferwa Awala v Attorney General*, Miscellaneous Application No 688 of 2003, High Court of Uganda (2 August 2005).

[15] Sharpe (n 7) 125–26. [16] See Sharpe (n 7) 127.

are rendered on a form that instructs the decision maker to proceed in this international then regional sequence.[17]

This sequential approach is supported by paragraph 9 of the preamble to the 1969 Convention, which recognizes the 1951 Convention as 'the basic and universal instrument relating to the status of refugees', as well as by the ordering of the two refugee definitions in article I of the 1969 Convention. It ensures that resettlement—which is usually contingent upon 1951 Convention refugee status—remains readily available among UNHCR's trio of 'durable solutions' for refugees.[18] Furthermore, the sequential approach contributes to the protection of refugees who move beyond Africa. Refugee status is of extraterritorial effect, meaning it should be recognized by third states, provided the state is party to the instrument pursuant to which status was recognized.[19] Because states outside Africa are not party to the 1969 Convention, article I(2) refugee status is not recognized beyond Africa. Once article I(2) refugees 'are out of the continent, their protection is ad hoc or non-existent'.[20]

In a second approach, the instrument applied is a function of the nature of the claimant's flight. Where the facts dictate the application of article I(2), individual circumstances of persecution are not considered. This approach is employed in Angola, Chad, Mozambique, Tanzania, Uganda, Zambia, and Zimbabwe.[21] In Angola and Mozambique, there is a tendency to conduct most RSD under article I(2), even when the 1951 Convention refugee definition would also apply legally and/or factually.[22] In Zimbabwe, RSD always occurs under article I(2), even though the 1983 Refugees Act incorporates both the 1951 and the 1969 Convention refugee definitions.[23] This tendency in Angola and Mozambique to employ—and in the case of Zimbabwe to automatically resort to—article I(2) likely relates to the nature of the refugee flows to these countries, which according to UNHCR is better reflected by article I(2) than by the 1951 Convention definition.[24]

In a third approach—which may overlap with the 'nature of flight' approach—the definition employed in RSD is based on pragmatic considerations. As discussed in Chapter 3, the article I(2) refugee definition is particularly suited to situations of large-scale influx given its compatibility with prima facie RSD.[25] In such situations, many states consider applying article I(2) prima facie to be more expedient

[17] Sharpe (n 7) 127.

[18] Non-African resettlement countries (principally Australia, Canada, and the United States) will typically only resettle refugees recognized under the 1951 Convention, because the 1969 Convention does not apply to them; see, generally, Kristin Sandvik, 'A Legal History: The Emergence of the African Resettlement Candidate in International Refugee Management' (2010) 22 IJRL 20.

[19] ExCom Conclusion No 12 (XXIX), 'Extraterritorial Effect of the Determination of Refugee Status' (1978).

[20] UNHCR, 'Persons Covered by the OAU Convention Governing the Specific Aspects of Refugee Problems in Africa and by the Cartagena Declaration on Refugees (Submitted by the African Group and the Latin American Group)' (1992) UNHCR EC/1992/SCP/CRP6 <http://www.refworld.org/topic,50ffbce51b1,50ffbce51ba,3ae68cd214,0,,SESSIONALREPORT,.html> accessed 25 January 2017, para 11.

[21] Sharpe (n 7) 127. [22] ibid 127–28. [23] ibid 128. [24] ibid.

[25] See section B.4.a.

and less resource intensive than applying article 1A(2) of the 1951 Convention.[26] Zambia, for example, has a policy of conducting RSD on a prima facie basis under the 1969 Convention in the borderlands, where most refugees arrive. Claims that are more aligned with the 1951 Convention are referred to the capital, Lusaka, for individual determination under article 1A(2). Those who arrive in Lusaka without having transited through the borderlands also have their claims processed under the 1951 Convention.[27]

In addition to the sequential, 'nature of flight', and pragmatic approaches, the decision about which refugee definition to apply in RSD may be unsystematic. In Nigeria, the refugee legislation of which includes both the 1951 and 1969 Convention refugee definitions,[28] an unreported case based on flight from unspecified insecurity was rejected under the 1951 Convention refugee definition without any subsequent consideration of the article I(2) definition. The same was true of an unreported decision from Guinea, regarding a woman who fled the conflict in Liberia in 1992.[29] As discussed in Chapter 3, the regional refugee definition is often not considered in adjudication in South Africa,[30] and several South African cases at the judicial review level recognized the refugee status of applicants from Burundi and the Democratic Republic of the Congo (DRC) without specifying the definition employed.[31]

Even worse than an unsystematic approach, decisions sometimes evidence misunderstanding about the distinct nature of the two refugee definitions. In two unreported Guinean cases, the reasoning combined the 1951 Convention's article 1A(2) 'membership of a particular social group' ground with the 1969 Convention article I(2) ground of 'events seriously disturbing public order'. This conflation was also evident in an unreported decision from Liberia.[32]

Such misunderstanding is unfortunate because the refugee definition pursuant to which an individual is recognized is important, in three principal respects. The first of these relates to the international opposability of refugee status. As discussed earlier in this section, article I(2) refugee status is not on its own sufficient for resettlement to Australia, Canada, and the United States (the principal resettlement countries),[33] nor is it opposable against states outside of Africa.

Secondly, as mentioned in Chapter 2, the 1969 Convention includes two cessation clauses that do not feature in its international counterpart: the 1969 Convention ceases to apply to any refugee who has 'committed a serious non-political crime

[26] George Okoth-Obbo, 'Thirty Years On: A Legal Review of the 1969 OAU Convention Governing the Specific Aspects of Refugee Problems in Africa' (2001) 20 RSQ 79, 120.

[27] Sharpe (n 7) 128.

[28] National Commission for Refugees (Establishment, etc) Act (1989, Nigeria).

[29] Sharpe (n 7) 128–29.

[30] See section B.3.

[31] *Abdul Shabani Akanakimana v The Chairperson of the Standing Committee for Refugee Affairs and Others*, Western Cape High Court 10970/13 (18 February 2015) <http://www.refworld.org/cases,ZAF_HC,54e5ed324.html> accessed 13 April 2017; *Christian Boketsa Bolanga v Refugee Status Determination Officer and Others*, Kwazulu-Natal High Court 5027/2012 (24 February 2015) <http://www.refworld.org/cases,ZAF_HC,54ecbc724.html> accessed 13 April 2017; *Deo Gracias Katsshingu v The Chairperson of the Standing Committee for Refugee Affairs and Others*, Western Cape High Court 19726/2010 (2 November 2011) <http://www.refworld.org/cases,ZAF_HC,50aba35a2.html> accessed 13 April 2011.

[32] Sharpe (n 7) 129.

[33] See n 18.

outside his country of refuge after his admission to that country as a refugee'[34] or has 'seriously infringed' the 1969 Convention's purposes and objectives.[35] According to Grahl-Madsen, these unique cessation clauses may result in an individual losing the 'benefit of the OAU [Organization of African Unity] Convention but not his refugee status, if that status is based on the [1951] Refugee Convention and Protocol, not merely on the special provisions of Art. I(2) of the OAU Convention'.[36] If, however, status were recognized only under the 1969 Convention and one of the regional cessation clauses were to apply, the individual would lose his or her refugee status.

Thirdly, the definition pursuant to which a refugee in Africa is recognized may be construed as relevant regarding the package of rights accompanying refugee status. Refugees within the meaning of the 1951 Convention definition are clearly entitled to the rights detailed in its articles 3 to 34. The rights to which refugees recognized only under the 1969 Convention—whether due to an application of the 'nature of flight' approach or the pragmatic approach, or due to rare circumstances in which an individual would fail to qualify for refugee status under the 1951 Convention but would meet the article I(2) definition[37]—are, by contrast, less immediately obvious. Section C explores this critical matter.

Before proceeding, however, it should be noted that in practice, issues that flow from the instrument of recognition are only salient where relevant records are reliably kept. A state's ability to deprive a 1969 Convention refugee of 1951 Convention rights would depend on state awareness that the refugee was recognized pursuant to the 1969 Convention. UNHCR used to collect such data, but no longer does.[38] Some states in Africa keep track of the legal basis for refugee status, while others do not. South Africa, for example, records the instrument of recognition, though its records are not consistently reliable.[39] Zambia also keeps track of the refugee

[34] 1969 Convention (n 2) art I(4)(f). [35] ibid art I(4)(g).

[36] Atle Grahl-Madsen, 'Political Rights and Freedoms of Refugees' in Goran Melander and Peter Nobel (eds), *African Refugees and the Law* (The Scandinavian Institute of African Studies 1978) 54.

[37] It should be noted that a refugee recognized under article I(2) will usually also meet the 1951 Convention (and the 1969 Convention article I(1)) refugee definition. However, some individuals will meet the 1969 Convention's regional refugee definition but not the 1951 Convention definition. Such individuals would include, for example, those fleeing the limited neo-colonial situations that continue to occur in Africa (see Chapter 3, section B.2.d) and those who, for evidentiary reasons, do not qualify under the 1951 Convention but whose country of origin is clearly affected by events seriously disturbing public order.

[38] Unpublished data collated by UNHCR's Field Information and Coordination Support Section recorded the legal basis for the refugee status of refugees in forty-one African countries as of October 2011. This data was provided to Tamara Wood, doctoral candidate at the University of New South Wales, on 21 October 2011. Wood shared this information on 24 August 2012. On 17 June 2015, Wood requested updated data in this regard. On 20 June 2015 she received a response from UNHCR's statistics unit indicating that data on the definition pursuant to which refugees in Africa were recognized was no longer being collected. Wood shared this correspondence on 21 June 2015.

[39] South African statistics seen by Wood indicated that all refugees recognized during the reporting period received status pursuant to the 1951 Convention refugee definition, though Wood was aware of individuals recognized during the same period under the 1969 Convention definition (email correspondence with Tamara Wood, 4 December 2013).

definition pursuant to which refugees on its territory are recognized.[40] Uganda, by contrast, does not record such information.[41]

C. The Rights of 1969 Convention Refugees

In what may be a remarkable case of constructive ambiguity, the 1969 Convention does not address refugees' civil, political, and socioeconomic rights, nor does it explicitly incorporate the 1951 Convention's articles 3 to 34 rights framework. Rather, it includes only a few rights: to RSD;[42] to non-refoulement;[43] to temporary protection in the first state of asylum;[44] protection from discrimination in the application of the Convention on the grounds of race, religion, nationality, membership of a particular social group or political opinions;[45] to voluntary repatriation;[46] and to a travel document.[47] This raises the issue of the additional rights applicable—on top of those provided by human rights law more generally—to refugees recognized under article I(2) of the 1969 Convention but who do not meet the 1951 Convention refugee definition[48] or to individuals whose status, for the procedural reasons described in section B, is recognized only pursuant to the regional instrument.

While this issue is salient for all 1969 Convention refugees (regardless of whether recognition is pursuant to article I(1) or article I(2)), it is starker in relation to article I(2) refugees, because refugees recognized pursuant to article I(1) of the 1969 Convention would also qualify for refugee status under article 1A(2) of the 1951 Convention; the two definitions are almost identical and the same exclusion clauses apply.[49] The regional refugee definition, by contrast, has no 1951 Convention parallel. The analysis below is therefore framed in relation to article I(2) refugees. Nevertheless, its conclusion that 1969 Convention refugees are entitled to 1951 Convention rights applies to all such refugees. This is important because the situation of article I(1) refugees has been overlooked by most among the handful of scholars who have addressed the rights of 1969 Convention refugees.

Remarkably little academic attention has been devoted to the rights of 1969 Convention refugees. This is perhaps because it seems obvious that, in states party to both the 1951 and 1969 Conventions, all refugees should benefit from 1951 Convention rights. Indeed, the scholars who have expressed this view have done so matter-of-factly or with very little supportive analysis.[50] Among them, Fitzpatrick notes only that the extension of the refugee definition under the 1969 Convention was done 'without any suggestion that the quality or durability of ... protection

40 Email correspondence with Chongo Chitupila, former officer with the Zambian Commissioner for Refugees, 25 October 2013.

41 Email correspondence with Salima Namusobya, Ugandan lawyer, 16 December 2013.

42 1969 Convention (n 2) art I(6). 43 ibid art II(3). 44 ibid art II(5).

45 ibid art IV. 46 ibid art V(1). 47 ibid art VI(1). 48 See n 37.

49 See Chapter 2, section C.

50 Admittedly none of the scholars discussed was explicitly addressing the question of the rights to which refugees recognized only under article I(2) of the 1969 Convention are entitled. Rather, in each case the issue arose as incidental to another question.

should be diminished as compared to that enjoyed by persons meeting the definition in the 1951 Convention'.[51] In discussing the domestic refugee laws of South Africa and Tanzania, Mandal mentions that the states' obligations under the 1969 Convention require them to guarantee the same rights to article I(2) refugees as to 1951 Convention refugees.[52] McAdam maintains simply that the 1969 Convention, 'as a regional complement to the [1951] Convention, applies [1951] Convention rights to persons fleeing external aggression, occupation, foreign domination or events seriously disturbing public order'.[53] Similarly, Abass and Mystris explain that the 1969 Convention

> seeks to place itself as a complementary instrument to that of the UN's 1951 Convention. It does this through encouraging those African States that have not acceded to the Convention to take such steps as well as calling on the OAU Members to apply the provisions within Africa. The result was a clear indication, from the OAU, that the 1951 UN Convention is applicable to refugees within Africa, and that international standards were to be met as a minimum, while the 1969 OAU Convention develops the standards further and in an African-specific context.[54]

Van Hövell tot Westerflier argues that 'The majority of Africa's refugees, though not falling within the stricter scope of the 1951 Convention, is, at least in theory, entitled to claim the rights set forth in this Convention'.[55] Weis maintains that the 1951 Convention, the Protocol relating to the Status of Refugees (1967 Protocol), and the 1969 Convention 'together, constitute a codification of the rights—and duties—of refugees in Africa'.[56] Rutinwa echoes these opinions, anchoring his perspective in conference proceedings:

> That refugees recognised under section I(2) of the OAU Convention are entitled to the same standards of treatment as those recognised under the 1951 Refugee Convention was confirmed by the Arusha Conference which recognised the definitions of the term 'refugee' contained in Article I, paragraphs 1 and 2 of the 1969 OAU Refugee Convention as the basis for determining refugee status in Africa and stressed 'the essential need for ensuring that African refugees are identified as such, so as to enable them to invoke the rights established for their benefit in the 1951 Refugee Convention and the 1967 Refugee Protocol and the

[51] Joan Fitzpatrick, 'Temporary Protection of Refugees: Elements of a Formalized Regime' (2000) 94 AJIL 279, 293.

[52] Ruma Mandal, 'Protection Mechanisms Outside the 1951 Convention ("Complementary Protection")' (2005) UNHCR Legal and Protection Policy Research Series <http://www.unhcr.org/435df0aa2.pdf> accessed 8 December 2010, xi–ii.

[53] Jane McAdam, *Complementary Protection in International Refugee Law* (OUP 2007) 38.

[54] Ademola Abass and Dominique Mystris, 'The African Union Legal Framework for Protecting Asylum Seekers' in Ademola Abass and Francesca Ippolito (eds), *Regional Approaches to the Protection of Asylum Seekers: An International Legal Perspective* (Ashgate 2014) 22.

[55] WJEM van Hövell tot Westerflier, 'Africa and Refugees: the OAU Refugee Convention in Theory and Practice' (1989) 7 NQHR 172, 174.

[56] Paul Weis, 'The Convention of the Organization of African Unity Governing the Specific Aspects of Refugee Problems in Africa' (1970) 3 Rev des droits de l'homme 449, 463.

1969 OAU Refugee Convention'. This was irrespective of the procedure by which they were recognised.[57]

Rutinwa concluded the same again more recently, finding that 'the juridical status of refugees recognized under any of the limbs of the refugee definition of the OAU Convention is the same as that of refugees recognized under the 1951 Convention, and [the] former refugees are entitled to the enjoyment of all the rights of refugees under the latter instrument'.[58] Durieux and Hurwitz also see 1969 Convention refugees as entitled to 1951 Convention rights. They rely on article VIII(2) of the 1969 Convention, which describes it as the 'regional complement' to the 1951 Convention, noting that 'On its face, the only possible interpretation of this provision is that a person recognized as a refugee under either branch of the definition in the complementary OAU Convention is entitled to the rights contained in the primary 1951 Convention'.[59] This view is reiterated in Durieux's later article with McAdam,[60] and by McAdam herself.[61] Rwelamira explains that in states that have ratified the universal and African refugee Conventions, the 'African refugee would then be able to enjoy the specific and well-defined rights relating to gainful employment, freedom of movement, welfare as well as rights relating to economic pursuit such as, labour legislation, acquisition of property, and other benefits related to employment'.[62] He concludes that 'In essence ... one should regard the two Conventions as cumulative'.[63] Beyani similarly noted that 'there exists a legal basis for the dual application of the principles contained in'[64] the 1951 and 1969 Conventions. UNHCR maintains simply that the 1951 and 1969 Conventions 'must be regarded as forming a whole'.[65] Naldi and D'Orsi find that the 1969 Convention 'does not seek to exclude the operation of the UN Convention from Africa, rather the substantive measures of protection provided for therein but not included in the OAU Convention apply'.[66]

Others, however, have adopted the opposite perspective, with a similar near absence of legal reasoning. Barutciski, describing the 1969 Convention as a

[57] Bonaventure Rutinwa, 'Prima Facie Status and Refugee Protection' (2002) UNHCR New Issues in Refugee Research Working Paper No 69 <http://www.unhcr.org/3db9636c4.pdf> accessed 8 December 2010, 14 (footnote omitted); on the Arusha Conference, see Chapter 6, section B.2.

[58] Bonaventure Rutinwa, 'Relationship Between the 1951 Refugee Convention and the 1969 OAU Convention on Refugees' in Volker Türk, Alice Edwards, and Cornelis Wouters (eds), *In Flight from Conflict and Violence: UNHCR's Consultations on Refugee Status and Other Forms of International Protection* (CUP 2017) 95–96.

[59] Jean-François Durieux and Agnes Hurwitz, 'How Many Is Too Many? African and European Legal Responses to Mass Influx of Refugees' (2004) 47 German YB Intl L 105, 126.

[60] Jean-François Durieux and Jane McAdam, 'Non-Refoulement through Time: The Case for a Derogation Clause to the Refugee Convention in Mass Influx Emergencies' (2004) 16 IJRL 4, 11.

[61] (n 53) 213.

[62] Medard RK Rwelamira, 'Some Reflections on the OAU Convention on Refugees: Some Pending Issues' (1983) 16 Comp & Intl LJ S Afr 155, 171.

[63] ibid 173.

[64] Chaloka Beyani, *Protection of the Right to Seek and Obtain Asylum Under the African Human Rights System* (Martinus Nijhoff 2013) 11.

[65] (n 20) para 1.

[66] Gino J Naldi and Cristiano D'Orsi, 'The Multi-faceted Aspects of Asylum-Law Applicable to Africa: Analysis for Reflection' (2014) 36 Loy LA Int'l & Comp L Rev 115, 127.

protection system 'meant to address mass flows'—an erroneous attribution discussed in Chapter 3—goes on to maintain that such system does 'not give refugees significant rights beyond *non-refoulement* guarantees'.[67] He further explains that, while the 1969 Convention's regional refugee definition 'means that it is the sole international refugee treaty which applies to most African refugees, it does not include the elaborate socioeconomic rights found in the 1951 Convention.... Limited rights apparently encourage a more liberal admission policy in situations of mass inflow, while elaborate rights that may lead to integration tend to discourage Governments from allowing refugees to access their territories'.[68] Barutciski is not alone in this perspective. Mendel maintains that 'the 1951 Convention may be described as guaranteeing extensive benefits, tending towards residence rights, to a narrowly defined class of individuals. The OAU Convention, on the other hand, provides relatively limited benefits, broadly consistent with maintenance in camps, to those fleeing a wide range of situations'.[69] Viljoen has also construed refugee rights in Africa narrowly, based, however, on different legal reasoning. He asserts that apart from non-refoulement, the 1969 Convention 'does not provide explicitly for the "rights" of refugees. Still, entitlements (or "indirect rights") are implied by the imposition of obligations on states, thus rendering the OAU Refugee Convention a "human rights related" treaty'.[70]

Chartrand had anticipated the emergence of this trend: 'The broadening of the definition of the term refugee could ... raise problems if it leads to the emergence of different classes of refugees—those who qualify for refugee status under all the relevant international instruments and those who qualify under only one—with confusion and disagreement among states and international agencies as to whom to accord which standard of treatment'.[71] De la Hunt confirmed Chartrand's prediction when she identified the emergence of an erroneous trend viewing the 1969 Convention as proposing 'an entirely different kind of refugee regime that [gives] fewer rights to more refugees'.[72] More recently, Rutinwa highlighted the 'tendency to treat refugees in or from Africa, particularly those from situations of conflict and generalized violence, as a distinct genre of refugees who do not fall under, nor are entitled to the benefits of, the 1951 Convention'.[73]

While most scholars who have addressed this issue, however briefly, agree that article I(2) refugees benefit from 1951 Convention rights in states party to both

[67] Michael Barutciski, 'The Development of Refugee Law and Policy in South Africa: a Commentary on the 1997 Green Paper and 1998 White Paper/Draft Bill' (1998) 10 IJRL 700, 714.

[68] ibid.

[69] Toby D Mendel, 'Refugee Law and Practice in Tanzania' (1995) 9 IJRL 35, 57.

[70] Frans Viljoen, *International Human Rights Law in Africa* (2nd edn, OUP 2012) 241–42.

[71] Philip E Chartrand, 'The Organization of African Unity and African Refugees: A Progress Report' (1975) 137 World Aff 265, 272.

[72] Lee Anne de la Hunt, 'Refugee Law in South Africa: Making the Road of the Refugee Longer' (2002) US Committee for Refugees and Immigrants <http://www.refugees.org/world/articles/safrica_wrs02.htm> accessed 6 May 2011, cited in Micah Bond Rankin, 'Extending the Limits or Narrowing the Scope? Deconstructing the OAU Refugee Definition Thirty Years On' (2005) 21 S Afr J Hum Rts 406, 417.

[73] (n 58) 95.

instruments, the existence of an opposite minority point of view, the widespread use of refugee camps in Africa, and the sparse legal reasoning on both sides of the issue mandate giving it sustained attention. Four principal arguments are advanced in support of the proposition that 1969 Convention refugees in states party to both the 1951 and 1969 Conventions are entitled to the full range of rights guaranteed by the former instrument: a treaty interpretation argument, certain general principles of international law, an equality argument, and, finally, a *lex specialis* argument. Each of these is addressed in turn below; they are in addition to the obvious points that viewing article I(2) refugees as not entitled to 1951 Convention rights empties the 1969 Convention's article II on asylum of all but the most base content, and that the procedural fact of which instrument a refugee is recognized under should not affect his or her substantive rights. Before proceeding, however, it is necessary to address ExCom's Conclusion No 22 on the Protection of Asylum-Seekers in Situations of Large-Scale Influx.[74]

1. ExCom Conclusion 22

ExCom Conclusion 22 may initially appear to support a circumscribed package of rights for article I(2) refugees. It could equally seem to support the incorrect position discussed in Chapter 3: that refugees recognized on a prima facie basis enjoy fewer rights than their counterparts recognized via ordinary status determination. Conclusion 22 begins by noting that large-scale influxes may include refugees within the meaning of the 1951 Convention or persons 'who, owing to external aggression, occupation, foreign domination or events seriously disturbing public order in either part or the whole of their country of origin or nationality are compelled to seek refuge outside that country'.[75] It then goes on to enumerate sixteen standards of treatment for 'asylum-seekers who have been temporarily admitted to a country pending arrangements for a durable solution'.[76] The list does not include certain rights guaranteed by the 1951 Convention, such as to education, to gainful employment, to social security, and to identity papers or a travel document.

The protection regime established by ExCom Conclusion 22 applies only, however, to large-scale influxes in which 'States, although committed to obtaining durable solutions, have only found it possible to admit asylum-seekers without undertaking at the time of admission to provide permanent settlement'.[77] In other words, the conclusion applies only to situations of temporary protection, and not to the circumstances of article I(2) refugees. Furthermore, even in temporary protection situations, according to Goodwin-Gill the conclusion provides 'a point of departure only'; in certain circumstances, 'even a "temporary" solution may require more substantial provision for refugees, including the opportunity to earn a living and to have access to education, housing, and social assistance'.[78] Goodwin-Gill's

[74] ExCom Conclusion No 22 (XXXII), 'Protection of Asylum-Seekers in Situations of Large-Scale Influx' (1981).

[75] ibid para I(1). [76] ibid para IIB. [77] ibid para I(2).

[78] Guy S Goodwin-Gill, 'Non-refoulement and the New Asylum Seekers' (1986) 26 Va J Intl L 897, 906.

view was affirmed during UNHCR's Global Consultations on International Protection, where it was noted that ExCom Conclusion 22 'was never intended as a substitute for standards of protection under the 1951 Convention'.[79]

Furthermore, McAdam explains that Conclusion No 22 must be understood within the context in which it was adopted: the mass exodus from Indochina beginning in the mid-seventies, when numbers overwhelmed individual processing and frontline states were not party to the 1951 Convention.[80] The conclusion, therefore, 'filled a gap by identifying existing normative standards for States not bound by the [1951] Convention or [1967] Protocol'.[81] In considering the particular circumstances to which it applies, it becomes clear that ExCom Conclusion 22 provides no support for the proposition that article I(2) refugees enjoy fewer rights than those recognized under the 1951 Convention. Nor does it support the idea that refugees recognized on a prima facie basis have fewer rights than those recognized in traditional RSD.

2. The law of treaties

Aspects of the text of the 1969 Convention, considered in light of the law of treaties, are instructive in determining the rights to which refugees recognized under article I(2) of the 1969 Convention are entitled. The relevant treaty law principles are the rule on the application of successive treaties relating to the same subject matter,[82] the general rule of interpretation[83] and the rule on supplementary means of interpretation.[84] Each is addressed in turn.

(a) Successive treaties relating to the same subject matter

Article 30 of the Vienna Convention on the Law of Treaties (VCLT) addresses the question of the relationship between successive treaties relating to the same subject matter. This provision, while primarily invoked to resolve explicit conflicts, is also applicable 'more generally to the rights and obligations of States parties to successive treaties relating to the same subject-matter'.[85] However, the strict construction[86] to be given to 'relating to the same subject matter'—language that appears in sub-paragraph 1 and addresses the general applicability of article 30—and the residuary character of article 30 in relation to conflict clauses[87] raises the threshold question of whether article 30 is even applicable.

[79] UNHCR Global Consultations, 'Protection of Refugees in Mass Influx Situations: Overall Protection Framework' UN Doc EC/GC/01/4 (19 February 2001) para 8.

[80] (n 53) 246–47. [81] ibid 247.

[82] Vienna Convention on the Law of Treaties (adopted 23 May 1969, entered into force 27 January 1980) 1155 UNTS 331, art 30.

[83] ibid art 31. [84] ibid art 32.

[85] Mark E Villiger, *Commentary on the 1969 Vienna Convention on the Law of Treaties* (Martinus Nijhoff 2009) 402.

[86] Anthony Aust, *Modern Treaty Law and Practice* (2nd edn, CUP 2007) 229; Ian Sinclair, *The Vienna Convention on the Law of Treaties* (2nd edn, Manchester University Press 1984) 98; contra: Fragmentation Report (n 5) paras 253–54.

[87] Aust (n 86) 227; Fragmentation Report (n 5) para 251; Sinclair (n 86) 97; Villiger (n 85) 403.

The 1969 Convention seeks only to regulate matters not already covered by the 1951 Convention,[88] calling into question whether it and the 1951 Convention can be construed as 'relating to the same subject matter'.[89] In this regard, the relationship between the 1951 and 1969 Conventions is an example of the main basis on which Sinclair critiques article 30. He notes that the 'rules laid down fail to take account of the many complications which arise when there coexist two treaties relating to the same subject-matter, one negotiated at the regional level ... and another negotiated within the framework of a universal organisation'.[90] Furthermore, article 30 is residual in the sense that it only applies 'in the absence of express treaty provisions regulating priority'.[91] Thus when a treaty expressly provides how it should relate to another instrument, article 30 does not apply. The 1969 Convention contains two provisions that may reasonably be viewed as conflict clauses.[92] Article VIII(2) provides that the 1969 Convention 'shall be the effective regional complement in Africa' of the 1951 Convention, while preambular paragraph 9 recognizes that the 1951 Convention 'constitutes the basic and universal instrument relating to the status of refugees and reflects the deep concern of States for refugees and their desire to establish common standards for their treatment'.

Thus while article 30's sub-paragraphs 3 and 4 on construing the relationship between successive treaties relating to the same subject matter do not apply, its second sub-paragraph confirms the primacy of the 1969 Convention's conflict clauses. Article 30(2) of the VCLT concerns conflict clauses aimed at giving priority to another treaty. It provides, 'When a treaty specifies that it is subject to, or that it is not to be considered as incompatible with, an earlier or later treaty, the provisions of that other treaty prevail'. According to Villiger, 'on the contractual level, the residual character of Article 30 vis-à-vis the conflict clause of another treaty may be based on its own para. 2—but only when that conflict clause grants priority to other treaties'.[93] The 1969 Convention's conflict clauses indeed acknowledge the primacy of the 1951 Convention. Article 30(2) therefore mandates that they should govern the issue at hand. The proper interpretation of the 1969 Convention's conflict clauses necessitates recourse to the general rule of interpretation.

(b) *The general rule of interpretation*

The general rule of interpretation provides, 'a treaty shall be interpreted in good faith in accordance with the ordinary meaning to be given to the terms of the treaty in their context and in the light of its object and purpose'.[94] This was elaborated in Chapter 3.[95] The general rule of interpretation must be applied to the clauses relevant to resolving the issue at hand which, as discussed earlier in this section, are the

[88] See Chapter 2, section D and Rwelamira (n 62) 167.
[89] See, generally, Christopher J Borgen, 'Resolving Treaty Conflicts' (2005) 37 Geo Wash Intl LR 573, 603; contra: Fragmentation Report (n 5) para 22.
[90] (n 86) 98. [91] ibid 97.
[92] According to Villiger, conflict clauses may appear 'in the treaty itself, in its preamble, or in an annex' ((n 85) 404).
[93] (n 85) 403. [94] VCLT (n 82) art 31(1). [95] See section B.2.a.

1969 Convention's conflict clauses: preambular paragraph 9 and article VIII(2). Preambular paragraph 10 is also relevant. 'Recalling Resolutions 26 and 104 of the OAU Assemblies of Heads of State and Government',[96] it calls on OAU member states 'who had not already done so to accede to the United Nations Convention of 1951 and to the Protocol of 1967 ... and meanwhile to apply their provisions to refugees in Africa'.

In interpreting these three provisions in line with their ordinary meaning in context, it becomes clear that article I(2) refugees are entitled to the rights contained in the 1951 Convention. In recognizing the 1951 Convention as 'the basic and universal instrument relating to the status of refugees',[97] the 1969 Convention establishes its predecessor instrument as the global reference point for refugee status in a general sense. In going on to recognize that the 1951 Convention 'reflects the deep concern of States for refugees and their desire to establish *common standards for their treatment*',[98] the 1969 Convention specifically establishes the 1951 Convention as the universal source of refugee rights. This is why, in the preambular paragraph that follows, the 1969 Convention calls on states that have 'not already done so to accede to' the 1951 Convention and 1967 Protocol. Moreover, preambular paragraph 10 calls on OAU member states to apply 1951 Convention and 1967 Protocol provisions to refugees in Africa. This clear call is unambiguous. Indeed, according to D'Sa,

> the fact that the OAU Convention expressly recognizes the legal status and validity of the UN Convention and encourages the OAU Member States to accede to the latter is ... evidence that the OAU Convention does not preclude the application by its Member States of the additional provisions of the UN Convention relating to such matters as gainful employment, welfare, housing, public education, administrative assistance and so on.[99]

This view is further evidenced by the 1969 Convention's title. According to Gardiner, titles 'may occasionally contribute to a specific interpretation'.[100] The reference in the 1969 Convention's title to its governance of the 'Specific Aspects of Refugee Problems in Africa' affirms the more general relevance of the 1951 Convention.

The co-application of the 1951 and 1969 Conventions that emerges from the latter instrument's conflict clause at preambular paragraph 9 is the meaning that

[96] The reference to OAHG resolution 104, which appears in all published versions of the 1969 Convention, seems to be in error. OAHG resolution 104 relates to the Western Sahara situation. Moreover, it was adopted in 1983, fourteen years after the 1969 Convention's adoption. The reference in preambular paragraph 10 is likely to OCM resolution 104 (CM/Res.104 (IX)), which was adopted in 1967 and relates to refugee problems in Africa. OCM resolution 104 recommends that states accede to the 1951 Convention and 1967 Protocol and apply them in Africa; recommends that the OAU adopt an African refugee convention; recommends that the OAU help countries of origin and host states 'devise ways and means for the return of the refugees to their country of origin, in complete security'; expresses gratitude to states, UNHCR, and non-governmental organizations 'and asks them to increase their assistance to refugees in African [sic] and facilitate their repatriation and resettlement'; and appeals to states 'adjacent to African territories under foreign domination to afford these refugees transit facilities, temporary residence and travel papers'. For the content of OAHG resolution 26, see Chapter 2, n 128.

[97] 1969 Convention (n 2) preambular para 9.

[98] ibid (emphasis added).

[99] Rose D'Sa, 'The African Refugee Problem, Relevant International Conventions and Recent Activities of the Organization of African Unity' (1984) 31 NILR 378, 390.

[100] Richard Gardiner, *Treaty Interpretation* (2nd edn, OUP 2010) 180.

must be similarly attributed to the article VIII(2) conflict clause. It provides that the 1969 Convention is the 'effective regional complement in Africa' of the 1951 Convention. As mentioned above, Durieux and Hurwitz find that 'on its face, the only possible interpretation of this provision is that a person recognized as a refugee under [either] branch of the definition in the complementary OAU Convention is entitled to the rights contained in the primary 1951 Convention'.[101] Durieux and McAdam,[102] and McAdam[103] reach the same conclusion. Okoth-Obbo explains that by describing itself as the regional complement to the 1951 Convention, the full scope of application of the 1969 Convention 'must be considered as also including the 1951 Convention'.[104] Similarly, Awuku views the language of article VIII(2) as implying that the 1969 Convention does not supersede, but rather supplements, the 1951 Convention.[105] Holborn considers article VIII(2), as well as preambular paragraphs 9 and 10, and finds, 'The final text of the 1969 ... Convention makes clear that it was drawn up to supplement and not to supersede or conflict with the 1951 Convention and the 1967 Protocol.... The substantive articles of the OAU Convention create obligations to be assumed by contracting states in addition to those they have accepted by becoming parties to the 1951 Convention and 1967 Protocol'.[106] These views suggest that the 1951 and 1969 Conventions are complementary in states party to both instruments: an individual can be recognized as a refugee under article I(2) of the 1969 Convention, and the rights associated with such status can be derived from the 1951 Convention.

This initial interpretation is not vitiated when considered in light of the 1969 Convention's object and purpose, which can be gleaned from the text of the 1969 Convention generally and from its preamble in particular.[107] The preamble begins by 'Noting with concern the constantly increasing numbers of refugees in Africa' and by stating that signatories are 'desirous of finding ways and means of alleviating ... [refugees'] misery and suffering as well as providing them with a better life and future'.[108] It goes on to articulate the 'need for an essentially humanitarian approach towards solving the problems of refugees'.[109] The preamble to the 1969 Convention then mentions the Charter of the United Nations (UN Charter) and the Universal Declaration of Human Rights (UDHR),[110] noting that they have 'affirmed the principle that human beings shall enjoy fundamental rights and freedoms without discrimination',[111] and states that African problems 'must be solved in the spirit of' the Charter of the Organization of African Unity (OAU Charter),[112] which itself affirms OAU member state adherence to the UN Charter and the UDHR.[113] These recitals suggest that a form of asylum featuring only the few rights explicitly recognized by the 1969 Convention would

[101] (n 59) 126. [102] (n 60) 11. [103] (n 53) 213. [104] (n 26) 98.

[105] Emmanuel Opoku Awuku, 'Refugee Movements in Africa and the OAU Convention on Refugees' (1995) 39 J Afr L 79, 81.

[106] Louise W Holborn, *Refugees: A Problem of our Time—The Work of the United Nations High Commissioner for Refugees, 1951–1972*, vol I and II (Scarecrow Press 1974) 188.

[107] Gardiner (n 100) 192. [108] 1969 Convention (n 2) preambular para 1.

[109] ibid preambular para 2. [110] UNGA Res 217A (III) (10 December 1948).

[111] 1969 Convention (n 2) preambular para 6. [112] ibid preambular para 8.

[113] Charter of the Organization of African Unity (25 May 1963) 479 UNTS 39, preambular para 9.

be manifestly inconsistent with the 1969 Convention's object and purpose of alleviating the suffering of refugees in a humanitarian manner in line with human rights. The preamble thus confirms the interpretation reached above: refugees recognized only under article I(2) of the 1969 Convention are entitled to 1951 Convention rights.

The regional refugee definition's opening words are also relevant. Article I(2) begins by noting that 'The term "refugee" shall also apply to' and it then goes on to provide the regional refugee definition. The word 'also' is a reference back to article I(1), which introduces the 1951 Convention's refugee definition by stating, 'For the purposes of this Convention, the term "refugee" shall mean every person who . . .'. Thus according to the 1969 Convention, the term 'refugee' is a single category, which includes individuals who meet the article I(1) international definition and also includes persons who meet the article I(2) regional definition. While the two prongs of article I provide two distinct points of entry into the refugee category, there is but one category; at no point does the 1969 Convention distinguish between article I(1) and article I(2) refugees. The ordinary meaning of this singularity is that all refugees in Africa must, according to the 1969 Convention, be treated equally.

The VCLT's article 31 general rule of interpretation includes an enumeration of the other elements that must be considered, together with the context. Among them are 'any relevant rules of international law applicable in the relations between the parties'[114] and 'any subsequent practice in the application of the treaty which establishes the agreement of the parties regarding its interpretation'.[115] Consideration of each of these elements affirms the conclusion that article I(2) refugees enjoy 1951 Convention rights.

(i) Relevant rules of international law

The VCLT's article 31(3)(c) mandates the consideration of 'relevant rules of international law' as part of the process of treaty interpretation. Chapter 3 parsed the meaning of this broad exhortation.[116] As a reminder, the international law that is 'relevant' consists of those rules—whether emanating from treaties, custom, general principles of international law, or the subsidiary sources of jurisprudence and scholarly commentary—that touch 'on the same subject matter as the treaty provision or provisions being interpreted or which in any way affect that interpretation'[117] and—given the evolutionary interpretive approach that may be applied regarding the 1969 Convention—that are in force at the time of interpretation.[118] The 1951 Convention and its 1967 Protocol, the UDHR, the International Covenant on Civil and Political Rights (ICCPR), the International Covenant on Economic, Social and

[114] VCLT (n 82) art 31(3)(c).

[115] ibid art 31(3)(b). In 2016 at its 68th session, the ILC adopted draft conclusions on 'Subsequent agreements [VCLT art 31(3)(a)] and subsequent practice [VCLT art 31(3)(b)] in relation to the interpretation of treaties' (International Law Commission, 'Subsequent Agreements and Subsequent Practice in Relation to the Interpretation of Treaties: Text of the Draft Conclusions Provisionally Adopted by the Drafting Committee on First Reading' (6 June 2016) UN Doc A/CN.4/L.874).

[116] See section B.2.a. [117] Gardiner (n 100) 260.

[118] ibid 251; Villiger (n 85) 433.

Cultural Rights[119] (ICESCR) and African human rights law[120] thus seem relevant to the interpretation of the 1969 Convention.[121] Their applicability is by no means, however, a foregone conclusion.

International refugee and human rights treaties cannot necessarily be applied to the interpretation of the 1969 Convention because—as discussed in Chapter 3[122]—according to article 31(3)(c), the 'relevant rules of international law' must be 'applicable in the relations between the parties'. This raises the question of whether it is 'necessary that *all* the parties to the treaty being interpreted are also parties to the treaty relied upon as the other source of international law for interpretation purposes'.[123] Jurisprudence and doctrine on this issue have not produced a clear answer,[124] though Pobjoy has outlined three dominant approaches.[125] That adopted here is that the rules that can be taken into account are those that 'can be said to be at least implicitly accepted or tolerated ... in the sense that [the rule] can reasonably be considered to express the common intentions or understandings of all members as to the meaning of the ... term concerned'.[126]

It is thus at the very least arguable that international refugee law and international and African human rights law currently prevailing are relevant to the interpretation of the 1969 Convention. Indeed, this is in line with the International Law Commission's (ILC) understanding of the principle of systemic integration, which lies at the core of article 31(3)(c) and requires that international obligations be 'interpreted by reference to their normative environment'.[127] Furthermore, Judge Weeramantry of the International Court of Justice has opined that 'Treaties that affect human rights cannot be applied in such a manner as to constitute a denial of human rights *as understood at the time of their application*'.[128]

Invoking present-day international refugee law and international and African human rights law to determine whether article I(2) refugees benefit from 1951 Convention rights reaffirms that they do; finding otherwise would be nonsensical, as it would effectively deny article I(2) refugees the human rights to which they are otherwise entitled. Of particular note in applying international refugee law to the interpretation of the 1969 Convention is the preamble to the 1967 Protocol, which provides that '*equal status* should be enjoyed by all refugees', including those who were recognized as a result of 'new refugee situations [that] have arisen since

[119] (Adopted 16 December 1966, entered into force 3 January 1976) 993 UNTS 3.

[120] See Chapter 5, section C.

[121] Tom Clark, 'Rights Based Refuge, the Potential of the 1951 Convention and the Need for Authoritative Interpretation' (2004) 16 IJRL 584, 594; James C Hathaway, *The Rights of Refugees Under International Law* (CUP 2005) 64–67.

[122] See section B.2.a.

[123] Fragmentation Report (n 5) para 470.

[124] Gardiner (n 100) 269. Note that the ILC proposes that considering this uncertainty, a better solution would be 'to permit reference to another treaty provided that the *parties in dispute* are also parties to that other treaty' (Fragmentation Report (n 5) para 472).

[125] See Chapter 3, section B.2.a.

[126] Joost Pauwelyn, 'The Role of Public International Law in the WTO: How Far Can We Go?' (2001) 95 AJIL 535, 576, cited in Jason Pobjoy, *The Child in International Refugee Law* (CUP 2017) 42.

[127] Fragmentation Report (n 5) para 413.

[128] *Gabcikovo-Nagymaros Project (Hungary/Slovakia)* [1997] ICJ Rep 7, 114–15 (emphasis added).

the [1951] Convention was adopted'.[129] Applying this provision in interpreting the 1969 Convention clearly suggests that the rights framework under the 1969 Convention should be derived from the 1951 Convention.

(ii) Subsequent practice

The subsequent state practice referred to in article 31(3)(b) includes domestic legislation.[130] Among the forty-seven African states with domestic refugee laws—Cape Verde, the Comoros, Egypt, Eritrea, Libya, Mauritius, São Tomé and Príncipe, and the Seychelles do not have national acts—the vast majority have incorporated the 1951 and 1969 Conventions in whole or in part.[131] Among these, the overwhelming majority have done so in a way that clearly affirms that 1951 Convention rights apply to article I(2) refugees. Specifically, the refugee acts of Angola,[132] Benin,[133] Burkina Faso,[134] Burundi,[135] Cameroon,[136] the Central African Republic,[137] Djibouti,[138] the DRC,[139] Ethiopia,[140] Gabon,[141] Gambia,[142] Ghana,[143] Guinea,[144] Guinea Bissau,[145] Kenya,[146] Lesotho,[147] Liberia,[148] Mali,[149] Mozambique,[150] Namibia,[151] Niger,[152] Nigeria,[153] Rwanda,[154] Sierra Leone,[155] South Africa,[156] South Sudan,[157] Tanzania,[158] Togo,[159] Uganda,[160] Zambia,[161] and Zimbabwe[162] include both the

129 Protocol relating to the Status of Refugees (adopted 31 January 1967, entered into force 4 October 1967) 606 UNTS 267, preambular paras 3 and 4 (emphasis added).

130 Gardiner (n 100) 228.

131 See Chapter 3, n 10, regarding Algeria, Botswana, and Morocco, whose refugee acts do not reflect their international obligations.

132 Law No 8 of 1990, Law on Refugee Status (Angola).

133 Ordonnance No 75-41 du 1975 portant status des réfugiés (Benin).

134 Loi no 042-2008/AN du 23 octobre 2008 portant statut des réfugiés au Burkina Faso.

135 Loi no 1/32 du 13 novembre 2008 sur l'asile et la protection des réfugiés au Burundi.

136 Loi no 2005/006 du 27 juillet 2005 portant statut des réfugiés au Cameroun.

137 Loi no 07.019 du 28 decembre 2007 portant statut des réfugiés en République centrafricaine.

138 Loi no 159/AN/16/7ième L du 5 janvier 2017 portant statut des réfugiés en République de Djibouti.

139 Loi no 021.2002 du 16 octobre 2002 portant statut des réfugiés en République démocratique du Congo.

140 Refugee Proclamation No 409/2004 (Ethiopia).

141 Loi no 5/98 du 5 mars 1998 portant statut des réfugiés en République gabonaise.

142 Refugee Act, 2008 (Gambia).

143 Refugee Law, 1992 (PNDCL 305D) (Ghana).

144 Loi L/2000/012/AN adoptant et promulguant le statut des réfugiés en République de guinée.

145 Loi no 6/2008 aprovado o estatuto do refugiado (Guinea Bissau).

146 The Refugees Act, 2006 (Kenya).

147 Refugee Act 1983 (Lesotho).

148 Refugee Act, 1993 (Liberia).

149 Loi no 98-40 du 20 juillet 1998 portant sur le statut des réfugiés (Mali).

150 Act No 21/1991 of 31 December 1991 (Refugee Act) (Mozambique).

151 Namibia Refugees (Recognition and Control) Act, 1999.

152 Loi no 97-016 du 20 juin 1997 portant statuts des réfugiés (Niger).

153 Nigeria (n 28).

154 Law No 13ter/2014 of 21/05/2014 Relating to Refugees (Rwanda).

155 The Refugees Protection Act, 2007 (Sierra Leone).

156 The Refugees Act 1998 No 130 of 1998 (South Africa).

157 Refugee Act, 2012, Act No 20 (South Sudan).

158 The Refugees Act, 1998 (Tanzania).

159 Loi no 2000-019 portant statut des réfugiés au Togo.

160 Uganda (n 6).

161 The Refugees Act, 2017 (Zambia).

162 Refugees Act [Chapter 4:03] (Zimbabwe, 2001).

1951 Convention refugee definition and that articulated at article I(2) of the 1969 Convention, and guarantee all refugees, however defined, a range of rights derived from the 1951 and 1969 Conventions.[163] In most states, all 1951 and 1969 Convention rights are reflected in the national act; however, some countries—Benin, Djibouti, Gabon, Gambia, Guinea, Mali, Mozambique, and Niger—guarantee only a subset of those rights (and the refugee acts of Malawi[164] and Senegal[165] are silent as to rights beyond non-refoulement). Some monist states have only secondary refugee laws, which deal with refugee issues in a procedural sense and are therefore naturally silent as to rights.[166] Variations in approach aside, the crucial point is that in no state law does the definition pursuant to which a refugee is recognized have any impact as to rights.

Kenya's Refugees Act is particularly instructive because, as mentioned in Chapter 3, it creates two types of refugee: 'statutory' refugees who meet the 1951 Convention definition and '*prima facie*' refugees who meet the article I(2) definition.[167] Both types of refugee receive identical rights, based—according to section 16 of the Refugees Act—on 'the international conventions to which Kenya is party'. In a Kenyan case relating to, inter alia, freedom of movement, the High Court invalidated a government encampment plan further to its reading of section 16 of the Refugees Act with article 26 of the 1951 Convention.[168] This decision was recently affirmed on appeal.[169] The operative portion of the judgment did not even invoke the 1969 Convention, despite the fact that the majority of the refugees who would have been affected by the encampment move were of the '*prima facie*' or article I(2) type; thus the court's approach was to derive the rights of '*prima facie*'/article I(2) refugees from domestic law based on the 1951 Convention.

[163] Sudan's refugee law was not analysed because it is only available in Arabic. Equatorial Guinea's refugee law could not be obtained.

[164] Refugee Act of 1989 (Malawi).

[165] Loi no 68-27 du 24 juillet 1968 modifiée portant statut des réfugiés, as amended (Senegal).

[166] The following monist states only have procedural or secondary legislation: Chad (Décret no 839/PR/PM/MAT/2011 portant création, organisation et attributions de la commission national d'accueil, de reinsertion des réfugiés et des apatrides (CNARR)), Côte d'Ivoire (Arreté no 47/MAE/AGH/DAH/AARA du 1 fevrier 2007 portant création, organisation et fonctionnement de la commission de recours au statut de réfugié), Madagascar (Décret no 1962-001 du 1962 portant creation d'un bureau des réfugiés et apatrides au Ministère de l'Intérieur (Direction de la Sécurité Nationale)), Mauritania (Décret no 2005-022 fixant les modalités d'application en République Islamique de Mauritanie des conventions internationals relatives aux réfugiés), Morocco (Décret no 2-57-1256 du 2 safar 1377 (29 août 1957) fixant les modalités d'application de la convention relative au statut des réfugiés signée à Genève le 28 juillet 1951), Republic of the Congo (Arreté no 8041 du 28 décembre 2001 portant création, organisation, attributions et fonctionnement de la commission d'éligibilité au statut du réfugié), Somalia (Presidential Decree No 25 of 1984, on Determination of Refugee Status), and Tunisia (Loi no 68-26 du 27 juillet 1968, portant adhesion de la Tunisie au protocole relative au statut des réfugiés; Loi no 89-77 du 2 septembre 1969, portant ratification de la convention de l'organisation de l'unité africaine régissant les aspects propres aux problèmes des réfugiés en Afrique).

[167] Kenya (n 146) s 3.

[168] *Kituo Cha Sheria, Abebe Dadi Tully, Ahmed Bashir Mohamed, Eugene Bwimana, Dachassa Galdi Nure, Muhima Sebihendo Joh, Mbuzukongire Nzabona and Said Abdullahi Abukar v the Attorney General*, Petition Nos 19 and 115 of 2013, High Court of Kenya (26 July 2013) para 59.

[169] *Attorney General v Kituo Cha Sheria & 7 Others* [2017] eKLR (*Kituo Cha Sheria*).

While the general position is that African refugee laws provide all refugees with 1951 Convention rights, freedom of movement is sometimes restricted.[170] The 1951 Convention guarantees this freedom.[171] Both Ethiopia and Kenya, however, (ware)house many of their refugees in camps. The latter's Refugees Act allows the Minister responsible for refugee affairs to 'designate places and areas in Kenya to be … refugee camps',[172] despite another provision guaranteeing refugees 'the rights … contained in the international conventions to which Kenya is party'.[173] Ethiopia's Refugee Proclamation allows the government to 'designate places and areas in Ethiopia within which recognized refugees … shall live'.[174] Like Kenya, section 21(1)(d) of Ethiopia's refugee law also guarantees to refugees the 'rights … contained in the [1951] Refugee Convention'; as a result, the provision allowing the establishment of camps states that it is 'Notwithstanding the provisions of Sub-Article (1)(d)'. Uganda also houses many of its refugees in camps, in accordance with section 44 of its Refugees Act on settlements and transit centres and section 30, which limits freedom of movement in line with 'reasonable restrictions specified in the laws of Uganda, or directions issued by the Commissioner' for refugees. The widespread housing of refugees in camps explains the above-mentioned perspectives viewing article I(2) refugees as entitled to fewer rights than their 1951 Convention counterparts, yet the specific contracting out of freedom of movement in the Ethiopian and Ugandan laws provides further evidence of the general or default legal position: all refugees are entitled to 1951 Convention rights. Thus Kenya's law should also carve out freedom of movement—indeed, as mentioned earlier in this section, a recent Kenyan decision invalidated a government encampment plan in part because the Refugees Act features no such carve-out[175]—and all three states should technically speaking have reserved article 26 of the 1951 Convention.

It must be noted that some commentary on the VCLT maintains that the subsequent practice referred to by article 31(3)(b) must be common to *all* parties to the treaty being interpreted.[176] As mentioned earlier in this section, the refugee laws of Malawi and Senegal are silent as to rights other than non-refoulement and Kenya houses refugees in camps without any acknowledgement in its Refugees Act—like those in the Ethiopian and Ugandan laws—of its obligation to guarantee freedom of movement under the 1951 Convention. This is not to say that domestic refugee legislation in Africa is of no value in interpreting the 1969 Convention. A recent authority concluded that 'the principle appears to be that there must be a sufficient nexus between the parties to the treaty and the practice, as distinct from actual participation of all parties in the practice concerned'.[177] Thus discordant Malawian, Senegalese, and Kenyan legislation do not necessarily undermine the otherwise widespread state practice of guaranteeing 1951 Convention rights for all

[170] See, generally, Nicholas Maple, 'Rights at Risk: A Thematic Investigation into how States Restrict the Freedom of Movement of Refugees on the African Continent' (2016) UNHCR New Issues in Refugee Research Paper No 281 <http://www.unhcr.org/57ee60d57.pdf> accessed 11 January 2018.

[171] 1951 Convention (n 1) art 26.

[172] Kenya (n 146) s 16(2)(b).

[173] ibid s 16(1)(a).

[174] Ethiopia (n 140).

[175] *Kituo Cha Sheria* (n 169).

[176] Aust (n 86) 241–43; Sinclair (n 86) 138.

[177] Gardiner (n 100) 236.

refugees. Moreover, the absence of any explicit distinction between 1951 and 1969 Convention refugees insofar as rights are concerned *is* common to all parties. Finally, subsequent practice that is not common to all parties may in any case 'constitute a supplementary means of interpretation within the meaning of Article 32 of the [Vienna] Convention'.[178] This is addressed in the following sub-section.

The subsequent practice referred to in article 31(3)(b) also includes judicial acts.[179] A Malawian case regarding expulsion invoked article 32 of the 1951 Convention without even raising the issue of whether the individuals concerned were refugees within the meaning of the 1951 Convention and therefore entitled to 1951 Convention rights.[180] This evidences that 1951 Convention rights apply to all refugees. A South African case relating to asylum seeker employment and education struck down a blanket prohibition on work and study prior to refugee recognition. In recognizing that these rights adhere prior to recognition, the court implicitly affirmed that the nature of status has no impact on rights.[181]

(c) Supplementary means of interpretation

Recourse may be had to supplementary means of interpretation to confirm the meaning flowing from the general rule of interpretation.[182] Supplementary means include the preparatory work of the treaty and the circumstances of its conclusion.[183] Three categories of source are relevant in this regard, beginning with OAU, African Union (AU), and UNHCR guidance or policy statements. In 1980 an OAU and UNHCR working group promulgated model legislation to assist states parties in incorporating their obligations under the 1969 Convention.[184] According to its section 11, 'persons considered as refugees according to the "extended" OAU refugee definition are entitled to the rights and are subject to the duties defined [in] the 1951 ... Convention'.[185] Similarly, in its 2006 Migration Policy Framework, the AU's Executive Council recommends that 'African refugees ... be given equal treatment with others from other parts of the world in line with [i]nternational [s]tandard as it applies to [r]efugees all over the world'.[186] UNHCR recently published guidance on 'the standards of treatment of refugees recognized under the 1969 OAU Convention'. Relying on an article on which this chapter draws,[187] this guidance states,

[178] Sinclair (n 86) 138. [179] Gardiner (n 100) 228.

[180] *Kambiningi Khazi Jones & 14 Others v The Refugee Committee (the Attorney General)*, Miscellaneous Civil Cause No 313 of 2005, High Court of Malawi (29 December 2005) 5.

[181] *Minister of Home Affairs and Others v Watchenuka and Others* [2004] 1 All SA 21 (SCA) (28 November 2003).

[182] VCLT (n 82) art 32. [183] ibid. [184] See Chapter 6, section B.2.

[185] Ivor C Jackson, *The Refugee Concept in Group Situations* (Martinus Nijhoff 1999) 195.

[186] AU (Executive Council), 'The Migration Policy Framework for Africa' (AU Banjul 25–29 June 2006) EX.CL/276 (IX) <http://www.unhcr.org/protection/migration/4d5258ab9/african-union-migration-policy-framework-africa.html> accessed 20 December 2017, 21.

[187] Sharpe (n 4).

> For most refugees in Africa who are recognized under the 1969 ... Convention, the limited package of rights included in the 1969 ... Convention does not pose a significant problem in practice, as the majority of ... [AU] Member States are party to both the 1951 Convention and/or its 1967 Protocol, as well as the 1969 ... Convention. In these countries, refugees recognised under the 1969 ... Convention, whether under Article I(1) or I(2), benefit from the 1951 Convention's rights framework.[188]

Finally, a recent United Nations (UN) General Assembly resolution affirmed that the 1951 Convention, together with the 1967 Protocol, 'remains the foundation of the international refugee protection regime in Africa'.[189]

The second category of supplementary means of interpretation is the domestic refugee legislation of states party to the 1969 Convention. As shown earlier in this section, this clearly affirms that 1969 Convention article I(2) refugees are entitled to 1951 Convention rights in states party to both instruments.

Third and finally is the history of the 1969 Convention. The drafting history detailed in Chapter 2 supports the interpretation here. That early drafts of the 1969 Convention included a detailed rights framework along the lines of the 1951 Convention certainly suggests that the 1969 Convention does not create second-class refugees. Only once the 1967 Protocol was adopted did drafts of the 1969 Convention cease to include the 1951 Convention's rights framework. Furthermore, during the drafting period, the OAU's Assembly of Heads of State and Government (OAHG) and its Council of Ministers (OCM) called on member states to ratify the 1951 Convention, at 'virtually every session in which they discussed the draft OAU Convention', indicating that the OAU 'did not see the developing African convention as an alternative to the 1951 Convention'.[190]

3. General principles of international law

This conclusion, reached by interpreting relevant clauses of the 1969 Convention in line with the VCLT, is confirmed by relevant general principles of international law. These are 'general principles of municipal jurisprudence, in particular of private law, in so far as they are applicable to relations of States'.[191] Two such general principles of international law relate to the possibility of characterizing the 1969 Convention as a special legal regime in relation to the 1951 Convention's more general regime.

Firstly, it is usually possible to contract out of a general international legal regime unless the general regime is *jus cogens*, or the special regime purports to deviate from law that benefits third parties (such as individuals), is of an *erga omnes* character[192]

[188] UNHCR, 'Key Legal Considerations on the Standards of Treatment of Refugees Recognized under the 1969 OAU Convention Governing the Specific Aspects of Refugee Problems in Africa' (19 December 2017) <http://www.refworld.org/docid/5a391d4f4.html> accessed 20 December 2017, para 6 (footnotes omitted).

[189] UNGA Res 71/173 (19 December 2016) UN Doc A/RES/71/173, preambular para 2.

[190] Rutinwa (n 58) 101.

[191] Ian Brownlie, *Principles of Public International Law* (6th edn, OUP 2003) 16.

[192] An obligation *erga omnes* is 'owed to the "international community as a whole" and all States—irrespective of their particular interest in the matter—are entitled to invoke State responsibility in case of breach' (Fragmentation Report (n 5) para 380).

or is of a public law nature.[193] The 1951 Convention legal regime possesses most of these characteristics: individual refugees benefit from it and the obligations under it are of a public law nature. The 1951 Convention legal regime is therefore one of the limited general international legal regimes that states may not contract out of by creating a special regime. Accordingly, African states may not, in the context of their regional refugee law regime, contract out of those refugee rights they agreed to protect under the more general 1951 Convention regime.

Secondly, according to the ILC, 'the scope of special laws is by definition narrower than that of general laws. It will thus frequently be the case that a matter not regulated by special law will arise in the institutions charged to administer it. In such cases, the relevant general law will apply'.[194] The special 1969 Convention regime does not detail the rights to which refugees are entitled once they are recognized as such because, as explained earlier in this section, to do so would represent an unlawful deviation from the more general 1951 Convention regime. Because the 1969 Convention does not detail post-recognition refugee rights, the 1951 Convention's general regime serves to fill the gap, as described in general terms by the ILC.

The principle of *lex posterior*, though not strictly applicable because the parties to the 1951 and 1969 Conventions are not identical, is nevertheless also instructive. It provides that an earlier treaty applies only to the extent that it is not inconsistent with a later treaty concluded among the same parties.[195] The application of 1951 Convention rights to article I(2) refugees is not inconsistent with the 1969 Convention; indeed, the applicability of the 1951 Convention's rights framework to 1969 Convention refugees is in keeping with the object and purpose of the 1969 Convention. This implies that in states party to both the 1951 and 1969 Conventions, there can be no suggestion that 1969 Convention refugees enjoy fewer rights than their 1951 Convention counterparts.

4. Equality

Several authors have found that the law of non-discrimination provides a basis for guaranteeing 1951 Convention rights to beneficiaries of complementary protection.[196] The thesis that the legal duty of non-discrimination mandates the equal treatment of refugees and beneficiaries of complementary protection was developed by Pobjoy,[197] while Hathaway has explored the role of non-discrimination regarding equal treatment between citizens and non-citizens[198] and among 1951 Convention refugees.[199] Furthermore, courts,[200] including courts in

[193] Fragmentation Report (n 5) para 154. [194] ibid para 15. [195] ibid para 24.

[196] See, for example, Tom Clark and François Crépeau, 'Mainstreaming Refugee Rights: The 1951 Refugee Convention and International Human Rights Law' (1999) 17 NQHR 389; Clark (n 121); Hathaway (n 121) 529; McAdam (n 53) 220–23.

[197] Jason Pobjoy, 'Treating Like Alike: The Principle of Non-Discrimination as a Tool to Mandate the Equal Treatment of Refugees and Beneficiaries of Complementary Protection' (2010) 34 MULR 181.

[198] (n 121) 123–47. [199] ibid 238–60.

[200] See, for example, *R (European Roma Rights Centre and others) v Immigration Officer at Prague Airport and another (United Nations High Commissioner for Refugees intervening)* [2004] UKHL 55.

Africa,[201] have invoked the universal proscription of discrimination in refugee protection contexts. An equality-based approach can equally be employed for the benefit of article I(2) refugees.

The legal duty of non-discrimination requires that 'irrelevant criteria not be taken into account in making allocations'.[202] Article 26 of the ICCPR[203] articulates this duty with particular force because the ambit of its guarantee is not limited to the ICCPR alone;[204] rather, it applies to the 'allocation of all public goods, including rights not stipulated by the Covenant itself'.[205] Article 26 provides: 'All persons are equal before the law and are entitled without any discrimination to the equal protection of the law. In this respect, the law shall prohibit any discrimination and guarantee to all persons equal and effective protection against discrimination on any ground such as race, colour, sex, language, religion, political or other opinion, national or social origin, property, birth or other status'. This ensures formal equality (equality before the law) as well as substantive equality (equal protection of the law).[206]

However, inspired by Justice Tanaka's seminal dissenting opinion in *South West Africa*, article 26 does not establish an unconditional guarantee of equality. Ruling on whether the racist government of South West Africa was in breach of the applicable League of Nations mandate, Tanaka observed,

> Equal treatment is a principle but its mechanical application ignoring all concrete factors engenders injustice. Accordingly, it requires different treatment, taken into consideration, of concrete circumstances of individual cases. The different treatment is permissible and required by the considerations of justice; it does not mean a disregard of justice. Equality being a principle and different treatment an exception, those who refer to the different treatment must prove its *raison d'être* and its reasonableness.[207]

Accordingly, not every instance of differential treatment amounts to discrimination; in many circumstances, it is reasonable for a state to differentiate between groups. Rather, equality requires that any unequal treatment be 'properly justified, according to consistently applied, persuasive, and acceptable criteria'.[208] The UN Human Rights Committee (HRC), which is the ICCPR's treaty-monitoring body, has thus observed 'that not every differentiation of treatment will constitute discrimination, if the criteria for such differentiation are reasonable and objective and if the aim is to achieve a purpose which is legitimate under the Covenant'.[209] Thus to

[201] *Kenya National Commission on Human Rights and Legal Advice Centre T/A Kituo Cha Sheria v The Hon. Attorney General, The Ministry of Interior & Coordination of National Government, Major General (RTD) Joseph Nkaissery and Dr. (ENG) Karanja Kibicho*, Petition No 227 of 2016, High Court of Kenya (9 February 2017).

[202] Hathaway (n 121) 124.

[203] International Covenant on Civil and Political Rights (adopted 19 December 1966, entered into force 23 March 1976) 999 UNTS 171.

[204] HRC 'General Comment No 18: Non-discrimination' (11 October 1989) para 12.

[205] Hathaway (n 121) 125.

[206] HRC (n 204) para 1.

[207] *South West Africa (Ethiopia v South Africa; Liberia v South Africa)* (Judgment) [1966] ICJ Rep 6, 308–09.

[208] Christopher McCrudden, 'Equality and Discrimination' in David Feldman (ed), *English Public Law*, vol XI (OUP 2004), cited in Hathaway (n 121) 124.

[209] HRC (n 204) para 13.

amount to discrimination under article 26, unequal treatment must be based on criteria that are neither reasonable nor objective, nor in pursuit of a legitimate aim.[210]

Pobjoy has distilled article 26 as qualified by the HRC into a convenient three-pronged test for establishing unlawful discrimination: '1. Has there been differential treatment between individuals in similar circumstances? In other words, is there an inequality *basis* for a discrimination claim? 2. Is the unequal treatment based on a ground captured by art 26? 3. Is the unequal treatment based on "reasonable and objective" criteria?'.[211] This test, with the 'pursuit of a legitimate aim' appended to its third prong, will be applied to determine whether article 26 prohibits the differential allocation of rights as between refugees recognized pursuant to article 1A(2) of the 1951 Convention and refugees recognized under article I(2) of the 1969 Convention. As a preliminary matter, however, it must be established that an article I(2) refugee can invoke the ICCPR vis-à-vis his or her host state, assuming that state has ratified the ICCPR and its optional protocol permitting individual communications.[212] The HRC has confirmed that as a general rule, the rights enshrined in the ICCPR 'must be guaranteed without discrimination between citizens and aliens'.[213] All refugees, therefore, benefit from ICCPR protection.

As a starting point, assume that a host state—party to the 1951 and 1969 Conventions as well as to the ICCPR and its optional protocol—guarantees the full range of 1951 Convention rights to refugees under that instrument but guarantees refugees recognized under article I(2) of the 1969 Convention only the few rights enumerated therein. The first prong of the test, which must establish that similarly situated individuals have been treated differently, is answered in the affirmative. Once in the host state, a refugee who fled individualized persecution is no different from one who fled a 1969 Event. The two, as refugees, are in similar circumstances, yet they do not enjoy the same allocation of rights.

To establish discrimination, the test's second prong must demonstrate that the unequal treatment is based on a ground captured by article 26. The unequal treatment by the host state is based on the source of the individual's refugee status. This is not among the grounds enumerated in article 26, however that list is not exhaustive; the source of the unequal treatment may fall within 'any other status'. The HRC has approached the meaning of 'any other status' on a case-by-case basis. The only general requirement is that the status in question must capture a distinct group, as opposed to an individual.[214] Refugees recognized under article I(2) of the 1969 Convention are a distinct group. Moreover, according to Pobjoy, because the HRC has repeatedly affirmed that distinctions based upon nationality or citizenship

[210] See, generally, Nisuke Ando, 'The Evolution and Problems of the Jurisprudence of the Human Rights Committee's Views Concerning Article 26' in Nisuke Ando (ed), *Towards Implementing Universal Human Rights: Festschrift for the Twenty-Fifth Anniversary of the Human Rights Committee* (Brill 2004).

[211] (n 197) 210.

[212] Optional Protocol to the ICCPR, UNGA Res 2200A (XXI) of 16 December 1966 (entered into force 23 March 1976) 999 UNTS 302.

[213] HRC, 'General Comment No 15: The Position of Aliens Under the Covenant' (11 April 1986) para 2.

[214] *Vos v Netherlands* comm no 218/1986 (29 March 1989) UN Doc CCPR/C/35/D/218/1986.

fall within the notion of 'other status' in article 26, it 'seems reasonable to assume that this principle would apply between different categories of non-citizens'.[215] The second prong of the test is therefore also answered affirmatively.

Under the test's third prong, to avoid running afoul of the ICCPR, the unequal allocation of rights must be based on reasonable and objective criteria and must be in pursuit of a legitimate aim. Owing to the paucity of jurisprudence on the issue, 'The extent to which the Committee is likely to consider differential treatment between categories of non-citizens to be reasonable and objective is unclear'.[216] In the absence of case law, Pobjoy finds that the most sensible approach is to 'identify the potential bases which a state may invoke to justify the differential allocation of rights . . . and . . . critically examine these bases to pre-empt the likelihood that they will be considered reasonable and objective'.[217] The only conceivable basis on which the host state might circumscribe the rights of article I(2) refugees would be the belief that their plight is inherently more temporary than refugees fleeing persecution. Such logic has been employed to justify the lower standards of treatment accorded to beneficiaries of subsidiary (complementary) protection under the European Union's Qualification Directive.[218] The logic is not, however, borne out in practice. The increasingly protracted nature of refugee situations in Africa[219] and the persistence of the conflicts giving rise to many of them have been amply documented.[220] Moreover, to accord fewer rights to refugees fleeing a 1969 Event on the theory that their plight is inherently temporary misconceives the nature of the universal regime of refugee protection, which itself is premised on temporariness. Because the denial of 1951 Convention rights to article I(2) refugees cannot be based on criteria that are objective and reasonable, there is no need to proceed to the test's second sub-prong regarding legitimate aims. The test's third prong is answered in the negative.

The application of this test suggests that distinguishing in the blanket allocation of rights between article I(2) refugees and refugees recognized under article 1A(2) of the 1951 Convention would be unlawful discrimination under the ICCPR. UNHCR takes a similar position in more general terms, finding it 'doubtful that international law would permit selective provision of international protection according to category'.[221] Indeed, in Europe certain migration status inequalities have been found to breach the European Convention for the Protection of Human Rights and Fundamental Freedoms (ECHR) article 14 non-discrimination guarantee.[222]

[215] (n 197) 215. [216] ibid 216. [217] ibid 218. [218] ibid 221.

[219] See, for example, Jeff Crisp, 'No Solution in Sight: The Problem of Protracted Refugee Situations in Africa' in Itaru Ohta and Yntiso D Gebre (eds), *Displacement Risks in Africa: Refugees, Resettlers and Their Host Population* (Kyoto University Press 2005); Edwin Odihambo Abuya, 'From Here to Where? Refugees Living in Protracted Situations in Africa' in Alice Edwards and Carla Ferstman (eds), *Human Security and Non-Citizens: Law, Policy and International Affairs* (CUP 2010).

[220] See, for example, Theo Farrell and Oliver Schmitt, 'The Causes, Character and Conduct of Internal Armed Conflict and the Effects on Civilian Populations, 1990–2010' in Volker Türk, Alice Edwards, and Cornelis Wouters (eds), *In Flight from Conflict and Violence: UNHCR's Consultations on Refugee Status and Other Forms of International Protection* (CUP 2017).

[221] UNHCR, 'Towards a Common European Asylum System' in CDU de Sousa and Philippe de Bruycker (eds), *The Emergence of a European Asylum Policy* (Bruylant 2004), cited in McAdam (n 53) 221.

[222] *Hode and Abdi v United Kingdom* app no 22341/09 (ECtHR, 6 November 2012); *Niedzwiecki v Germany* app no 58453/00 (ECtHR, 25 October 2005).

Moreover, the 1969 Convention itself recalls that the UN 'Charter ... and the Universal Declaration of Human Rights have affirmed the principle that human beings shall enjoy fundamental rights and freedoms *without discrimination*'.[223]

This conclusion is, however, tentative, as the HRC has never ruled on the issue and there is limited jurisprudence concerning the differential allocation of rights among categories of non-citizen. Indeed, it is unlikely that the issue of discrimination against article I(2) refugees would ever come before the HRC, since states in Africa do not, in their practice, distinguish between refugees recognized under article 1A(2) of the 1951 Convention and those recognized under article I(2) of the 1969 Convention, nor does domestic refugee legislation in Africa make such a formal distinction.[224] Furthermore, it should be noted that while status-based distinctions in the blanket allocation of rights would likely be prohibited by article 26 of the ICCPR, certain individual distinctions may be permissible, in line with the proviso articulated above.[225] For example, depriving an article I(2) refugee of recourse to the 1951 Convention's article 1C(5) 'compelling reasons' proviso should be allowed; this is discussed further below.[226]

5. The 1951 Convention as *lex specialis*

'Complementary protection' describes the protection from refoulement 'granted by States on the basis of an international protection need outside the 1951 Convention framework'.[227] The prohibitions against refoulement subsumed by the concept of complementary protection generally arise from, or have been read into, international and regional human rights instruments, such as the Convention against Torture and Other Cruel, Inhuman or Degrading Treatment or Punishment[228] (CAT) and the ECHR.[229]

In her study of complementary protection, McAdam argues that the 1951 Convention 'functions as a form of *lex specialis* (specialist law) for all those in need of international protection, and provides an appropriate legal status irrespective of the source of the State's protection obligation'.[230] In other words, McAdam views the content of complementary protected status as derived from the 1951 Convention, regardless of the fact that the beneficiaries of such status are not refugees within

[223] 1969 Convention (n 2) preambular para 6 (emphasis added).

[224] See section C.2.b of this chapter.

[225] See text attached to n 209.

[226] See section D.1.a of this chapter.

[227] McAdam (n 53) 21.

[228] (Adopted 10 December 1984, entered into force 26 June 1987) 1465 UNTS 85, art 3(1).

[229] Convention for the Protection of Human Rights and Fundamental Freedoms (European Convention on Human Rights, as amended) (4 November 1950) art 3.

[230] McAdam (n 53) 1. However, the 1951 Convention cannot be said to provide beneficiaries of complementary protection with status as such, because the status accorded by the 1951 Convention is refugee status, for which beneficiaries of complementary protection by definition do not qualify. McAdam's argument would have been more convincing had she argued that the 1951 Convention articulates the *content* of complementary protected status, rather than any status as such. Furthermore, her designation of the 1951 Convention's rights framework as the *lex specialis* for all persons in need of international protection is problematic because it may be taken to suggest that refugees are not also entitled to rights derived from human rights law.

the meaning of article 1A(2). McAdam advances several propositions in support of this thesis, but the core of her argument is that the 1951 Convention's 'application has been extended through the expansion of *non-refoulement* under human rights law ... rather than by the conventional means of a Protocol.... Since the scope of *non-refoulement* has been broadened by subsequent human rights instruments, this necessarily widens the Convention's application'.[231]

If the 1951 Convention provides the rights blueprint for all beneficiaries of complementary protection, then such rights must apply equally to refugees within the meaning of article I(2). McAdam argues that the progressive development of human rights-based non-refoulement, in extending the range of individuals entitled to international protection, also extended the applicability of the 1951 Convention. Surely the 1969 Convention's extension of protection from refoulement to individuals fleeing a 1969 Event extends the 1951 Convention's applicability in a similar fashion, especially because, as refugees, individuals recognized under article I(2) of the 1969 Convention are conceptually more similar to 1951 Convention refugees than are beneficiaries of complementary protection.

This argument is of even more force when one considers McAdam's reasoning in relation to why human rights instruments themselves do not, in addition to protection from refoulement, also provide for status. She argues that it would be 'futile for instruments like the CAT to enumerate the legal status arising from the application of *non-refoulement*, since the Refugee Convention (as the *lex specialis*) already provides an appropriate status for any person protected by that principle'.[232] It would be similarly futile for the 1969 Convention to enumerate an exhaustive list of refugee rights, since the 1951 Convention, as the *lex specialis* on the content of refugee status, already does so. Indeed, Bakwesegha explains that the 'issue of rights of refugees is not raised [in the 1969 Convention] because they were adequately covered in the 1951 ... Convention'.[233]

The argument that beneficiaries of complementary protection, and hence article I(2) refugees, enjoy 1951 Convention rights by virtue of that instrument being the *lex specialis* for individuals in need of international protection must, however, be approached with some caution in light of Hathaway's critique of McAdam's position.[234] Hathaway rejects McAdam's thesis on two principal grounds. Firstly, he argues that 'there is no basis to suggest that the Refugee Convention exists to delineate the entitlements of persons granted protection against *refoulement*'.[235] In other words, he asserts that McAdam's argument is simply not substantiated, an assertion to which McAdam has responded.[236]

Secondly, Hathaway maintains that McAdam's contention is premised on an incorrect application of *lex specialis*. 'Lex specialis', short for '*lex specialis derogare lege*

[231] (n 53) 209. [232] ibid 209–10.

[233] Chris J Bakwesegha, 'The OAU and African Refugees' in Yassin El-Ayouty (ed), *The Organization of African Unity after Thirty Years* (Greenwood Publishing Group 1994) 11.

[234] James C Hathaway, 'Leveraging Asylum' (2009) 45 Texas Intl LJ 503. [235] ibid 531.

[236] Jane McAdam, 'Status Anxiety: Complementary Protection and the Rights of Non-Convention Refugees' (2010) University of New South Wales Faculty of Law Research Series <http://law.bepress.com/unswwps/flrps10/art1/> accessed 13 October 2011.

generali',[237] is a widely accepted maxim of legal interpretation used to resolve norm conflicts.[238] Hathaway accepts this primary understanding of *lex specialis* and explains that the maxim can also be employed 'to assist in the construction of a general provision in relation to a matter also governed by a more specific norm'.[239] He argues that McAdam, however, employs *lex specialis* in quite a different sense: to extend the 1951 Convention's 'beneficiary class to embrace persons outside its textual ambit'.[240] According to Hathaway, 'Because there is simply a legal void to be filled in relation to non-refugees, there is no conflict of rules that lex specialis can assist to resolve'.[241] Hathaway further argues that the secondary usage of *lex specialis* similarly provides no support for McAdam's position: 'the importance of interpreting general rules in harmony with more specific rules does not advance McAdam's thesis that the absence of rules defining the status of the broader class of non-returnable persons must be filled by effectively recasting the Refugee Convention's beneficiary class'.[242] McAdam has responded to these critiques as well[243] and Hathaway's critique of McAdam has itself been criticized.[244] Yet if Hathaway is correct and the 1951 Convention is not the *lex specialis* for all persons in need of international protection, then it clearly becomes impossible to argue that 1951 Convention rights apply to article I(2) refugees on that basis.

D. Other Aspects of the Relationship between the Conventions

In addition to the major procedural and substantive issues discussed in sections B and C above, the simultaneous applicability of the 1951 and 1969 Conventions in many African jurisdictions gives rise to several more isolated relationship issues. These can be grouped into two categories. In the first, the relationships are complementary: one instrument makes provision for an issue on which the other is silent or addresses a common issue more generously. The ILC terms these 'relationships of interpretation', in which 'one norm assists in the interpretation of another'.[245] In the second category are conflicts between the 1951 and 1969 Conventions. In relationships of conflict 'two incompatible norms point to opposite conclusions'.[246] Each category is addressed in turn.

[237] Which means special law derogates from general law.

[238] Fragmentation Report (n 5) paras 56–57.

[239] Hathaway (n 121) 533; see, also, Fragmentation Report (n 5) para 56.

[240] Hathaway (n 121) 532. [241] ibid 533. [242] ibid 534.

[243] McAdam (n 236).

[244] Guy S Goodwin-Gill, 'Non-refoulement, Temporary Refuge, and the "New" Asylum Seekers' in David James Cantor and Jean-François Durieux (eds), *Refuge from Inhumanity? War Refugees and International Humanitarian Law* (Brill Nijhoff 2014) 447–57.

[245] International Law Commission, 'Conclusions of the Work of the Study Group on the Fragmentation of International Law: Difficulties Arising from the Diversification and Expansion of International Law' (2006) 2 UNYBILC 175, para 2.

[246] ibid.

1. Relationships of interpretation

When it is the 1969 Convention that affords refugees more generous or robust protection than the 1951 Convention, the latter's article 5 is dispositive. Chapters 2 and 3 discuss aspects of the 1969 Convention that are somewhat more generous than the 1951 Convention—the scope of the non-discrimination and non-refoulement provisions—or address issues about which the 1951 Convention is silent—temporary protection and voluntary repatriation. The 1951 Convention's article 5 speaks directly to such provisions: 'Nothing in this Convention shall be deemed to impair any rights and benefits granted by a Contracting State to refugees apart from this Convention'. Such 'rights and benefits' may result from, inter alia, another treaty.[247] It is thus clear that when the 1969 Convention puts refugees in a more favourable position than they would have been under the 1951 Convention alone, the more generous provisions of the regional instrument apply.

The 1969 Convention does not contain any provision analogous to the 1951 Convention's article 5. Thus when the 1951 Convention is the more generous or robust instrument, the relationship between the treaties must be articulated through a process of treaty interpretation.

(a) *The 'compelling reasons' proviso*

Besides the 1969 Convention's lack of a refugee rights framework and the 1951 Convention's detailed provisions in this regard, which was addressed in section C above, the other significant instance in which the 1951 Convention addresses an issue on which the 1969 Convention is silent relates to cessation. As noted in Chapter 2, the 1969 Convention does not include the 1951 Convention proviso preventing the cessation of an individual's refugee status if he or she can 'invoke compelling reasons arising out of previous persecution for refusing to avail himself of the protection of the country of nationality'.[248] This leads to the question of whether a refugee recognized only under article I(1) of the 1969 Convention could raise such 'compelling reasons' in the face of an invocation by his or her country of asylum of the 1951 Convention article 1C(5) ceased circumstances clause, assuming the host state invoked the clause in respect of all refugees, not just those recognized pursuant to the 1951 Convention.

In answering the question of whether a 1969 Convention refugee could invoke 'compelling reasons arising out of previous persecution' to mitigate the applicability of the ceased circumstances cessation clause, it is useful to begin by considering why the 1969 Convention does not include the 1951 Convention's 'compelling reasons' proviso. The answer seems clear: the 1969 Convention's article I(4) cessation clauses—which except for the omission of the 'compelling reasons' proviso otherwise mirror the 1951 Convention provisions—apply to both article I(1) and

[247] Atle Grahl-Madsen, 'Commentary on the Refugee Convention 1951: Articles 2–11, 13–37' (1997) UNHCR <http://www.refworld.org/pdfid/4785ee9d2.pdf> accessed 13 January 2017, 14.

[248] 1951 Convention (n 1) art 1C(5).

article I(2) refugees. Refugee status under the regional definition does not depend on persecution. The 'compelling reasons' proviso, by contrast, relates to past persecution. It would have been incoherent to include this proviso in a generally applicable cessation clause, given that it could only ever be invoked by a sub-set of 1969 Convention refugees. Furthermore, the 1951 Convention's cessation clauses were likely included in the 1969 Convention to make them apply to the article I(2) refugee definition. Because there was no need to make the 'compelling reasons' proviso applicable to article I(2)—and indeed to do so would not have made sense—there was no reason to include the proviso in the 1969 Convention. Finally, on the language of article 1C(5) alone, the 'compelling reasons' proviso applies only to article 1A(1) statutory refugees; as interpreted today, the proviso applies equally to article 1A(2) refugees.[249] If in the sixties, when the 1969 Convention was being drafted, the proviso was still interpreted textually as applying only to statutory refugees, it would have had no bearing in the context of the regional instrument. Thus the 1951 Convention's 'compelling reasons' proviso was not omitted from the 1969 Convention to prevent 1969 Convention refugees from benefitting from it. Rather, it was omitted because the proviso is incompatible with, or at the time of drafting was irrelevant to, the article I(2) refugee definition.

Given that there was never any intention to deprive refugees in Africa of the ability to invoke the 'compelling reasons' proviso, it becomes clear that the issue of whether 1969 Convention article I(1) refugees may invoke it can be resolved in the same manner as the issue of the rights to which 1969 Convention refugees are entitled. The interpretation of the 1969 Convention[250]—which makes clear that the 1951 Convention is the 'basic and universal instrument relating to the status of refugees'[251] and the 1969 Convention its 'regional complement in Africa'[252]—the equality principle[253] and the possibility that the 1951 Convention is the *lex specialis* for all persons in need of international protection[254] indicate that 1969 Convention article I(1) refugees may invoke the 1951 Convention's 'compelling reasons' proviso. Moreover, the instrument and definition under which a refugee from persecution is recognized—whether the 1951 Convention's article 1A(2) or the 1969 Convention's article I(1)—is a procedural question that often depends on purely pragmatic considerations;[255] such a procedural issue should have no effect on substantive rights.

State practice affirms this conclusion. Further to UNHCR's recommendation, on 30 June 2013, Zambia (along with Malawi, the Republic of the Congo, and Zimbabwe) terminated the refugee status of Rwandans who fled between 1959 and 1998. All refugees affected by this declaration of cessation—regardless of the instrument and provision of recognition—were, in the context of exemption procedures developed in line with relevant UNHCR[256] and ExCom[257] guidance, given

[249] Guy S Goodwin-Gill and Jane McAdam, *The Refugee in International Law* (3rd edn, OUP 2007) 145–49.

[250] See section C.2 of this chapter.

[251] 1969 Convention (n 2) preambular para 9.

[252] ibid art VIII(2).

[253] See section C.4 of this chapter.

[254] See section C.5 of this chapter.

[255] See section B of this chapter.

[256] UNHCR, 'Guidelines on Exemption Procedures in respect of Cessation Declarations' (2011).

[257] ExCom Conclusion No 69 (XLIII), 'Cessation of Status' (1992).

the opportunity to present compelling reasons mitigating against cessation.[258] Municipal refugee legislation also makes the 'compelling reasons' proviso available to all refugees. Uganda's Refugees Act, 2006, for example, includes the 1951 Convention and regional refugee definitions and makes its ceased circumstances cessation clause applicable only to those among them 'without compelling reasons arising out of previous persecution'.[259] Similarly, South Africa's Refugees Act, 1998 includes both refugee definitions and makes its ceased circumstances cessation clause inapplicable to any refugee with compelling reasons arising out of previous persecution for refusing to avail him or herself of the protection of his or her country of nationality.[260]

UNHCR shares this view. Its Guidelines on Exemption Procedures in respect of Cessation Declarations note that although the 1969 Convention 'does not contain a provision which allows for exemption due to "compelling reasons" ', this exception should be viewed as subsumed by article I(4)(e) of the 1969 Convention because 'the OAU Convention complements the 1951 Convention and the close connection between the purposes of the African Union and the United Nations are recognized'.[261]

2. Relationships of conflict

The drafting history of the 1969 Convention presented in Chapter 2 demonstrated that the initiative to create a regional refugee treaty was initially directed at making the 1951 Convention applicable in Africa. After the adoption of the 1967 Protocol, it became about addressing refugee issues particular to Africa. As a result, the 1951 and 1969 Conventions are a mutually supportive set of instruments, or what Fitzmaurice has called a 'chain' of treaties, which 'grapple with the same type of problem at different levels or from particular (technical, geographical) points of view'.[262] In such contexts, 'specific norms must be read against other norms bearing upon those same facts as the treaty under interpretation'.[263] Thus while there are some inconsistencies between the two instruments, these can usually be reconciled by seeking a harmonizing interpretation.

In isolated instances, however, such inconsistencies rise to the level of a norm conflict. The appropriate interpretive maxims for resolving such conflicts are discussed in Chapter 1. Regarding the inconsistencies discussed later in this section, *lex specialis* is the appropriate interpretive maxim; *lex posterior* is not applicable because the parties to the later 1969 Convention are different from the parties to the earlier 1951 Convention,[264] and *lex superior* is not applicable because none of the norms at issue is a hierarchically superior norm. It is important to recall, however, that the invocation of *lex specialis* does not result in the more specialist 1969 Convention

[258] Electronic correspondence with Katele Kalumba, Senior Legal Advisor, Office of the Commissioner for Refugees, Ministry of Home Affairs, Zambia, 6 November 2013.

[259] Uganda (n 6) s 6(1)(e).

[260] South Africa (n 156) s 5(2).

[261] UNHCR (n 256) n 7.

[262] GG Fitzmaurice, 'Third Report' (1958) II UNYBILC 44, cited in Fragmentation Report (n 5) para 416.

[263] Fragmentation Report (n 5) para 416.

[264] ibid para 243.

norm simply extinguishing the conflicting 1951 Convention rule. When *lex specialis* is applied, the special indeed steps in to become applicable instead of the general, but such 'replacement remains ... always only partial. The more general rule remains in the background providing interpretative direction to the special one'.[265] With this background in place, each of the inconsistencies between the 1951 and 1969 Conventions is addressed in turn.

(a) *Freedom of movement*

The 1951 Convention's article 26 on freedom of movement provides that each 'Contracting State shall accord to refugees lawfully in its territory the right to choose their place of residence and to move freely within its territory, subject to any regulations applicable to aliens generally in the same circumstances'.[266] Aliens should not generally face restrictions, as the article 12(1) of the African Charter on Human and Peoples' Rights (African Charter) guarantees freedom of movement and residence to 'every individual'.[267] Refugees who are not lawfully present are covered by the 1951 Convention's article 31(2), which only permits restrictions on movement 'which are necessary'. Article II(6) of the 1969 Convention, by contrast, provides that for 'reasons of security, countries of asylum shall, as far as possible, settle refugees at a reasonable distance from the frontier of their country of origin'. Article II(6) suggests that the 1969 Convention permits states parties to determine where refugees shall reside, and indeed such is the practice of some African states.

As discussed in section C, refugees in Africa often experience restrictions on their freedom of movement.[268] Under Uganda's Refugees Act, 2006, many refugees must live in one of the country's several rural refugee 'settlements' and Ethiopia's Refugee Proclamation allows the government to designate certain places as refugee camps. In 2006 the government of Malawi ordered all refugees living outside the Dzaleka and Luwani camps to return to them.[269] In 2012 the Kenyan Department of Refugee Affairs instituted an encampment policy by halting the reception and registration of refugees in urban areas, ordering all refugees to move to camps and directing UNHCR and other refugee-assisting organizations to cease providing services in urban areas.[270] The policy was quashed by the courts in 2013.[271] In 2014 the Kenyan government issued a slightly narrower directive, ordering all 'refugees

[265] ibid para 102.

[266] Angola, Botswana, Malawi, Mozambique, Namibia, Rwanda, Sudan, Zambia, and Zimbabwe have reserved this provision.

[267] See Chapter 5, section D.2.b.

[268] See, generally, Maple (n 170).

[269] *Frodovard Nsabimana and 83 Others v the State and the Department of Poverty and Disaster Management Affairs and the Commissioner for Disaster Preparedness, Relief and Rehabilitation*, Miscellaneous Civil Application No 19 of 2006, High Court of Malawi (17 April 2008) (*Frodovard Nsabimana*) 2.

[270] Kenya Department of Refugee Affairs Press Release (18 December 2012) cited in *Kituo Cha Sheria, Abebe Dadi Tully, Ahmed Bashir Mohamed, Eugene Bwimana, Dachassa Galdi Nure, Muhima Sebihendo Joh, Mbuzukongire Nzabona and Said Abdullahi Abukar v the Attorney General*, Petition Nos 19 and 115 of 2013, High Court of Kenya (26 July 2013) para 48.

[271] ibid para 100; see Chapter 5, section D.2.b.

outside the designated refugee camps of Kakuma and Dadaab ... to return to their respective camps with immediate effect' and closing all refugee registration centres in the urban areas of Nairobi, Mombasa, Malindi, Isiolo, and Nakuru.[272] (Ironically, in May 2016 Kenya announced its intention to close Dadaab, due in large part to a perceived connection between it and increasing terrorist attacks in Kenya.) It is notable that among these four states, only Malawi has reserved article 26 of the 1951 Convention.

As mentioned in the introductory chapter, this work employs a wide notion of norm conflict, in line with the ILC's approach. Thus a conflict exists 'where two rules or principles suggest different ways of dealing with a problem'.[273] Under this definition, article II(6) of the 1969 Convention is in conflict with article 26 of the 1951 Convention. The VCLT's general rule of interpretation mandates consideration of the ordinary meaning of treaty terms in their context and in light of the instrument's object and purpose.[274] Article II(6) does not mandate states to settle refugees; the provision merely notes that if states do so—which presumably would be in extenuating circumstances—it should be at a reasonable distance from the border with the country of origin. This ordinary meaning is affirmed by the context and by the 1969 Convention's object and purpose, both of which can be gleaned from the instrument's preamble. In stressing the humanitarian approach that should be taken to refugee problems[275] and human rights, which are mentioned directly[276] and invoked by reference to the OAU Charter,[277] the preamble confirms that the 1969 Convention should not be interpreted to deprive refugees of freedom of movement. This is further confirmed by the application of the VCLT's article 31(3)(c), which mandates a consideration of 'relevant rules of international law applicable in the relations between the parties'. While certain aspects of this exhortation remain unclear, as discussed in section C it is at least arguable that this mandates a consideration of international refugee law and international and African human rights law.[278] All of these enshrine freedom of movement,[279] with the 1951 Convention limiting the freedom only insofar as it is limited with respect to aliens generally in the same circumstances, the ICCPR permitting derogations from freedom of movement only where necessary to protect critical national interests[280] and the African Charter limiting freedom of movement only to the extent that the individual in question does not abide by the law.[281]

The same interpretive result is reached using *lex specialis*. While the 1969 Convention is the *lex specialis* on the freedom of movement of refugees in Africa, as

[272] *Samow Mumin Mohamed and Others v Cabinet Secretary, Minister of Interior Security and Co-ordination and others*, Petition No 206 of 2011, High Court of Kenya (30 June 2014) para 3.

[273] Fragmentation Report (n 5) para 25.

[274] VCLT (n 82) art 31(1).

[275] 1969 Convention (n 2) preambular para 2.

[276] ibid preambular para 6.

[277] ibid preambular para 8; preambular para 9 of the OAU Charter (n 113) reaffirms OAU member state adherence to the UN Charter and the UDHR.

[278] See section C.2.b of this chapter.

[279] 1951 Convention (n 1) art 26; ICCPR (n 203) art 12(1); African Charter on Human and Peoples' Rights (adopted 27 June 1981, entered into force 21 October 1986) 21 ILM 58, art 12(1).

[280] ICCPR (n 203) art 12(3).

[281] African Charter (n 279) art 12(1).

mentioned earlier in this section, its article II(6) must be interpreted in light of the associated 1951 Convention rule. Elaborating on this point, the ILC stresses that the 'important point ... is that when *lex specialis* is invoked as an exception to the general law then what is being suggested is that the special nature of the facts justifies a deviation from what otherwise would be the "normal" course of action'.[282] This suggests that the joint effect of the 1951 and 1969 Conventions is that in 'normal' circumstances, refugees are free to move and establish residence within their host state; however, the 1969 Convention acknowledges that in certain unusual circumstances, such may not be possible. The 1951 Convention provides the general rule, and the 1969 Convention applies only when the facts render the general rule untenable. The refugee crisis that engulfed the DRC during and following the 1994 Rwandan genocide provides an example. In the aftermath of the genocide, camps in the eastern DRC hosted approximately 1.5 million Rwandan refugees.[283] Clearly it would have been difficult, if not impossible, for the DRC to accommodate so many refugees on a self-settlement basis. The 1969 Convention acknowledges that when circumstances such as these necessitate the coordinated settlement of refugees, their safety is best ensured by situating them far from the border with the country of origin.

A Malawian case that considered the issue affirmed this approach to encampment, though the court interpreted the circumstances that would justify encampment broadly. It found that the 'State does not have to wait until there is an actual breakdown of national security or public order. It is prudent upon the State to set up appropriate security structures and measures, than to be overtaken by events'.[284] That said, the decision—which upheld the government's encampment policy—largely relied upon Malawi's reservation to article 26 of the 1951 Convention, thereby affirming refugees' freedom of movement as the default position in the absence of any relevant treaty reservation.

The same conclusion was reached by Grahl-Madsen in his brief consideration of this issue, which constitutes a rare example of scholarly reflection on the relationship between the 1951 and 1969 Conventions. Interestingly, Grahl-Madsen found that the settlement of refugees would only be permissible 'in cases where there exists a real concern that the refugees in question may engage in subversive activities'.[285] Unfortunately, he does not explain this focus on subversion at the expense of other considerations that might warrant encampment, such as refugees' safety or facilitating the provision of humanitarian assistance. He goes on to conclude, as above, that in the absence of a concern about subversion, the 'application of Article II(6) would probably conflict with the provisions of Article 26 of the Refugee Convention'.[286]

[282] Fragmentation Report (n 5) para 105.

[283] Gérard Prunier, *From Genocide to Continental War: The 'Congolese' Conflict and the Crisis of Contemporary Africa* (Hurst 2009) 25.

[284] *Frodovard Nsabimana* (n 269) 18–19.

[285] (n 36) 48.

[286] ibid.

(b) Freedom of association

The 1951 Convention includes a provision on the 'right of association'.[287] At the same time, as discussed in Chapter 3, the 1969 Convention prohibits refugees from engaging in 'any subversive activities against any Member State of the OAU'[288] and exhorts contracting states to prohibit refugees on their territories from 'attacking any State Member of the OAU', where 'attack' is broadly construed as including any 'activity likely to cause tension between Member States, in particular by use of arms, through the press, or by radio'.[289] This is further to the 1969 Convention's general aim of discouraging the activities of 'subversive elements'.[290] This initially suggests a norm conflict. However, the 1951 Convention's article 15 protection of the right of association is so circumscribed that achieving a harmonized interpretation of the two instruments is fairly straightforward.

Article 15 of the 1951 Convention relates only to 'non-political and non-profit-making associations and trade unions', reflecting the instrument's essential rejection of the more generous conception of freedom of association prevailing under international human rights law.[291] According to Hathaway, 'the best that can be said for Art. 15 is that it is an important affirmation of the rights of refugees—at least once they are lawfully staying, and to the same extent as most-favored foreigners—to undertake quite a broad range of associated activities, including not only the right to join trade unions, but also to participate in the activities of a diverse array of associations, including those with cultural, sporting, social, or philanthropic aims'.[292] It is difficult to conceive of trade union or sporting association activities, for example, that would constitute 'subversion' within the meaning of the 1969 Convention. The real conflict arises between international and regional refugee law, on the one hand, and international and regional human rights law, on the other. This is considered in Chapter 5.[293]

(c) Travel documents

Article 28 of the 1951 Convention mandates contracting states to 'issue to refugees lawfully staying in their territory travel documents ... unless compelling reasons of national security or public order otherwise require'. Article VI of the 1969 Convention provides substantially the same, except the entire provision is made 'Subject to Article III'—the prohibition of subversive activities—presumably to prevent travel undertaken with the objective of fomenting subversion. This implies that states parties to the 1969 Convention need not issue a travel document to any refugee who has engaged, or is likely to engage, in subversive activities. It might seem that these provisions are in conflict insofar as 'subversive elements' are concerned, however, as with freedom of association, it is not difficult to reach a

287 1951 Convention (n 1) art 15. 288 1969 Convention (n 2) art III(1).
289 ibid art III(2). 290 ibid preambular para 5.
291 See, for example, ICCPR (n 203) art 22(1). 292 (n 121) 891.
293 See section D.2.a.

harmonized interpretation of the two articles. All that is required is that the 'compelling reasons of national security or public order' referred to in the 1951 Convention's article 28 are understood to include 'subversive activities' within the meaning of the 1969 Convention, with the result that article III of the 1969 Convention should be strictly construed.

E. Conclusions

This chapter has addressed the numerous procedural and substantive aspects of the relationship between the 1951 and 1969 Conventions. On the procedural side, the various approaches to RSD in states party to both Conventions were surveyed. Then substantive aspects of the relationship were addressed. The most salient among these is the rights to which refugees recognized only under the 1969 Convention are entitled; a more isolated issue is whether 1969 Convention article I(1) refugees may invoke the 1951 Convention's 'compelling reasons' proviso to mitigate the application of the ceased circumstances cessation clause.

The analysis demonstrated that the 1969 Convention was not drafted with a view to providing an expanded class of individuals in Africa with a more restricted set of rights than their international counterparts, in terms of refugee rights in general and in terms of a refugee's rights in the face of cessation in particular. Rather, 'The substantive articles of the … regional agreement are intended to create obligations to be assumed by states which are parties to it *in addition* to those undertaken by becoming parties to the [1951] Convention and the [1967] Protocol.'[294] Thus the 1969 Convention was innovative not only in addressing refugee issues particular to Africa, most notably by incrementally expanding the range of individuals who could qualify for refugee status. In applying the content of the existing universal instrument's status to this expanded class of individuals, the drafters also found a pioneering yet pragmatic way of ensuring that refugees in Africa are guaranteed the same rights as refugees elsewhere.

This approach has been referred to as 'novel',[295] and as with all novelties, it is not without its complications. Yet this chapter also demonstrated that apparent conflicts between the 1951 and 1969 Conventions can be resolved through a harmonizing interpretation of the two instruments. This was the case regarding the freedoms of movement and association, and regarding the provision of travel documents.

That all refugees in Africa are entitled to 1951 Convention rights is particularly important in relation to the critical right to work. The African Charter does not protect the right to work as such,[296] and the ICESCR allows developing countries to limit the extent to which they protect non-nationals' economic rights.[297] Article 17 of the 1951 Convention, however, provides that states 'shall accord to refugees lawfully

[294] Chartrand (n 71) 271 (emphasis added).

[295] Bahame Tom Mukirya Nyanduga, 'Refugee Protection Under the 1969 OAU Convention Governing the Specific Aspects of Refugee Problems in Africa' (2004) 47 German YB Intl L 85, 93.

[296] See Chapter 5, section C.1. [297] (n 119) art 2(3).

staying in their territory the most favourable treatment accorded to nationals of a foreign country ... as regards ... wage-earning employment'. Many African states are part of regional economic communities (RECs) that allow sub-regional freedom of movement and establishment, such as the East African Community (EAC) and the Economic Community of West African States. Thus within such communities, the most-favoured foreigner standard by which refugees' right to work is determined under the 1951 Convention is a generous one. The combined effect of the 1951 and 1969 Conventions is that refugees in states that are part of RECs offering sub-regional freedom of movement and establishment should be allowed to work on the same basis as nationals of REC member states. This played out recently in Uganda, where refugees 'are allowed to engage in gainful or wage earning employment on the most favourable treatment according to foreign residents'.[298] This standard was for a time unclear,[299] however article 10 of the Protocol on the Establishment of the East African Community Common Market, which allows EAC citizens to work in any EAC member state, established unambiguously that Uganda's most favoured foreigner standard is one that allows refugees there to work. This sub-regional effect may eventually extend to the whole continent, as the AU just adopted an instrument governing continental freedom of movement and establishment.[300]

The complementary relationship between the 1951 and 1969 Conventions leaves certain refugees—those in states party to the 1969 Convention but not its universal counterpart, or in states that are party to the 1951 and 1969 Conventions but not the 1967 Protocol, or in states party to the 1951 and 1969 Conventions that have retained the former's geographical limit[301]—in a precarious situation. Rwelamira explains, 'because the OAU Convention is regarded as complementary to the UN Convention it has no provisions dealing with substantive or minimum rights, a problem which becomes real when a state member of the OAU Convention is not a party to the UN Convention'.[302] Thus Goundiam argues that to be effective, the 1969 Convention must be 'completed by states ratifying ... other more exhaustive instruments'.[303] Writing around 1970, Goundiam probably had the 1951 Convention in mind. Today, however, international and regional human rights law has an important role to play. The role of regional human rights law in articulating standards of treatment for refugees is addressed in Chapter 5.

298 Statutory Instruments 2010 No 9, The Refugees Regulations, 2010 (26 February 2010) (Uganda) s 64.

299 See Sharpe and Namusobya (n 9) 577–78.

300 See Chapter 6, section C.4.a.

301 Among African states, the Comoros and Libya are party to the 1969 Convention, but not the 1951 Convention; Madagascar is not party to the 1967 Protocol, and it and the Republic of the Congo recognize the 1951 Convention's geographical limitation to Europe.

302 (n 62) 178.

303 Ousmane Goundiam, 'African Refugee Convention' [1970] Migr News 3, 12.

5

Regional Human Rights Law

A. Introduction

Chapters 1 to 4 focus on refugee-specific legal instruments. These, however, constitute only part of the regional legal regime. Human rights law also plays a role. In his treatise on international human rights law in refugee protection, Hathaway called on scholars to 'build upon' his analysis—grounded in the Convention relating to the Status of Refugees[1] (1951 Convention) and the two international human rights covenants—to 'define the entitlements of sub-groups of the refugee population entitled to claim additional protections'.[2] This chapter does this for Africa by demonstrating how regional human rights law—principally the African Charter on Human and Peoples' Rights (African Charter)[3]—is an important source of rights for refugees.

This is particularly relevant in the African context, because domestic refugee laws often give refugees only a limited package of rights founded exclusively in the 1951 Convention and the Organization of African Unity Convention Governing the Specific Aspects of Refugee Problems in Africa (1969 Convention).[4] For example, Ghana's Refugee Law, 1992, provides simply that a 'person granted refugee status in Ghana shall be entitled to the rights and be subject to the duties specified in (a) ... [the 1951 Convention]; (b) the Protocol Relating to the Status of Refugees of 1967 [1967 Protocol] ... and (c) the ... [1969 Convention]'.[5] Similarly, Ethiopia's Refugee Proclamation entitles refugees to the rights 'contained in the [1951] Refugee Convention and the OAU Refugee Convention'.[6] Angola's Law on Refugee Status provides only that refugees are 'entitled to engage in gainful activities' and 'have the right to education and health assistance';[7] the 1951 Convention, the Protocol relating to the Status of Refugees and the 1969 Convention apply to 'all situations not provided for' by the Law.[8]

Furthermore, the rights of refugees in Africa are regularly violated. For example, in response to a 2012 complaint lodged by Médecins Sans Frontières and others, the South African Human Rights Commission found that conditions at the Lindela

[1] (Adopted 28 July 1951, entered into force 22 April 1954) 189 UNTS 137.
[2] James C Hathaway, *The Rights of Refugees Under International Law* (CUP 2005) 8.
[3] (Adopted 27 June 1981, entered into force 21 October 1986) 21 ILM 58.
[4] (Adopted 10 September 1969, entered into force 20 June 1974) 1001 UNTS 45.
[5] Refugee Law, 1992 (Ghana) PNDCL 305D, s 11.
[6] Refugee Proclamation No. 409/2004 (Ethiopia) art 21(1)(d).
[7] Law No 8 of 1990, Law on Refugee Status (Angola) art 8.
[8] ibid art 21.

pre-removal detention facility near Johannesburg, which likely housed a number of refugees, violated the constitutional rights to freedom and security of the person and the rights to health care, food, water, and social security, among others.[9] A 2017 Scalabrini Institute Report detailed violations of refugees' rights to health, basic education, and work in the Democratic Republic of the Congo (DRC), Ethiopia, Kenya, Nigeria, South Africa, and Sudan.[10] According to Crisp, refugees in Africa 'increasingly find that by crossing an international border, they exchange one form and degree of vulnerability for another'.[11] His description of the situation for refugees in Africa is worth quoting:

> refugee-populated areas may be the target of direct military attacks, sometimes in the form of aerial bombing but more usually by means of land-based attacks. . . . there is [also] evidence to suggest that refugee-populated areas in Africa are now increasingly affected by a variety of non-military security threats . . . [including] rape and armed robbery; conscription into militia forces; abductions for the purpose of forced marriage; arbitrary arrest and punishment by refugee community leaders and members of the local security forces; fighting between different clans and sub-tribes within the same refugee community; and armed confrontations between refugees of different nationalities.[12]

Crisp goes on to describe the conditions for refugees in protracted situations, which are characterized by 'the inability of exiled populations to avail themselves of basic human rights'.[13] Refugees in protracted situations suffer from 'limited physical security; limited freedom of movement; limited civil and political rights; limited legal [due process] rights; limited freedom of choice; and limited economic opportunities'.[14] The African Charter has a key role to play in preventing and redressing such violations.

This chapter begins with a review of the literature on the relationship between international human rights law and international refugee law, which charts the evolution of human rights in refugee protection. Section C then goes on to address regional human rights law, beginning with the African Charter overall, followed by its provisions of particular relevance to refugees, in terms of both non-refoulement and asylum and rights during exile. This is followed by surveys of relevant aspects of the Protocol to the African Charter on the Rights of Women in Africa[15] (Women's Protocol) and the African Charter on the Rights and Welfare of the Child (Children's Charter).[16] Having articulated the human rights component of the regional legal

[9] Gauteng/2012/0134, South African Human Rights Commission Investigative Reports Volume 4.

[10] Sergio Carciotto and Cristiano D'Orsi, 'Access to Socio-Economic Rights for Refugees: A Comparison Across Six African Countries' (March 2017) The Scalabrini Institute for Human Mobility in Africa <http://sihma.org.za/wp-content/uploads/2017/03/Access-to-socio-economic-rights_refugees.pdf> accessed 28 March 2017.

[11] Jeff Crisp, 'Forced Displacement in Africa: Dimensions, Difficulties, and Policy Directions' (2010) 29 RSQ 1, 7.

[12] ibid 7–8. [13] ibid 15. [14] ibid.

[15] (Adopted 11 July 2003, entered into force 25 November 2005) AU Doc CAB/LEG/66.6.

[16] (Adopted 11 July 1990, entered into force 29 November 1999) OAU Doc CAB/LEG/24.9/49(1990).

regime for refugee protection, section D then goes on to analyse how it interacts with regional refugee law. A final section concludes.

B. The Role of Human Rights Law in Refugee Protection

The role of human rights law in refugee protection has been steadily evolving. The link between the two fields was initially conceptualized causally: violations create refugees.[17] Goodwin-Gill paved the way for a more interactive approach when, in 1989, he viewed refugee protection through the lens of human rights,[18] but developments in this regard progressed slowly. In 1993 Matas explained that while human rights had begun to penetrate the refugee domain, this was occurring 'only fitfully and intermittently. Regrettably, the human rights world and the refugee world, on a day-to-day basis, function separately and apart from one another'.[19] Clark and Crépeau made a similar observation in 1999, noting that the 1951 Convention had for too long 'been treated as a piece of international legislation that could only be interpreted according to its own internal logic and objectives in isolation from international human rights law'.[20] During the nineties scholars did, however, begin to use human rights norms to inform their interpretation of refugee law concepts, including persecution[21] and non-refoulement;[22] by the turn of the millenium, human rights had significantly broadened the latter concept.[23] Human rights law also began to be invoked to provide the redress absent from refugee law, because the 1951 Convention lacks a supervisory treaty body with jurisdiction to hear complaints.[24]

[17] Vincent Chetail, 'Are Refugee Rights Human Rights? An Unorthodox Questioning of the Relations between Refugee Law and Human Rights Law' in Ruth Rubio-Marin (ed), *Human Rights and Immigration, Collected Courses of the Academy of European Law* (OUP 2014) 19.

[18] Guy S Goodwin-Gill, 'International Law and Human Rights: Trends Concerning International Migrants and Refugees' (1989) 23 Intl Migr Rev 526.

[19] David Matas, 'A History of the Politics of Refugee Protection' in Kathleen Mahoney and Paul Mahoney (eds), *Human Rights in the Twenty-first Century: A Global Challenge* (Martinus Nijhoff 1993) 622.

[20] Tom Clark and François Crépeau, 'Mainstreaming Refugee Rights: The 1951 Refugee Convention and International Human Rights Law' (1999) 17 NQHR 389, 389.

[21] James C Hathaway, 'Fear of Persecution and the Law of Human Rights' (1992) 91 Bull Hum Rts 98; James C Hathaway, *The Law of Refugee Status* (Butterworths 1991) chap 4.

[22] See, for example, Clark and Crépeau (n 20); Richard Plender and Nuala Mole, 'Beyond the Geneva Convention: Constructing a De Facto Right of Asylum from International Human Rights Instruments' in Frances Nicholson and Patrick Twomey (eds), *Refugee Rights and Realities: Evolving International Concepts and Regimes* (CUP 1999).

[23] For a complete account, see Jane McAdam, *Complementary Protection in International Refugee Law* (OUP 2007).

[24] See, for example, Oldrich Andrysek, 'Gaps in International Protection and the Potential for Redress through Individual Complaints Procedures' (1997) 9 IJRL 392; Joan Fitzpatrick (ed), *Human Rights Protection for Refugees, Asylum-Seekers and Internally Displaced Persons: A Guide to International Mechanisms and Procedures* (Transnational 2002); Saul Takahashi, 'Recourse to Human Rights Treaty Bodies for Monitoring of the Refugee Convention' (2002) 20 NQHR 53; Chaloka Beyani, 'The Role of Human Rights Bodies in Protecting Refugees' in Anne Bayefsky (ed), *Human Rights and Refugees, Internally Displaced Persons and Migrant Workers: Essays in Memory of Joan Fitzpatrick and Arthur Helton* (Martinus Nijhoff 2005). See also the March 2015 (vol 34) special issue of RSQ on 'The Role of International Organizations and Human Rights Monitoring Bodies in Refugee Protection'.

More recently, academics have invoked human rights as a source of standards of treatment during the period of asylum, both in a general sense and in relation to specific issues.[25] Today, the study of human rights in refugee protection has advanced to the point of critical analysis.[26]

Human rights have, of course, always applied to refugees. According to Gilbert, 'the idea that refugees deserve the traditional human rights in addition to the rights established in the 1951 Convention is not open to dispute'.[27] But the literature has not always approached refugee protection in this way, perhaps because of the gap of fifteen years between the adoption of the 1951 Convention and the adoption of the two international human rights covenants. This temporal gap also explains why the 1951 Convention is framed as a duty-based rather than as a human rights-based instrument: 'framing refugee status as involving obligations of states rather than rights of individuals ... emerged as a necessity in the absence of legally binding human rights' when the 1951 Convention was being drafted.[28] Clark and Crépeau were not, therefore, stating the obvious when they explained in 1999 that 'a range of protections beyond the Refugee Convention supplement the Refugee Convention protections against expulsion and refoulement. When on State territory, while claiming refugee status or with recognised refugee status, "everyone" may claim other treaty human rights without discrimination'.[29]

Such treaty human rights are important in five general ways. Firstly, international human rights law protects rights about which the 1951 Convention is mostly silent, such as the freedoms of association and expression. Secondly, where both international refugee law and international human rights law speak to a particular right, the latter generally protects the right to a higher standard. For example, protection from discrimination is broader under the International Covenant on Civil and Political Rights (ICCPR)[30] than under the 1951 Convention. Thirdly, international human rights law protects rights on an absolute basis. Rights under the 1951 Convention, by contrast, are contingent upon the refugee's degree of attachment to his or her host state and are guaranteed only to the extent that a particular reference group also enjoys the right in question.[31] Fourthly, international human rights law must inform how the 1951 Convention is interpreted and implemented.[32] Finally, because it is supervised by treaty bodies with the capacity to adjudicate individual communications, international human rights law can provide redress where international refugee law cannot.[33]

In addition to these general contributions, certain human rights treaty standards are of particular relevance to refugees. These are discussed in section C in the specific

[25] The seminal work in this regard is Hathaway (n 2).

[26] See, for example, Colin Harvey, 'Time for Reform? Refugees, Asylum-seekers, and Protection Under International Human Rights Law' (2015) 34 RSQ 43.

[27] Geoff Gilbert, 'Rights, Legitimate Expectations, Needs and Responsibilities: UNHCR and the New World Order' (1998) 10 IJRL 349, 387.

[28] Chetail (n 17) 40.

[29] (n 20) 392.

[30] International Covenant on Civil and Political Rights (adopted 16 December 1966, entered into force 23 March 1976) 999 UNTS 171.

[31] See Marina Sharpe, 'The 1951 Refugee Convention's Contingent Rights Framework and Article 26 of the ICCPR: A Fundamental Incompatibility?' (2014) 30 Refuge 5.

[32] Clark and Crépeau (n 20).

[33] Chetail (n 17) 61–68; see, also, n 24.

context of the African Charter and include procedural rights, which apply during status determination;[34] equality rights, which ensure equality among refugees[35] and between refugees and other non-citizens;[36] and liberty rights, which are important in relation to immigration detention.

These general and specific contributions of international human rights to refugee protection have led to the now universally held view that refugee rights under international law are derived from both refugee and human rights law. Hathaway led the charge in this regard. His treatise on the topic explains that 'the development of a pervasive treaty-based system of international human rights law has filled many critical gaps in the Refugee Convention's rights regime'.[37] This is not to say, however, that the 1951 Convention has been supplanted by human rights law. To the contrary, in Hathaway's view, the 1951 Convention remains of critical importance because 'treaty-based human rights are framed in generic terms' and as such, 'there is a continuing role for the Refugee Convention in responding to the particular disabilities that derive from involuntary migration'.[38]

This approach to the role of human rights in refugee protection, which views the standards of treatment applicable to refugees as deriving from both the 1951 Convention and international human rights law, is not without its detractors. Chetail argues that human rights law is now the core of refugee protection:

> human rights law has radically informed and transformed the distinctive tenets of the [1951] Geneva Convention to such an extent that the normative frame of forced migration has been displaced from refugee law to human rights law. As a result of this systemic evolution, the terms of the debate should be inversed: human rights law is *the* primary source of refugee protection, while the [1951] Geneva Convention is bound to play a complementary and secondary role.[39]

At the other end of the spectrum lies McAdam, who argues that the 1951 Convention should remain the primary source of refugee rights because human rights law fails to provide refugees with a status,[40] and because of the 'gap between the theory of human rights and the ability to enjoy those rights'.[41] These debates about the relative weight that should be accorded to each legal regime aside, it is now beyond dispute that human rights are integral to refugee protection. The remainder of this chapter addresses how African human rights law can contribute to refugee protection on the continent, and the relationships of interpretation and of conflict that these contributions raise.

[34] Chetail (n 17) 35 and 51–54.
[35] Sharpe (n 31).
[36] Jason Pobjoy, 'Treating Like Alike: The Principle of Non-Discrimination as a Tool to Mandate the Equal Treatment of Refugees and Beneficiaries of Complementary Protection' (2010) 34 MULR 181.
[37] (n 2) 110.
[38] ibid.
[39] (n 17) 22.
[40] (n 23) 198.
[41] ibid 202.

C. Regional Human Rights Law

The corpus of international human rights law in Africa includes several instruments. The leading treatise covers what may be termed the three core instruments: the African Charter, the Women's Protocol, and the Children's Charter, as well as the 1969 Convention and instruments relating to internally displaced persons (IDPs), indigenous peoples, and the environment.[42] Furthermore, in addition to addressing regional human rights law, it also treats a range of instruments that have emerged at the sub-regional level, an increasingly important plane for human rights protection in Africa.[43] The discussion of regional human rights law here is limited to the three core instruments, beginning with the most widely applicable.

1. The African Charter

The African Charter was an Organization of African Unity (OAU) initiative. A reference to human rights in its constitutive act notwithstanding,[44] the African Charter was the organization's first significant foray into the field. The OAU's interest in human rights at the end of the seventies was a result of the increased attention being paid to human rights internationally, especially by American President Carter in the Cold War context and by the United Nations (UN) to condemn South Africa's apartheid regime, and as a reaction to unchecked violations in post-independence Central African Republic, Equatorial Guinea, and Uganda.[45]

Work towards the African Charter began in 1979 with a proposal by President Léopold Senghor of Senegal and the Mauritian representative, supported by Nigeria and Uganda, that the OAU resolve to commence a process that would lead to the adoption of an African human rights instrument.[46] Drafting began in December of that year when a group of experts, led by Senegalese jurist Keba Mbaye,[47] met in Dakar with a mandate to 'prepare an African charter on human rights based upon an African legal philosophy and responsive to African needs'.[48] They had, as a blueprint for their work, the 'Monrovia Proposal for the Setting up of an African Commission on Human Rights', which was the outcome of the UN-sponsored 'Seminar on the

[42] See Frans Viljoen, *International Human Rights Law in Africa* (2nd edn, OUP 2012).

[43] ibid 469–514; see, generally, Frans Viljoen, 'The Realization of Human Rights in Africa Through Sub-regional Institutions' (1999) 7 Afr YB Intl L 186.

[44] Article II(1)(e) of the OAU Charter (Charter of the Organization of African Unity (25 May 1963) 479 UNTS 39) lists the promotion of 'international cooperation, having due regard to the Charter of the United Nations and the Universal Declaration of Human Rights' as among the OAU's purposes.

[45] Christof Heyns, 'The African Regional Human Rights System: The African Charter' (2003–04) 108 Penn State L Rev 679, 685; Viljoen (n 42) 158–59.

[46] Viljoen (n 42) 160.

[47] Christof Heyns and Frans Viljoen, 'An Overview of International Human Rights Protection in Africa' (1999) 15 S Afr J Hum Rts 421, 433.

[48] Richard Gittleman, 'African Charter on Human and Peoples' Rights: A Legal Analysis' (1981–82) 22 Va J Intl L 667, 668; this article contains a brief but excellent drafting history of the African Charter.

Establishment of Regional Commissions on Human Rights with Special Reference to Africa' held in Liberia in September 1979.[49]

The Monrovia Proposal was directed at establishing a human rights body and, as a result, did not articulate any new standards; rather, it merely referred to norms already contained in international instruments.[50] Mbaye's group rejected this approach, preferring to draft a new instrument that would articulate standards suited to the African context.[51] According to D'Sa, the necessity for such specific standards stemmed from cultural differences, such as the African emphasis on community over individuals, and from the stage of Africa's development.[52] Heyns points to the continental experiences of slavery and colonialism as necessitating region-specific standards.[53]

Despite the drafters' insistence on an instrument reflecting uniquely African norms, the Charter ultimately affirmed international human rights law[54] and international law more generally[55] as relevant sources within the regional system. This is but one example of how elements that have been separated in other contexts coexist within the African Charter. The Charter also includes civil and political rights as well as economic, social, and cultural rights; protects individuals and peoples; and enumerates rights as well as duties. Perhaps this balance has contributed to the African Charter's almost universal acceptance among African Union (AU) member states. The Charter was adopted in 1981 and entered into force five years later, and has now been ratified by all AU member states except Morocco, which only recently joined the AU.

The African Charter is set out in three parts. Chapters I and II of part I deal with rights and duties respectively. Part II includes four chapters, the first of which creates the African Commission on Human and Peoples' Rights (African Commission), which was ultimately established in 1987 and was supplemented, by way of a 1998 Protocol,[56] by the African Court on Human and Peoples' Rights (African Court). This latter body may eventually be replaced by the African Court of Justice and Human and Peoples' Rights (New Merged Court) (the African Commission and these courts are the subject of Chapter 7, though the African Commission's treatment of relevant Charter provisions is discussed here). Chapter II of part II sets out the African Commission's mandate, while chapter III establishes its procedure. The final chapter of part II articulates the principles governing the African Commission. Part III of the Charter contains general provisions.

The African Charter contains several distinctive features. As mentioned earlier in this section, it includes protections that have elsewhere been bifurcated. The inclusion of civil and political rights alongside economic, social, and cultural rights has been praised for stressing the indivisibility and justiciability of all rights.[57] The

[49] ibid 672. [50] ibid. [51] ibid 673.

[52] Rose D'Sa, 'Human and Peoples Rights: Distinctive Features of the African Charter' (1985) 29 J Afr L 72, 74.

[53] (n 45) 680. [54] African Charter (n 3) art 60. [55] ibid art 61.

[56] Protocol to the African Charter on Human and Peoples' Rights on the Establishment of the African Court on Human and Peoples' Rights (adopted 10 June 1998, entered into force 25 January 2004) OAU Doc OAU/LEG/EXP/AGCHPR/PROT.

[57] Viljoen (n 42) 214.

Charter's inclusion of socioeconomic rights has, however, also been criticized. Heyns notes that only a modest number of such rights have been included:[58] to work under 'equitable and satisfactory conditions' and receive equal pay for equal work, to health, and to education.[59] Furthermore, the Charter's socioeconomic rights are not framed with the usual qualifiers that make them subject only to the standards of 'progressive realization' and 'available resources'. On the one hand, this renders these socioeconomic rights immediately justiciable, however on the other, it sets what might be an unattainable standard, thereby emptying the rights of meaningful content. The omission of certain civil and political rights has also been criticized. Heyns and Viljoen note that the Charter fails to protect the rights to privacy, to form trade unions, to free and fair elections and to freedom from forced labour.[60]

The Charter does not include limitation and derogation clauses. Thus, under conditions of scarcity or emergency, the Charter is often simply ignored. Moreover, many Charter protections contain clawback clauses, which allow states to restrict the right in question to the extent permitted by domestic law. Clawback clauses are imprecise and therefore do not provide the external check on state action afforded by derogation clauses. Heyns has gone so far as to argue that clawback clauses 'undermine the whole idea of international supervision of domestic law and practices and render the Charter meaningless'.[61] The African Commission has, however, prevented this absurdity by interpreting limitations of rights in the complainant's favour.[62] For example, it has interpreted clawback clauses as limiting rights only insofar as the domestic law in question complies with international human rights standards.[63] The African Commission has also interpreted one of the Charter's duty provisions as a general limitation clause, as explained later in this section in the discussion of duties.

The African Charter protects peoples' rights, in particular their rights to existence, to self-determination, to freely dispose of their natural resources, to development, to international peace and security and to a satisfactory environment.[64] D'Sa explains that the inclusion of peoples' rights was a result of the importance the drafters placed on creating a document that would reflect a particularly African conception of human rights.[65] The Charter does not, however, define the concept of a 'people', nor is the term defined in international law more generally, leading Viljoen to characterize it as 'a concept in need of clarity'.[66] The ability of a people to enforce its rights under the Charter depends on a distinctive procedural feature: unlike other regional and international human rights instruments, the African Charter has no individual victim requirement. This has allowed representatives of a people, as well as individuals and non-governmental organizations (NGOs), to bring complaints

[58] (n 45) 690–91. [59] African Charter (n 3) arts 15–17. [60] (n 47) 434.

[61] (n 45) 688.

[62] Gino J Naldi, 'Limitation of Rights Under the African Charter on Human and Peoples' Rights: The Contribution of the African Commission on Human and Peoples' Rights' (2001) 17 S Afr J Hum Rts 109, 112.

[63] *Media Rights Agenda & Others v Nigeria* comm nos 105/93, 128/94, 130/94 and 152/96, 12th Annual Activity Report of the Af Cm HRP (1998) (*Media Rights Agenda*) para 66.

[64] African Charter (n 3) arts 20–24. [65] (n 52) 77. [66] (n 42) 219.

to the African Commission regarding violations of their rights and/or the rights of others.[67]

The final unique feature of the African Charter is its inclusion of individual duties. These duties are owed to others, one's family, one's community, the state, and the African and international communities.[68] Different explanations have been proffered for the inclusion of duties. According to D'Sa, duties reflect African cultural values,[69] and this is how Senghor characterized them.[70] Gittleman, by contrast, explains that duties were included to ensure the Charter's broad acceptance: 'the notion of "individual" in a socialist State differs markedly from the notion in a capitalist State. As a result, to ensure the eventual adoption of the Charter by all States, the drafters in Dakar stated that if the individual is to have rights "recognized" by the State, he also must have obligations flowing back to the State'.[71]

While some of the Charter's duties are enforceable—for example the duty to pay taxes[72]—others create moral, as opposed to legal, obligations. One seemingly moral duty has, however, been imbued by the African Commission with significant legal meaning. Article 27(2) provides that the 'rights and freedoms of each individual shall be exercised with due regard to the rights of others, collective security, morality and common interest'. The African Commission has interpreted this duty provision innovatively as a general limitation clause, stating that 'the only legitimate reasons for limitations to the rights and freedoms of the African Charter are found in article 27(2)'.[73]

2. The African Charter in refugee protection

The African Charter's guarantees are owed to 'Every individual ... without distinction of any kind such as ... national ... origin ... or any status'.[74] The African Commission has confirmed that Charter rights are owed to nationals and non-nationals alike,[75] and to refugees in particular.[76] Doctrine also confirms this.[77] It is thus settled law that refugees benefit from the protection of the Charter during the period of asylum,[78] and a refugee whose rights have been violated by his or her

[67] Rachel Murray, 'International Human Rights: Neglect of Perspective from African Institutions' (2006) 55 Intl & Comp LQ 193, 199.

[68] African Charter (n 3) arts 27–29.

[69] (n 52) 77.

[70] Viljoen (n 42) 239.

[71] (n 48) 676–77.

[72] African Charter (n 3) art 29(6).

[73] *Media Rights Agenda* (n 63) para 68; see, also, *Constitutional Rights Project and Others v Nigeria* comm nos 140/94, 141/94 and 145/95, 13th Annual Activity Report of the Af Cm HRP (1999) para 41.

[74] African Charter (n 3) art 2.

[75] *Rencontre Africaine pour la defense des droits de l'homme (RADDHO) v Zambia* comm no 71/92, 10th Annual Activity Report of the Af Cm HPR (2000) (*RADDHO*) para 22.

[76] *African Institute for Human Rights and Development (on behalf of Sierra Leonean refugees in Guinea) v Guinea* comm no 249/2002, 20th Annual Activity Report of the Af Cm HRP (2005–06) (*African Institute*) para 68.

[77] See, for example, Gino J Naldi and Cristiano D'Orsi, 'The Role of the African Human Rights System with Reference to Asylum Seekers' in Ademola Abass and Francesca Ippolito (eds), *Regional Approaches to the Protection of Asylum Seekers: An International Legal Perspective* (Ashgate 2014) 56.

[78] Except the article 13 rights to political participation and access to the public service, which are owed to 'every citizen'.

host state has recourse to the African Commission's individual communications procedure.[79] Indeed, communications have been lodged by individual refugees, by refugee associations, and by NGOs on behalf of refugees. The range of human rights protected by the African Charter means that refugees may invoke Charter protections regarding non-refoulement and asylum as such, and regarding their rights during exile. Each is addressed in turn.

(a) Non-refoulement and asylum

International refugee law provides that an individual may not be returned to a state where his or her life or freedom would be threatened for a 1951 Convention reason.[80] African refugee law similarly provides that an individual may not be subjected to measures that would compel him or her to return to, or remain in, a territory where his or her life, physical integrity, or liberty would be threatened for a 1969 Convention reason.[81] International human rights law has expanded the scope of non-refoulement such that it now also prohibits return to torture; to cruel, inhuman, or degrading treatment or punishment; and to arbitrary deprivations of life,[82] as well as to enforced disappearance.[83] This human rights form of non-refoulement is typically known as 'complementary protection' because it extends, and is hence complementary to, refugee law's non-refoulement protection. It is now widely accepted that both the refugee and the human rights law forms of non-refoulement have attained the status of customary international law.[84]

Regional human rights law also provides for complementary protection,[85] though the precise ambit of the guarantee is unclear. Article 5 of the African Charter prohibits 'torture' as well as 'cruel, inhuman or degrading punishment and treatment' (CIDT). The African Commission has held that return to face torture, CIDT, and/or death is equally prohibited. *John K Modise v Botswana*, concerning a complainant who was rendered stateless by Botswana, repeatedly forcibly moved between Botswana and South Africa, and forced by Botswana to remain on a strip of no man's

[79] Bahame Tom Mukirya Nyanduga, 'Refugee Protection Under the 1969 OAU Convention Governing the Specific Aspects of Refugee Problems in Africa' (2004) 47 German YB Intl L 85, 101.

[80] 1951 Convention (n 1) art 33(1).

[81] 1969 Convention (n 4) art II(3).

[82] Convention against Torture and Other Cruel, Inhuman or Degrading Treatment or Punishment (adopted 10 December 1984, entered into force 26 June 1987) 1465 UNTS 85, art 3(1); ICCPR (n 30) art 7, read with HRC, 'General Comment No 31: The Nature of the General Legal Obligation Imposed on States Parties to the Covenant' (29 March 2004) para 12 (see Chapter 3, n 287).

[83] International Convention for the Protection of All Persons from Enforced Disappearance (adopted 20 December 2006, entered into force 23 December 2010) 2716 UNTS 3, art 16(1).

[84] *Kituo Cha Sheria, Abebe Dadi Tully, Ahmed Bashir Mohamed, Eugene Bwimana, Dachassa Galdi Nure, Muhima Sebihendo Joh, Mbuzukongire Nzabona and Said Abdullahi Abukar v the Attorney General*, Petition Nos 19 and 115 of 2013, High Court of Kenya (26 July 2013) para 44; Elihu Lauterpacht and Daniel Bethlehem, 'The Scope and Content of the Principle of Non-refoulement: Opinion' in Erika Feller, Volker Türk, and Frances Nicholson (eds), *Refugee Protection in International Law: UNHCR's Global Consultations on International Protection* (CUP 2003); Cathryn Costello and Michelle Foster, 'Non-refoulement as Custom and Jus Cogens? Putting the Prohibition to the Test' (2016) 46 NYIL 2015 273; contra: James C Hathaway, 'Leveraging Asylum' (2009) 45 Texas Intl LJ 503.

[85] Rachel Murray, 'Refugees and Internally Displaced Persons and Human Rights: the African System' (2005) 24 RSQ 56, 59; Chetail (n 17) 35.

land between the two countries, addressed CIDT. The African Commission found that the removals (and the homelessness) exposed Modise 'to personal suffering and indignity in violation of the right to freedom from cruel, inhuman or degrading treatment guaranteed under Article 5 of the Charter'.[86] *Institute for Human Rights and Development in Africa v Republic of Angola* (*Institute for Human Rights and Development*) addressed CIDT as well as torture and death, even though article 5 does not mention the latter. In its decision, the African Commission stressed the importance of procedural safeguards in removal contexts, to ensure that non-nationals 'are not sent back/deported/expelled to countries or places they are likely to suffer from torture, inhuman or degrading treatment, or death, among others'.[87] Thus African Commission jurisprudence suggests that article 5 protects from return to torture, CIDT, and death.

Yet the African Commission's Guidelines and Measures for the Prohibition and Prevention of Torture, Cruel, Inhuman or Degrading Treatment or Punishment in Africa forbid only return to torture. The Guidelines instruct states to 'ensure no one is expelled or extradited to a country where he or she is at risk of being subjected to torture'.[88] CIDT is absent from the prohibition, which is particularly conspicuous given that other elements of the Guidelines do mention CIDT. The broadest understanding of complementary protection—the *Institute for Human Rights and Development* conception including torture, CIDT, and death—is also the most recent, suggesting complementary protection can be understood expansively in Africa. In practice, however, the scope of complementary protection makes little difference to refugees, as they rarely if ever rely on it. The protection gap the concept fills in other regions is in Africa addressed through article I(2) of the 1969 Convention.

In addition to article 5, according to Wood article 18 may also contribute to non-refoulement in Africa.[89] It provides that the 'family shall be the natural unit and basis of society. It shall be protected by the State which shall take care of its physical health and moral' health. In *Union inter-Africaine des droits de l'homme v Angola* (*Union inter-Africaine des droits de l'homme*), the mass expulsion of West Africans from Angola, which fractured several families, was found to offend article 18.[90] Subsequently, in *Sudan Human Rights Organisation & Centre on Housing Rights and Evictions (COHRE) v Sudan*, the article 18 duty of protection was interpreted as requiring 'that States refrain from any action that will affect the family unit, including arbitrary separation of family members and involuntary displacement of families'.[91]

[86] *John K Modise v Botswana* comm no 97/93, 10th Annual Activity Report of the Af Cm HPR (2000) para 92.

[87] Comm no 292/2004, 24th Annual Activity Report of the Af Cm HPR (2008) para 84.

[88] African Commission, 'Resolution on Guidelines and Measures for the Prohibition and Prevention of Torture, Cruel, Inhuman or Degrading Treatment or Punishment in Africa' (32nd Ordinary Session, 17–23 October 2002) art 15.

[89] Tamara Wood, 'Protection and Disasters in the Horn of Africa: Norms and Practice for Addressing Cross-Border Displacement in Disaster Contexts' (2015) The Nansen Initiative <http://www.nanseninitiative.org/wp-content/uploads/2015/03/190215_Technical_Paper_Tamara_Wood.pdf> accessed 23 January 2017, 33–34.

[90] Comm no 292/04, 23rd and 24th Annual Activity Report of the Af Cm HPR (2004) para 17.

[91] *Sudan Human Rights Organisation & Centre on Housing Rights and Evictions (COHRE) v Sudan* comm no 279/03–296/05, 45th Annual Activity Report of the Af Cm HPR (2009) para 214. Separating

Wood has argued that article 18, considered alongside Children's Charter provisions requiring states to protect and support families and guarantee the right of every child to reside with his or her parents,[92] may 'give rise to a prohibition on forcible return to one's country of origin' when such return would compromise family life.[93]

While articles 5 and 18 of the African Charter support non-refoulement, article 12 contributes to its corollary: asylum. Various aspects of the African Charter's article 12 support asylum. Article 12(3) protects the right to 'seek and obtain' asylum, article 12(4) prohibits the arbitrary expulsion of non-nationals, and article 12(5) forbids the mass expulsion of non-nationals. Each is addressed in turn.

Article 12(3) of the African Charter protects the right of every individual 'when persecuted, to seek and obtain asylum in other countries in accordance with the law of those countries and international conventions'. This regional right to seek and *obtain* asylum is broader than the cognate right on the international plane. Article 14 of the Universal Declaration of Human Rights protects only the right 'to seek and to *enjoy* in other countries asylum from persecution'.[94] The UN Declaration on Territorial Asylum is similarly circumscribed.[95] The broader African wording was perhaps inspired by the inter-American provision that preceded it: the American Convention on Human Rights protects the right 'to seek and be *granted* asylum in a foreign territory, in accordance with the legislation of the state and international conventions, in the event he is being pursued for political offences or related common crimes'.[96] Gittleman maintains that the recognition of the right to asylum in both regional conventions is 'far-reaching in light of the earlier attitude of the international community that individuals had no such right of any legal significance'.[97] Despite this advance, the grant of asylum remains in international law within the exclusive discretion of states.[98] Indeed, 'it has long been recognised that, according to customary international law, the right of asylum is a right of States, not of the individual'.[99] That individuals have no right to be granted asylum is reflected in the language of article 12(3), which features a clawback clause subjecting the right

families has even been found to constitute inhuman treatment within the meaning of article 5 of the African Charter. In *Amnesty International and Others v Sudan*, the Commission found that 'holding an individual without permitting him or her to have any contact with his or her family, and refusing to inform the family if and where the individual is being held, is inhuman treatment of both the detainee and the family concerned' (comm nos 48/90, 50/91, 52/91, and 83/93, 13th Annual Activity Report of the Af Cm HPR (1999) para 54).

92 Children's Charter (n 16) arts 18(1) and 19(1).

93 Wood (n 89) 33.

94 UNGA Res 217 A (III) (10 December 1948) (emphasis added); see, generally, Alice Edwards, 'Human Rights, Refugees, and The Right "To Enjoy" Asylum' (2005) 17 IJRL 293.

95 UNGA Res 2312 (XXII) (14 December 1967).

96 (Adopted 21 November 1969, entered into force 18 July 1978) 1144 UNTS 123 (emphasis added).

97 Gittleman (n 48) 698.

98 Guy S Goodwin-Gill and Jane McAdam, *The Refugee in International Law* (3rd edn, OUP 2007) 358.

99 *Minister for Immigration and Multicultural Affairs v Khawar* [2002] HCA 14, para 42.

to 'obtain' asylum to the domestic laws of the state where protection is sought. The African Charter has thus advanced—but has not enshrined—the recognition of an individual right to asylum on the international plane.

Although article 12(3) represents progressive development towards the international recognition of an individual right to asylum, it could have been broader still. Drafting of the African Charter began in the late seventies, at which point the 1969 Convention was already in force. The regional refugee instrument protects individuals fleeing 'external aggression, occupation, foreign domination or events seriously disturbing public order',[100] in addition to those in flight from persecution.[101] It is curious, therefore, that the African Charter right to seek and obtain asylum is limited to individuals who have been persecuted. The African Commission could have aligned article 12(3) with the 1969 Convention in *Organisational mondiale contre la torture v Rwanda* (*OMT*), a case about the expulsion of four Burundian refugees from Rwanda on ostensible security grounds. The African Commission, however, merely held that article 12(3) provides 'a general protection of all those who are subject to *persecution*, that they may seek refuge in another state'.[102] Article 12(3) is also unduly narrow in that the right to seek and obtain asylum applies only 'when persecuted', which Naldi and d'Orsi argue is susceptible to a restrictive interpretation pursuant to which 'refugees are required to have suffered actual persecution rather than simply demonstrating the more generous [international] standard of a well-founded fear of persecution'.[103] Again, *OMT* gave the African Commission the opportunity to broaden the scope of article 12(3), but it remained true to the letter of the Charter, interpreting the provision as providing 'a general protection of all those *who are subject to* persecution'.[104]

While the African Commission has interpreted article 12(3) narrowly, Beyani has taken a more expansive approach, interpreting the right to 'seek and obtain asylum' in light of the African Charter's article 7(1) on fair trial rights. Applying the constitutive theory of interpretation, pursuant to which a treaty is interpreted as an integral whole, he argues that the language of article 7(1) and the African Commission's approach to it imply that states have an obligation to establish institutions and fair procedures for refugee status determination, including legal aid.[105] This position received a measure of support when article 7(1) was applied in a refugee context. In *OMT* the African Commission held that Rwanda's expulsion of four Burundian refugees violated their article 7(1) due process rights.[106] Beyani's argument is further strengthened by the African Charter's article 26, which provides that states 'shall allow the establishment and improvement of appropriate national institutions

[100] 1969 Convention (n 4) art I(2). [101] ibid art I(1).

[102] *Organisation mondiale contre la torture and Others v Rwanda* comm nos 27/89, 46/91, 49/91, 99/93, 10th Annual Activity Report of the Af Cm HPR (1996) (*OMT*) para 31 (emphasis added).

[103] Naldi and D'Orsi (n 77) 62. [104] *OMT* (n 102) para 31 (emphasis added).

[105] Chaloka Beyani, *Protection of the Right to Seek and Obtain Asylum Under the African Human Rights System* (Martinus Nijhoff 2013) 52–53. Note, however, that the European Convention on Human Rights' fair trial guarantee was found not to apply to asylum proceedings (*Katani v Germany* app no 67679/01 (ECtHR 31 May 2001)).

[106] *OMT* (n 102) para 34.

entrusted with the promotion and protection of the rights and freedoms guaranteed by the present Charter'.

Article 12(3) may also render important refugee protection provisions applicable to circumstances in which they might not otherwise apply. In guaranteeing the right of every individual 'to seek and obtain asylum in other countries in accordance with the law of those countries and international conventions', article 12(3) draws such 'international conventions' into the normative environment. For example, refugees in Libya are often detained without cause, a practice prohibited by the 1951 Convention's article 31. While Libya is not party to the 1951 Convention, it has ratified the African Charter. It is therefore bound to respect refugees' right 'to seek and obtain asylum ... in accordance with ... international conventions', which would include the 1951 Convention's article 31 provision on non-penalization for unlawful entry.[107]

Articles 12(4) and 12(5) are the source of an emerging line of African Commission jurisprudence relating to the expulsion of refugees and migrants more generally. Article 12(4) prohibits the arbitrary expulsion of non-citizens, providing that a 'non-national legally admitted in a territory of a State Party ... may only be expelled from it by virtue of a decision taken in accordance with the law'. The above-mentioned expulsion of four Burundian refugees from Rwanda was found to violate article 12(4).[108] The provision was also applied in favour of refugees in *African Institute*,[109] which addressed allegations that the Guinean President incited discrimination against Sierra Leonean refugees in a speech urging their arrest and confinement to camps. As a result of the speech, thousands of Sierra Leonean refugees fled their homes in Guinea and many had no choice but to return to Sierra Leone, while others were forced back there by Guinean authorities.

Article 12(5) of the Charter also prohibits the expulsion of non-nationals but relates in particular to mass expulsion, which is characterized as discriminatory expulsion 'aimed at national, racial, ethnic or religious groups'. Demonstrating a qualitative, as opposed to quantitative, approach to mass expulsion, article 12(5) was found to have been violated in *OMT*, which related to just four refugees.[110] It was similarly violated in *Institute for Human Rights and Development*, which concerned fourteen Gambians who had been living and working legally in Angola but were deported as part of the government's *Operaçao Brilhante*.[111] *Institute for Human Rights and Development* also demonstrated the African Commission's willingness to apply article 12(5) to groups not specifically mentioned by the provision. The African Commission found article 12(5) to have been violated on the basis of the Gambians'

107 See, in this regard, UNHCR, 'Key Legal Considerations on the Standards of Treatment of Refugees Recognized Under the 1969 OAU Convention Governing the Specific Aspects of Refugee Problems in Africa' (19 December 2017) <http://www.refworld.org/docid/5a391d4f4.html> accessed 5 January 2017, para 9.

108 *OMT* (n 102) para 30.

109 *African Institute* (n 76).

110 *OMT* (n 102) paras 31–32.

111 *Institute for Human Rights and Development* (n 87).

status as non-nationals from West and Central African countries,[112] paving 'the way for the possibility of categories not specifically mentioned in article 12(5) ... being afforded protection in terms of this provision'.[113]

Violations of article 12(5) have also been found in larger scale expulsions. In *Union inter-Africaine des droits de l'homme*, the mass expulsion of West Africans from Angola violated article 12(5).[114] In *RADDHO*, the detention and subsequent deportation of 517 West Africans from Zambia contravened the prohibition of mass expulsion.[115] These cases also illustrate that the expulsion need not have occurred at one point in time to violate article 12(5);[116] in each of *Institute for Human Rights and Development*, *Union inter-Africaine des droits de l'homme* and *RADDHO*, a number of separate deportations occurred over a period of several months. According to Bekker, the latter two cases also evidence the African Commission's view that mass expulsion constitutes a gateway human rights violation. She argues that implicit in *Union inter-Africaine des droits de l'homme* and *RADDHO* is 'acknowledgement that the prohibition against mass expulsions is a right upon which a number of other rights are predicated'.[117] Indeed, in an earlier communication the African Commission had noted that mass expulsion 'calls into question a whole series of rights recognized and guaranteed by the Charter'.[118]

The article 12 prohibitions on expulsion clearly support asylum when they are invoked in favour of refugees. In view of *Institute for Human Rights and Development*, they now also contribute to non-refoulement. In that case, the African Commission explained that 'a state's right to expel individuals is not absolute and it is subject to certain restraints'.[119] According to the African Commission, procedural safeguards must ensure that non-nationals 'are not sent back/deported/expelled to countries or places they are likely to suffer from torture, inhuman or degrading treatment, or death, among others'.[120] Thus while article 5 of the Charter has been interpreted to prohibit return to torture or other ill-treatment, article 12 requires procedural safeguards to prevent the same. The overall contribution of article 12 to non-refoulement may have been implicitly acknowledged by the African Commission in *Curtis Francis Doebbler v Sudan*, which concerned the repatriation of Ethiopian refugees by virtue of Sudan's 1999 invocation of the 1951 Convention's article 1C(5) cessation clause.[121] The African Commission held that the return of the refugees to Ethiopia

[112] ibid para 69.

[113] Gina Bekker, 'Mass Expulsion of Foriegn Nationals: A "Special Violation of Human Rights" – Communication 292/2004 Institute for Human Rights and Development in Africa v Republic of Angola' (2009) 9 Afr Hum Rts LJ 262, 270.

[114] (n 90). [115] *RADDHO* (n 75) paras 19–28. [116] Bekker (n 113) 270.

[117] ibid 264.

[118] *Union inter-Africaine des droits de l'homme, Federation internationale des ligues des droits de l'homme, Rencontre Africaine des droits de l'homme, Organisation nationale des droits de l'homme au Sénégal and Association Malienne des droits de l'homme v Angola* comm no 159/96, 11th Annual Activity Report of the Af Cm HPR (1997) para 17.

[119] *Institute for Human Rights and Development* (n 87) para 79. [120] ibid para 84.

[121] *Curtis Francis Doebbler v Sudan* comm no 235/00, 27th Annual Activity Report of the Af Cm HPR (2009) (*Doebbler*).

where they feared *persecution* would constitute a violation of the Charter.[122] The African Commission did not indicate which Charter provision it was relying upon, however it is likely the members had article 12 in mind, because article 5 relates to torture and cruel, inhuman, or degrading punishment and treatment, rather than to persecution.

(b) *Rights in the country of asylum*

Except for the African Charter's article 13 political participation guarantee, refugees benefit from all Charter rights during displacement, as discussed earlier in this section. Because of their unique circumstances, certain rights are, however, particularly relevant to refugees during exile. Among these, the guarantee of non-discrimination is paramount. According to Hathaway, 'to the extent that the main concern of refugees is to be accepted by a host community, a guarantee of non-discrimination might in fact be virtually the only legal guarantee that many refugees require'.[123] The African Charter includes an accessory protection from discrimination at article 2, which provides that 'Every individual shall be entitled to the enjoyment of the rights and freedoms recognised and guaranteed in the present Charter without distinction of any kind such as race, ethnic group, colour, sex, language, religion, political or any other opinion, national and social origin, fortune, birth or any status'. This provision was applied in *African Institute* in the context of the mass expulsion of Sierra Leonean refugees from Guinea,[124] as well as in the context of the expulsion of four Burundian refugees from Rwanda.[125]

The African Charter also includes a free-standing right to equality, at article 3. It guarantees that every individual shall be 'equal before the law' and 'entitled to equal protection of the law'. Like the corresponding right on the international plane—article 26 of the ICCPR, discussed in Chapter 4[126]—this ensures formal equality (equality before the law) as well as substantive equality (equal protection of the law) in respect of rights not articulated by the Charter itself. Moreover, the Charter goes beyond the ICCPR in that its prohibition of discrimination is not limited to enumerated grounds. Hathaway has noted that ICCPR article 26 might 'be a sufficient basis to require asylum states to bring an end to any laws or practices that set refugees apart from the rest of their community'.[127] If this is true of the ICCPR, it must be equally true of the African Charter, especially because the article 3 protection is not limited to enumerated grounds of discrimination. Article 3 has, however, been surprisingly overlooked by the African Commission in its decisions and by scholarly accounts of refugee protection under African human rights law.

In addition to freedom from discrimination and the right to equality, other civil and political rights are particularly important to refugees. Although 'no combined study on the conditions faced by refugees ... in Africa exists',[128] there is ample

[122] ibid para 146. [123] Hathaway (n 2) 123. [124] *African Institute* (n 76) para 69.
[125] *OMT* (n 102) para 32. [126] See section C.4.
[127] Hathaway (n 2) 127–28; see, also, Sharpe (n 31).
[128] Zachary A Lomo, 'The Struggle for the Protection of the Rights of Refugees and IDPs in Africa: Making the Existing International Legal Regime Work' (2000) 18 Berk J Intl L 268, 272.

evidence that refugees in Africa regularly experience violations of their *most fundamental* human rights.[129] For example, according to Lomo, the 'greatest danger to refugees ... in Africa has been the threat of violence to their persons'.[130] Verdirame and Harrell-Bond catalogue instances of torture and CIDT experienced by refugees in Kenya and Uganda.[131] Refugees in Africa are also often confined to camps.[132] In view of these fundamental violations, first generation Charter rights are particularly salient.[133] Indeed, African Commission communications concerning violations of refugees' rights during exile generally relate to civil and political rights, including the article 4 right to life and personal integrity,[134] the article 5 prohibition of torture and CIDT,[135] the article 6 right to liberty and security of the person,[136] the article 7 right to a fair trial,[137] and the article 14 right to property.[138] The violation of refugees' article 12(1) right to freedom of movement and residence has never been litigated before the African Commission, despite the widespread use of refugee camps in Africa. Nor has article 12(2), protecting the right of every individual to leave any country and to return to his or her own country, ever been applied in a refugee context.

In addition to specific protections provided by the Children's Charter and the Women's Protocol, which are discussed later in this section, article 18(4) of the African Charter recognizes the specific needs of elderly and disabled individuals, who may be particularly vulnerable in refugee contexts. However, this provision has yet to be invoked in a refugee protection context.

3. Other core human rights instruments

Article 18(3) of the African Charter requires that states 'ensure the elimination of every discrimination against women and also ensure the protection of the rights of women and the child as stipulated in international declarations and conventions'. This obligation was strengthened in 1990 with the adoption of the Children's Charter, and again in 2003 with the supplementation of the African Charter by a protocol on the rights of women in Africa.

Like the African Charter, the Children's Charter—its article 4 best interests provision in particular—is relevant to refugee minors in a general sense. Its provisions

[129] See Jeff Crisp, 'Africa's Refugees: Patterns, Problems and Policy Challenges' (2000) 8 Afr YB Intl L 93; Lomo (n 128) 272–75; Bonaventure Rutinwa, 'The End of Asylum? The Changing Nature of Refugee Policies in Africa' (2002) 21 RSQ 12; Guglielmo Verdirame and Barbara Harrell-Bond, *Rights in Exile: Janus Faced Humanitarianism* (Berghahn Books 2005); Edwin Odihambo Abuya, 'From Here to Where? Refugees Living in Protracted Situations in Africa' in Alice Edwards and Carla Ferstman (eds), *Human Security and Non-Citizens: Law, Policy and International Affairs* (CUP 2010).

[130] Lomo (n 128) 277.

[131] Verdirame and Harrell-Bond (n 129) 133–51.

[132] Lomo (n 128) 281–83; see also Chapter 4, section D.2.a.

[133] Recent research has explored the extent to which refugees enjoy their socioeconomic rights during exile; see Carciotto and D'Orsi (n 10).

[134] *African Institute* (n 76); *OMT* (n 102); *Doebbler* (n 121), however, the Commission found no violation of article 4.

[135] *African Institute* (n 76); *OMT* (n 102); *Doebbler* (n 121), however the Commission found no violation of article 5.

[136] *OMT* (n 102); *Doebbler* (n 121), however, the Commission found no violation of article 6.

[137] *OMT* (n 102).

[138] *African Institute* (n 76).

protecting the family and addressing separation from it may be particularly relevant to refugees, given the family unity issues that often arise in refugee contexts.[139] Article 18(1) positions the family as 'the natural unit and basis of society'. Accordingly, it 'shall enjoy the protection and support of the State for its establishment and development'. Relatedly, article 19(1) provides that every 'child shall be entitled to the enjoyment of parental care and protection and shall, whenever possible, have the right to reside with his or her parents'. Article 25 on separation from parents entitles any child deprived of the family environment 'for any reason' to 'special protection and assistance', including 'alternative family care'. Addressing refugee contexts specifically, article 25 further provides that states 'shall take all necessary measures to trace and re-unite children with parents or relatives where separation is caused by internal and external displacement arising from armed conflicts or natural disasters'.

The Children's Charter article 6(3) nationality guarantee, which gives every child the 'right to acquire a nationality', is also highly relevant in refugee contexts, particularly to refugees who bear children in host states that do not offer or operationalize *jus soli* citizenship.[140] Article 6(3) may have been considered by Tanzania in 2008,[141] when it naturalized Burundian refugees who had fled to Tanzania in the seventies and their descendants (who were technically already Tanzanian under the *jus soli* provision of Tanzania's Citizenship Act).[142]

The Children's Charter also contains a refugee-specific provision, which is very similar to the Convention on the Rights of the Child's article 22.[143] It requires, inter alia, that states provide refugee children with 'appropriate protection and humanitarian assistance in the enjoyment of the rights set out' in the Charter and in 'other international human rights and humanitarian instruments to which the States are Parties'. It also mandates state cooperation with international organisations' child protection and family reunification work and prohibits states from discriminating against unaccompanied refugee children in the provision of protection.[144]

The Children's Charter has a dedicated treaty monitoring body: the African Committee of Experts on the Rights and Welfare of the Child. It engages primarily in promotional activities and has only issued five decisions (including two relating solely to admissibility), none of which pertains to refugees. The Children's Charter was, however, invoked regarding the effects on refugee children of a March 2014 Kenyan government press statement ordering refugees to relocate to the Dadaab and Kakuma camps. The Refugee Consortium of Kenya, together with a parent suing on behalf of her six children and forty-two other minors, alleged that the relocation

[139] See, generally, Thoko Kaime, 'From Lofty Jargon to Durable Solutions: Unaccompanied Refugee Children and the African Charter on the Rights and Welfare of the Child' (2004) 16 IJRL 336.

[140] See, generally, Gerard-Rene de Groot, 'Children, Their Right to a Nationality and Child Statelessness' in Alice Edwards and Laura van Waas (eds), *Nationality and Statelessness Under International Law* (CUP 2014).

[141] See, generally, Amelia Kuch, 'Naturalization of Burundian Refugees in Tanzania: The Debates on Local Integration and the Meaning of Citizenship Revisited' (2017) 30 JRS 468.

[142] Tanzania Citizenship Act, 1995, s 5(1).

[143] (Adopted 20 November 1989, entered into force 2 September 1990) 1577 UNTS 3.

[144] Chilren's Charter (n 16) art 23(1)–(3).

order was enforced against parents with the effect of separating them from their children, who were left behind in Nairobi. The decision invokes the Children's Charter's best interests provision,[145] which among other things led the court to find in the petitioners' favour.

The Women's Protocol protects refugee women in a general sense and also contains several provisions devoted to refugees. Article 4 on the right to life, integrity, and security of the person commits states parties to ensuring that 'women and men enjoy equal rights in terms of access to refugee status determination procedures and that women refugees are accorded the full protection and benefits guaranteed under international refugee law, including their own identity and other documents'.[146] Article 10 on the right to peace further commits states parties to ensuring the increased participation of women 'in the local, national, regional, continental and international decision making structures to ensure physical, psychological, social and legal protection of asylum seekers, refugees, returnees and displaced persons, in particular women'[147] and 'in all levels of the structures established for the management of camps and settlements for asylum seekers, refugees, returnees and displaced persons, in particular, women'.[148] Finally, with article 11 on the protection of women in armed conflict states parties undertake 'to protect asylum seeking women, refugees, returnees and internally displaced persons, against all forms of violence, rape and other forms of sexual exploitation, and to ensure that such acts are considered war crimes, genocide and/or crimes against humanity and that their perpetrators are brought to justice before a competent criminal jurisdiction'.[149] As a Protocol to the African Charter, the Women's Protocol is supervised by the African Commission, rather than by its own treaty monitoring body. The African Commission has yet to apply the Women's Protocol in a refugee context.

D. The Relationship between Regional Human Rights Law and the 1969 Convention

That human rights apply to refugees is settled law and in recent years scholars have elaborated the role of human rights in refugee protection on both the international[150] and regional planes.[151] Yet the precise relationships between human rights and refugee law, and particularly relationships of conflict, remain largely unexamined. For example, Naldi and D'Orsi note only that international refugee law has had to adapt to comply with international human rights law's often superior norms,[152]

[145] *Refugee Consortium of Kenya and NT v the Attorney General, the Cabinet Secretary Ministry of Interior and National Co-ordination and the Commissioner of Refugee Affairs*, Petition No 382 of 2014, High Court of Kenya (18 December 2015) para 50.

[146] Women's Protocol (n 15) art 4(2)(k).

[147] ibid art 10(2)(c).

[148] ibid art 10(2)(d).

[149] ibid art 11(3).

[150] See section B of this chapter.

[151] See, for example, Rachel Murray, *Human Rights in Africa: From the OAU to the African Union* (CUP 2004) chap 7; Gina Bekker, 'The Protection of Asylum Seekers and Refugees within the African Regional Human Rights System' (2013) 13 Afr Hum Rts LJ 1; Beyani (n 105); Naldi and D'Orsi (n 77).

[152] Naldi and D'Orsi (n 77) 56.

without explaining how refugee law has adapted. Similarly, Murray's treatment of the 'relationship between human rights and refugee law' is limited to a description of how the African Commission and the AU have addressed refugee issues.[153] An expert meeting on 'Complementarities between International Refugee Law, International Criminal Law and International Human Rights Law' tackled these relationships thematically but did not address specific norm conflicts, beyond implying that these should be addressed in accordance with the International Law Commission (ILC) approach.[154]

The lack of specific relationship analysis is particularly surprising given recent academic[155] and practical[156] interest in the relationships between specific bodies of international law, such as human rights and humanitarian law.[157] International refugee law has not been exempted from this line of enquiry, but it has largely examined the regime's relationships with international humanitarian law, international human rights law, and international criminal law in a general[158] or thematic[159] sense; specific relationships between refugee law on the one hand and human rights law on the other, and relationships of conflict in particular, have gone largely unexplored in relation to both the international and regional planes.[160]

This gap is perhaps due to the fact that international norms of refugee and human rights law generally do not conflict. International human rights law in most cases provides more robust protection than international refugee law, and the 1951

[153] Murray (n 151) 185–86.

[154] UNHCR, 'Expert Meeting on Complementarities between International Refugee law, International Criminal Law and International Human Rights Law, Arusha, Tanzania, 11–13 April 2011' (2011) 23 IJRL 860, para 4.

[155] See, for example, Martti Koskenniemi and Päivi Leino, 'Fragmentation of International Law: Postmodern Anxieties?' (2002) 15 Leiden J of Intl L 553; Andreas Fischer-Lescano and Gunther Teubner, 'Regime-Collisions: The Vain Search for Legal Unity in the Fragmentation of Global Law' (2004) 25 Mich J Intl L 999; Anne van Aaken, 'Defragmentation of Public International Law Through Interpretation: A Methodological Proposal' (2009) 16 Indiana J of Global Leg Stud 483; Mads Andenas and Eirik Bjorge (eds), *A Farewell to Fragmentation: Reassertion and Convergence in International Law* (CUP 2015).

[156] International Law Commission, 'Fragmentation of International Law: Difficulties Arising From the Diversification and Expansion of International Law – Report of the Study Group of the International Law Commission' (13 April 2006) A/CN4/L682 (Fragmentation Report).

[157] See, for example, Michaela Hailbronner, 'Laws in Conflict: The Relationship Between Human Rights and International Humanitarian Law under the African Charter on Human and Peoples' Rights' (2016) 16 Afr Hum Rts LJ 339; Marko Milanovic, 'Norm Conflicts, International Humanitarian Law and Human Rights Law' in Orna Ben-Naftali (ed), *Human Rights and International Humanitarian Law, Collected Courses of the Academy of European Law*, vol XIX/1 (OUP 2010).

[158] See, for example, David James Cantor and Jean-François Durieux (eds), *Refuge from Inhumanity? War Refugees and International Humanitarian Law* (Brill 2014); Violeta Moreno-Lax, 'Systematising Systemic Integration: "War Refugees", Regime Relations, and a Proposal for a Cumulative Approach to International Commitments' (2014) 12 J Intl Crim Justice 907.

[159] See, for example, Idil Atak and James Simeon, 'Human Trafficking: Mapping the Legal Boundaries of International Refugee Law and Criminal Justice' (2014) 12 J Intl Crim Justice 1019; Valerie Oosterveld, 'Gender at the Intersection of International Refugee Law and International Criminal Law' (2014) 12 J Intl Crim Justice 953.

[160] Chetail (n 17) is a notable exception. He examines specific relationships of interpretation, but not specific relationships of conflict, as these do not arise on the international plane.

Convention makes plain that such higher standards should apply alongside it.[161] Hathaway explains that article 5 of the 1951 Convention

should be read as requiring governments to respect the array of important international human rights accords negotiated in recent years. These international human rights conventions generally regulate the treatment of all persons subject to a state's jurisdiction, and are therefore critical sources of enhanced protection for refugees. Art. 5 of the Refugee Convention makes clear that the drafters were aware that refugees would be protected by additional rights acquired under the terms of other international agreements, and that they specifically intended that this should be so.[162]

Based on his review of the 1951 Convention's *travaux préparatoires*, Hathaway explains further that article 5 applies to rights that pre-date the 1951 Convention, as well as to rights that accrued after its adoption.[163]

This apparently straightforward parallelism between the 1951 Convention and international human rights law's higher standards of treatment obfuscates several important relationship issues on the regional plane. The simultaneous applicability of the 1969 Convention and the African Charter to refugees in Africa raises two relationships of interpretation and two relationships of conflict. The relationships of interpretation relate to the 1969 Convention's and the African Charter's respective provisions on asylum,[164] as well as to the 1969 Convention's voluntary repatriation provision[165] and the Charter right to leave and return.[166] There are relationships of conflict between the 1969 Convention's prohibition of subversive activities[167] and the African Charter's freedoms of expression[168] and association,[169] as well as between the 1969 Convention's provision on settlement[170] and the Charter's freedom of movement guarantee.[171] These are analysed or resolved here in line with the ILC approach. This approach is detailed in the introductory chapter. It essentially views articulating the relationship between legal instruments as a contextual process of treaty interpretation, supplemented by relevant interpretive maxims when interpretation does not yield a harmonized result.

The propriety of the ILC approach in this context is confirmed by a rare reference to specific norm conflicts between refugee law on the one hand and human rights law on the other, made by the African Commission in *Curtis Francis Doebbler v Sudan*. The complainant raised the issue, as recounted in the decision:

The Complainant argues that since the African Charter is a treaty that is *later in time*, than either the UN Refugees Convention, or the African refugees convention, the general principle of international law to be applied to resolve any conflict between treaties is that the latter treaty prevails over the former treaty that are not compatible. The Complainant relies on

[161] 1951 Convention (n 1) art 5, which provides: 'Nothing in this Convention shall be deemed to impair any rights and benefits granted by a Contracting State to refugees apart from this Convention'.

[162] (n 2) 110.

[163] ibid.

[164] 1969 Convention (n 4) art II(1) and African Charter (n 3) art 12(3).

[165] 1969 Convention (n 4) art V(1).

[166] African Charter (n 3) art 12(2).

[167] 1969 Convention (n 4) art III.

[168] African Charter (n 3) art 9(2).

[169] ibid art 10(1).

[170] 1969 Convention (n 4) art II(6).

[171] African Charter (n 3) art 12(1).

Article 30(3) of the Vienna Convention on the Law of Treaties, which states that 'the earlier treaty applies only to the extent that its provisions are compatible with those of the latter treaty.' He argues that by applying this principle, any provisions of the UN refugees convention that are incompatible with either the African refugee convention or the Charter must be deemed to be overridden by these latter two instruments.[172]

The African Commission, however, rejected the complainant's reliance on *lex posterior*—which does not usually apply unless the parties to the treaties under consideration are the same[173]—in favour of the ILC-sanctioned approach, which prioritizes a harmonizing interpretation. Though it did not mention the ILC specifically, the African Commission's strong presumption against normative conflict suggests ILC influence:

> The Commission wishes to state that it does not find any conflict or incompatibility between the African Charter and the two refugees' convention, or between the UN and the OAU refugees conventions. The 1969 OAU Convention stipulates that it is a complement to the 1951 UN Refugees Convention. Paragraph 9 of its preamble recognises the 1951 UN Convention and the 1967 Protocol as the basic and universal instruments relating to the status of refugees. Article VIII of the OAU Convention enjoins Member States to cooperate with the UNHCR, and states further that the OAU Convention is a regional complement to the 1951 UN Convention. In that respect the Commission shall read the provisions of the three instruments as complementing each other. The Complainant's argument that the provisions of the latter convention prevail over the former do not in any way affect the interpretation the Commission will give to the applicable provisions, should it be necessary to do so under this communication. This is because the provisions are at most complementary to each other and not mutually exclusive.[174]

Following this lead, the ILC approach is applied here, in the first instance to relationships of interpretation.

1. Relationships of interpretation

(a) *Asylum*

The 1969 Convention and African Charter provisions on asylum are discussed in Chapter 3 and in section C. The latter instrument gives every individual 'the right, when persecuted, to seek and obtain asylum in other countries in accordance with the law of those countries and international conventions'.[175] The former exhorts member states to 'use their best endeavours consistent with their respective legislations to receive refugees and to secure the settlement of those refugees who, for

[172] *Doebbler* (n 121) para 124.

[173] International Law Commission, 'Conclusions of the Work of the Study Group on the Fragmentation of International Law: Difficulties Arising from the Diversification and Expansion of International Law' (2006) 2 UNYBILC 175 (ILC) para 25.

[174] *Doebbler* (n 121) paras 125–26; this reasoning also supports the argument in favour of article I(2) refugees' entitlement to 1951 Convention rights, which is advanced in Chapter 4.

[175] African Charter (n 3) art 12(3).

well-founded reasons, are unable or unwilling to return to their country of origin or nationality'.[176]

The reference to international conventions in the African Charter's provision on asylum makes plain that it must be interpreted in light of international law, including the 1969 Convention. States' obligation under the 1969 Convention is one of means, not of result. Thus when analysed together, the outcome is the same as when each instrument is interpreted in isolation: there is no individual right to asylum in Africa, however states must do their utmost to provide asylum. Moreover, interpreting the African Charter in light of the 1969 Convention goes some way to remedying the issue identified in section C: that the African Charter seems to limit the right of asylum to individuals who have been 'persecuted'. Under the 1969 Convention, states must 'use their best endeavours' to grant asylum to all refugees 'who, for well-founded reasons, are unable or unwilling to return to their country'.[177] Such 'well-founded reasons' presumably include both persecution as well as 'external aggression, occupation, foreign domination or events seriously disturbing public order'.[178]

(b) The right to return and voluntary repatriation

Article 12(2) of the African Charter gives every individual the 'right to leave any country including his own, and to return to his country'. The 1969 Convention speaks of return in the refugee context, providing that the 'essentially voluntary character of repatriation shall be respected in all cases and no refugee shall be repatriated against his will'.[179] It then goes on to provide for the modalities of such voluntary repatriation.[180] Extrapolating from *John D Ouko v Kenya* (*Ouko*),[181] Beyani insists on the importance of interpreting article 12(2) of the African Charter in light of the 1969 Convention's provisions on voluntary repatriation.

In *Ouko*, the African Commission found that the persecution the claimant experienced in Kenya and during his subsequent exile in Uganda and the DRC violated his Charter rights to leave and to return, among others.[182] The African Commission also urged Kenya to facilitate Ouko's safe return.[183] According to Beyani, such return cannot be understood in isolation; rather, it must be viewed in light of the 1969 Convention's article V on voluntary repatriation. Beyani explains that voluntary repatriation is normally implemented through tripartite agreements between the country of origin, the host state, and the Office of the United Nations High Commissioner for Refugees (UNHCR)[184] and argues that, following *Ouko*, 'repatriation agreements which do not satisfy the conditions stipulated in' article V of the

[176] 1969 Convention (n 4) art II(1). [177] ibid. [178] ibid art I(2).
[179] ibid art V(1). [180] ibid arts V(2)–(5).
[181] *John D Ouko v Kenya* comm no 232/99, 14th Annual Activity Report of the AfCm HPR (2000).
[182] ibid para 31; see Chapter 7, section B.3.b.
[183] ibid; Beyani misstates the African Commission's holding, recounting that it 'further determined that the State of origin has a duty to facilitate safe return' (Beyani (n 105) 43), while in fact, the African Commission only 'urged' Kenya to facilitate the claimant's return.
[184] See Chapter 3, section C.3.

1969 Convention may 'be challenged as a breach of the duty to ensure safe return under Article 12 of the African Charter'.[185]

Chetail made the same argument in the international context. Further to the Human Rights Committee view that 'the right of a person to enter his or her own country ... includes ... the right to return after having left one's own country' which 'is of the utmost importance for refugees seeking voluntary repatriation',[186] Chetail argues that the right 'to return proves to be crucial for ensuring both the voluntary nature of repatriation and the correlative obligation of states of origin to admit their nationals'.[187]

2. Relationships of conflict

(a) Political rights and the prohibition of subversive activities

Hathaway explains that the 1969 Convention purports 'to deny some forms of political free speech as the cost of enhanced basic protection rights'.[188] He is referring to the 1969 Convention's article III, titled the 'Prohibition of Subversive Activities'. In its first paragraph, it exhorts every refugee to 'abstain from any subversive activities against any Member State of the OAU' and goes on in paragraph 2 to call on signatory states to 'prohibit refugees residing in their respective territories from attacking any State Member of the OAU, by any activity likely to cause tension between Member States, and in particular by use of arms, through the press, or by radio'. As discussed in Chapters 2 and 3, the prohibition of subversive activities was the result of member state concern that refugee activists operating on their territories would undermine relations among newly independent African states.[189]

The prohibition of subversive activities regularly plays out in practice, though restrictions are not necessarily explicitly linked to article III. For example, in a communication the African Commission ultimately deemed inadmissible, Mauritanian refugees complained that their freedoms of expression and assembly had been violated when the town of Podor in Senegal banned their planned demonstration.[190] Refugees have been expelled from Zimbabwe for merely criticizing the government, and Tanzania at one time prohibited meetings of more than five refugees.[191] According to Mandal, 'there is evidence that some OAU States have adopted a rather sweeping approach to Article III, interpreting it as prohibiting any political activity with respect to the refugee's country of origin, or indeed any political activity whatsoever'.[192]

[185] Beyani (n 105) 43. See, however, n 183 above; Beyani's characterization of the African Commission's holding as a 'duty', when in fact it merely 'urged' Kenya to facilitate Ouko's return to Kenya, might mean that his argument is somewhat overstated.

[186] HRC 'General Comment No 27: Freedom of Movement' (2 November 1999) para 19.

[187] Chetail (n 17) 47.

[188] Hathaway (n 2) 119.

[189] See Chapter 2, section D and Chapter 3, section C.4.

[190] *Mouvement des réfugiés mauritaniens au Sénégal pour la defense des droits de l'homme v Sénégal* comm no 254/02, sixteenth Annual Activity Report of the Af Cm HPR (2003).

[191] Ruma Mandal, 'Political Rights of Refugees' (2003) UNHCR Legal and Protection Policy Research Series <http://www.refworld.org/pdfid/3fe820794.pdf> accessed 12 January 2015, 20–21.

[192] ibid 2.

It must be determined whether the prohibition of subversive activities conflicts with the African Charter guarantees of expression, association, and assembly.[193] Each of these features a clawback clause. Every individual has the right to 'express and disseminate his opinions *within the law*',[194] to 'free association *provided that he abides by the law*',[195] and to 'assemble freely with others' subject to 'necessary restrictions provided for by law, in particular those enacted in the interest of national security, the safety, health, ethics and rights and freedoms of others'.[196] These restrictions on the freedoms of expression, association, and assembly make the rights in question contingent upon domestic laws. However, as explained in section C, the African Commission interprets clawback clauses as limiting rights only insofar as the relevant domestic law complies with international human rights standards,[197] and these international standards protect expression, association, and assembly robustly. The ICCPR protects expression subject only to such restrictions as are necessary to protect the 'rights or reputations of others' and for 'the protection of national security or of public order (*ordre public*), or of public health or morals'.[198] Similarly, the rights of association and peaceful assembly may only be limited insofar as is 'necessary in a democratic society in the interests of national security or public safety, public order (*ordre public*), the protection of public health or morals or the protection of the rights and freedoms of others'.[199]

Also relevant to the analysis is article 23(2) of the African Charter, which provides,

> For the purpose of strengthening peace, solidarity and friendly relations, State Parties to the present Charter shall ensure that: (a) any individual enjoying the right of asylum under Article 12 . . . shall not engage in subversive activities against his country of origin or any other State Party to the present Charter; (b) their territories shall not be used as bases for subversive or terrorist activities against the people of any other State Party to the present Charter.[200]

The African Commission has never engaged substantively with this provision,[201] so the meaning of 'subversive activities' is as unclear in the Charter as it is under the 1969 Convention.[202] What is clear is that the Charter's article 23(2) prohibition of subversive activities 'has to be compatible with the lawful restrictions provided in the other relevant provisions (Arts. 8 to 11 of the African Charter)',[203] and as explained earlier in this section, such lawful restrictions flow from the ICCPR.[204]

The question thus becomes whether the 1969 Convention's prohibition of subversive activities can be reconciled with the permissible limitations on the Charter freedoms of expression, association, and assembly, where the allowable limitations are those in the ICCPR. It is difficult to answer this question with any certainty,

[193] For related analysis of a similar issue on the international plane, considering the duty owed by a host state to the country of origin in relation to hostile activities undertaken by exiled dissidents, see Steven Corliss, 'Asylum State Responsibility for the Hostile Acts of Foreign Exiles' (1990) 2 IJRL 181.

[194] African Charter (n 3) art 9(2) (emphasis added).

[195] ibid art 10(1) (emphasis added).

[196] ibid art 11.

[197] *Media Rights Agenda* (n 63) para 66.

[198] ICCPR (n 30) art 19.

[199] ibid arts 21–22.

[200] African Charter (n 3) art 23(2).

[201] Bekker (n 151) 17.

[202] See Chapter 3, section C.4.

[203] Chetail (n 17) n 143.

[204] Moreover, article 23(2) is open to challenge as it purports to limit rights on the basis of refugee status, which is arguably prohibited by the Charter's article 2 accessory non-discrimination provision.

because the precise meanings of 'subversive activities' and 'any activity likely to cause tension between Member States' have never been clarified by a court. It is likely, however, that article III of the 1969 Convention purports to restrict refugees' political rights beyond the ICCPR limitations on expression, association, and assembly. The prohibition of subversive activities begins by noting that every refugee 'has duties to the country in which he finds himself, which require in particular that he conforms with its laws and regulations as well as with measures taken for the maintenance of public order'. That article III mentions public order and then goes on to explicitly prohibit 'subversive activities' and 'any activity likely to cause tension between Member States' suggests that the drafters intended that article III should prohibit political activities lesser than those that rise to the level of threatening public order.

There is some commentary on the relationship between the 1969 Convention's prohibition of subversive activities and political rights under the African Charter. Writing before *Media Rights Agenda* clarified how the Charter's imprecise clawback clauses should be understood, the Lawyers Committee for Human Rights found that article III of the 1969 Convention did not impugn the Charter guarantees of expression and association,[205] because these may be limited 'within the law'. The Lawyers Committee did, however, find the prohibition of subversive activities in clear violation of the ICCPR guarantees of expression and association.[206] Hathaway concluded the same, finding that the 1969 Convention's 'sweeping prohibition on political activities cannot be reconciled to duties under the Covenant on Civil and Political Rights'.[207] The *Media Rights Agenda* approach to clawback clauses—which requires that any limitations on the Charter guarantees of expression and association comply with the limitations permissible under the ICCPR—suggests that today, the African Charter is similarly violated.

The conclusion reached by the Lawyers Committee and by Hathaway, however, ignores the ILC exhortation to seek a harmonizing interpretation, which came after the Lawyers Committee and Hathaway works were published. Such a harmonizing interpretation can be achieved by narrowly construing the 1969 Convention and Charter subversion prohibitions, such that they would not catch the vast majority of refugees' political activity, thereby limiting genuine norm conflicts to the rare instances in which refugee political activity is truly 'subversive'. Indeed, this is Chetail's approach to the issue. He argues that 'as any exception to a right (ie, freedoms of expression, of association and of peaceful assembly), the very notion of "subversive activities" must be interpreted restrictively and must not impair the essence of the rights in question'.[208] This was also the result reached in a South African analysis of the issue.[209]

[205] The Lawyers Committee did not consider that the prohibition of subversive activities might also impugn freedom of assembly.

[206] Lawyers Committee for Human Rights, *African Exodus: Refugee Crisis, Human Rights and the 1969 OAU Convention* (Lawyers Committee for Human Rights 1995) 93.

[207] Hathaway (n 2) 119, n 177.

[208] Chetail (n 17) n 143.

[209] Alison Vadachalam, 'Does the 1969 OAU Convention Governing the Specific Aspects of Refugee Problems in Africa Article III Provision Prohibiting "Subversive Activities" Unjustifiably Limit the Freedom of Expression of a Refugee?: A South African Answer' (2014) University of Cape Town

Such a narrow construction of the 1969 Convention and Charter subversion prohibitions also finds support in the principle of systemic integration,[210] pursuant to which 'international obligations are interpreted by reference to their normative environment'.[211] This environment includes norms such as the African Commission's Principles on Freedom of Expression in Africa. The Principles affirm freedom of expression as 'a fundamental and inalienable human right and an indispensable component of democracy'[212] and provide that any restrictions on freedom of expression must 'serve a legitimate interest and be necessary in a democratic society'.[213]

In instances in which truly 'subversive' political activity creates genuine norm conflicts, these must be resolved by way of *lex specialis* or *lex posterior*. However, as discussed in Chapter 1, these maxims are not of absolute validity and cannot therefore be applied mechanically. According to the ILC, whether 'a rule's speciality or generality should be decisive, or whether priority should be given to the earlier or to the later rule' depends on factors such as 'the will of the parties, the nature of the instruments and their object and purpose as well as what would be a reasonable way to apply them with minimal disturbance to the operation of the legal system'.[214] It could be argued that the 1969 Convention is the *lex specialis* regarding refugees' political rights, with the result that article III of the 1969 Convention trumps the African Charter protections of expression, association, and assembly. However, such a mechanistic application of *lex specialis* ignores the importance of teleological interpretation in human rights contexts,[215] as well as the ILC's caution that *lex specialis* cannot be invoked to deprive third parties of rights guaranteed by the more general law.[216] These considerations suggests that *lex posterior* is the appropriate maxim. Pursuant to *lex posterior*, the earlier-in-time article III prohibition of subversive activities must yield to the later-in-time Charter protections of expression, association, and assembly. Thus refugees' political activity must be permitted unless it is caught by the ICCPR's limitation clauses. While this approach likely permits more refugee political activity than the drafters of the 1969 Convention intended, it reflects the current normative environment, which is different than that which existed in the years leading up to 1969.

(b) Freedom of movement

Article II(6) of the 1969 Convention provides that 'for reasons of security, countries of asylum shall, as far as possible, settle refugees at a reasonable distance from the frontier of their country of origin'.[217] Similarly, article 10(2) of the Women's

Refugee Rights Unit Working Paper No 1 <http://www.refugeerights.uct.ac.za/usr/refugee/Working_papers/Working_Paper_1_of_2014.pdf> accessed 12 January 2015.

210 Vienna Convention on the Law of Treaties (adopted 23 May 1969, entered into force 27 January 1980) 1155 UNTS 331, art 31(3)(c).

211 Fragmentation Report (n 156) para 413.

212 Adopted at the 32nd Ordinary Session (17–23 October 2002) art I(1).

213 ibid art II(2).

214 Fragmentation Report (n 156) paras 410–11.

215 ibid paras 130–31.

216 ILC (n 173) para 10.

217 During drafting of the 1969 Convention, 50 kilometres was raised as being a 'reasonable distance'; however, the drafters ultimately decided not to specify a particular distance, including because

Protocol provides that states 'shall take all appropriate measures to ensure the increased participation of women ... in ... structures established for the management of camps and settlements for asylum seekers, refugees, returnees and displaced persons'. These mentions of organized settlement are at least suggestive of a deprivation of refugees' freedom of movement and residence. Furthermore, in practice African states regularly confine refugees to camps.[218] The refugee laws of major refugee hosting states Ethiopia, Kenya, and Uganda allow for the settlement of refugees in camps, and four of the biggest refugee camps in the world—Bidi Bidi in Uganda, Dadaab and Kakuma in Kenya, and Dollo Ado in Ethiopia—are in Africa. Freedom of movement and residence is, however, guaranteed by the African Charter. It provides that 'every individual shall have the right to freedom of movement and residence within the borders of a State *provided he abides by the law*'.[219] This clawback clause has been interpreted by the African Commission in a way that suggests that permissible limitations cannot be based on the violation of an arbitrary or discriminatory law.[220]

A similar apparent conflict, between article II(6) of the 1969 Convention and the 1951 Convention's freedom of movement provision, was addressed in Chapter 4,[221] and there a harmonizing interpretation was found. The same result applies in this context. As discussed in Chapter 4, article II(6) does not require states to settle refugees; the provision merely states that if states do so—which presumably would be in extenuating circumstances—it should be at a reasonable distance from the frontier with the country of origin, in order to ensure refugees' safety. The context and object and purpose of the 1969 Convention, and the wider normative environment, affirm this interpretation of settlement as an exceptional measure,[222] as does the Charter's freedom of movement guarantee. When exceptional circumstances warrant refugee settlement—such as when 1.5 million Rwandan refugees arrived in the DRC in 1994—laws, orders, or regulations detailing the modalities of this could be promulgated. Provided such laws, orders, or regulations were neither arbitrary nor discriminatory and were enacted considering the exceptional circumstances at hand, refugee settlement would be within the permissible limitations on article 12(1) of the African Charter.

The relationship between freedom of movement and encampment recently played out in a line of four Kenyan cases. The first stemmed from a 2012 policy halting reception and registration in urban centres, ordering all refugees to move to camps

this would have not made sense in the context of small states such as Gambia, Lesotho, and Swaziland (UNHCR Representative Cosmas Chanda, Third AU Humanitarian Law and Policy Training, Livingstone, Zambia, 21 March 2018).

218 See, generally, Lucy Hovil and Moses C Okello, 'The Right to Freedom of Movement for Refugees in Uganda' in David Hollenbach (ed), *Refugee Rights: Ethics, Advocacy and Africa* (Georgetown University Press 2008) 78.

219 African Charter (n 3) art 12(1) (emphasis added).

220 *Malawi African Association and Others v Mauritania* comm nos 54/91, 61/91, 98/93, 164/97 to 196/97 and 210/98, 13th Annual Activity Report of the Af Cm HPR (2000) para 126.

221 See section D.2.a.

222 See Chapter 4, section D.2.a.

and directing UNHCR and others to cease providing services in urban areas.[223] The NGO Kituo Cha Sheria and several individual petitioners challenged the policy, arguing inter alia that it violated Kenya's constitutional free movement guarantee and its international obligations under the 1951 Convention and the ICCPR.[224] The court introduced, inter alia, the 1969 Convention and the African Charter.[225] In its reasoning, the court held that while article 39 of Kenya's constitution limits 'the right to enter, remain in and reside anywhere in Kenya' to citizens, this guarantee must be read together with international free movement provisions: article 26 of the 1951 Convention, article 12 of the ICCPR, and article 12 of the African Charter, which are guaranteed to refugees by section 16 of Kenya's Refugees Act, 2006.[226] As a result, any limitation on refugees' movement must comply with article 24 of Kenya's constitution, which delineates permissible limitations on constitutional rights. Ultimately, the court held that the encampment violated article 24, finding it 'a threat to ... [refugees'] right to movement enshrined in Article 26 of the 1951 Convention as read with section 16 of the [Refugees] Act'.[227]

Refugees' freedom of movement in Kenya arose again in a case decided in 2014 and relating in part to a March 2014 government press statement ordering all refugees to return immediately to Kakuma or Dadaab. The ten refugee petitioners alleged among other things that the order violated their right to freedom from discrimination as well as their rights to property and to work under the African Charter; the petitioners did not raise freedom of movement under the African Charter but they did raise it in relation to the Constitution. The court found in favour of the government not because the order was constitutional or compliant with Kenya's international obligations, but because the 'petitioners did not demonstrate by way [of] affidavit evidence how the Directive affects their individual circumstances to the extent that their fundamental rights and freedoms are violated'.[228] This suggests that had the petitioners' case been more persuasively argued, they would have prevailed.

Refugees' freedom of movement arose for the third time in a 2015 case addressing the Security Laws (Amendment) Act of 2014, which amended twenty-two legislative acts in response to terrorist attacks in Kenya. The changes included the addition of section 14(c) to The Refugees Act, 2006, preventing a refugee from leaving his or her designated camp without the permission of a camp officer.[229] Reversing its position in *Kituo Cha Sheria*, the court upheld section 14(c) based on the limitation of Kenya's constitutional freedom of movement guarantee to citizens.[230] The decision considered neither the *Kituo Cha Sheria* precedent nor Kenya's international

[223] *Kituo Cha Sheria, Abebe Dadi Tully, Ahmed Bashir Mohamed, Eugene Bwimana, Dachassa Galdi Nure, Muhima Sebihendo Joh, Mbuzukongire Nzabona and Said Abdullahi Abukar v the Attorney General*, Petition Nos 19 and 115 of 2013, High Court of Kenya (26 July 2013) para 48.

[224] ibid para 12. [225] ibid paras 37–38. [226] ibid paras 50–57.

[227] ibid para 59.

[228] *Samow Mumin Mohamed and Others v Cabinet Secretary, Minister of Interior Security and Coordination and others*, Petition No 206 of 2011, High Court of Kenya (30 June 2014) para 27.

[229] Security Laws (Amendment) Act, No 19 of 2014 (Kenya) s 47.

[230] *Coalition for Reform and Democracy, Kenya National Commission on Human Rights and Samuel Njuguna Ng'ang'a v Republic of Kenya and Attorney General*, Petition Nos 628 and 630 of 2014 and Petition No 12 of 2015, High Court of Kenya (23 February 2015) paras 394–403.

obligations, other than article 2 of the 1951 Convention and article 3 of the 1969 Convention on refugee duties. The court did, however, point out that section 14(c) applies only to refugees residing in the designated camps, perhaps to distinguish the facts at bar from the more widespread and blanket restriction at issue in *Kituo Cha Sheria*.[231] Moreover, the decision in *Kituo Cha Sheria* was upheld on appeal in 2017.[232] Thus the most recent and the highest Kenyan judicial authority on refugees' freedom of movement affirms the general conclusion reached above: refugees in Africa should generally enjoy freedom of movement.

While this appellate decision suggests that the Kenyan refugee camps are unlawful, their ongoing existence exemplifies the wide gulf between the law and practice of refugee protection in Africa. A principal challenge for refugee advocates is to work to narrow this gulf. There is positive news from Ethiopia in this regard. The country began implementing its Out of Camp policy in 2010. The policy allows some refugees from Eritrea with a sponsor to live in urban areas, though without access to waged labour.[233] At the UN-sponsored Leaders' Summit on Refugees, held in September 2016, Ethiopia pledged to expand its Out of Camp policy to benefit a further 75,000 refugees, which represents about ten per cent of Ethiopia's refugee population.[234]

E. Conclusions

This chapter began by tracing the role of human rights law in refugee protection, situating the current moment as one in which both bodies of law have a role to play. Some scholars disagree about the extent of each body's role, with McAdam coming out on the side of the 1951 Convention,[235] Chetail favouring international human rights law,[236] and Hathaway sitting somewhere in between.[237] The approach adopted here is the middle and generally accepted one, in which standards of treatment during all phases of displacement derive from both the 1951 Convention and international and regional human rights law.

This chapter has sketched this latter body of law, highlighted the aspects of it that contribute to non-refoulement and asylum and rights during displacement, and articulated the relationships of interpretation—regarding asylum and regarding the right to return and voluntary repatriation—and of conflict—regarding the prohibition of subversive activities and political rights and regarding freedom of movement—between regional refugee law on the one hand and regional human

[231] ibid para 400. [232] *Attorney General v Kituo Cha Sheria & 7 Others* [2017] eKLR.

[233] Norwegian Refugee Council and Samuel Hall, 'Living Out of Camp: Alternative to Camp-Based Assistance for Eritrean Refugees in Ethiopia' (2014) <http://samuelhall.org/wp-content/uploads/2014/05/Living-Out-of-Camp-Alternative-to-Camp-based-Assistance-in-Ethiopia.pdf> accessed 25 April 2017, 16.

[234] UN, 'Summary Overview Document: Leaders' Summit on Refugees' (2016) <https://refugeesmigrants.un.org/sites/default/files/public_summary_document_refugee_summit_final_11-11-2016.pdf> accessed 25 April 2017.

[235] (n 23) chap 6. [236] (n 17). [237] (n 2) chap 2.

rights law on the other. Together, this has established how regional human rights law contributes to refugee protection in Africa, while also making sense of the legal issues that arise from these two sometimes divergent bodies of law applying to the same population.

However, these issues are largely theoretical, while the 'divergence between the theory and the reality of international human rights law is strikingly apparent',[238] with some questioning whether international human rights law even makes a difference.[239] Such questions are especially salient in Africa, where Viljoen and Louw found a modest record of state compliance with African Commission recommendations.[240] This and other implementation issues will be addressed in Part II.

This marks the end of Part I on the treaty framework for refugee protection in Africa. Part II is devoted to the institutional architecture supportive of this framework, with Chapter 6 focusing on the OAU and the AU, and the final Part II chapter focusing on the roles of African Commission and the African human rights courts in refugee protection.

[238] James C Hathaway, 'Reconceiving Refugee Law as Human Rights Protection' (1991) 4 JRS 113, 113.

[239] See, for example, Oona A Hathaway, 'Do Human Rights Treaties Make a Difference?' (2002) 111 Yale LJ 1935; Eric Posner, 'The Case Against Human Rights' (*The Guardian*, 4 December 2014) <https://www.theguardian.com/news/2014/dec/04/-sp-case-against-human-rights> accessed 6 December 2017.

[240] Frans Viljoen and Lirette Louw, 'State Compliance with the Recommendations of the African Commission on Human and Peoples' Rights 1994–2004' (2007) 101 AJIL 1.

PART II

THE INSTITUTIONAL ARCHITECTURE

6

The Organization of African Unity and the African Union

A. Introduction

The Organization of African Unity Convention Governing the Specific Aspects of Refugee Problems in Africa (1969 Convention) was an Organization of African Unity (OAU) project, as described in Chapter 2. While the Convention's adoption was lauded, both the OAU and the African Union (AU) have been criticized for failing to create any self-sustaining institutional implementation mechanism such as a treaty body.[1] However, while the 1969 Convention has indeed not been operationalized in this sense, it has underpinned all OAU and AU efforts in favour of refugees, reinforcing diplomacy, advocacy, and policy.[2] In other words, the Convention has been implemented in a general sense by OAU and AU political organs.[3] These bodies have highlighted refugee issues through resolutions, decisions, and declarations;[4] the OAU's Secretary-General regularly reported on refugees to the OAU's

[1] See, for example, Medard RK Rwelamira, 'Some Reflections on the OAU Convention on Refugees: Some Pending Issues' (1983) 16 Comp & Intl LJ S Afr 155, 162; Joe Oloka-Onyango, 'Human Rights, the OAU Convention and the Refugee Crisis in Africa: Forty Years After Geneva' (1991) 3 IJRL 453, 459; Jacob van Garderen and Julie Ebenstein, 'Regional Developments: Africa' in Andreas Zimmermann (ed), *The 1951 Convention Relating to the Status of Refugees and its 1967 Protocol* (OUP 2011) 203; Frans Viljoen, *International Human Rights Law in Africa* (2nd edn, OUP 2012) 158.

[2] Interview with George Okoth-Obbo, Director, Africa Bureau, UNHCR, 20 June 2011, Geneva.

[3] Bahame Tom Mukirya Nyanduga, 'Refugee Protection Under the 1969 OAU Convention Governing the Specific Aspects of Refugee Problems in Africa' (2004) 47 German YB Intl L 85, 96.

[4] The OAU's Assembly of Heads of State and Government (OAHG) issued only a handful of resolutions and decisions relating to refugees: that relating to the drafting of the 1969 Convention, discussed in Chapter 2; a 1983 resolution on ICARA II (defined and described below); a 1995 resolution endorsing President Mobutu's proposal to host a World Conference on Refugees and Displaced Persons in what was then Zaire (the conference never eventuated); a 2001 decision marking the fiftieth anniversary of the 1951 Convention; and a decision on the report of the Secretary-General on the Situation of Refugees, Returnees and Displaced Persons, adopted at the OAHG's very last session in Durban in 2002. In addition, in 1994, on the occasion of the twenty-fifth anniversary of the adoption of the 1969 Convention, the OAHG adopted the Tunis Declaration (OAU (OAHG) 'Tunis Declaration on the 1969 Convention Governing the Specific Aspects of Refugee Problems in Africa' (OAU Tunis 1994) AHG/Decl 216). The OAU Council of Ministers, by contrast, adopted many refugee-related resolutions and decisions. Most of these served to take note of reports, or establish or direct particular bodies or initiatives, and are cited where relevant throughout this chapter, but several served the more general purpose of, among other things, highlighting refugee protection issues on the continent and/or calling on member states to ratify and implement the 1951 and 1969 Conventions.

Council of Ministers (OCM); and both the OAU and the AU have established refugee-related bodies, organized conferences focused on refugee issues, and addressed refugees within more general instruments and initiatives. Such engagement is the focus of this chapter.

Analysis in this regard is critical because accounts of AU engagement with refugee issues are few.[5] Similarly, evaluations of the OAU's refugee work are either out of date or focus on only one aspect of engagement.[6] Informed by these few secondary sources, primary archival and interview research conducted at the Office of the United Nations High Commissioner for Refugees (UNHCR) in Geneva in June 2011 and in Addis Ababa in January 2012, primary interview research conducted at the AU Commission in Addis Ababa in January 2012 and December 2016, and primary research using OAU and AU materials, this chapter consolidates knowledge of OAU and AU refugee engagement from the time of the continental organization's founding in 1963 up to 1 January 2018.[7]

The section following this introduction relates to OAU engagement with refugee issues subsequent to the adoption of the Convention in 1969, beginning with the OAU's refugee-related bodies.[8] Each is addressed in turn, beginning with the Commission of Ten (later of Fifteen, then of Twenty, and finally of all member states) on Refugee Problems in Africa (Commission). This is followed by the Bureau for the Placement and Education of African Refugees (BPEAR or the Bureau) and then the Coordinating Committee on Assistance to Refugees (CCAR). Select special refugee initiatives, in the form of conferences and summits, are then addressed, with specific attention devoted to the OAU's commemorations of significant anniversaries of the 1969 Convention.

Section C relates to the AU, beginning with an overview of its constituent organs. Among these, the Executive Council has engaged most frequently with refugee policy; its activities in this regard are therefore covered in a dedicated section. The AU's refugee-related bodies are then discussed, starting with the Specialized Technical Committee (STC) on Migration, Refugees and Internally Displaced Persons (STC on Migration, Refugees and IDPs). This is followed by discussions of the Permanent Representatives' Committee (PRC) Sub-Committee on Refugees, Returnees and

[5] See Ademola Abass and Dominique Mystris, 'The African Union Legal Framework for Protecting Asylum Seekers' in Ademola Abass and Francesca Ippolito (eds), *Regional Approaches to the Protection of Asylum Seekers: An International Legal Perspective* (Ashgate 2014), as well as an article on which this chapter draws: Marina Sharpe, 'Organization of African Unity and African Union Engagement with Refugee Protection: 1963–2011' (2013) 21 Afr J Intl Comp L 50.

[6] See Philip E Chartrand, 'The Organization of African Unity and African Refugees: A Progress Report' (1975) 137 World Aff 265; Rose D'Sa, 'The African Refugee Problem, Relevant International Conventions and Recent Activities of the Organization of African Unity' (1984) 31 NILR 378; Richard Greenfield, 'The OAU and Africa's Refugees' in Yassin El-Ayouty and I William Zartman (eds), *The OAU After Twenty Years* (Praeger 1984); Joe Oloka-Onyango, 'The Place and Role of the OAU Bureau for Refugees in the African Refugee Crisis' (1994) 6 IJRL 34; Rachel Murray, *Human Rights in Africa: From the OAU to the African Union* (CUP 2004) chap 7.

[7] As of 1 January 2018, the most recent Assembly and Executive Council decisions publicly available were from the twenty-eighth AU Summit held in January 2017. Decisions from the Executive Council's 31st Ordinary Session, held at the 29th AU Summit in July 2017, were obtained directly from the AU.

[8] For an overview of the OAU itself and of the drafting of the 1969 Convention, see Chapter 2.

Internally Displaced Persons in Africa (PRC Sub-Committee); the Coordinating Committee on Forced Displacement and Humanitarian Action (CCFDHA); and the Department of Political Affairs' Division of Humanitarian Affairs, Refugees and Displaced Persons (HARDP). The final sub-section within section C relates to AU initiatives that are not refugee specific but nevertheless devote some attention to, or impact upon, refugees. These are the Conference on Security, Stability, Development and Cooperation in Africa (CSSDCA); the Peace and Security Council (PSC); the Solemn Declaration on a Common African Defence and Security Policy and the related AU Non-Aggression and Common Defence Pact; the African Charter on Democracy, Elections and Governance; Agenda 2063, which envisions the continental free movement of persons; and, finally, the AU's recent major humanitarian initiatives: its Humanitarian Policy Framework (HPF) and the Common African Position on Humanitarian Effectiveness (CAP). Section D concludes and includes a discussion of ongoing AU reform efforts.

B. OAU Engagement with Refugee Issues: 1963 to 2001

The 1969 Convention clearly contemplates OAU involvement with refugees. 'In order to enable the Administrative Secretary-General of the ... [OAU] to make reports to the competent organs of the' OAU, article VII of the Convention requires that member states 'provide the Secretariat ... with information and statistical data requested concerning: (a) the condition of refugees; (b) the implementation' of the Convention and '(c) laws, regulations and decrees which are, or may hereafter be, in force relating to refugees'. In addition to this role for the Secretary-General, the OAU also created a number of dedicated refugee-related bodies. Each is addressed in turn.

1. The OAU's refugee-related bodies

(a) The Commission of Ten/Fifteen/Twenty/the Whole on Refugee Problems in Africa

Following the OCM's 1964 recommendation that the Commission become a permanent OAU body, discussed in Chapter 2, its work focused on drafting the regional instrument. Once the 1969 Convention was adopted, the Commission's work ceased. It was revived at the OCM's 19th Ordinary Session, held in Rabat, Morocco, in June 1972, when the OCM called on the OAU Secretariat to reconvene the Commission 'to consider the current situation of refugees in Africa and the necessary measures to be taken with a view to their assistance and voluntary repatriation and their resettlement'.[9]

[9] OAU (OCM), 'Resolution on the Bureau for the Placement and Education of African Refugees' (OAU Rabat 5–12 June 1972) CM/Res 266 (XIX) para 1.

The Commission duly reconvened in Addis Ababa in December 1972, producing a report that was adopted by the OCM at its 20th Ordinary Session in February 1973.[10] The resolution adopting the Commission's report was the first to officially refer to it as the 'Commission of Ten on Refugee Problems in Africa'.[11] Thereafter, the Commission began to meet annually and submit regular reports to the OCM on 'the situation of refugees, returnees and displaced persons in Africa, focusing on the contribution of the ... [OAU] in favour of those uprooted'.[12] The Commission thus became the main OAU policy-making organ on refugee matters, shaping the continental body's response to refugee issues.[13] Its activities included undertaking fact-finding missions, providing governments with advice, and the provision of emergency financial assistance to states in need.[14] Okoth-Obbo compares the Commission to UNHCR's Executive Committee (ExCom).[15]

In 1980 it was decided that the Commission's membership should rotate and be expanded to include fifteen states.[16] Initial members were Angola, Cameroon, Mali, Niger, Nigeria, Senegal, Sudan, Swaziland, Tanzania, Uganda, Zaire (now the Democratic Republic of the Congo), Zambia, Zimbabwe, and two further countries, to be selected by North African states.[17] In 1994 the Commission membership was further expanded to twenty states, whose tenure did not rotate.[18] These states were Algeria, Angola, Cameroon, Côte d'Ivoire, Egypt, Gabon, Kenya, Libya, Malawi, Mali, Mozambique, Niger, Nigeria, Senegal, Sudan, Uganda, Tanzania, Zaire, Zambia, and Zimbabwe.[19] Soon after its expansion to twenty states, the Commission's workings were formalized through the adoption of Rules of Procedure, which defined the functions of the Commission in almost exactly the same terms as had been used in 1964, when the Commission was first convened as an ad hoc body.[20] In 1998 the Commission was again enlarged, this time to include all OAU member states;[21] its Rules of Procedure were revised accordingly.

[10] OAU (OCM), 'Resolution on the Commission of Ten on Refugees' (OAU Addis Ababa 5–9 February 1973) CM/Res 296 (XX) preambular para 3.

[11] ibid preambular para 2.

[12] EM Ngung, 'The Role of Regional and Sub-Regional Organizations in Situations of Conflict or Displacement' (1999) 18 RSQ 97, 98.

[13] ibid.

[14] Monette Zard, 'African Union' in Matthew Gibney and Randall Hansen (eds), *Immigration and Asylum From 1900 to the Present* (ABC-CLIO 2005) 7.

[15] George Okoth-Obbo, 'The OAU/UNHCR Symposium on Refugees and Forced Population Displacements in Africa—A Review Article' [Special Issue Summer 1995] IJRL 274, 283.

[16] OAU (OCM), 'Resolution on the Situation of Refugees in Africa' (OAU Freetown 18–28 June 1980) CM/Res 814 (XXXV) para 5.

[17] Murray (n 6) 196.

[18] OAU (OCM), 'Resolution on Refugees, Returnees and Displaced Persons in Africa' (OAU Tunis 6–11 June 1994) CM/Res 1521 (LX) para 10.

[19] ibid.

[20] OAU (OCM), 'Rules of Procedure of the OAU Commission of Twenty on Refugees in Africa' (OAU Addis Ababa 23–27 February 1998) in accordance with CM/Res 388 (LXVII).

[21] OAU (OCM), 'Decision on the Report of the Commission of Twenty on the Situation of Refugees, Returnees and Displaced Persons in Africa' (OAU Addis Ababa 23–27 February 1998) CM/Res 388 (LXVII) para 13.

The Commission played an important role in shaping and communicating the OAU's approach to specific refugee situations.[22] Notably, it adopted the 1990 Khartoum Declaration on Africa's Refugee Crisis, which assessed national, subregional, regional, and international responses to refugees in Africa and recommended follow-up action to be taken by the OAU and the international community.[23] At its 64th Ordinary Session in 1996, the OCM adopted a 'Programme of Action' for the Commission. The activities proposed were grouped under four themes: the mobilization of resources; public sensitization; building the capacity of African states to manage emergency situations; and 'other activities', a deceptively simple heading for what was actually the massive task of implementing OCM and OAHG resolutions on refugees and displacement.[24]

Oloka-Onyango judged the Commission as ineffective, finding it 'constrained by its very composition and relationship to the OAU decision-making processes, which are ultimately politically controlled.... Thus the extent of the impact of the ... [Commission] is clearly limited by considerations of *Realpolitik*, as well as by the very real constraint of the "non-interference" clause that still holds considerable sway in Africa'.[25] The Commission nevertheless survived the OAU's transformation into the AU,[26] though it was renamed the PRC Sub-Committee, which is discussed in section C.[27]

(b) The Bureau for the Placement and Education of African Refugees

The BPEAR[28] was created on 1 March 1968 further to recommendation XI of the 1967 Conference on the Legal, Economic and Social Aspects of African Refugee Problems,[29] which is discussed later in this section, with the task of promoting the resettlement and employment of African refugees and collecting and disseminating information concerning educational, training, and employment opportunities for them.[30] The intention was that the Bureau would function as a continental academic and occupational placement system for refugees.[31] Its mandate, however, expanded in practice over time to include functioning as an information conduit to member states and the international community on the patterns, causes, and consequences of refugee movements in Africa, equipping refugees with resources to

[22] Oloka-Onyango (n 6) 39.

[23] OAU (Commission of Fifteen on Refugees), 'Khartoum Declaration on Africa's Refugee Crisis' (OAU Khartoum 22–24 September 1990) OAU Doc BR/COM/XV/5590.

[24] OAU (OCM), 'Programme of Action for the OAU Commission of Twenty on Refugees' (OAU Yaoundé 1–5 July 1996).

[25] Oloka-Onyango (n 6) 39. [26] Murray (n 6) 196. [27] See section C.3.b.

[28] For a detailed analysis of BPEAR's functions and effectiveness, see Oloka-Onyango (n 6); see, also, Louise W Holborn, *Refugees: A Problem of our Time—The Work of the United Nations High Commissioner for Refugees, 1951–1972*, vol I and II (Scarecrow Press 1974) 942–47; Murray (n 6) 197–200.

[29] Chartrand (n 6) 280; Chaloka Beyani, *Protection of the Right to Seek and Obtain Asylum Under the African Human Rights System* (Martinus Nijhoff 2013) 9.

[30] UNECA and others, 'Final Report of the Conference on the Legal, Economic and Social Aspects of the African Refugee Problems' December 1968, 115 (on file with the author).

[31] Holborn (n 28) 943.

assist them in coping with their displacement and eventual repatriation, mediating between host states and refugees regarding alleged violations of national law and working with UNHCR, voluntary agencies, and member states to further the objectives of the 1969 Convention.[32]

Initially, BPEAR undertook these tasks as an autonomous body. It was entirely independent of the OAU, funded by outside sources (principally UNHCR) and operated through a system of Bureau representatives, known as national correspondents, placed within the executives of OAU member states. A standing committee of UN agencies—namely UNHCR; the International Labour Organization; the Economic Commission for Africa (UNECA); the Educational, Scientific and Cultural Organization; and the Development Programme—advised it on operational matters and the Bureau received policy advice from a consultative board composed of the same agencies plus an OAU representative and non-governmental organization (NGO) observers.[33] In 1970, BPEAR's standing committee and consultative board merged and became known as the Bureau's coordinating committee.

In 1971 BPEAR was placed under the supervision of the OAU's Assistant Secretary-General for Political Affairs.[34] In 1974 the Bureau was further integrated into the OAU Secretariat pursuant to the recommendations of a Commission report, becoming part of the OAU Secretariat's political department both organizationally and financially.[35] The 1974 restructuring also enlarged BPEAR's mandate to include legal assistance to refugees and rural resettlement programmes, and gave the Bureau a formal role in assisting the Commission in the formulation of OAU refugee policy.[36]

Oloka-Onyango's extensive analysis of the BPEAR concluded that it had

> great difficulty in meeting the conditions of its establishing mandate, and effectively expanding that mandate to deal with the critical issues concerning African refugees presently. The problems of the Bureau for Refugees basically stem from two factors: first, the fashion in which it has conceptualized its role, which is also a function of the influence of the OAU over its programming. The second issue relates to the question of finances.[37]

Others have echoed his view. Nobel, for example, explains that while 'potentially helpful, the BPEAR has been a disappointment due to what appears to be incompetence and mismanagement. A critical analysis has identified problems in the lack of efficient correspondents in member states, lack of economic support, and perhaps, weaknesses inherent in the OAU system itself'.[38] Such generalized problems translated into quite specific failures. For example, the Bureau started but ultimately abandoned a project on domestic implementation of the 1969 Convention.[39]

32 Oloka-Onyango (n 6) 35. 33 UNECA (n 30) 115; Holborn (n 28) 943.

34 OAU (OCM), 'Resolution on the Bureau for the Placement and Education of African Refugees' (OAU Addis Ababa 15–19 June 1971) CM/Res 244 (XVII) para 1(a).

35 OAU (OCM), 'Resolution on the OAU Bureau for the Placement and Education of African Refugees' (OAU Mogadishu 6–11 June 1974) CM/Res 346 (XXIII) para 1.

36 ibid. 37 Oloka-Onyango (n 6) 47.

38 Peter Nobel, 'Refugees, Law, and Development in Africa' (1982) 3 Mich YB Intl L Stud 255, 258.

39 Oloka-Onyango (n 6) 49.

Furthermore, Chartrand observed a disjuncture between the efforts of and investment in the Bureau on the one hand, and the number of refugees actually placed in employment or education on the other.[40]

In the early nineties BPEAR was renamed the Bureau for Refugees, Displaced Persons and Humanitarian Assistance.[41] This further change did not solve its problems: 'conceptually, the successive changes in the nomenclature of the bureau may reflect a metamorphosing mandate, and are in part reflective of the role that the bureau was supposed to play in the ever-changing refugee situation on the continent. However, in practical terms the operations of the office have remained largely the same since its inception'.[42] Thus, not surprisingly, the transition from the OAU to the AU marked the Bureau's demise.[43] Its coordinating committee did, however, survive, but under another name, as explained in the next sub-section.

(c) The Coordinating Committee on Assistance to Refugees

As mentioned above, the standing committee and consultative board formed to advise BPEAR merged in 1970 to form the Bureau's coordinating committee.[44] In 1974 as part of the BPEAR restructuring described earlier in this section, the coordinating committee's membership was expanded to include representatives from the Executive Secretariat of the OAU's Liberation Committee and the Chairman of the Annual Conference of Liberation Movements, and its role was formalized.[45] Then, in 1981, the coordinating committee was renamed the CCAR and given a specific mandate to assist the OAU's Secretary-General with the organization of the International Conference on Assistance to Refugees in Africa (ICARA), which is described later in this section. In spite of this specific mandate, the CCAR also evolved into an advisory committee to the Commission and a liaison body between BPEAR and the outside agencies that provided it with organizational support and funding.[46]

According to Oloka-Onyango, the CCAR was not as successful as it might have been in fulfilling its broader mandate. He explains that

> even in the admission of members of the CCAR, it is clear that the Committee has not done as much as it could have, particularly in terms of meeting financial commitments made to Bureau programmes. At present, this body is largely inactive, in part because of the relative malaise of the Bureau, but also because the members of the committee do not fully believe in its effectiveness, or in the capacity of the OAU to tackle the refugee question in a forthright, non-political fashion.[47]

Despite these issues, the CCAR, like the Commission, survived the transition to the AU, becoming the Coordinating Committee on Assistance and Protection to Refugees, Returnees and Internally Displaced Persons (CCAPRRI). It is now known as the CCFDHA. Its role is described in section C.

[40] (n 6) 280. [41] Murray (n 6) 197.

[42] Lawyers Committee for Human Rights, *African Exodus: Refugee Crisis, Human Rights and the 1969 OAU Convention* (Lawyers Committee for Human Rights 1995) 140.

[43] Murray (n 6) 200. [44] Holborn (n 28) 943. [45] OAU (n 35) para 1.

[46] Oloka-Onyango (n 6) 39. [47] ibid 40.

2. Special refugee initiatives

In addition to establishing bodies dedicated to refugees, the OAU convened or co-convened several major conferences and meetings devoted to aspects of refugee protection in Africa. Twelve years after the 1967 Addis Ababa conference discussed in Chapter 2,[48] the OAU co-hosted its next significant gathering devoted to refugees: the Pan-African Conference on the African Refugee Problem, held in Arusha, Tanzania, on 7–17 May 1979.[49] While the conference was hosted by the OAU and UNHCR, with assistance from UNECA, it was an initiative of the All African Conference of Churches. The umbrella organization

> sensed that a new refugee conference was needed primarily to document the sufferings and problems of large numbers of refugees before their existence could be denied completely by many political leaders of independent Africa. Equally important was the task of discussing these difficulties and possible solutions with the international community, the intergovernmental organizations, the nongovernmental organizations, and the voluntary agencies.[50]

The conference was attended at ministerial level by thirty-eight OAU member states, as well as by twenty non-African countries, five officially recognized liberation movements, sixteen intergovernmental and regional organizations and thirty-seven NGOs.[51] It adopted a range of recommendations, which can be divided into two categories: legal and protection issues, and the socioeconomic, institutional, administrative, and financial issues refugees can create.[52] Among recommendations in the first category, recommendation seven called on OAU member states that had not already done so to ratify the 1951 Convention, the Protocol relating to the Status of Refugees (1967 Protocol), and the 1969 Convention and to incorporate them into domestic law.[53] The OCM endorsed the conference's recommendations,[54] which subsequently received the support of the General Assembly of the UN (UNGA).[55]

Following the Arusha conference, the OAU and UNHCR constituted a joint working party for the implementation of its recommendations. The working group met for the first time in May 1980 in Addis Ababa and ultimately recommended a plan of action.[56] At its second meeting, the working party adopted model legislation for the domestic implementation of the 1969 Convention, which ultimately influenced how many states incorporated the treaty.[57]

The next major conference to address refugees in Africa was convened not by the OAU but by the UN Secretary-General further to an OCM resolution, which

[48] See section D.5.

[49] Extensive documentation and analysis of this gathering can be found in Lars-Gunnar Eriksson, Goran Melander, and Peter Nobel, *An Analysing Account of the Conference on the African Refugee Problem, Arusha, May 1979* (Scandinavian Institute of African Studies 1981).

[50] Nobel (n 38) 259. [51] Greenfield (n 6) 225.

[52] D'Sa (n 6) 391; for a summary of the conference's recommendations, see D'Sa (n 6) 391–94; the recommendations are reproduced in their entirety in Eriksson, Melander, and Nobel (n 49) 47–62.

[53] Eriksson, Melander, and Nobel (n 49) 52.

[54] OAU (OCM), 'Resolution on the Situation of Refugees in Africa and on Prospective Solutions to their Problems in the 1980s' (OAU Monrovia 6–20 July 1979) CM/Res 727 (XXXIII) Rev 1, para 2.

[55] UNGA Res 34/61 (29 November 1979). [56] D'Sa (n 6) 394.

[57] Ivor C Jackson, *The Refugee Concept in Group Situations* (Martinus Nijhoff 1999) 194–96.

invited the 'Secretary-General of the OAU in collaboration with the UN Secretary-General and … [UNHCR] to hold consultations with governmental and non-governmental organizations as well as governments of countries which are likely to offer contributions and the UN Specialized Agencies, in order to assess the possibility of holding a pledging conference for African refugees under the auspices of the' UN.[58] The UNGA subsequently noted the inadequacy of the assistance provided to African refugees[59] and the UN Secretary-General, in cooperation with the OAU and UNHCR, accordingly convened ICARA to 'mobilize assistance for refugees in Africa'.[60] ICARA was held on 9–10 April 1981 in Geneva and raised US$558 million,[61] however none of these funds was allocated directly to the OAU. Rather, they went to cover UNHCR programmes in Africa. The OAU had by then, however, established a Special Refugee Contingency Fund, which received two per cent of the OAU's regular budget[62] and which UNHCR contributed to.

The OAU Secretariat convened a meeting of NGOs involved in assisting refugees in Africa on 21–25 March 1983 in Arusha. While not on the same scale as the Arusha meeting before it, the gathering's opening address was delivered by Tanzanian President Julius Nyerere, suggesting that the refugee issue remained high profile. The meeting produced a range of recommendations under twelve broad headings,[63] including 'Preparation for ICARA II'. Indeed, further to the success of ICARA, a second fundraising conference was at the request of the UNGA[64] convened by the UN Secretary-General, the OAU, and UNHCR in Geneva from 9–11 July 1984. This time, however, funds were raised for UNHCR as well as to assist African host countries, fourteen of which submitted 128 proposals for specific infrastructural projects.[65] ICARA II also resulted in the adoption of a Declaration and Programme of Action aimed at an effective long-term strategy for African refugees.[66]

While preparations for ICARA II were ongoing, the OAU turned its attention from fundraising back to substantive issues, in particular to the situation of refugees from the racist regime in South Africa. At its 40th Ordinary Session, held in Addis Ababa in February and March 1984, the OCM called on the Southern African Development Co-ordinating Conference (now the Southern African Development Community) to organize, in collaboration with the OAU, UN, and UNHCR, 'an

[58] OAU (n 16) para 8. [59] UNGA Res 35/42 (25 November 1980) preambular para 8.

[60] ibid para 3.

[61] UN Secretary-General, 'Report of the Secretary General on the International Conference on Assistance to Refugees in Africa' UN Doc A/37/522 (1982) 11; see, also, OAU (Secretary-General), 'Report of the Secretary General on the International Conference on Assistance to Refugees in Africa' CM/1130 (XXXVII) Rev 1.

[62] OAU, 'Second OAU/ICRC Seminar for African Ambassadors Accredited to Ethiopia: The OAU and Humanitarian Problem' (OAU Addis Ababa 11–12 April 1995) BR/58/LM/9/95, 5.

[63] Preparation for ICARA II; protection; voluntary repatriation; awareness building and public information; cooperation in refugee assistance at the national, regional and international levels; root causes; education, training and scholarships; employment; counselling; settlement and resettlement; role of voluntary agencies during emergencies; and general (OAU, 'Recommendations of the Meeting of the OAU Secretariat and Voluntary Agencies on African Refugees' (OAU Arusha 21–25 March 1983)).

[64] UNGA Res 37/197 (18 December 1982) para 5. [65] D'Sa (n 6) 396.

[66] UN, 'Declaration and Program of Action of the Second International Conference on Assistance to Refugees in Africa' UN Doc A/CONF.125/L.1 (10 July 1984).

international conference on all aspects of the refugee problem in Southern Africa, in order to co-ordinate and harmonize approaches to refugee matters'.[67] In July 1986 the OCM called for substantive preparations to begin.[68] The conference, titled 'International Conference on the Plight of Refugees, Returnees and Displaced Persons in Southern Africa' (SARRED), was held in Oslo, Norway, on 22–24 August 1988. It resulted in the adoption of the Oslo Resolution, Declaration and Plan of Action on the Plight of Refugees, Returnees and Displaced Persons in Southern Africa,[69] which was subsequently endorsed by the OCM.[70]

Just as South Africa's apartheid regime had focused OAU attention on refugees in southern Africa, resulting in SARRED, the 1994 Rwandan genocide and ensuing refugee crisis led to a series of initiatives focused on the Great Lakes region. First was the OAU/UNHCR Regional Conference on Assistance to Refugees, Returnees and Displaced Persons in the Great Lakes Region, held in Bujumbura, Burundi, on 12–17 February 1995. This meeting resulted in a plan of action; the UNGA later reiterated that the plan continued 'to be a viable framework for the resolution of the refugee and humanitarian problems in that region'.[71] Its implementation led to a series of follow-up meetings.[72] On 8–9 May 1998 the OAU and UNHCR held another regional meeting on refugee issues in the Great Lakes region, this time in Kampala. Around the same time, there was also a focus on refugee women and children as particular populations of concern: on 12–15 October 1998 the OAU convened in Addis Ababa its Regional Seminar on Enhancing the Participation of Returnee, Refugee and Internally Displaced Women and Children in Reconstruction, Rehabilitation and Peace-Building. The seminar adopted a plan of action.[73]

[67] OAU (OCM), 'Resolution on the Situation of Refugees in Africa' (OAU Addis Ababa 27 February to 5 March 1984) CM/Res 939 (XL) para 5.

[68] OAU (OCM), 'Resolution on the Situation of Refugees in Africa' (OAU Addis Ababa 21–26 July 1986) CM/Res 1040 (XLIV) para 14; see, also, OAU (OCM), 'Resolution on International Conference on the Plight of Refugees, Returnees and Displaced Persons in Southern Africa, Oslo, Norway 22–24 August 1988' (OAU Addis Ababa 19–23 May 1988) CM/Res 1150 (XLVIII).

[69] OAU, 'Oslo Resolution, Declaration and Plan of Action on the Plight of Refugees, Returnees and Displaced Persons in Southern Africa' (OAU Oslo 22–24 August 1988) <http://www.unhcr.org/refworld/category,POLICY,UNGA,,,3ae68f410,0.html> accessed 10 October 2011; the declaration portion of the Oslo document addressed root causes; basic principles on humanitarian assistance (the linkage between relief, recovery, and development assistance and burden sharing); and specific refugee-related issues (asylum and military and armed attacks on refugees). The plan of action addressed humanitarian and rehabilitation assistance (emergency preparedness; needs assessment; the delivery of assistance, recovery, and development; and the mobilization of resources); durable solutions (voluntary repatriation and return, local integration and resettlement); public information and dissemination; and follow-up and evaluation.

[70] OAU (OCM), 'Resolution on the International Conference on the Plight of Refugees, Returnees and Displaced Persons in Southern Africa' (OAU Addis Ababa 20–25 February 1989) CM/Res 1181 (XLIX) para 3.

[71] UNGA Res 51/71 (12 December 1996) para 9.

[72] For example, in February 1996, the Second Meeting of the Follow-Up Committee on the Implementation of the Bujumbura Conference Plan of Action on Assistance to Refugees, Returnees and Displaced Persons in the Great Lakes Region.

[73] OAU, 'Plan of Action for Enhancing the Participation of Refugee, Returnee and Internally Displaced Women and Children in Rehabilitation, Reintegration, Reconstruction and Peace-Building' (OAU Addis Ababa 12–15 October 1998).

Many of the OAU's special refugee initiatives were organized in partnership with UNHCR and other UN agencies. However, one of the last refugee-related gatherings before the OAU became the AU was an exclusively OAU affair: the OAU Ministerial Meeting on Refugees, Returnees and Internally Displaced Persons in Africa, held in Khartoum, Sudan, on 13–14 December 1998. The meeting produced both a declaration[74] and recommendations.[75] The former included an appeal for states to ratify the 1951 Convention, its 1967 Protocol, and the 1969 Convention, and to domesticate and implement them. The latter consisted of thirty-four recommendations grouped under seven broad themes.[76]

(a) Commemorations

The OAU has marked significant anniversaries of the 1969 Convention's adoption. The first such initiative was held further to an OCM resolution, to mark the twenty-fifth anniversary of the Convention's adoption and twenty years since its entry into force.[77] The gathering was co-convened by the OAU and UNHCR and titled 'Commemorative Symposium on Refugees and the Problems of Forced Population Displacements in Africa'.[78] UNHCR's ExCom called the Symposium 'one effective way of highlighting the contribution of the OAU Convention to refugee protection and solutions in Africa and indeed in other regions of the world' and noted that it would 'highlight the continuing crises of forced displacements in Africa'.[79]

Held on 8–11 September 1994 in Addis Ababa, the symposium produced the Addis Ababa Document on Refugees and Forced Population Movements in Africa.[80] It included thirty-four recommendations grouped under ten headings.[81] Among the recommendations, number five called on states to ratify, uphold, domesticate, and implement the 1969 Convention. While the symposium was a success

[74] OAU, 'Khartoum Declaration of the OAU Ministerial Meeting on Refugees, Returnees and Internally Displaced Persons in Africa' (OAU Khartoum 14 December 1998); not to be confused with the Khartoum Declaration of 1990 (n 23).

[75] OAU, 'Khartoum Recommendations of the OAU Ministerial Meeting on Refugees, Returnees and Internally Displaced Persons in Africa' (OAU Khartoum 14 December 1998).

[76] Root causes; refugee instruments; strengthening refugee protection in Africa; durable solutions; consolidating the reintegration process; building Africa's capacity to respond to refugee and internal displacement situations; and assistance and resolving the problem of IDPs in Africa.

[77] OAU (OCM), 'Resolution on Refugees, Returnees and Displaced Persons in Africa' (OAU Addis Ababa 31 January to 4 February 1994) CM/Res 1489 (LIX) para 10.

[78] Okoth-Obbo (n 15) provides an extensive analysis of this symposium.

[79] UNHCR, 'Note on Preparations for the Commemoration of the 25th Anniversary of the Adoption of the 1969 OAU Convention Governing the Specific Aspects of Refugee Problems in Africa and the Twentieth Year of its Entry into Force' (15 September 1994) EC/1994/SCP/CRP.7 <http://www.unhcr.org/excom/scip/3ae68cbb0/note-preparations-commemoration-25th-anniversary-adoption-1969-oau-convention.html> accessed 22 December 2017, para 9.

[80] OAU and UNHCR, 'The Addis Ababa Document on Refugees and Forced Population Displacements in Africa, adopted by the OAU/UNHCR Symposium on Refugees and Forced Population Displacements in Africa, 8–10 September 1994, Addis Ababa, Ethiopia' [Special Issue Summer 1995] IJRL 303.

[81] Root causes; the 1969 Convention; refugee protection in Africa; material assistance; internal displacement; solutions; other populations in need of protection and assistance; emergency preparedness and response; the relief to development continuum; and institutional aspects.

in terms of the number of participants it attracted—340 from OAU member states, other states, UN agencies, and NGOs—it failed to advance thinking on substantive issues. Rather, it 'succeeded mainly only in echoing the familiar call urgently to address the root causes of refugee flows and other forms of coerced population movements. Having not tackled root causes with any rigour, it also could not etch out clearly the essential legal, policy, and operational groundmarks for tackling those issues in a concrete and result-producing manner'.[82]

In addition, to mark the 1969 Convention's 1994 anniversaries, the OAHG adopted the 'Tunis Declaration on the 1969 Convention Governing the Specific Aspects of Refugee Problems in Africa'. The Tunis Declaration remarks upon 'the wisdom' of the 1969 Convention, given that it has 'ensured the very survival of the institution of asylum itself and its humanitarian character where the character of refugee flows has sometimes threatened the very fabric of brotherhood and peaceful coexistence between States'.[83] The Declaration goes on to state that the 1969 Convention provides 'a solid cornerstone for refugee policy and state practice in the reception of, grant of asylum to, and treatment of, asylum seekers and refugees, as well as for the implementation of voluntary repatriation'. However, the Declaration also recognizes 'the continuing crises of displacement in the continent' and the heads of state and government 'reiterate' their 'unflinching determination to eradicate the root causes of refugee flows in Africa'.[84]

The next commemorative initiative was a meeting of government and non-governmental experts in Conakry, Guinea, on 27–29 March 2000, to mark the thirtieth anniversary of the 1969 Convention's adoption.[85] This meeting, co-convened by the OAU and UNHCR, 'consolidated the OAU's approach [to refugees] and directed the way in which it would operate in the future'[86] and resulted in the Comprehensive Implementation Plan.[87] This was subsequently endorsed by the OCM,[88] referred to by the OAHG,[89] and is considered the regional complement to the 2002 Agenda for Protection,[90] which resulted from the Global Consultations on International Protection convened by UNHCR in 2000.[91]

[82] Okoth-Obbo (n 15) 281.

[83] OAU (OAHG), 'Tunis Declaration on the 1969 Convention Governing the Specific Aspects of Refugee Problems in Africa' (OAU Tunis 13–15 June 1994) AHG/Decl 216, para 4.

[84] ibid para 5.

[85] The excellent 2001 RSQ article by George Okoth-Obbo cited throughout this work was one of three background papers prepared for this meeting (Bonaventure Rutinwa, 'Relationship Between the 1951 Refugee Convetion and the 1969 OAU Convention on Refugees' in Volker Türk, Alice Edwards, and Cornelis Wouters (eds), *In Flight from Conflict and Violence: UNHCR's Consultations on Refugee Status and Other Forms of International Protection* (CUP 2017) 96).

[86] Murray (n 6) 192.

[87] OAU, 'Comprehensive Implementation Plan Adopted by the Special OAU/UNHCR Meeting of Government and Non-Government Technical Experts on the Thirtieth Anniversary of the 1969 OAU Refugee Convention' CONF.P/OAU30th/Report—Annex II, reprinted in RSQ 21 (2001) 31; all documentation related to the Conakry meeting is reprinted in volume 20(1) (2001) of RSQ.

[88] OAU (OCM), 'Decision on the Situation of Refugees, Returnees and Displaced Persons in Africa' (OAU Lomé 6–8 July 2000) CM/Res 2171 (LXXII) para 8.

[89] OAU (OAHG), 'Decision on the Fiftieth Anniversary of the Adoption of the 1951 Convention on the Status of Refugees' (OAU Lusaka 9–11 July 2001) AHG/Dec 6 (XXXVII) preambular para 6.

[90] Beyani (n 29) 7.

[91] UNGA, 'Agenda for Protection' UN Doc A/AC.96/965/Add.1 (26 June 2002).

The recommendations contained in the Comprehensive Implementation Plan suggested that UNHCR and the OAU convene a working group to consider amendments to the 1969 Convention,[92] including the designation of an oversight body.[93] Another directed UNHCR to conclude a memorandum of understanding with the African Commission on Human and Peoples' Rights (African Commission), in order to strengthen 'its monitoring capacity and programme of work with respect to the human rights of refugees and asylum-seekers'.[94] This memorandum of understanding was ultimately concluded in 2003; it is discussed in Chapter 7.[95]

The recommendations concerning amendments to, and oversight of, the 1969 Convention, by contrast, were not implemented as a direct result of the Comprehensive Implementation Plan. However, an expert report emanating from the AU's First Ministerial Meeting on Human Rights, held in Kigali in May 2003, identified the African Commission as having oversight of the 1969 Convention;[96] this is also discussed in Chapter 7.[97] Additionally, in May 2004, a group of experts met in Addis Ababa to review all OAU and AU treaties and consider the conclusion of new treaties. The AU's Executive Council took note of the experts' report and decided that 'the 1969 ... Convention ... should be retained in its present form', that the 'safety and security of refugees and host countries as well as all other areas not covered by the OAU 1969 Convention should be addressed through soft law; through the adoption of annual decisions of the Assembly' and that the 'specific needs of ... [IDPs] such as protection and assistance should be addressed through a separate legal instrument'.[98] This 'separate legal instrument', the Convention for the Protection and Assistance of Internally Displaced Persons in Africa (Kampala Convention), was adopted in 2009.[99] More generally, in 2004 the AU's Executive Council requested that the AU Commission 'continue the implementation of the Comprehensive Implementation Plan (CIP) adopted in Conakry (Guinea) in March 2000, in close partnership with the UNHCR'.[100]

The thirtieth anniversary of the 1969 Convention's adoption was the last time the instrument was commemorated in any major way. However, the AU's Executive Council recently recognized that 2019 is the fiftieth anniversary of the Convention's adoption; this is discussed below.[101]

[92] OAU (n 87) action two. [93] ibid action four. [94] ibid action fifteen.

[95] See section B.3.a.

[96] OAU, 'Report of the Meeting of Experts of the First AU Ministerial Conference on Human Rights in Africa' (OAU Kigali 5–6 May 2003) EXP/CONF/HRA/RPT (II) para 40(2), cited in Rachel Murray, 'Refugees and Internally Displaced Persons and Human Rights: the African System' (2005) 24 RSQ 56, 62.

[97] See section B.3.a.

[98] AU (Executive Council), 'Decision on the Meeting of Experts on the Review of OAU/AU Treaties' (AU Addis Ababa 25 June to 3 July 2004) EX.CL/95 (V) paras 2–4.

[99] (Adopted 23 October 2009, entered into force 6 December 2012) 49 ILM 86.

[100] AU (Executive Council), 'Decision on the Situation of Refugees, Returnees and Displaced Persons' (AU Addis Ababa 25 June to 3 July 2004) EX.CL/108 (V) para 11.

[101] See section C.2.

The Comprehensive Implementation Plan adopted in Conakry and indeed most recommendations flowing from the OAU's various special refugee initiatives are sound. However, there is reason to be sceptical. As an NGO delegate to the 1994 Commemorative Symposium remarked, 'there is no shortage of declarations, recommendations, or plans of action to solve the refugee and displacement crisis in Africa. If even half of these were to be implemented, there would be virtually no refugees or displaced persons in Africa today and none for the whole of the twenty-first century'.[102] The number of declarations, recommendations, and plans of action emanating from African gatherings devoted to refugees—whether commemorative or otherwise—evidences the essential truth of this somewhat sweeping observation. If even one plan of action were successfully implemented, there would be little need for those coming after it. Indeed, Okoth-Obbo notes that conference documents have not shown a record of implementation commensurate with the effort and cost of their elaboration.[103]

Such documents do, however, provide a historical record of the OAU's evolving approach to refugees. The OAU initially viewed refugees predominantly as a threat to interstate relations, an approach discussed in Chapters 2 and 3 and reflected in the 1969 Convention. Later, the relationship between refugees and development came to the fore.[104] Finally, increasing regard for human rights resulted in recognition of the linkages between human rights violations and forced population displacement.[105] Indeed, recognition of the importance of human rights—for which the OAU had no clear mandate—contributed to the decision to replace the OAU with the AU. Not surprisingly, therefore, the connection between the protection and promotion of human rights on the one hand and refugees on the other was a salient feature of the AU's initial engagement with refugees. Such engagement is detailed in the next section.

C. AU Engagement with Refugee Issues: 2001 to 2018

The end of the Cold War precipitated major political change in Africa. Democracy began to take root and in 1990 Namibia, the last African country under colonial rule, gained its independence. The first formal indication of the OAU's declining relevance within this new political landscape came in the form of the 1990 Declaration on the Political and Socio-Economic Situation in Africa,[106] which acknowledged that the 'era of focusing mainly on "political liberation and nation building" should

[102] Cited in Okoth-Obbo (n 15) 297. [103] ibid 298. [104] Nyanduga (n 3) 99.

[105] See, for example, OAU, 'Grand Bay (Mauritius) Declaration and Plan of Action' (OAU Grand Bay 12–16 April 1999) CONF/HRA/Dec 1, para 9, which provides: 'While welcoming the improvements which have taken place in addressing the refugee problem, the conference believes that the high number of refugees, displaced persons and returnees in Africa constitutes an impediment to development. It recognizes the link between human rights violations and population displacement and calls for redoubled and concerted efforts by States and the OAU to address the problem'.

[106] OAU (OAHG), 'Declaration on the Political and Socio-Economic Situation in Africa' (OAU Addis Ababa 9–11 July 1990) AHG/Dec.1(XXVI).

make way for a new era of greater emphasis on economic development and integration'.[107] This economic development agenda was concretized in 1991 with the adoption of the Treaty Establishing the African Economic Community (Abuja Treaty),[108] which created the African Economic Community (AEC). Its primary objective was 'to promote economic, social and cultural development and the integration of African economies'[109] through the gradual coordination of the continent's existing subregional economic communities and the establishment of new policies, programmes, and institutions over thirty-four years.[110] Only eight years later, however, African leaders committed to forming an African union that would fast track the creation and implementation of the institutions contemplated by the Abuja Treaty.[111]

1. The AU

This new norm-setting continental institution superseded the OAU and incorporated the AEC on 26 May 2001, when its Constitutive Act entered into force.[112] Viljoen describes it as 'essentially a merger of the largely political ambitions of the OAU and the mainly economically minded AEC, with the addition of some organs and with an acceleration of pace in economic integration'.[113] The AU's objectives thus reflect the Abuja Treaty's economic development agenda while also recognizing the importance of social and democratic development and according particular prominence to human rights. Of the AU's sixteen 'guiding principles', six make either explicit or implicit reference to human rights,[114] and the AU's 'objectives' are similarly human rights focused. According to its Constitutive Act, the AU aims to achieve unity and solidarity among African states and peoples; defend the sovereignty, territorial integrity, and independence of its member states; accelerate African political and socioeconomic integration; promote and defend common African positions; encourage international cooperation; promote peace, security, stability, democracy, good governance, and human and peoples' rights; foster strong African participation in the global economy and international relations; promote sustainable development, the integration of African economies, and cooperation in all fields of human activity; coordinate and harmonize policies across the various regional economic communities; promote research; and engage in international cooperation for public health.[115] According to Viljoen, the AU 'not only sets out to attain human rights *objectives* but also intends to use human rights-based means (or *principles*) to achieve those objectives', which 'evidences its resolve to make a clean break from the OAU's *modus operandi*'.[116]

[107] ibid para 12.
[108] (Adopted 3 June 1991, entered into force 12 May 1994) 30 ILM 1241.
[109] ibid art 4(1)(a). [110] ibid art 4(2).
[111] OAU (OAHG), 'Sirte Declaration' (OAU Sirte 9 Sept 1999) AHG/Draft/Decl (IV) Rev 1.
[112] Constitutive Act of the African Union (adopted 11 July 2000, entered into force 26 May 2001) 2158 UNTS 3 (AU Constitutive Act).
[113] Viljoen (n 1) 164. [114] ibid 165. [115] AU Constitutive Act (n 112) art 3.
[116] Viljoen (n 1) 165.

The AU's machinery to achieve its range of goals is more extensive than was that of the OAU.[117] The AU Commission is the regional body's Addis Ababa-based secretariat.[118] It is headed by the chairperson, under whom sits a deputy chairperson and eight commissioners. The AU Commission has twelve departments, each of which handles a discrete portfolio,[119] one of which is political affairs. Commission responsibility for humanitarian affairs generally and refugees in particular is located within the Department of Political Affairs.

The AU's supreme organ is its Assembly of Heads of State and Government (Assembly), which determines AU policies.[120] The Executive Council is composed of member state foreign ministers. It also sets AU policies and monitors policy implementation.[121] AU summits, at which the Assembly and Executive Council convene to set AU policy by way of decisions, declarations, and resolutions, occur twice per year in January and July. The January summit is always held at the AU Commission in Addis Ababa, while the July summit is often held elsewhere on the continent.

The PRC is composed of Addis Ababa-based diplomats accredited to the AU and is charged with preparing the work of the Executive Council and executing its instructions.[122] In practice, however, the PRC supervises day-to-day AU Commission operations. The STCs are composed of relevant member state ministers and senior officials. STCs set policy as instructed by the Executive Council and work on policy implementation.[123] The PSC makes decisions on the prevention, management, and resolution of conflicts.[124] The Pan-African Parliament is the AU's legislative arm, with members elected by member state legislatures.[125] The AU's financial institutions are the African Central Bank, the African Investment Bank, and the African Monetary Fund.[126] The Economic, Social and Cultural Council is an advisory organ composed of social and professional groups from member states.[127] The AU also includes ad hoc bodies, such as the Panel of the Wise, a panel of eminent persons mandated to prevent conflict.

[117] See, generally, AU Commission and New Zealand Ministry of Foreign Affairs and Trade, *African Union Handbook 2017: A Guide for Those Working With and Within the African Union* (2017) <https://au.int/sites/default/files/pages/31829-file-african-union-handbook-2017-edited.pdf> accessed 23 December 2017.

[118] AU Constitutive Act (n 112) art 20.

[119] Agenda 2063; civil society and diaspora; economic affairs; human resources, science and technology; infrastructure and energy; legal affairs; peace and security; political affairs; rural economy and agriculture; social affairs; trade and industry; and women, gender and development.

[120] AU Constitutive Act (n 112) arts 6–9.

[121] ibid arts 10–13.

[122] ibid art 21; the PRC has eleven sub-committees: the Advisory Sub-Committee on Administrative, Budgetary and Financial Matters; the Sub-Committee on Audit Matters; the Sub-Committee on Contributions; the Sub-Committee on Economic and Trade Matters; the Sub-Committee on Headquarters and Host Agreements; the Sub-Committee on Multilateral Cooperation and Strategic Partnerships; the Sub-Committee on the New Partnership for Africa's Economic Development; the Sub-Committee on Programmes and Conferences; the Sub-Committee on Refugees, Returnees and Internally Displaced Persons in Africa; the Policy Sub-Committee of the Special Emergency Assistance Fund for Drought and Famine Relief in Africa; and the Sub-Committee on Structures.

[123] AU Constitutive Act (n 112) arts 14–16.

[124] Protocol Relating to the Establishment of the Peace and Security Council of the African Union (adopted 9 July 2002, entered into force 26 December 2003) (PSC Protocol).

[125] AU Constitutive Act (n 112) art 17.

[126] ibid art 19.

[127] ibid art 22.

The legal organs are the AU Advisory Board on Corruption and the AU Commission on International Law; the African Court of Justice, mandated to adjudicate member state disputes under AU treaties, exists only on paper[128] and in practice any such disputes would be resolved using ad hoc mechanisms such as arbitration. The human rights institutions are the African Commission, the African Court on Human and Peoples' Rights (African Court), and the African Committee of Experts on the Rights and Welfare of the Child.

The AU's approach to refugees was initially strongly linked to its focus on human rights. This connection was first evidenced in the Kigali Declaration, the outcome of the First AU Ministerial Conference on Human Rights. The Declaration called on member states to recognize forced displacement as a grave violation of the human rights to peace, security, and dignity.[129] The centrality of human rights in the AU's approach to refugees was in part the result of changing patterns of forced displacement. When the OAU first addressed refugee protection with the 1969 Convention, the major cause of forced displacement was colonial occupation, but as time progressed, civil war became a major cause of refugee outflow. In addition to focusing attention on human rights, this new cause of displacement also served to widen the AU's focus: whereas the OAU had primarily been focused on refugees, the AU pays equal attention to IDPs and returnees, and has recently viewed all three within a broader humanitarian context.

While the transformation of the OAU into the AU heralded a more rights-based approach to refugees and brought IDPs and returnees to the fore, the transition was also a missed opportunity. The adoption of the AU's Constitutive Act raised the prospect of creating a dedicated continental refugee body,[130] or at the very least the opportunity of creating a body to formally supervise the 1969 Convention. Neither of these opportunities was seized. Instead, the AU developed several bodies responsible for refugee issues with distinct political, advisory, and technical roles. These are discussed in turn below, following a general discussion of refugee policy-making by the AU's Executive Council and in other ministerial fora.

2. Executive Council and ministerial refugee policymaking

The AU's Executive Council is composed of member state foreign ministers. It meets biannually at AU summits, and sometimes at extraordinary summits, to set AU policy or to delegate policymaking to the STCs and to direct the AU Commission's policy implementation work. The Executive Council's refugee-related decisions are cited as relevant throughout this chapter, however its most significant refugee policy decisions are addressed here.

[128] See Chapter 7, section D.

[129] OAU, 'Kigali Declaration of the First AU Ministerial Conference on Human Rights in Africa' (OAU Kigali 8 May 2003) MIN/CONF/HRA/Decl1 (I) para 11.

[130] Nierum S Okogbule, 'The Legal Dimensions of the Refugee Problem in Africa' (2004) 10 E Afr J Peace & Hum Rts 176, 189.

Most recently, at its 31st Ordinary Session, held at the 29th AU Summit in June and July 2017, the Executive Council adopted its 'Decision on [the] Humanitarian Situation in Africa', which paid particular attention to refugees. In the decision, the Executive Council expressed 'deep concern ... regarding [the] situation of refugees in Africa' and called on 'all stakeholders, Member States and international organizations to look at the root causes of refugees in Africa, working collectively on finding solutions to conflicts on the continent'.[131] It also commended member states for their 'invaluable efforts ... in hosting refugees and facilitating the delivery of humanitarian assistance' and called on 'all stakeholders to provide the necessary support in handling the refugee situation in Africa'.[132] The Executive Council went on to call on the AU Commission, in collaboration with the PRC Policy Sub-Committee on the Special Emergency Assistance Fund for Drought and Famine Relief in Africa and the PRC Sub-Committee, to organize a 'Donors'/Pledging Conference to raise resources to replenish the Special Emergency Fund for humanitarian response'.[133] The decision also recognized that 2019 is the fiftieth anniversary of the adoption of the 1969 Convention and the tenth anniversary of the adoption of the Kampala Convention. In this connection, the Executive Council called on 'the Union to declare 2019 as the Year of Refugees, Returnees and Internally Displaced Persons in Africa: "towards durable solutions to forced displacement in Africa," and [to] develop an implementation road map'.[134] The Executive Council also called on the AU to work with the regional economic communities (RECs), the UN Secretary-General, and UNHCR 'to organize an activity that will bring global visibility to forced displacements in Africa'.[135]

Prior to this 2017 decision, the Executive Council's most significant refugee-related policy decision was its adoption, in 2006, of the AU's Migration Policy Framework for Africa. The policy framework addresses a range of migration issues, including labour migration, border management, irregular migration, internal migration, migration data, migration and development, regional cooperation, and forced displacement. In the latter context, the policy framework notes that strengthening state responses to refugee crises requires 'further efforts at the national level to establish legislative frameworks, policies, and structures giving effect to international protection obligations; redoubling efforts to find durable solutions for refugees in collaboration with UNHCR and other national and international partners; and addressing root causes of refugee movements including conflict and instability'.[136] The policy framework goes on to recommend a number of strategies to improve state refugee responses, including ratification of the 1951 Convention, 1967 Protocol, and 1969 Convention and their effective implementation. In this connection, the Executive Council highlights that the policy framework's 'most important' recommendation is that the Assembly 'and respective governments must be

[131] AU (Executive Council), 'Decision on Humanitarian Situation in Africa' (AU Addis Ababa 1 July 2017) EX.CL/Dec.968(XXXI) para 2.

[132] ibid para 3. [133] ibid para 6. [134] AU (n 131) para 8. [135] ibid para 9.

[136] AU (Executive Council), 'The Migration Policy Framework for Africa' (AU Banjul 25–29 June 2006) EX.CL/276 (IX) <http://www.unhcr.org/protection/migration/4d5258ab9/african-union-migration-policy-framework-africa.html> accessed 20 December 2017, 19.

monitored as to their compliance to ratified instruments and be held accountable in the event of apparent failure to comply'.[137] No monitoring mechanism was ever established to give effect to this recommendation.

The Executive Council can delegate policymaking to the relevant STC.[138] In theory, therefore, AU refugee policy can be set by the STC on Migration, Refugees and IDPs. However, this Committee—which is discussed in sub-section 3 below—was not established until 2009 and did not meet for the first time until 2015. Prior to this, alongside Executive Council policymaking, AU refugee policy was also formulated ad hoc at ministerial meetings. The first such AU meeting was held in Ouagadougou, Burkina Faso, on 1–2 June 2006—eight years after the OAU's last ministerial meeting on refugees—at the behest of a 2005 Executive Council decision.[139] The meeting resulted in the adoption of the Ouagadougou Declaration[140] and during the gathering it was decided that ministerial meetings devoted to forced displacement should be convened every two years.

Accordingly, ministers met again in November 2008 in Addis Ababa. There they worked towards an even higher level gathering: the AU Special Summit on Refugees, Returnees and Internally Displaced Persons in Africa, which was ultimately held on 19–23 October 2009 in Kampala. The Special Summit produced the Kampala Declaration, which addressed prevention; protection; women, children and other vulnerable groups; the forging of partnerships to address forced displacement;[141] and, most importantly, adopted the landmark Kampala Convention, perhaps the most significant illustration of the way in which internal displacement has come to the fore in the AU.

The AU Commission, specifically its Department of Political Affairs' HARDP, was tasked with implementing the Kampala Declaration and was requested to formulate a plan of action in this regard.[142] To build consensus around and formalize its draft plan of action, on 4–5 June 2010 HARDP convened in Addis Ababa the third meeting of ministers in charge of forced displacement matters. The ministers adopted HARDP's plan of action, which was subsequently welcomed by the Executive Council.[143] A consultative meeting aimed at implementing the plan of action was convened by HARDP on 20–21 May 2011 in Kinshasa. After this 2011 meeting, ministerial meetings on refugees were replaced by the more formal STC on Migration, Refugees and IDPs,[144] in accordance with a June 2014 Assembly

[137] ibid 21. [138] AU Constitutive Act (n 112) art 13(3).

[139] AU (Executive Council), 'Decision on the Situation of Refugees, Returnees and Displaced Persons' (AU Abuja 24–28 January 2005) EX/CL/Dec179 (VI) para 8.

[140] AU, 'Ouagadougou Declaration of the Ministerial Meeting on Refugees, Returnees and Internally Displaced Persons in Africa' (AU Ouagadougou 1–2 June 2006) AU/MIN/HARDP/Decl1.

[141] AU, 'Kampala Declaration on Refugees, Returnees and Internally Displaced Persons in Africa' (AU Kampala 22–23 October 2009) Ext/Assembly/AU/PA/Draft/Decl (I) Rev1.

[142] AU (Executive Council), 'Decision on the Situation of Refugees, Returnees and Internally Displaced Persons in Africa' (AU Addis Ababa 25–29 January 2010) EX/CL/Dec529 (XVI) para 6.

[143] AU (Executive Council), 'Decision on the Situation of Refugees, Returnees and Internally Displaced Persons in Africa' (AU Kampala 19–23 July 2010) EX/CL/Dec558 (XVII) para 4.

[144] Interview with Olabisi Dare, Head, HARDP, 6 December 2016, Addis Ababa.

decision calling on the AU Commission to operationalize all STCs by December 2014.[145]

3. The AU's refugee-related bodies

(a) The STC on Migration, Refugees and IDPs

The AU's Constitutive Act provides for seven STCs composed of member state ministers and senior officials.[146] The role of each STC is to

a. Prepare projects and programmes of the Union and submit in to the Executive Council;
b. Ensure the supervision, follow-up and the evaluation of the implementation of decisions taken by the organs of the Union;
c. Ensure the coordination and harmonization of projects and programmes of the Union;
d. Submit to the Executive Council either on its own initiative or at the request of the Executive Council, reports and recommendations on the implementation of the provisions of… [the AU's Constitutive Act]; and
e. Carry out any other functions assigned to it for the purpose of ensuring the implementation of the provisions of [the AU's Constitutive Act].[147]

In February 2009 the Assembly doubled the initial number of committees[148] to better align the STCs with the AU Commission's discrete portfolios.[149] Among these fourteen committees is the STC on Migration, Refugees and IDPs, currently chaired by Rwanda. In June 2011, the Assembly decided the STCs should meet once every two years.[150]

In addition to the general STC functions cited earlier in this section, article 5 of the STC on Migration, Refugees and IDPs' Rules of Procedure mandates the Committee to strengthen mechanisms for effective humanitarian response on the continent by establishing an African humanitarian agency;[151] strengthen the

[145] AU (Assembly), 'Decision on the Operationalization of the Specialized Technical Committees' (AU Malabo 26–27 June 2014) Assembly/AU/Dec.526(XXIII) para 2.

[146] The Committee on Rural Economy and Agricultural Matters; the Committee on Monetary and Financial Affairs; the Committee on Trade, Customs and Immigration Matters; the Committee on Industry, Science and Technology, Natural Resources and Environment; the Committee on Transport, Communications and Tourism; the Committee on Health, Labour and Social Affairs; and the Committee on Education, Culture and Human Resources (AU Constitutive Act (n 112) art 14).

[147] AU Constitutive Act (n 112) art 15.

[148] AU (Assembly), 'Decision on the Specialized Technical Committees' (AU Addis Ababa 1–3 February 2009) Assembly/AU/Dec.227(XII) para 2.

[149] The new STCs are: agriculture, rural development, water, and environment; finance, monetary affairs, economic planning, and integration; trade, industry, and minerals; transport, transcontinental, and interregional infrastructures, energy and tourism; gender and women empowerment; justice and legal affairs; social development, labour, and employment; the public service, local government, urban development, and decentralization; health, population, and drug control; migration, refugees and IDPs; youth, culture, and sports; education, science, and technology; communication, and information and communication technologies; and defence, safety, and security.

[150] AU (Assembly), 'Decision on the Specialized Technical Committees' (AU Malabo 30 June to 1 July 2011) Assembly/AU/Dec.365(XVII) para 3.

[151] See section C.4.b. of this chapter.

protection of, and assistance to, populations in need of humanitarian assistance, including through the formulation and implementation of AU guidelines; strengthen measures to popularize international humanitarian law and principled action; discuss the AU's Humanitarian Policy Framework, including guidelines on disaster management, epidemic response, and the role of the African Standby Force in humanitarian emergencies.[152]

Despite its constitution in 2009, for several years the STC on Migration, Refugees and IDPs was—like other STCs—not formally established, its functions instead fulfilled at the sectoral ministerial meetings discussed earlier in this section.[153] The first session of the STC on Migration, Refugees and IDPs occurred in November 2015, when it met over one week at the AU Commission in Addis Ababa. The meeting, which followed the usual format of an expert meeting followed by a ministerial meeting, was themed 'Towards Humanitarian Effectiveness in Africa'. Its agenda was to adopt its Rules of Procedure; the CAP, which was to be presented to the World Humanitarian Summit (WHS) in Istanbul, Turkey in May 2016; the HPF; and the AU's Disaster Management Guidelines.[154] The report of this first session is not publicly available, but the AU Assembly took note of and approved it at its 26th Ordinary Session in January 2016,[155] in the same decision in which it also adopted the CAP and resolved to establish an African Humanitarian Agency.[156] These humanitarian initiatives are addressed later in this section.[157]

The second STC session was held in October 2017 in Kigali, Rwanda. The meeting, themed 'Opportunities for Migration and Free Movement of Persons in Africa and Mitigating Challenges', addressed ongoing work towards the adoption of a Protocol to the Abuja Treaty on the free movement of persons in Africa;[158] the Migration Policy Framework discussed earlier in this section and a related plan of action;[159] Africa's common position in relation to the Global Compact for Safe, Orderly and Regular Migration;[160] and the situation in the Horn of Africa.[161] The second session of the AU's STC on Migration, Refugees and IDPs thus focused on migration and not on refugee issues.

152 AU Commission (n 117) 53–54.

153 See section C.2.

154 AU, 'Press Release No 342/2015: Specialized Technical Committee (STC) on Migration, Refugees and Internally Displaced Persons convenes at the African Union Commission, Headquarters' (16 November 2015) <https://www.au.int/en/newsevents/16832/specialized-technical-committee-stc-migration-refugees-and-internally-displaced> accessed 28 March 2017.

155 AU (Assembly), 'Decision on the Common African Position on Humanitarian Effectiveness' (AU Addis Ababa 30–31 January 2016) Assembly/AU/Dec.604(XXVI) para 1.

156 ibid para 9.

157 See section C.4.b.

158 See section C.4.a.

159 See section C.2.

160 AU (STC), 'Draft Common African Position (CAP) on the Global Compact for Safe, Orderly and Regular Migration' (October 2017) AU/STC/MRIDP/4(II) <https://au.int/sites/default/files/newsevents/workingdocuments/33023-wd-draft_cap_migration19_oct_e.pdf> accessed 20 December 2017.

161 AU (Directorate of Information and Communication), 'Experts Session of the STC on Migration, Refugees and Displaced Persons Opens' (17 October 2017) Press Release No 158/2017.

(b) The PRC Sub-Committee on Refugees, Returnees and IDPs

The PRC Sub-Committee is the AU incarnation of the OAU's Commission. It is a Committee of the whole currently chaired by Equatorial Guinea and represented by a Bureau of five member states.[162] It is a decision-making body, acting on its own as well as by raising issues to the Executive Council.[163] Its role includes assisting AU organs in developing and coordinating refugee policy and proposing policy to the AU's Executive Council. Sub-Committee sessions are supposed to be held at the AU Commission at least once per month,[164] but in practice they may occur less frequently.

Despite its refugee-focused nomenclature, the PRC Sub-Committee views its mandate in broader terms, as encompassing humanitarian affairs more generally.[165] This may be due in part to the degree to which it relies on and defers to HARDP. Lacking in refugee experts among its ambassador members, the PRC Sub-Committee relies heavily on HARDP, with which it works closely and which is its secretariat. HARDP's mandate is not limited to refugees but includes humanitarian affairs more generally; it is thus not surprising that this broader focus has impacted HARDP's political counterpart. In January 2014 an Executive Council decision stressed 'the need to review and clarify' the PRC Sub-Committee's role to enable it to effectively fulfil its mandate.[166]

The PRC Sub-Committee reports regularly to the AU's Executive Council. The Executive Council's responses to Sub-Committee activities provide an indication of those activities. At its 26th Ordinary Session in January 2015, the Executive Council took note of PRC Sub-Committee missions to the Central African Republic, Kenya, Madagascar, and Zimbabwe; encouraged the Sub-Committee to 'intensify its efforts' to promote relevant AU legal instruments with member states, particularly the Kampala Convention; and invited the Sub-Committee to 'continuously update its statistics on refugees, returnees' and IDPs 'through a mechanism for coordination with all the field players', including member states, UNHCR, and humanitarian agencies.[167] The same Executive Council decision also requested that the AU Commission 'rationalize the activities and operations' of the PRC Sub-Committee on the AU's Special Emergency Assistance Fund for Drought and Famine in Africa with those of the PRC Sub-Committee.[168] This call was reiterated at the 28th

[162] AU, 'The Permanent Representatives' Committee' <https://au.int/web/en/organs/prc> accessed 21 April 2017.

[163] Patrick Tigere and Rita Amukhobu, 'The African Union's Institutional Framework for Responding to Forced Displacement in Africa' [2005] Conflict Trends 48, 53.

[164] AU, 'The Permanent Representatives' Committee (PRC)' <https://au.int/organs/prc> accessed 4 August 2017.

[165] Interview with Olabisi Dare, Head, HARDP, 16 January 2012, Addis Ababa.

[166] AU (Executive Council), 'Decision on the Report of the Sub-Committee on Refugees, Returnees and Internally Displaced Persons in Africa' (AU Addis Ababa 21–28 January 2014) EX.CL/Dec.802 (XXIV) para 4.

[167] AU (Executive Council), 'Decision on the Reports of the PRC Sub-Committees' (AU Addis Ababa 23–27 January 2015) EX.CL/Dec.854 (XXVI) paras 18–21.

[168] ibid para 40.

Ordinary Session in January 2016,[169] as well as at the 27th Ordinary Session in June 2015.[170] At this latter meeting, the Executive Council also took note of PRC Sub-Committee missions to Malawi, South Sudan, and Uganda and encouraged the Sub-Committee to visit Cape Verde, Ethiopia, Nigeria and the Saharawi Arab Democratic Republic, as well as Guinea, Liberia, and Sierra Leone in view of the ebola outbreak.[171]

Executive Council responses to PRC Sub-Committee reports sometimes also evidence AU thinking on refugees. For example, in response to one such report, the Executive Council noted the 'positive developments that continue to take place in the area of forced displacement' while also expressing 'concern over the large number of refugees' and IDPs in Africa.[172] The Executive Council also used the opportunity to express its 'gratitude to countries of asylum that continue to meet their international obligations and most importantly commit themselves to extend hospitality to refugees in spite of the environmental, security and social impact of such hospitality upon their countries'[173] as well as to appeal to the 'international community to exert all efforts to extend the financial and material assistance to the forcibly displaced ... in the spirit of solidarity and burden sharing'.[174] Additionally, the Executive Council commended Uganda 'for its laudable Refugee Integration Policy' and urged 'other refugee hosting countries to emulate' it,[175] and noted 'the challenges posed by the presence of the Dadaab Refugee Camp in Kenya'.[176] Finally, the Executive Council recommended 'the holding of an international Conference to address the issue of migration'.[177]

(c) *The Coordinating Committee on Forced Displacement and Humanitarian Action*

The CCFDHA was born under the OAU as the BPEAR's coordinating committee, and later became the CCAR. As an AU organ, it was initially known as the CCAPRRI, though it was subsequently renamed the CCFDHA. The CCAPRRI/CCFDHA was intended to be the AU's main advisory body on humanitarian issues, with membership open to AU member states, relevant UN agencies, intergovernmental organizations, and NGOs.[178] A subset of members resident in Addis Ababa were to

[169] AU (Executive Council), 'Decision on the Activities of the Permanent Representatives' Committee' (AU Addis Ababa 23–28 January 2016) EX.CL/Dec.899 (XXVIII) Rev.2, paras 55 and 57.

[170] AU (Executive Council), 'Decision on the Reports of the PRC Sub-Committees' (AU Johannesburg 7–12 June 2015) EX.CL/Dec.877 (XXVII) para 32(iii).

[171] ibid paras 31 and 32(i). [172] ibid para 26. [173] ibid para 27.

[174] ibid para 29.

[175] ibid para 33; on Uganda's approach to refugees, see The World Bank Group, 'An Assessment of Uganda's Progressive Approach to Refugee Management' (2016) <https://openknowledge.worldbank.org/handle/10986/24736> accessed 27 April 2017.

[176] ibid para 37. [177] ibid para 35.

[178] CCAPRRI, 'Rules of Procedure of the AU Coordinating Committee on Assistance and Protection to Refugees, Returnees and Internally Displaced Persons in Africa' (CCAPRRI Addis Ababa 9 November 2006) POL/DIR/113/2927 (XXVIII) art II.

form the body's working group, which had a mandate to assist HARDP in its day-to-day activities[179] and prepare the work of the Committee as a whole.[180]

The CCFDHA's broad functions are derived from the CCAPRRI's 2006 Rules of Procedure, which due to their scope are worth reproducing:

(a) advise the AU Commission, the PRC Sub-Committee on Refugees, … [regional economic communities] and relevant … [AU] organs, including the African Commission … on matters that promote the better protection, assistance and the search for durable solutions for refugees, returnees and … [IDPs] in Africa, with particular focus on the special needs of vulnerable groups …;
(b) perform as an advisory group that promotes policies on the protection and assistance of refugees, returnees and IDPs as well as propose strategies for mainstreaming of various principles contained in the relevant regional and international legal instruments including the 1969 … Convention …;
(c) provide a platform for the exchange of data and information, experiences, best practices and lessons learnt as well as analyze policy formulation and recommendations and advise on areas of intervention, modalities of engagement and strategies of implementation in order to improve concerned human protection and relief assistance at country level;
(d) ensure wide dissemination of important resolutions and decisions adopted by relevant AU organs;
(e) establish modalities and/or plans of action, including a mechanism for monitoring and reporting to the PRC Sub-Committee on Refugees on the implementation of relevant resolutions and decisions;
(f) coordinate efforts of members of the CCAR in order to harmonize their policies and activities and ensure complementarity in their programmes relating to refugees, returnees and IDPs;
(g) mobilize support for capacity and institution building activities of member organizations, refugee hosting countries and other organizations particularly indigenous African NGOs involved in the protection and assistance to refugee, returnees and IDPs;
(h) assist and support the AU and member organizations in mobilizing resources necessary to ensure the smooth functioning of the Coordinating Committee and the implementation of planned activities;
(i) assist and support the AU and member organizations in mobilizing support and resources for refugees, returnees, IDPs and other related humanitarian activities;
(j) provide early warning and advice on the prevention of large-scale forced population displacement and humanitarian catastrophes, and support African countries and communities hosting refugees and IDPs on adequate, timely and appropriate preparedness, and response to emergency situations; as well as advocate for comprehensive peace building, reconstruction and development for countries emerging out of conflict to ensure that the needs of displaced persons are addressed;
(k) undertake any other assignment as, and when, necessary and requested by the AU Commission and/or the AU decision-making organs;
(l) play the role of advocacy on issues related to refugees, returnees and … [IDPs] regarding their assistance and protection on humanitarian needs.[181]

[179] ibid art VI.

[180] Interview with Millicent Mutuli, Deputy Representative, UNHCR Representation to the AU and the UNECA, 16 January 2012, Addis Ababa.

[181] CCAPRRI (n 178) art I.

Despite this wide mandate, in practice the CCAPRRI/CCFDHA has focused on its function as an advisory body to the PRC Sub-Committee, providing 'a forum and interface between the practitioners and the [AU's] decision-making and policy organs'.[182] Activities that would fall under its other functions have been overlooked. For example, at a 2003 meeting between UNHCR and the African Commission, it was suggested that the CCAPRRI (as it was then known) should 'examine the feasibility of promoting the adoption of a Protocol to the 1969 … Convention which would expand its scope to cover issues not adequately addressed therein'.[183] This never occurred. Moreover, even in its limited role as an advisory body to the PRC Sub-Committee, the CCAPRRI/CCFDHA has been remarkably weak and has recently been entirely non-functional.

In 2004, further to a request from the Executive Council, the AU Commission and UNHCR began working together to revitalize the CCAPRRI, in particular by updating its membership.[184] The request was reiterated in January 2005 'as a matter of urgency'.[185] According to Tigere and Amukhobu, new members were secured by mid-2005,[186] when the Executive Council commended the AU Commission and UNHCR for their efforts in this regard.[187] Further revitalization followed: the CCAPRRI's 2006 Rules of Procedure entered into force when they were adopted by the AU's Executive Council in 2008[188] and a renewed search for additional members began in 2009.[189]

Despite these procedural revitalizations, the CCAPRRI/CCFDHA has in practice been dormant since at least 2008. In the 2008 decision that adopted the CCAPRRI's revised Rules of Procedure, the Executive Council also requested that the AU Commission 'reactivate the Coordinating Committee as soon as possible'.[190] Such has not occurred in any meaningful way. In 2011 the Committee's working group convened a task force to revitalize it,[191] yet in early 2012, relevant officials in Addis Ababa described the CCAPRRI/CCFDHA as 'dormant' at best and, at worst, as 'defunct'. As of late 2017, the CCFDHA was still not operational.

(d) The Division of Humanitarian Affairs, Refugees and Displaced Persons

HARDP is a division of the AU Commission's Department of Political Affairs. It functions as a secretariat to the political PRC Sub-Committee and to the advisory (but dormant) CCFDHA, in particular by facilitating their activities, decision

182 Tigere and Amukhobu (n 163) 53. 183 Murray (n 6) 195.

184 AU (Executive Council), 'Decision on the Situation of Refugees, Returnees and Displaced Persons' (AU Addis Ababa 30 June to 3 July 2004) EX/CL/Dec127 (V) para 12.

185 AU (n 139) para 7. 186 Tigere and Amukhobu (n 163) 53.

187 AU (Executive Council), 'Decision on the Situation of Refugees, Returnees and Displaced Persons' (AU Sirte 28 June to 2 July 2005) EX/CL/Dec197 (VII) para 10.

188 AU (Executive Council), 'Decision on the Rules of Procedure of the Revitalized African Union Coordinating Committee on Assistance and Protection to Refugees, Returnees and Internally Displaced Persons in Africa' (AU Addis Ababa 25–29 January 2008) EC/CL/Dec382 (XII) para 1.

189 AU, 'Statement of HE Mrs Julia Dolly Joiner AU Commissioner for Political Affairs to the 59th Session of the Executive Committee of the High Commissioner's Programme' (6–10 October 2009) 1.

190 AU (Executive Council) (n 188) para 2. 191 Mutuli interview (n 180).

making, and policy development.[192] For example, when the CCAPRRI/CCFDHA was operational, HARDP prepared the first draft of its annual report,[193] as well as drafts all PRC Sub-Committee reports for AU summits.[194] HARDP also coordinates the interface between the AU's humanitarian actors and its decision makers,[195] and takes the lead on all technical aspects of AU policy regarding refugees in particular and humanitarian affairs in general. For example, HARDP led the drafting of the HPF. According to Tigere and Amukhobu, HARDP is central to the 'coordination, documentation and liaison of the work of the AU Commission, AU organs and other partners on matters related to forced displacements'.[196]

Despite its largely technical mandate, HARDP is enormously powerful. Due to the CCFDHA's inactivity and the lack of significant refugee expertise among the diplomats on the PRC Sub-Committee, HARDP has extensive control over the PRC Sub-Committee's programme of work. Among its agenda items, the PRC Sub-Committee selects certain of them to raise to the AU's Executive Council, which may in turn raise issues with the Assembly. Thus HARDP—a technical division meant to serve as a secretariat to the political and advisory arms of the AU's refugee apparatus and staffed by just a few individuals—essentially exercises quite a bit of control over the AU's entire refugee agenda. In this connection, it is important to note that refugees are but one of HARDP's several concerns. As is evident from its name, the division also has a broader humanitarian affairs mandate, which its head is keen to embrace,[197] and which has recently become an AU priority, as discussed later in this section. Thus the AU's engagement with refugee issues is effectively controlled by a few individuals for whom refugees are but one among several concerns.

4. Refugees within other AU initiatives

In addition to these special organs devoted at least in part to them, refugees have also received attention within, or might be impacted by, more general AU initiatives. The CSSDCA, a policy development process commenced under the OAU, noted among its 'core values' that the 'plight of African refugees and internally displaced persons constitutes a scar on the conscience of African governments and people' and provided an undertaking to strengthen refugee protection.[198] Moreover, among the Conference's key performance indicators, all AU member states were expected to have ratified and implemented the 1969 Convention by 2003; it was proposed that the AU should review the 1969 Convention's scope by 2005, ensuring in particular the strength of oversight mechanisms; and states were requested to provide the Conference with information on the condition of refugees, the protection of their human rights, and mechanisms for the mitigation of their situation.[199] Unfortunately, however, the CSSDCA was 'consigned to the rubbish heap of lofty declarations without implementation', and was overtaken by other institutional developments, principally the PSC.[200]

[192] Tigere and Amukhobu (n 163) 53. [193] CCAPRRI (n 178) art VII.
[194] Dare interview (n 165). [195] Tigere and Amukhobu (n 163) 53. [196] ibid.
[197] Dare interview (n 165).
[198] Murray (n 6) 193. [199] ibid. [200] Viljoen (n 1) 168.

The PSC is charged with decision making for the prevention, management, and resolution of conflict on the continent.[201] It was established by a 2002 Protocol to the AU's Constitutive Act,[202] which entered into force in 2003, replacing the OAU's Mechanism for Conflict Prevention, Management and Resolution. The PSC's responsibilities include 'the management of catastrophes and humanitarian actions that encompass situations where refugees, asylum seekers and IDPs will be present'.[203] Not surprisingly, then, the eleventh preambular paragraph of the Protocol establishing the PSC notes African states' concern that 'conflicts have forced millions of our people, including women and children, into a drifting life as refugees and internally displaced persons, deprived of their means of livelihood, human dignity and hope', and it commits the PSC to assisting member states affected by violent conflict through activities including the 'resettlement and reintegration of refugees' once hostilities have ceased;[204] no mention is made of asylum during the period of conflict. The role of the PSC in assisting with the resettlement and reintegration of refugees was reiterated two years following the PSC Protocol's adoption in the AU's Solemn Declaration on a Common African Defence and Security Policy.[205]

The AU's Constitutive Act envisioned the establishment of a common African defence policy.[206] In 2004 AU member states adopted the Solemn Declaration on a Common African Defence and Security Policy, which articulates the scope and objectives of the policy and charges the PSC with its implementation,[207] but does not clearly establish the policy as such. The Declaration lists the 'plight of refugees and internally displaced persons and the insecurity caused by their presence'[208] as among the factors that 'engender insecurity' in Africa,[209] and lists the 'plight of African refugees and internally displaced persons'[210] as among the 'principles and values forming the basis of' the policy.[211] The Declaration goes on to provide that a goal of the Common African Defence and Security Policy is to 'provide a framework for addressing the problems of refugees and internally displaced persons at the continental, regional and national levels'[212] and, relatedly, recognizes the 1969 Convention as among the 'building blocks' of the policy.[213]

The common defence policy envisaged by the Declaration was put on a legal footing with the 2005 adoption of the African Union Non-Aggression and Common Defence Pact.[214] The Pact is principally a collective security arrangement, construing aggression against any member state as 'a threat or aggression against all [AU] Member States'.[215] The Pact does not deliver specifically on the Declaration's promise to 'provide a framework for addressing the problems of refugees'; the Pact's

[201] Jeremy Levitt, 'The Peace and Security Council of the African Union: The Known Unknowns' (2003) 13 Transnat'l L & Contemp Probs 109, 110.

[202] PSC Protocol (n 124). [203] Abass and Mystris (n 5) 31.

[204] PSC Protocol (n 124) art 14(3)(d).

[205] AU (Assembly), 'Solemn Declaration on a Common African Defence and Security Policy' (AU Sirte 28 February 2004) para 22.

[206] AU Constitutive Act (n 112) art 4(d). [207] AU (n 205) para 3.

[208] ibid para I(8)(iv)(n). [209] ibid para I(8)(iv).

[210] ibid para II(12)(v). [211] ibid para II(12). [212] ibid para III(13)(v).

[213] ibid para VI(A)(1)(xxi).

[214] (Adopted 31 January 2005, entered into force 18 December 2009). [215] ibid art 2(c).

only specific mention of refugees is as a provision that the 'Pact shall not derogate from, and shall not be interpreted as derogating in any way whatsoever, from the rights of refugees guaranteed by the relevant continental and international instruments'.[216] However, averting conflict would clearly prevent much displacement. Furthermore, the Pact creates several institutions that could benefit refugees indirectly: the African Peace Academy, the African Centre for the Study and Research on Terrorism, and the AU Commission on International Law.[217] The latter is mandated to 'undertake activities relating to codification and progressive development of international law in the African continent', draft treaties, conduct relevant studies, and encourage scholarly activity in relation to AU law.[218] The AU Commission on International Law's Sixth Forum, held in Malabo, Equatorial Guinea on 4–5 December 2017, focused on the 'legal & socio-economic consequences of immigration, refugees and internally displaced persons in Africa'.

Another AU initiative that is not directed at, but still considers, refugees is the African Charter on Democracy, Elections and Governance.[219] Its article 8(2) provides that states parties 'shall adopt legislative and administrative measures to guarantee the rights of women, ethnic minorities, migrants, people with disabilities, refugees and displaced persons and other marginalized and vulnerable social groups'. This does not add much to the human rights obligations states have already assumed under the African Charter.

(a) *Continental free movement of persons*

The first legal contemplation of the free movement of persons in Africa was in the 1991 Abuja Treaty. The then OAU member states agreed to the 'gradual removal ... of obstacles to the free movement of persons ... and the right of residence and establishment'.[220] To realize this objective, they agreed

> to adopt, individually, at bilateral or regional levels, the necessary measures, in order to achieve progressively the free movement of persons, and to ensure the enjoyment of the right of residence and the right of establishment by their nationals within the Community.
>
> (2) For this purpose, Member State agree to conclude a Protocol on the Free Movement of Persons, Right of Residence and Right of Establishment.[221]

Agenda 2063, which articulates a vision for Africa's future (to be implemented in a series of ten-year plans), resurrected this idea. Agenda 2063 was formally adopted by the Assembly at its 24th Ordinary Session in January 2015.[222] It lists seven

[216] ibid art 17(b). [217] ibid arts 12–14.

[218] Statute of the African Union Commission on International Law (adopted 4 February 2009, entered into force 4 February 2009) EX.CL/478(XIV)a, art 4.

[219] African Charter on Democracy, Elections and Governance (adopted 30 January 2007, entered into force 15 February 2012).

[220] (n 108) art 4(2)(i). [221] ibid art 43.

[222] AU (Assembly), 'Decision on the Report of the Commission on Development of the African Union Agenda 2063 and the Report of the Ministerial Follow-Up Committee on the Bahr Dar Retreat' (AU Addis Ababa 30–31 January 2015) Assembly/AU/Dec.565(XXIV) para 6.

'aspirations'. Aspiration 2 is for an 'integrated continent', including 'seamless borders'[223] and 'the free movement of people'.[224] This aspiration was concretized six months after the adoption of Agenda 2063 in the AU's Declaration on Migration.

The Declaration on Migration committed member states to work towards goals including the introduction of an African passport[225] and the continental free movement of persons,[226] and called on the AU Commission to organize an Executive Council retreat focused on mobility and free movement in Africa. The retreat occurred on 24–25 January 2016 in Mekele, Ethiopia, where the Executive Council considered an AU Commission report on the issue. Thereafter, the Executive Council urged member states to adopt the 'process outlined towards the adoption of a Protocol [to the Abuja Treaty] on Free Movement of People by January 2018, which should come into immediate effect in Member States'.[227]

The 'Protocol to the Treaty Establishing the African Economic Community Relating to Free Movement of Persons, Right of Residence and Right of Establishment' (Free Movement Protocol) was drafted by law professor Vincent Chetail. According to Chetail, the Free Movement Protocol 'facilitates entry, residence and establishment of all nationals of ... [AU] Member States ... [and] governs many other key issues, including an African passport, the principle of non-discrimination, the mutual recognition of academic and professional qualifications, the protection of property rights and the portability of social security benefits'.[228] The African passport Chetail mentions was launched before the Free Movement Protocol was submitted to states, at the AU's 27th Ordinary Session in Kigali, Rwanda in July 2016.[229] It allows holders visa-free entry to all states on the continent, but for the time being is available exclusively to heads of state and government, ministers of foreign affairs, and Addis Ababa-based permanent representatives of AU member states.[230]

Chetail's draft of the Free Movement Protocol was submitted to AU member states in late March 2017 and underwent three rounds of negotiation—in Accra, Ghana; Kigali, Rwanda; and Port Louis, Mauritius—during that year. The Port Louis meeting focused on elaborating a roadmap for the Free Movement Protocol's eventual implementation.

223 AU Commission, 'Agenda 2063: The Africa We Want—Popular Version' (April 2015) para 20.

224 ibid para 23.

225 AU (Assembly), 'Declaration on Migration' (AU Johannesburg 14–15 June 2015) Assembly/AU/Decl.6(XXV) para iii.

226 ibid para i.

227 AU (Executive Council), 'Decision on the Mekele Retreat of the Executive Council' (AU Addis Ababa 23–28 January 2016) EX.CL.Dec.908(XXVIII)Rev.1, para 18.

228 Graduate Institute of International and Development Studies, 'Vincent Chetail has Drafted the Future Treaty on the Free Movement of Persons in Africa' (3 April 2017) <http://graduateinstitute.ch/home/research/research-news.html/_/news/research/2017/prof-chetail-has-drafted-the-fut> accessed 2 August 2017.

229 AU (Assembly), 'Decision on Free Movement of Persons and the African Passport' (AU Kigali 17–18 July 2016) Assembly/AU/Dec.607(XXVII) para 3.

230 AU (Commission), 'Press Release: African Union Set to Launch e-Passport at July Summit in Rwanda' (13 June 2016) <https://au.int/en/pressreleases/30770/african-union-set-launch-e-passport-july-summit-rwanda> accessed 12 April 2017.

The 30th AU summit, held on 29–30 January 2018, focused in part on free movement, specifically on reaching consensus around contested issues so that the Free Movement Protocol could be adopted. The sticking points related to the Free Movement Protocol's entry into force and to the specifics of the Port Louis implementation plan. Regarding entry into force, some states wanted the Free Movement Protocol to enter into force immediately upon adoption, while others favoured entry into force with the fifteenth ratification. Regarding implementation, some states wanted the implementation plan to form part of the Free Movement Protocol, which would make it binding, while others preferred annexing the implementation plan to the Free Movement Protocol, which would afford flexibility.[231] The Free Movement Protocol was adopted at the 30th AU summit, just as this book was going to press. At this time, neither the Free Movement Protocol as adopted nor official decisions indicating how the aforementioned issues were resolved was available.

However, a draft of the Free Movement Protocol dated July 2017 was public. It is arranged in seven parts: definitions, objectives and principles, free movement of persons, right of establishment and right of residence, general provisions, implementation, and final provisions.[232] Part V on general provisions contains several articles relevant to refugee protection. Article 20 prohibits the mass expulsion of non-nationals. Article 21 provides that a 'national of a Member State lawfully admitted into the territory of a host Member State may only be expelled, deported or repatriated ... by virtue of a decision taken in accordance with the law in force in the host Member State'. Article 24 covers 'procedures for movement of specific groups'. It provides that a 'Member State may in addition to the measures provided for by international, regional and continental instruments, establish specific procedures for the movement of specific vulnerable groups including refugees, victims of human trafficking, asylum seekers and pastoralists'. Its second paragraph goes on to state that 'Procedures established by a Member State under this article shall be consistent with the obligations of that Member State under the international, regional and continental instruments relating to the protection of each group of persons referred to in paragraph 1'.[233]

These provisions support existing refugee and human rights law protections. Article 20 reiterates the African Charter article 12(5) prohibition of mass expulsion. Article 21 reinforces the African Charter article 12(4) prohibition of arbitrary expulsion and supports non-refoulement by subjecting any expulsion to 'the law in force in the host Member State'. Most importantly, in requiring

[231] Institute for Security Studies Peace and Security Council Report, '30th AU Summit: Time to Implement First AU Reforms' (9 January 2018) <https://issafrica.org/pscreport/on-the-agenda/30th-au-summit-time-to-implement-first-au-reforms?utm_source=BenchmarkEmail&utm_campaign=PSC_Report&utm_medium=email> accessed 12 January 2018.

[232] AU, 'Draft Protocol to the Treaty Establishing the African Economic Community Relating to Free Movement of Persons, Right of Residence and Right of Establishment' (July 2017) <https://au.int/sites/default/files/newsevents/workingdocuments/33023-wd-pa20330_e_original_free_movement_protocol.pdf> accessed 21 December 2017.

[233] ibid art 24.

that any 'procedures for movement of specific groups' be consistent with cognate international and regional obligations, the Free Movement Protocol's article 24(2) ensures that any measures adopted in the context of the emerging continental free movement regime will reinforce pre-existing refugee protection obligations. While these provisions represent a positive start, scholars and advocates must remain vigilant regarding the possibility that the emerging continental free movement regime may end up compromising refugee protection. The EU precedent is instructive in this regard.

Citizens of EU member states enjoy freedom of movement and establishment within the border-free single market.[234] Under Europe's Protocol on Asylum for Nationals of Member States of the European Union[235] (Aznar Protocol), EU member states may declare as inadmissible any refugee claim from the national of another EU member state.[236] While this is premised upon the assumption that the level of human rights protection within the EU renders all member states 'safe countries of origin' for asylum purposes,[237] the Aznar Protocol cannot be divorced from the EU's free movement regime. Indeed, the Aznar Protocol's seventh preambular paragraph bears in mind that the 'Constitution establishes an area without internal frontiers and grants every citizen of the Union the right to move and reside freely within the territory of the Member States'. While an EU national who experiences persecution at home may indeed relocate to any other EU member state and enjoy rights of establishment there, the most important refugee right—non-refoulement—does not form part of the establishment rights bundle. Regional free movement regimes may therefore complement,[238] but are no substitute for, refugee protection. As the AU develops its free movement system, it is critical that it not adopt any Aznar-style instrument that positions free movement as a substitute for refugee protection.

Once it enters into force and is fully implemented, the Free Movement Protocol may even benefit refugees. Chapter 4 demonstrated that all refugees in Africa, including those recognized exclusively under the 1969 Convention's article I(2), are entitled to 1951 Convention rights. Such rights are, however, often contingent.

[234] Consolidated Version of the Treaty on the Functioning of the European Union, 26 October 2012, OJ 326/01, arts 20, 21, and 45.

[235] Protocol on Asylum for Nationals of Member States, 16 December 2004, OJ C 310/362, sole article.

[236] Relatedly, the EU's Qualification Directive applies only to third country nationals and stateless persons.

[237] The Aznar Protocol's sole article provides, 'Given the level of protection of fundamental rights and freedoms by the Member States of the European Union, Member States shall be regarded as constituting safe countries of origin in respect of each other for all legal and practical purposes in relation to asylum matters'. The case of *MSS v Belgium and Greece* (App No 30696/09 (Grand Chamber, 21 January 2011)) has highlighted that human rights are not in fact uniformly protected across Europe, and in so doing has underlined just how problematic the Aznar Protocol is.

[238] How rights of establishment may complement refugee protection can be seen in Uganda. Section 9 of that country's Refugees Regulations provide that a 'person who applies and is granted refugee status in Uganda and is a national of the East Africa Community shall enjoy all the rights and privileges bestowed on the "Community nationals" and as set out in the Treaty and Protocols for the establishment of the East Africa Community'.

Many 1951 Convention rights are guaranteed to a refugee only to the extent that they are enjoyed by a particular reference group: aliens generally in the same circumstances, most favoured foreigners or nationals.[239] Two sets of 1951 Convention rights that are critical to refugees' well-being are subject to such legal contingencies and are also regularly restricted in practice: the article 17–19 rights to gainful employment and the article 26 freedom of movement and residence. Article 17 on waged employment is guaranteed to refugees to the extent of 'the most favourable treatment accorded to nationals of a foreign country in the same circumstances'. Article 18 on self-employment, article 19 on the exercise of liberal professions, and article 26 on freedom of movement and residence are guaranteed to refugees only to the extent they are enjoyed by aliens generally in the same circumstances.[240] When the Free Movement Protocol enters into force, it will likely amplify these critical yet contingent rights in adhering states, by improving the standard of treatment owed to relevant reference groups. Under a fully implemented free movement regime, African 'aliens generally in the same circumstances' and African 'nationals of a foreign country in the same circumstances' will be able to work and move within state territory on favourable terms,[241] thereby raising the standard of treatment owed to refugees under the 1951 Convention.[242]

(b) The AU's humanitarian agenda

The AU finalized its HPF in 2015 after a HARDP-led drafting process. The HPF defines humanitarian action as action 'to preserve, protect and save lives, alleviate suffering and enhance physical security and human dignity'.[243] The HPF's 'strategic vision' is to

> strengthen African's humanitarian governance by enhancing the AU's leadership role and mandate through providing strategic approaches and guidelines for ... [AU] led efforts in conformity with African shared values, and the norms and standards for humanitarian action on the African continent; in full respect of international law; and on the other hand in strengthening the primary responsibility of Member States by strengthening their predictive, preventive, response and adaptive capabilities.[244]

This vision is broken down into nine objectives, relating to the protection of and assistance for 'persons in need of humanitarian assistance'; prevention; support for Africa's RECs; promotion of dialogue; enhanced coordination; protection for

[239] See Marina Sharpe, 'The 1951 Refugee Convention's Contingent Rights Framework and Article 26 of the ICCPR: A Fundamental Incompatibility?' (2014) 30 Refuge 5.

[240] Regarding the meaning of 'in the same circumstances', see the 1951 Convention ((adopted 28 July 1951, entered into force 22 April 1954) 189 UNTS 137) art 6.

[241] Free Movement Protocol (n 232) arts 14, 16, and 17.

[242] Such improved treatment is of course in addition to the African Charter's robust protection of freedom of movement and residence under article 12(1).

[243] AU (HARDP), 'African Union Humanitarian Policy Framework' (November 2015) <http://www.peaceau.org/uploads/humanitarian-policy-framework-rev-final-version.pdf> accessed 6 April 2017, para 3.

[244] ibid para 13.

stateless persons and the reduction of statelessness; improved planning; support for host communities; and enhanced partnerships and resource mobilization.[245] These objectives are to be achieved through 'a strategic approach and guidelines for coordinating and supporting [the] AU's involvement in its early warning and prevention efforts, in addressing root causes and durable solutions, ensuring adequate preparations to respond to and deal with root causes and the aftermaths of humanitarian challenges on the continent'.[246]

The HPF includes two points of 'strategic focus': coordination and the 'phases of AU's humanitarian action', which include 'protection and assistance'. The protection discussion—which covers refugees, asylum seekers, returnees, stateless persons, and IDPs—does not mention non-refoulement but notes that all 'displaced people are entitled to the protection of their human rights and assistance accorded to them by relevant laws'. The document then goes on to list several vulnerable groups, such as unaccompanied minors. The section on 'assistance', which essentially covers humanitarian aid, is much more detailed than its predecessor on protection. While the AU should be lauded for taking steps to address the humanitarian situation in Africa, stressing aid over protection and the related failure to mention non-refoulement represent a step backwards. In her seminal 1986 book, Harrell-Bond warned of the dangers of treating refugees as passive victims in need of little more than humanitarian assistance.[247] The AU's institutional foundation seemed to heed that warning by entrenching a rights-based approach, from which the HPF unfortunately departs.

The CAP 'builds on' the HPF[248] and the HPF in turn 'anchors' the CAP.[249] The two are, however, quite distinct. While the HPF focuses on humanitarian action in Africa specifically, the CAP is Africa's united call for, and contribution to, a 'global humanitarian architecture',[250] made at the first ever WHS in Istanbul, Turkey, in May 2016. The process of drafting the CAP began with a June 2014 Executive Council decision requesting that the AU Commission, 'in close collaboration with the PRC Sub-Committee on Refugees ... engage Member States in a Political Process ... to establish an African Position that will be presented at the World Humanitarian Summit'.[251] This resulted in the CAP, which the Assembly formally adopted at its 26th Ordinary Session in January 2016.[252] At this time, the Assembly also resolved to establish an African Humanitarian Agency,[253] which is mentioned in the CAP but has yet to be operationalized.

245 ibid para 17. 246 ibid para 14.

247 Barbara Harrell-Bond, *Imposing Aid: Emergency Assistance to Refugees* (OUP 1986).

248 AU, 'Common African Position (CAP) on Humanitarian Effectiveness: One Africa, One Voice, One Message at the World Humanitarian Summit' (March 2016) 12.

249 ibid.

250 ibid 13.

251 AU (Executive Council), 'Decision on the Humanitarian Situation in Africa' (AU Malabo 20–24 June 2014) EX.CL/Dec.817(XXV) para 8.

252 AU (n 155) para 9.

253 See, generally, Romola Adeola, 'Africa Has Some Work to do Before it Starts its own Humanitarian Agency' (10 October 2016) <http://theconversation.com/africa-has-some-work-to-do-before-it-starts-its-own-humanitarian-agency-65960> accessed 6 April 2017.

While the CAP represents Africa's call for reform of the international humanitarian system, it is nevertheless naturally focused on Africa's 'peculiarities'.[254] With these in mind, the CAP groups Africa's humanitarian priorities into ten pillars: the primary responsibility of the state; root causes and durable solutions; governance and human rights; the connection between development, peace, and security; institutional architecture; the domestication and implementation of normative and policy frameworks; protection and assistance; evidence base; promoting the role of the private sector, African civil society, the diaspora, and youth; and financing partnerships.[255]

Pillar seven on 'protection and assistance of affected populations' remarkably fails to mention refugees. Instead, it focuses on 'vulnerable groups', specifically women, children, the elderly, and persons with disabilities. Similarly, pillar six, calling for the domestication and implementation of normative frameworks, mentions the Kampala Convention and the Protocol to the African Charter on Human and Peoples' Rights on the Right to a Nationality in Africa (Nationality Protocol), which has yet to be adopted, but not the 1969 Convention.[256] The 1969 Convention is similarly not invoked under pillar three on human rights. This is particularly surprising given the PRC Sub-Committee's leadership role in drafting the CAP.

To the extent refugee issues are reflected in the CAP, the underlying theme is one of easing the burden refugees are seen to represent by focusing on solutions and international responsibility sharing. Pillar two on root causes mentions protracted refugee situations and identifies voluntary repatriation, local integration, and resettlement as solutions.[257] Pillar ten on financing partnerships calls on the international community to 'share the burden imposed on host countries in Africa and ensure a much fairer means of burden sharing globally' and welcomes the WHS global consultation recommendation of a 'New Deal for Refugees' emphasizing the provision of support to host countries; the CAP adds to this by calling for hosts' contributions to refugee protection to be quantified and recognized in the same way a pecuniary contribution would be. Pillar ten also calls on AU member states to 'shift the focus from measures for strengthening strategies for management of . . . refugees, and place such emphasis and focus on finding durable and sustainable solutions'.[258] Solutions and responsibility sharing are of course important, but the fact that they are not mentioned alongside calls on states to uphold the 1969 Convention, non-refoulement, and other foundational refugee protection principles represents the culmination of a major shift in the AU's approach to refugees, addressed in the conclusion below.

D. Conclusions

The OAU and AU have engaged consistently with refugee issues. Both organizations have adopted legal instruments, created bodies with refugee-focused mandates, and staged political and other gatherings resulting in resolutions, declarations,

[254] AU (n 248) 13. [255] ibid. [256] ibid 21. [257] ibid 15. [258] ibid 25.

decisions, recommendations, and plans of action. Whether these initiatives have been effective is, however, another matter. Authors who have examined specific OAU and AU refugee initiatives in depth have consistently questioned their efficacy. According to Nyanduga, for example, the 'Unenforceability of resolutions and decisions of regional political ... bodies remains a major handicap for the legal protection mechanism'.[259] Indeed, the number of refugees in Africa has recently been on the rise,[260] many refugees remain trapped in protracted situations, violations of refugees' rights abound,[261] and, as discussed in Chapter 1, states' commitment to refugee protection is waning. Thus, it may be a question of quantity over quality and rhetoric over reality; while there is no shortage of norms, bodies, and initiatives, it is not clear that they have been effectively implemented by member states, prevented or resolved forced displacement or produced better protection outcomes for refugees.

The transition from the OAU to the AU represented an opportunity to remedy this. The AU's focus on democracy, social and economic development, peace and security, and human rights is more in line with refugee protection than was its predecessor's preoccupation with decolonization and the consolidation of post-colonial states, and the establishment of the AU created the possibility of building new AU institutions. Indeed, the AU established bodies focused at least in part on refugees, with neatly parsed out political (PRC Sub-Committee), advisory (the dormant CCFDHA), and technical (STC on Migration, Refugees and IDPs and HARDP) mandates. Yet these bodies have not produced unequivocal results. Moreover, while there are four AU bodies focused at least in part on refugee issues, in practice much control seems to lie with HARDP.

These issues of implementation and effectiveness are in keeping with broader critiques of the AU, which have come from both outside and inside the organization. The AU has not been unresponsive. In July 2007 the Assembly called for an audit of the organization.[262] The report in this connection, known as the Adedeji Report,[263] was delivered before the year was out, however its recommendations were for the most part not implemented.[264]

259 Nyanduga (n 3) 102.

260 UNGA, 'Assistance to Refugees, Returnees and Displaced Persons in Africa, Report of the Secretary General' (20 August 2015) UN Doc A/70/337, para 2.

261 See, for example, Bonaventure Rutinwa, 'The End of Asylum? The Changing Nature of Refugee Policies in Africa' (2002) 21 RSQ 12; Jeff Crisp, 'No Solution in Sight: The Problem of Protracted Refugee Situations in Africa' in Itaru Ohta and Yntiso Gebre (eds), *Displacement Risks in Africa: Refugees, Resettlers and Their Host Population* (Kyoto University Press 2005); Guglielmo Verdirame and Barbara Harrell-Bond, *Rights in Exile: Janus Faced Humanitarianism* (Berghahn Books 2005).

262 AU (Assembly), 'Accra Declaration on the Union Government of Africa' (AU Accra 3 July 2007) <http://www.dirco.gov.za/docs/2007/ghan_decl0706.htm> accessed 23 December 2017.

263 Abedabo Adedeji et al, 'Audit of the African Union' (2007) <http://osf.org.za/wp-content/uploads/2015/08/Audit-of-the-African-Union-Report-of-the-High-Level-Panel.pdf> accessed 23 December 2017.

264 Paul Kagame, 'The Imperative to Strengthen our Union: Report on the Proposed Recommendations of the Institutional Reform of the African Union' (29 January 2017) <http://www.rci.uct.ac.za/sites/default/files/image_tool/images/78/News/FInal%20AU%20Reform%20Combined%20report_28012017.pdf> accessed 23 December 2017, 15.

In July 2016 heads of state and government, ministers of foreign affairs, and ministers of finance met in Kigali to discuss the need for institutional reform, and subsequently entrusted the endeavour to Rwandan President Paul Kagame.[265] He delivered his report early in 2017. It unequivocally states that 'The chronic failure to see through African Union decisions has resulted in a crisis of implementation'.[266] Kagame goes on to point out that while the Assembly has adopted over 1,500 resolutions, 'there is no easy way to determine how many of those have actually been implemented. By consistently failing to follow up on the implementation of the decisions we have made, the signal has been sent that they don't matter. As a result, we have a dysfunctional organization in which member states see limited value, global partners find little credibility, and our citizens have no trust'.[267] Kagame made four concrete proposals to address this and the other issues he identifies, which were adopted by the Assembly.[268] First among Kagame's proposed reforms is that the AU focus on 'key priorities with continental scope'.[269]

Refugees should be among the 'key priorities' Kagame proposes, simply because of the sheer number of, and abysmal conditions for, refugees on the continent. It is time for the AU to either rehabilitate or officially retire its moribund CCFDHA, and for all bodies to focus on the quality or effectiveness of initiatives over their quantity. This might be achieved by addressing a limited number of defined issues, such as root causes, non-refoulement or local integration, rather than by allowing norms to proliferate beyond any reasonable capacity to implement them. Follow-up or accountability mechanisms must also be developed and implemented. Just as Kagame argues that the AU must focus on key priorities, the many issues arising within each such key priority must also be addressed with focus and with accountability.

There is hope in this regard. Rwanda took over chairmanship of the AU on 1 January 2018 and the thirtieth AU summit on 29–30 January 2018 focused in part on Kagame's proposed reforms. The AU Commission has already established a Reform Implementation Unit, and according to Kagame's implementation matrix, four further recommendations are to be implemented in January 2018: a mechanism to ensure the implementation of legally binding decisions; the strengthening and enforcement of a sanctions mechanism; the completion of an audit of bureaucratic inefficiency; and the adoption of quotas for women and youth among AU Commission staff.[270]

Finally, and perhaps most importantly, the AU must ensure that the issues it has recently prioritized—the continental free movement of persons, humanitarian affairs generally and the foundational social, economic and security issues encapsulated in Agenda 2063—do not come at the expense of refugees' specific rights.

[265] AU (Assembly), 'Decision on the Institutional Reform of the African Union' (AU Kigali 17–18 July 2016) AU/Dec/606 (XXVII) para 2.

[266] Kagame (n 264) 4. [267] ibid 5.

[268] AU (Assembly), 'Decision on the Outcome of the Retreat of the Assembly of the African Union on the Institutional Reform of the African Union' (AU Addis Ababa 30–31 January 2017) Assembly/AU/Dec.635 (XXVIII) para 5.

[269] Kagame (n 264) 5.

[270] Institute for Security Studies Peace and Security Council Report (n 231).

Certainly, if the Agenda 2063 goals of a prosperous, peaceful, and secure continent characterized by good governance, democracy, respect for human rights, justice, and the rule of law are achieved,[271] it will benefit all Africans, not least refugees. However, these ambitious long-term goals cannot come at the expense of the immediate and still critical issues of preventing forced displacement, protecting refugees' rights during exile, and fostering durable solutions.

The AU's political and administrative machinery is not alone in facing a crisis of effectiveness. The African Commission also has a robust record of refugee engagement and similarly equivocal results. It and other AU judicial institutions with human rights mandates are addressed in Chapter 7.

[271] AU Commission (n 223) aspirations 1, 3, and 4.

7
The African Commission and Human Rights Courts

A. Introduction

The regional institutional architecture supportive of refugee protection in Africa consists of African Union (AU) bodies with political, advisory, and technical mandates, which were the subject of Chapter 6, as well as judicial organs with human rights mandates. This chapter focuses on how these have engaged with refugee issues. Four institutions are addressed: the African Commission on Human and Peoples' Rights (African Commission), the African Court on Human and Peoples' Rights (African Court), the African Court of Justice and Human Rights (Merged Court), and the African Court of Justice and Human and Peoples' Rights (New Merged Court). They are previewed in this introduction, with the remainder of the chapter devoted to addressing each body and its refugee engagement in more depth. The African Commission's promotional and protective mandates and its refugee-related activities within each are the focus of section B. Specific issues addressed in the promotional context include the Commission's collaboration with the Office of the United Nations High Commissioner for Refugees (UNHCR), its supervision (or not) of the Organization of African Unity Convention Governing the Specific Aspects of Refugee Problems in Africa (1969 Convention), its promotional activities and the mandate of the Special Rapporteur on Refugees, Asylum Seekers, Internally Displaced Persons and Migrants in Africa (Special Rapporteur). Section C is devoted to the African Court and its engagement with refugee issues, while section D covers the Merged Court and the New Merged Court. A final section concludes.

The African Commission is a supervisory treaty body created by the African Charter on Human and Peoples' Rights (African Charter) to 'promote human and peoples' rights and ensure their protection in Africa'.[1] It began operating in 1987. The African Commission's decisions in individual and interstate complaints are often viewed as not being legally binding, a problem the African Court was created in part to address. The African Court was created by way of a 1998 protocol to the

[1] African Charter on Human and Peoples' Rights (adopted 27 June 1981, entered into force 21 October 1986) 21 ILM 58, art 30.

African Charter[2] (African Court Protocol) and became operational in June 2006, when its first cohort of judges was sworn in.

Between the 1998 adoption of the African Court Protocol and the Court's creation in 2006, the then AU Assembly of Heads of State and Government (Assembly) Chair and Nigerian President, Olusegun Obasanjo, revived a dormant idea to merge the African Court with the African Court of Justice, to save on costs and rationalize pan-African institutions.[3] The African Court of Justice was to be the AU's principal judicial organ, mandated to address issues related to the application or implementation of the AU's Constitutive Act. At the time of Obasanjo's proposal, a protocol establishing the African Court of Justice had been adopted but had yet to enter into force.[4] The Assembly adopted Obasanjo's suggestion in July 2004,[5] which will prevent the African Court of Justice from ever being established, despite the entry into force of its establishing protocol on 11 February 2009.[6] A protocol establishing the Merged Court, with the Merged Court's statute annexed to it, was adopted in 2008 (Merged Court Protocol).[7]

Six states have ratified the Merged Court Protocol,[8] nine ratifications short of the fifteen required for its entry into force.[9] The Merged Court Protocol will not, however, enter into force in its original form. In June 2014 the Merged Court Protocol was amended by way of a further protocol (Malabo Protocol),[10] which created—on paper—the New Merged Court. The New Merged Court is substantially the same as the Merged Court, except its jurisdiction was extended to cover international crimes[11] (though not those committed by sitting heads of state and other senior officials),[12] due in part to debate in Africa surrounding the International Criminal Court. The Malabo Protocol has been signed by ten states[13] but has not received any ratifications; it needs fifteen ratifications for entry into force.

[2] Protocol to the African Charter on Human and Peoples' Rights on the Establishment of an African Court on Human and Peoples' Rights (adopted 10 June 1998, entered into force 25 January 2004) OAU Doc OAU/LEG/EXP/AFCHPR/PROT.

[3] Sonia Sceats, 'Africa's New Human Rights Court: Whistling in the Wind?' (2009) Chatham House <https://www.chathamhouse.org/publications/papers/view/109010> accessed 26 January 2018, 5.

[4] Protocol of the Court of Justice of the African Union (adopted 11 July 2003, entered into force 11 February 2009).

[5] AU (AHG), 'Decision on the Seats of the African Union' (AU Addis Ababa 6–8 July 2004) Assembly/AU/Dec 45 (III) Rev 1, para 4.

[6] As a result of the practical non-existence of the African Court of Justice, states must employ alternative dispute resolution mechanisms, such as arbitration, to resolve issues within the African Court of Justice's theoretical jurisdiction.

[7] Protocol on the Statute of the African Court of Justice and Human Rights (adopted 1 July 2008) AU Doc Assembly/AU/Dec 196 (XI).

[8] Benin, Burkina Faso, the Republic of Congo, Liberia, Libya, and Mali.

[9] Merged Court Protocol (n 7) art 9(1).

[10] Protocol on Amendments to the Protocol on the Statute of the African Court of Justice and Human Rights (adopted 27 June 2014). Note that the Malabo Protocol only amends, and does not replace, the Merged Court Protocol; many aspects of the New Merged Court's jurisdiction and functioning continue to be regulated by the Merged Court Protocol.

[11] ibid art 3(1).

[12] ibid, Annex, art 46A *bis*.

[13] Benin, Chad, Ghana, Guinea-Bissau, Kenya, Mauritania, the Republic of the Congo, São Tomé and Príncipe, Sierra Leone, and Uganda.

B. The African Commission on Human and Peoples' Rights

Despite the existence of the African Court, much of the general and refugee-related human rights work in Africa is still performed by the African Commission. The Commission has a dual promotional and protective mandate. The latter consists mainly of the consideration of individual complaints, known as communications, while the former consists primarily of the examination of state party reports.

Article 60 of the African Charter articulates the Commission's sources of law. It provides that the African Commission

> shall draw inspiration from international law on human and peoples' rights, particularly from the provisions of various African instruments on Human and Peoples' Rights, the Charter of the United Nations, the Charter of the Organization of African Unity, the Universal Declaration of Human Rights, other instruments adopted by the United Nations and by African countries in the field of Human and Peoples' Rights, as well as from the provisions of various instruments adopted within the Specialised Agencies of the United Nations of which the Parties to the present Charter are members.

Additionally, according to article 61, the African Commission shall

> take into consideration, as subsidiary measures to determine the principles of law, other general or special international conventions, laying down rules expressly recognised by Member States of the Organization of African Unity, African practices consistent with international norms on Human and Peoples' Rights, customs generally accepted as law, general principles of law recognised by African States as well as legal precedents and doctrine.

These two provisions made their way into the African Charter by way of the Monrovia Proposal, which, as explained in Chapter 5,[14] was a blueprint for the establishment of an African human rights body. The Monrovia Proposal included this range of international human rights sources 'to ensure that the proposed Commission would have a substantive basis on which to operate, *in the absence of any African human rights convention or charter*'.[15] Although the African Charter ultimately included substantive rights and duties, articles 60 and 61 were nevertheless retained.[16] The African Commission may thus draw on African and international human rights treaties—including the 1969 Convention—customary international law, jurisprudence, doctrine and general principles of law. In practice, however, the African Commission primarily applies the African Charter.

The African Commission's functioning is regulated by its Rules of Procedure, which were adopted in 1988[17] and amended in 1995. New Rules of Procedure, which currently govern the Commission, were adopted in 2010. The African Commission is comprised of eleven commissioners, who are elected by the AU

[14] See section C.1.

[15] Frans Viljoen, *International Human Rights Law in Africa* (2nd edn, OUP 2012) 325.

[16] ibid.

[17] Reproduced in Rachel Murray and Malcolm Evans (eds), *Documents of the African Commission on Human and Peoples' Rights*, vol 1 (Hart 2001) 136–64.

Assembly to serve part-time and in a personal capacity.[18] They meet twice per year for ten to fifteen days, usually at the African Commission's seat in Banjul, Gambia, where there is also a small Commission secretariat.

Despite the distance between Banjul and Addis Ababa, where the AU is headquartered, the African Commission was created 'within' the Organization of African Unity (OAU).[19] The nature of the relationship between the African Commission and the AU is not articulated beyond this. While the African Charter established the African Commission 'within' the OAU, according to the French language version of the Charter, the African Commission was established '*auprès*', or 'close to', the OAU.[20] When the AU supplanted the OAU, the Assembly decided that the African Commission would 'henceforth operate within the framework of'[21] the AU, a similarly imprecise formulation. At the very least, it is clear that the African Commission is not an AU organ as such, but rather a body within an autonomous treaty regime. In the absence of a clear relationship among the African Commission and AU organs with concurrent human rights mandates, 'the resolution and governance of the resulting diversification of institutional responsibilities pertaining to the African Charter must be left to a study of the practices and decisions of these institutions'.[22] Viljoen has found that the African Commission is isolated from the AU.[23]

1. Promotional mandate

The African Commission's promotional functions are non-adversarial public activities entailing education about, and the creation of a culture of respect for, human rights. A principal activity in this regard is addressing state reports. The African Charter's article 62 requires states parties to submit biennial reports on legislative or other measures taken to give effect to the rights and freedoms guaranteed under the Charter. Interestingly, however, the consideration of state party reports is not mentioned by the African Charter's article 45, which lists the African Commission's functions. Moreover, article 62 does not specify the body to which reports should be submitted. In 1988 the African Commission requested a mandate to examine state reports, which was granted by the OAU's Assembly of Heads of State and Government (OAHG) based on the power implied by article 62.[24] Soon thereafter, the African Commission adopted guidelines on state reporting; in 1998 these were amended and also supplemented by a more concise set of additional guidelines.[25]

[18] African Charter (n 1) arts 31 and 33. [19] ibid art 30. [20] ibid.

[21] AU (AHG), 'Decision on the Interim Period' (AU Durban 9–10 July 2002) ASS/AU/Dec.1-8(I) para 2.

[22] Chidi Odinkalu, 'From Architecture to Geometry: The Relationship Between the African Commission on Human and Peoples' Rights and Organs of the African Union' (2013) 35 Hum Rts Q 850, 856.

[23] Viljoen (n 15) 169. [24] ibid 356.

[25] Christof Heyns, 'The African Regional Human Rights System: The African Charter' (2003–2004) 108 Penn State L Rev 679, 682; the guidelines are reprinted in Christof Heyns, *Human Rights Law in Africa*, vol 3 (Brill 1998) 125.

Broadly speaking, the guidelines require reports to be publicly examined, and then commented upon, by the African Commission. Despite the fact that state reporting forms the 'backbone' of the African Commission's mission,[26] reports are often overdue, as is their consideration by the Commission.[27] For example, after the African Commission's 24th Ordinary Session, 258 state reports were due, however only thirty had been submitted and only twenty-five had been examined;[28] as of 2012, no state had ever met the article 62 requirement to report every two years.[29] In this context, promotional activities that do not depend on regular state participation are of increased importance. These include the issuing of resolutions;[30] undertaking fact-finding and promotional missions; disseminating information; convening seminars, symposia, and conferences; and creating subsidiary bodies such as special rapporteurs, working groups, and committees.[31]

2. Protective mandate

The African Commission discharges its protective mandate primarily by hearing oral arguments and issuing findings in adversarial proceedings regarding alleged Charter violations. Communications may be instituted by one state party to the Charter against another,[32] or by an individual or a legal person (such as a non-governmental organization (NGO)) against a state party. As with state party reports, the African Charter provides no explicit legal basis for individual complaints, as the consideration of individual communications is not explicitly provided by article 45 on the African Commission's mandate. Moreover, article 58 provides,

1. When it appears after deliberations of the Commission that one or more Communications apparently relate to special cases which reveal the existence of a series of serious or massive violations of human and peoples' rights, the Commission shall draw the attention of the Assembly of Heads of State and Government to these special cases.
2. The Assembly of Heads of State and Government may then request the Commission to undertake an in-depth study of these cases and make a factual report, accompanied by its finding and recommendations.

Neither the OAHG nor the AU Assembly has ever responded to this procedure, so the African Commission no longer pursues it.[33] Nevertheless, it has been read as indicating that the African Commission may only consider communications regarding 'serious or massive violations' and further to instructions from the Assembly.[34] Drawing on the language of article 55, which refers to communications 'other than those of State Parties', the African Commission has always, however, interpreted its mandate as including the power to consider communications authored by individuals or legal persons.[35]

[26] Viljoen (n 15) 349.
[27] Christof Heyns and Frans Viljoen, 'An Overview of International Human Rights Protection in Africa' (1999) 15 S Afr J Hum Rts 421, 430.
[28] ibid. [29] Viljoen (n 15) 355. [30] African Charter (n 1) art 45(1)(b).
[31] ibid art 45(1)(a). [32] ibid arts 47–59. [33] Heyns (n 25) 695.
[34] ibid 694. [35] ibid.

Before the African Commission can consider a communication on its merits, the author's standing must be established, followed by the communication's admissibility. States parties to the African Charter have automatic standing. The African Charter does not include any individual victim requirement and the current Rules of Procedure are silent as to standing. Under the original 1988 Rules, legal persons had standing to submit communications on behalf of an alleged victim if the victim was 'unable to submit the communication' him or herself.[36] The Commission still permits this and indeed has taken an expansive approach to individual standing: the legal person need not have the victim's express consent, nor must it have observer status before the Commission.[37]

Admissibility is assessed after the threshold requirement of standing. The admissibility criteria are set out at article 56 of the Charter. Communications may not be submitted anonymously,[38] use 'disparaging or insulting language',[39] be based solely on information disseminated by mass media,[40] or deal with issues already settled in another forum.[41] With several exceptions,[42] communications may only be submitted after, and within a reasonable period of time from,[43] the exhaustion of domestic remedies.[44]

The Charter is silent as to whether a complainant who has fled the respondent state must nevertheless meet the article 56(5) exhaustion of domestic remedies admissibility requirement. Bekker reviewed the jurisprudence in this regard, finding it inconsistent. She explains that a distinction, however, 'appears to be drawn between cases where an individual filing an application has been granted refugee status and those where the complainant is merely an asylum seeker'.[45] In the latter case, the African Commission appears reluctant to view the exhaustion of domestic remedies constructively.[46]

Finally, communications must be 'compatible with' the OAU (now AU) Charter, or with the African Charter.[47] This admissibility criterion relates to the rights-holder(s), the duty-bearer(s), the time and place at which the violation is alleged to have occurred, and the substantive issues involved.[48] Thus the author must be someone protected by the Charter (or be a legal person representing the interests of a protected individual), the respondent state must be bound by the Charter, the violation must have occurred after the Charter's entry into force for the respondent state and the right or rights violated must be 'located within the Charter'.[49] The latter does not, however, require that the communication invoke a particular Charter right. According to Viljoen, the Commission can consider alleged violations of any AU human rights treaty without an autonomous treaty monitoring body, such as the 1969 Convention.[50] Indeed, in *African Institute for Human Rights and Development (on Behalf of Sierra Leone Refugees in Guinea) v Guinea (African Institute)*, the African Commission found

[36] 1988 Rules of Procedure (n 17) r 114(1)(a). [37] Viljoen (n 15) 304.
[38] African Charter (n 1) art 56(1). [39] ibid art 56(3). [40] ibid art 56(4).
[41] ibid art 56(7). [42] See Viljoen (n 15) 316–19.
[43] African Charter (n 1) art 56(6). [44] ibid art 56(5).
[45] Gina Bekker, 'The Protection of Asylum Seekers and Refugees within the African Regional Human Rights System' (2013) 13 Afr Hum Rts LJ 1, 10.
[46] ibid. [47] African Charter (n 1) art 56(2). [48] Viljoen (n 15) 311.
[49] ibid 312. [50] ibid.

that the mass expulsion of refugees violated the 1969 Convention's article IV non-discrimination provision.[51]

The African Commission's willingness to pronounce upon human rights treaties other than the African Charter reflects its innovative approach to both substantive and procedural matters. In the latter connection, the African Commission's Rules of Procedure provide for the individual complaints procedure described earlier in this section, despite the Charter's silence in this regard. In a substantive sense, African Commission resolutions and decisions have 'provided clarity about vaguely formulated rights and expanded the normative scope of the Charter'.[52] This has been within a largely textual interpretive approach, balanced by recognition of the importance of giving effect to rights.[53]

This recognition is but one aspect of whether rights are realized. Equally important are remedies, their legal status and whether they are implemented. The Charter is silent regarding remedies, noting only that the African Commission may make 'recommendations to the [OAU's, now AU's] Assembly of Heads of State and Government' (rather than to the respondent state).[54] This has led to the widely held, and at the very least arguable,[55] view that African Commission decisions are not legally binding,[56] and resulted in early jurisprudence that found violations without providing an associated remedy.[57] Eventually, however, the African Commission began to order both open-ended remedies admonishing the state to bring its laws in line with the Charter and specific remedies prescribing measures to correct violations or provide compensation. Viljoen argues that states should not be able to opt out of such remedies, and views the issue of whether African Commission decisions are binding as a red herring: the 'contention is ... not so much that the Commission's findings should be characterized as "binding", but rather that states are treaty-bound to give effect to the Charter as interpreted by the treaty body in individual cases'.[58] The African Commission has expressed the same view, based on article 1 of the Charter, pursuant to which states parties agree to 'give effect' to Charter rights.[59]

The implementation record of African Commission decisions, however, unfortunately suggests that states do not share this view. In their seminal study of state compliance with the forty-four African Commission decisions issued between 1994 and 2004, Viljoen and Louw found full compliance in only fourteen per cent of cases. In thirty per cent of cases, the respondent state did not comply with the African Commission's decision, and thirty-two per cent of cases featured only partial

[51] *African Institute for Human Rights and Development (on Behalf of Sierra Leonean Refugees in Guinea) v Guinea* comm no 249/2002, 20th Annual Activity Report of the Af Cm HPR (2004) para 74.

[52] Viljoen (n 15) 323. [53] ibid 323–24. [54] African Charter (n 1) art 53.

[55] See Frans Viljoen and Lirette Louw, 'The Status of the Findings of the African Commission: From Moral Persuasion to Legal Obligation' (2004) 48 J Afr L 1, 13–18.

[56] See, for example, Rose D'Sa, 'Human and Peoples Rights: Distinctive Features of the African Charter' (1985) 29 J Afr L 72, 79–80.

[57] Viljoen (n 15) 337. [58] ibid 339.

[59] *Civil Liberties Organisation v Nigeria* comm no 129/94, 9th Annual Activity Report of the Af Cm HPR (1995) para 16.

compliance. In the remaining nine per cent of cases, compliance was unclear.[60] This poor record must be borne in mind as the African Commission's refugee engagement is surveyed.

3. Engagement with refugee issues

The African Commission's promotional and protective engagement with refugee issues began in the nineties, when the African Commission held its first refugee-related event and heard its first refugee-focused case.[61] How the African Commission has addressed refugees within its promotional and protective mandates is addressed in this section.

(a) Refugees within the promotional mandate

One of the earliest examples of the African Commission's promotional engagement with refugees was the appearance of the issue on the agenda of its 8th Ordinary Session in 1990.[62] Four years later, in February 1994, the African Commission co-hosted, with the Southern African Centre for Research and Documentation, a Harare seminar titled 'African Refugees and Internally Displaced Persons'.[63] It concluded that the 'plight of African refugees and internally displaced persons is a flagrant violation of human dignity and basic human rights'.[64] However, beyond highlighting refugees as a vulnerable group in need of special protection, little came of the seminar; African Commission engagement with refugee issues did not commence in earnest until it began collaborating with UNHCR.[65]

(i) Collaboration with UNHCR

An early example of collaboration between the organizations was a December 1998 workshop in Dakar, Senegal.[66] The following year, UNHCR attended the African Commission's 26th Ordinary Session, where discussions were held about formal co-operation between them.[67] In March 2000 UNHCR and the OAU co-organized a Conakry meeting of government and non-governmental experts, convened to mark the thirtieth anniversary of the 1969 Convention's adoption.[68] The meeting resulted

[60] Frans Viljoen and Lirette Louw, 'State Compliance with the Recommendations of the African Commission on Human and Peoples' Rights 1994–2004' (2007) 101 AJIL 1, 5–7; see, also, Rachel Murray and Debra Long, *The Implementation of the Findings of the African Commission on Human and Peoples' Rights* (CUP 2015).

[61] *Organisation mondiale contre la torture et al v Rwanda* comm nos 27/89, 46/91, 49/91, and 99/93, 10th Annual Activity Report of the Af Cm HPR (1996) (*OMT*).

[62] Rachel Murray, 'Refugees and Internally Displaced Persons and Human Rights: the African System' (2005) 24 RSQ 56, 58.

[63] ibid; the conference's recommendations are attached to the 7th Annual Activity Report of the Af Cm HPR.

[64] Cited in Bekker (n 45) 20–21.

[65] Bekker (n 45) 21.

[66] Rachel Murray, *Human Rights in Africa: From the OAU to the African Union* (CUP 2004) 194.

[67] Murray (n 62) 61.

[68] See Chapter 6, section B.2.a.

in a Comprehensive Implementation Plan,[69] which suggested that UNHCR and the African Commission conclude an agreement aimed at strengthening the African Commission's monitoring capacity and programme of work regarding refugee and asylum seeker rights.[70]

Further discussions were held in March 2003 at an Addis Ababa meeting of UNHCR and the African Commission. It concluded that 'refugees are endowed with the same rights and responsibilities as all other human beings. The specific rights of refugees are an integral part of human rights and are universal, indivisible, inter-dependent and inter-related. Where national laws on refugees are inadequate or non-existent, general human rights law should therefore be invoked to protect refugees'.[71] The Addis Ababa meeting also recommended that the African Commission become a member of the AU's Coordinating Committee on Assistance and Protection to Refugees, Returnees and Internally Displaced Persons (CCAPRRI, now the Coordinating Committee on Forced Displacement and Humanitarian Action),[72] which is discussed in Chapter 6,[73] and, importantly, that the African Commission monitor the implementation of the 1969 Convention.[74] Just two months later, an expert report prepared in connection with the AU's First Ministerial Meeting on Human Rights, held in Kigali in May 2003, identified the African Commission as having oversight of the 1969 Convention.[75] The legal basis of this identification is not clear.

The memorandum of understanding between the African Commission and UNHCR was signed on 26 May 2003 during the African Commission's 33rd Ordinary Session;[76] its imminent signature had been 'welcomed' by the Ministerial Meeting's Kigali Declaration.[77] The memorandum identifies several areas of cooperation, including information sharing; joint dissemination and provision of training in international human rights, refugee, and humanitarian law; joint research and publication; joint action to implement African Commission resolutions on refugees; the promotion of closer cooperation between UNHCR, the African Commission, and the AU; and the promotion of communication between UNHCR and the African Commission.[78] The memorandum also provides that both organizations

[69] The papers produced for, and all documents resulting from, this meeting were published in 2001 in volume 20(1) of RSQ.

[70] OAU and UNHCR, 'Comprehensive Implementation Plan' (2001) 20 RSQ 31, action 15.

[71] Cited in Murray (n 66) 194.

[72] Murray (n 66) 195.

[73] See section C.3.c.

[74] Murray (n 66) 194.

[75] OAU, 'Report of the Meeting of Experts of the First AU Ministerial Confernece on Human Rights in Africa' (OAU Kigali 5–6 May 2003) EXP/CONF/HRA/RPT (II) para 40(2), cited in Murray (n 62) 62.

[76] Amanda Lloyd and Rachel Murray, 'Institutions with Responsibility for Human Rights Protection under the African Union' (2004) 48 J Afr L 165, 174.

[77] OAU, 'Kigali Declaration of the First AU Ministerial Conference on Human Rights in Africa' (OAU Kigali 8 May 2003) MIN/CONF/HRA/Decl1 (I) para 15.

[78] African Commission and UNHCR, 'Memorandum of Understanding Between the African Commission on Human and Peoples' Rights and the United Nations High Commissioner for Refugees' (26 May 2003) <http://www.africa-union.org/Structure_of_the_Commission/Political%20Affairs/x/achpr-unhcr%20agreement,%20english.pdf> accessed 15 October 2011, art 2.

should draw inspiration from United Nations (UN) treaty monitoring and Charter-based bodies, UNHCR's Executive Committee, and relevant AU organs.[79]

A document detailing the 'modalities for the operationalization of the memorandum of understanding' between the African Commission and UNHCR was adopted at the African Commission's 34th Ordinary Session, held in November 2003.[80] According to this document, the 'joint mechanism' for implementing the memorandum was the appointment of a focal person within each institution. Commissioner Bahame Tom Nyanduga, then African Commission Focal Point on Refugees and Displaced Persons in Africa, was appointed on the Commission side. He met with officials from UNHCR's liaison office in Addis Ababa in May 2004, during which 'a more detailed plan of future activities to be undertaken based on the areas of interaction' was developed.[81] The operationalization document also repeated the recommendation that had emerged from the above-mentioned March 2003 African Commission–UNHCR meeting: that the Commission should join CCAPRRI (as it was then known). The document further recommended that the Commission and UNHCR should 'involve the Department of Political Affairs' Division of Humanitarian Affairs, Refugees and Displaced Persons [(HARDP)] as much as possible'.[82]

The operationalization document also detailed African Commission–UNHCR 'areas of interaction'. These state that the Commission will encourage NGOs and others to submit communications relating to refugees' rights; ensure that refugee rights are an integral part of promotional missions; request that state parties include information on refugee rights in their periodic reports; include a standing item on refugees on each ordinary session agenda; include a refugee rights report in each annual activity report submitted to the AU Assembly; and hold bi-annual meetings with UNHCR.[83]

While these things may have happened in the years following the conclusion of the memorandum of understanding and the adoption of the related operationalization document, it seems they are not occurring of late. Among the most recent Commission activity reports available,[84] refugee issues were not addressed in any depth. The 40th Activity Report, from the Commission's 58th Ordinary Session in December 2015, notes the 'increasing number of refugees and internally displaced persons [(IDPs)] as a result of political instability, acts of terrorism and conflict in some African countries' as an area of concern; recommending that states ensure 'respect for ... international refugee law in efforts to combat terrorism'; and recommending that the AU Assembly address 'the issue of migrants, refugees and ... [IDPs], by dealing with the root causes of this population movement with tragic consequences'.[85] The

[79] ibid.

[80] African Commission, '17th Annual Activity Report of the African Commission on Human and Peoples' Rights' (2003–04) <http://www.achpr.org/files/activity-reports/17/achpr34and35_actrep17_20032004_eng.pdf> accessed 3 April 2017, Annex IV.

[81] ibid para 44. [82] ibid para 1. [83] ibid para 2.

[84] The 40th, 41st, and 42nd Activity Reports, which cover 2015, 2016, and part of 2017.

[85] African Commission, '40th Activity Report of the African Commission on Human and Peoples' Rights' (December 2015) <http://www.achpr.org/files/activity-reports/40/actrep40_2016_eng.pdf> accessed 21 December 2017, 14, 16, and 18.

41st Activity Report, from the Commission's 59th Ordinary Session in May 2016, highlighted 'increasing numbers of refugees and ... [IDPs], including old people, unaccompanied children, victims of sexual violence and disabled people' as an area of concern.[86] The 42nd Activity Report, from the Commission's 60th Ordinary Session in February 2017, does not mention refugees, however, the Commission did, at its 60th Session, adopt its 'Resolution on the Implementation of the New York Declaration for Refugees and Migrants'.[87]

According to Naldi and D'Orsi, while on paper the relationship between the African Commission and UNHCR 'looks like it goes a long way in helping to promote and protect asylum seekers and refugees', in fact 'there has been little cooperation between the two and a lack of undertaking in the areas of cooperation'.[88] Bekker agrees, arguing ten years after the memorandum was concluded that 'little progress has been achieved'.[89] When asked about the current status of the memorandum of understanding, Commissioner Maya Sahli-Fadel—the Commission's current Special Rapporteur—indicated that the Commission has been working with UNHCR towards the adoption of the draft Protocol to the African Charter on the Right to a Nationality in Africa (Nationality Protocol) and that in future the organizations will collaborate on IDPs.[90] As explained earlier in this section, the Comprehensive Action Plan adopted in 2000 recommended cooperation between the African Commission and UNHCR in order to strengthen the Commission's capacity in relation to *refugees' and asylum seekers'* human rights.[91] It seems that, today, collaboration between the two organizations is focused on other issues.

(ii) Supervision of the 1969 Convention?

While the Conakry recommendation that the African Commission should conclude an agreement with UNHCR did come to fruition, there were no further developments regarding the 2003 Addis Ababa recommendation that the Commission should have, and the 2003 Kigali expert report identification that the Commission does have, responsibility for oversight of the 1969 Convention. Yet several scholars have identified the African Commission as having supervisory authority over the 1969 Convention. Naldi and D'Orsi note that while there 'was originally no regional mechanism tasked with implementation and enforcement ... this has changed with the ... [African Commission] mandate being extended to cover the 1969 OAU

[86] African Commission, '41st Activity Report of the African Commission on Human and Peoples' Rights' (May 2016) <http://www.achpr.org/files/activity-reports/41/actrep41_2016_eng.pdf> accessed 21 December 2017, 16.

[87] African Commission, 'Resolution on the Implementation of the New York Declaration for Refugees and Migrants' (60th Ordinary Session, 8–22 May 2017) ACHPR/Res.371.

[88] Gino J Naldi and Cristiano D'Orsi, 'The Role of the African Human Rights System with Reference to Asylum Seekers' in Ademola Abass and Francesca Ippolito (eds), *Regional Approaches to the Protection of Asylum Seekers: An International Legal Perspective* (Ashgate 2014) 41.

[89] Bekker (n 45) 21.

[90] Interview with Commissioner Maya Sahli-Fadel, Special Rapporteur on Refugees, Asylum Seekers, Internally Displaced Persons and Migrants in Africa, African Commission, 12 August 2015, Geneva.

[91] OAU and UNHCR (n 70).

Convention'.[92] Van Garderen and Ebenstein similarly describe the AU as having 'mandated the . . . African Commission to enforce the OAU Refugee Convention'.[93]

There is, however, no legal basis for these statements, nor do they reflect actual African Commission practice. Only one African Commission decision has pronounced upon the 1969 Convention,[94] and this was likely pursuant to articles 56(2) and 60 of the African Charter rather than because of any supervisory authority.[95] Indeed, Commissioner Sahli-Fadel indicated that the Commission's jurisdiction over the 1969 Convention flows from article 12(3) and article 60 of the African Charter, rather than from any official supervisory authority.[96] An expert report identifying the African Commission as having oversight of the 1969 Convention is meaningless in the absence of a clear legal basis for this identification and formal activity in this regard. Thus, while the African Commission can issue findings in relation to the 1969 Convention, in practice the treaty remains without formal supervision.[97]

(iii) Promotional activities

Beginning in 1990—and with increasing frequency since the 2003 creation of the Focal Point, then Special Rapporteur, mandate discussed later in this section—the African Commission has raised refugee issues during its promotional and fact-finding missions, including on visits to Botswana,[98] Burkina Faso,[99] Burundi,[100] Gabon,[101]

[92] Naldi and D'Orsi (n 88) 26.

[93] Jacob van Garderen and Julie Ebenstein, 'Regional Developments: Africa' in Andreas Zimmermann (ed), *The 1951 Convention Relating to the Status of Refugees and its 1967 Protocol* (OUP 2011) 201.

[94] *African Institute* (n 51).

[95] As a reminder, article 60 of the African Charter allows the African Commission to 'draw inspiration from international law on human and peoples' rights', while, according to Viljoen, the Charter's article 56(2) admissibility requirement allows the Commission to consider alleged violations of any AU human rights treaty without an autonomous treaty monitoring body ((n 15) 312).

[96] Fadel interview (n 90); article 12(3) relates to the right to seek and obtain asylum.

[97] Note, however, that UNHCR recently began issuing interpretive guidance regarding the 1969 Convention, pursuant to article 8 of its statute (UNGA Res 428 (V) (14 December 1950)). See, in this regard, UNHCR, 'Guidelines on International Protection No. 12: Claims for Refugee Status Related to Situation of Armed Conflict and Violence under Article 1A(2) of the 1951 Convention and/or 1969 Protocol relating to the Status of Refugees and the Regional Refugee Definitions' (2 December 2016) HCR/GIP/16/12, section III; UNHCR, 'Key Legal Considerations on the Standards of Treatment of Refugees Recognized under the 1969 OAU Convention Governing the Specific Aspects of Refugee Problems in Africa' (19 December 2017).

[98] African Commission, 'Mission Report to the Republic of Botswana' (February 2005) <http://www.achpr.org/files/sessions/38th/mission-reports/botswana/misrep_promo_botswana_2005_eng.pdf> accessed 3 April 2017.

[99] African Commission, 'Report of a Promotion Mission of Commissioner Rezag Bara to Burkina Faso' (March 2007) <http://www.achpr.org/files/sessions/46th/mission-reports/burkina-faso/misrep_promo_burkinafaso_2007_eng.pdf> accessed 3 April 2017.

[100] African Commission, 'Report of the Mission of Promotion to Burundi by Commissioner Mohamed Abdellahi Ould Babana' (February 2004) <http://www.achpr.org/files/sessions/41st/mission-reports/burundi/misrep_promo_burundi_2004_eng.pdf> accessed 3 April 2017.

[101] African Commission, 'Report of the Human Rights Promotion Mission to the Gabonese Republic' (January 2014) <http://www.achpr.org/files/sessions/54th/mission-reports/gabon-promo-2014/achpr54os_misrep_promo_gabon_2014_eng.pdf> accessed 3 April 2017.

Lesotho,[102] Mali,[103] Rwanda,[104] Senegal,[105] Sudan,[106] and Uganda.[107] The African Commission has also adopted resolutions relating in whole or in part to refugees. Among its country-specific resolutions covering refugee issues, the Commission has addressed the situations in Burundi,[108] Côte D'Ivoire,[109] Mali,[110] South Africa,[111] Sudan,[112] and Zaire (now the Democratic Republic of the Congo (DRC)).[113] Among its thematic resolutions on refugees, the Commission has addressed refugees in a general sense,[114] as well as refugees' educational needs,[115] anniversaries of the 1969 Convention,[116] refugees' human rights,[117] and the 'situation of migrants in Africa'.[118] In May 2015 the Commission issued a 'Statement on the Deteriorating

[102] African Commission, 'Report of the Promotional Mission to the Kingdom of Lesotho' (April 2006) <http://www.achpr.org/files/sessions/40th/mission-reports/promo-lesotho-2006/misrep_promo_lesotho_2006_eng.pdf> accessed 3 April 2017.

[103] African Commission, 'Report of the Fact-Finding Mission to the Republic of Mali' (June 2013) <http://www.achpr.org/files/sessions/53rd/mission-reports/mali-fact-finding-2013/misrep_fact-finding_mali_2013_eng.pdf> accessed 3 April 2017.

[104] African Commission, 'Report of Promotional Mission Undertaken by Commissioner Mohamed Abdellahi Ould Babana in Rwanda' (February 2004) <http://www.achpr.org/files/sessions/41st/mission-reports/rwanda/misrep_promo_rwanda_2004_eng.pdf> accessed 3 April 2017.

[105] African Commission, 'Press Release on the Promotion Mission to the Republic of Senegal' (June 1996) <http://www.achpr.org/files/sessions/20th/mission-reports/senegal/achpr20_misrep_promo_senegal_1996_eng.pdf> accessed 3 April 2017.

[106] African Commission, 'Report of the African Commission on Human and Peoples' Rights' Fact-Finding mission to the Republic of Sudan in the Darfur Region' (July 2004) <http://old.achpr.org/english/Mission_reports/Sudan/report_darfur%20region_eng.pdf> accessed 3 April 2017.

[107] African Commission, 'Report of the Joint Promotion Mission Undertaken to the Republic of Uganda' (August 2013) <http://www.achpr.org/files/sessions/14th-eo/mission-reports/uganda-promo-2013/achpr14eos_misrep_promo_uganda_2013_eng.pdf> accessed 3 April 2017.

[108] African Commission, 'Resolution on Burundi' (19th Ordinary Session, 26 March to 4 April 1996) ACHPR/Res.24.

[109] African Commission, 'Resolution on the Human Rights Situation in Côte D'Ivoire' (9th Extraordinary Session, 23 February to 3 March 2011) ACHPR/Res.182.

[110] African Commission, 'Resolution on the Situation of the North of the Republic of Mali' (51st Ordinary Session, 18 April to 2 May 2012) ACHPR/Res.217.

[111] African Commission, 'Resolution on the Situation of Migrants in South Africa' (43rd Ordinary Session, 7–22 May 2008) ACHPR/Res.131; African Commission, 'Resolution Condemning the Xenophobic Attacks in the Republic of South Africa' (56th Ordinary Session, 21 April to 7 May 2015) ACHPR/Res.304.

[112] African Commission, 'Resolution on Sudan' (17th Ordinary Session, 13–22 March 1995) ACHPR/Res.15; African Commission, 'Resolution on the Situation of Human Rights in Darfur, Sudan' (35th Ordinary Session, 21 May to 4 June 2004) ACHPR/Res.68; African Commission, 'Resolution on the Situation of Human Rights in the Darfur Region of Sudan' (38th Ordinary Session, 21 November to 5 December 2005) ACHPR/Res.93.

[113] African Commission, 'Resolution on Zaire' (21st Ordinary Session, 15–24 April 1997).

[114] African Commission, 'Resolution on the Situation of Human Rights in Africa' (16th Ordinary Session, 25 October to 3 November 1994) ACHPR/Res.15, para 3.

[115] African Commission, 'Resolution on Human Rights Education' (14th Ordinary Session, 1–10 December 1993) ACHPR/Res.6, para 3.

[116] African Commission, 'Resolution on the Observance of the 30th Anniversary of the OAU Convention Governing the Specific Aspects of Refugees in Africa' (26th Ordinary Session, 1–5 November 1999) ACHPR/Res.43.

[117] African Commission, 'Resolution on Migration and Human Rights' (42nd Ordinary Session, 15–28 November 2007) ACHPR/Res.114.

[118] African Commission, 'Resolution on the Situation of Migrants in Africa' (19th Extraordinary Session, 16–25 February 2016) ACHPR/Res.333.

Situation of African Migrants in the Mediterranean'.[119] At its 56th Ordinary Session in April and May 2015, the Commission issued a resolution on the terrorist attacks in Kenya, highlighting problematic 'retaliatory measures such as ... expulsion of refugees in the urban areas ... and the threat of closure of refugee camps' and calling on Kenya to 'Take all necessary measures to protect refugees in conformity with regional and international commitments'.[120]

Most recently, in May 2017, the Commission issued its 'Resolution on the Implementation of the New York Declaration for Refugees and Migrants'. The resolution recommends that states parties 'adopt a comprehensive approach to issues relating to population displacement regardless of the cause'; calls upon states parties and the AU to participate in consultations related to the two Global Compacts; urges the AU, refugee hosting states, and countries of origin to implement the New York Declaration; calls upon the AU to implement the Common African Position on Humanitarian Effectiveness (CAP) and to expedite the establishment of the African Humanitarian Agency; and urges the AU to 'take into account the recommendations of the New York Declaration during implementation of the ... [CAP] with the aim of aligning them with the global response strategy emanating from the Declaration'.[121] Due to the absence of mechanisms to follow up these resolutions, it is difficult to know whether they have been of any practical effect.

In addition to raising refugee issues within its missions and within its country and thematic resolutions, the African Commission has since 2004 included refugee issues within its state reporting procedure, highlighting refugee matters in some among the few of its concluding observations that have been made public.[122] These include reports on Côte D'Ivoire, Ethiopia, Kenya, Mauritius, Rwanda, South Africa, and Sudan.[123] The effectiveness of the Commission's refugee work within the state reporting procedure has, however, been limited. Poor state compliance with reporting obligations and the lack of publicity for, and follow up on, recommendations and concluding observations have hampered their effectiveness.[124] In this regard, it is worth noting that according to Commissioner Sahli-Fadel, much valuable discussion with states occurs outside of official reporting channels.[125]

The Commission's promotional work in favour of refugees is largely divorced from AU efforts in this regard.[126] The African Commission has largely failed to collaborate with the AU's refugee-related entities detailed in Chapter 6. When the African Commission began to engage with refugee issues, the 'OAU's Refugee Division [HARDP] was suggested as a possible partner, but the African Commission chose to

[119] African Commission, 'Statement on the Deteriorating Situation of African Migrants in the Mediterranean' (3 May 2015) <http://www.achpr.org/news/2015/05/d176/> accessed 3 April 2017.

[120] African Commission, 'Resolution on Terrorist Acts in the Republic of Kenya' (56th Ordinary Session, 21 April to 7 May 2015) ACHPR/Res.302.

[121] African Commission (n 87) paras 1–5.

[122] Bekker (n 45) 21.

[123] ibid 21–23.

[124] ibid 23–24.

[125] Fadel interview (n 90).

[126] See, generally, Curtis Doebbler, 'Complex Ambiguity: The Relationship between the African Comission on Human and Peoples' Rights and Other African Union Initiatives Affecting Respect for Human Rights' (2003) 13 Transnat'l L & Contemp Probs 7.

determine its own procedures first before collaborating with the Division'.[127] This marked the beginning of a pattern. For a long time 'the OAU/AU organs and the African Commission ... seemed to operate, in this [refugee] area as well as many others, in splendid isolation. Neither referred to the other's documents or jurisprudence, nor did they collaborate to enforce decisions or recommendations'.[128]

This is not to say that the African Commission and the AU have never worked together. In November 2002 the African Commission and HARDP co-hosted the 'Conference on Refugee Protection in Africa: How to Ensure Security and Development for Refugees and Local Hosts'.[129] More recently, the AU undertook in its Humanitarian Policy Framework to 'encourage Member States to cooperate with and support the Special Rapporteur ... in addressing issues of displaced persons'[130] and the CAP called for the Special Rapporteur mandate to be upgraded to the UN level.[131] While this AU recognition of the Special Rapporteur is encouraging, it hardly amounts to fruitful collaboration. Indeed, the following discussion of the Special Rapporteur demonstrates that the mandate largely operates separately from the AU.

(iv) The Special Rapporteur

The African Commission appointed Tanzanian Commissioner Bahame Tom Nyanduga as its first Focal Point on Refugees and Displaced Persons in Africa at its 34th Ordinary Session in November 2003,[132] just six months after the expert report prepared for the ministerial meeting in Kigali identified the African Commission as having oversight of the 1969 Convention.[133] The Focal Point role was upgraded the following year during the African Commission's 36th Ordinary Session, when Nyanduga was made the first Special Rapporteur on Refugees, Asylum Seekers and IDPs in Africa.[134] As mentioned earlier in this section, the current (and fourth)

[127] Rachel Murray, 'The African Charter on Human and Peoples' Rights 1987–2000: An Overview of its Progress and Problems' (2001) 1 Afr Hum Rts LJ 1, 16.

[128] Murray (n 62) 61; see, also, Viljoen (n 15) 297.

[129] Lloyd and Murray (n 76) 174.

[130] AU (HARDP), 'African Union Humanitarian Policy Framework' (November 2015) <http://www.peaceau.org/uploads/humanitarian-policy-framewrok-rev-final-version.pdf> accessed 6 April 2017, para 4.

[131] AU, 'Common African Position (CAP) on Humanitarian Effectiveness: One Africa, One Voice, One Message at the World Humanitarian Summit' (March 2016) 21.

[132] According to Viljoen, this thematic approach goes beyond the Commission's explicit mandate (Viljoen (n 15) 297). See, also, Julia Harrington, 'Special Rapporteurs of the African Commission on Human and Peoples' Rights' (2001) 1 Afr Hum Rts LJ 247, 249–54.

[133] While the appointment of a Focal Point on refugees may have been related to the expert report's identification of the African Commission as having oversight of the 1969 Convention, the mere existence of a Focal Point or Special Rapporteur on refugees is not in itself sufficient to discharge the full responsibility of supervising the 1969 Convention, especially when one considers the Special Rapporteur's mandate. It is broader and more general than typical supervisory functions, and moreover the responsibilities are located in one individual, who serves part-time and in a personal capacity.

[134] African Commission, 'Resolution on the Mandate of the Special Rapporteur on Refugees, Asylum Seekers and Internally Displaced Persons in Africa' (36th Ordinary Session, 23 November to 7 December 2004) ACHPR/Res.72; for a detailed account of Nyanduga's activities as Special Rapporteur, see Jamil Ddamulira Mujuzi, 'The African Commission on Human and Peoples' Rights and the Promotion and Protection of Refugees' Rights' (2009) 9 Afr Hum Rts LJ 160, 168–71.

Special Rapporteur is Algerian Commissioner Maya Sahli-Fadel. She took up the role in November 2011; her current two-year mandate expires in November 2019.[135]

The Special Rapporteur has a mandate to

a. seek, receive, examine and act upon information on the situation of refugees, asylum seekers and internally displaced persons in Africa;
b. undertake studies, research and other related activities to examine appropriate ways to enhance the protection of refugees, asylum seekers and internally displaced persons in Africa;
c. undertake fact-finding missions, investigations, visits and other appropriate activities to refugee camps and camps for internally displaced persons;
d. assist Member States of the African Union to develop appropriate policies, regulations and laws for the effective protection of refugees, asylum seekers and internally displaced persons in Africa;
e. cooperate and engage in dialogue with Member States, National Human Rights Institutions, relevant intergovernmental and non governmental bodies, international and regional mechanisms involved in the promotion and protection of the rights of refugees, asylum seekers and internally displaced persons;
f. develop and recommend effective strategies to better protect the rights of refugees, asylum seekers and internally displaced persons in Africa and to follow up on his recommendations;
g. raise awareness and promote the implementation of the UN Convention on Refugees of 1951 as well as the 1969 OAU Convention Governing the Specific Aspects of Refugees Problems in Africa;
h. submit reports at every ordinary session of the African Commission on the situation of refugees, asylum seekers and internally displaced persons in Africa.[136]

The Special Rapporteur mandate was extended at the African Commission's 39th Ordinary Session in May 2006 to include migration issues.[137] When Commissioner Sahli-Fadel's mandate was renewed in November 2017, the Commission noted several factors, including: the need for work with states towards the adoption of the draft Nationality Protocol; the 'constantly worsening situation of refugees, asylum seekers and' IDPs in Africa; and the need for advocacy for the ratification and implementation of the Kampala Convention.[138]

Among mandate activities, which have been limited by budgetary constraints,[139] Special Rapporteurs have undertaken fact-finding missions, such as to Senegal to investigate the situation of Mauritanian refugees and to Zimbabwe following the government's eviction operation Murambatsvina, and participated in an AU humanitarian and security assessment mission to Darfur, Sudan.[140] Special Rapporteurs have also issued statements regarding particular occasions or situations, written to governments and participated in relevant seminars and conferences. Regarding

[135] African Commission, 'Resolution on the Renewal of the Mandate of the Special Rapporteur on Refugees, Asylum Seekers and Internally Displaced Persons in Africa' (61st Ordinary Session, 1–15 November 2017) ACHPR/Res.379.

[136] African Commission (n 134) para 1.

[137] Chaloka Beyani, 'Recent Developments in the African Human Rights System 2004–2006' (2007) 7 Hum Rts L Rev 582, 588–89.

[138] African Commission (n 135). [139] Bekker (n 45) 24. [140] Viljoen (n 15) 376.

standard setting, the first Special Rapporteur contributed to the adoption of the Kampala Convention.[141]

The current Special Rapporteur is playing a major role in relation to nationality issues.[142] In this connection, Commissioner Sahli-Fadel authored a major study[143] and led the drafting of the Nationality Protocol;[144] as mentioned earlier in this section, she is now promoting its adoption.[145] Indeed, Commissioner Sahli-Fadel explained that most of the time she spends on her Special Rapporteur mandate is devoted to this nationality and statelessness work.[146] Among her other activities, Commissioner Sahli-Fadel has issued statements and press releases and participated in promotional and fact-finding missions. In March 2017 Commissioner Sahli-Fadel, together with the Commissioner responsible for South Africa, issued a press release condemning the xenophobic attacks on migrants in South Africa.[147] In 2015 she issued a press release on the ratification of the Kampala Convention.[148] Her most recent statements were released on the occasions of International Migrants Day (18 December) and World Refugee Day (20 June).[149] The most recent African Commission missions in which Commissioner Sahli-Fadel participated were to Mauritania, in December 2016, and to Senegal, in September 2015; she also participated in a mission of the UN independent investigation on Burundi.[150] While mission reports from the African Commission visits to Mauritania and Senegal were not available, it is notable that neither of the press releases issued at the conclusion of each mission mentioned refugee issues.[151]

141 ibid.

142 African Commission, 'Resolution on the Right to Nationality' (53rd Ordinary Session, 9–23 April 2013) ACHPR/Res.234.

143 African Commission, 'The Right to a Nationality in Africa' (2014) <http://www.achpr.org/files/special-mechanisms/refugees-and-internally-displaced-persons/the_right_to_nationality_in_africa.pdf> accessed 28 April 2015.

144 African Commission, 'Resolution on the Drafting of a Protocol to the African Charter on Human and Peoples' Rights on the Right to a Nationality in Africa' (55th Ordinary Session, 28 April to 12 May 2014) ACHPR/Res.277.

145 See n 135.

146 Fadel interview (n 90).

147 African Commission, 'Joint Press-Release on the Xenophobic Attacks on Migrants in South Africa' (17 March 2017) <http://www.achpr.org/press/2017/03/d350/> accessed 4 April 2017.

148 African Commission, '38th Activity Report of the African Commission on Human and Peoples' Rights' (May 2015) <http://www.achpr.org/files/activity-reports/38/actrep38_2015_eng.pdf> accessed 4 April 2017, para 38.

149 African Commission, 'Statement by the Special Rapporteur on Refugees, Asylum Seekers, Internally Displaced Persons and Migrants in Africa on the Occasion of World Refugee Day' (20 June 2017) <http://www.achpr.org/news/2017/06/d292> accessed 21 December 2017; African Commission, 'Statement by the Special Rapporteur on Refugees, Asylum Seekers, Internally Displaced Persons and Migrants in Africa on the Occasion of International Migrants Day' (18 December 2017) <http://www.achpr.org/press/2017/12/d382/> accessed 21 December 2017.

150 African Commission, 'Inter-session Report of Mrs Maya Sahli-Fadel' (April 2016) <http://www.achpr.org/files/sessions/58th/inter-act-reps/257/58os_inter_session_report_maya_eng.pdf> accessed 4 April 2017, 5.

151 African Commission, '*Communiqué de presse sur la mission de promotion de le Commission Africaine des droits de l'homme et des peoples en République islamique de mauritanie*' (27 December 2016) <http://www.achpr.org/fr/press/2016/12/d342/> accessed 4 April 2017; African Commission, 'Press Release on the African Commission on Human and Peoples' Rights Promotion Mission to the Republic of Senegal' (5 October 2015) <http://www.achpr.org/press/2015/10/d277/> accessed 4 April 2017.

Commissioner Sahli-Fadel's most recent publicly available inter-session activity report, presented at the Commission's 58th Ordinary Session in April 2016, listed several additional activities undertaken in her capacity as Special Rapporteur. She attended a joint AU Commission, UNHCR, and civil society workshop on the Kampala Convention, held at the AU Commission in late 2015; in November 2015 she participated in a consultation to consolidate the AU's CAP; in February 2016 Commissioner Sahli-Fadel participated in a civil society meeting in Dakar, Senegal, aimed at building a coalition to advocate for the eradication of statelessness in Africa and promoting the draft Nationality Protocol; finally, she participated in panel discussions on nationality and statelessness, and on the human rights situation in Burundi.[152]

Naldi and D'Orsi conclude that the mandate is of limited effect and call for a rethink of the Special Rapporteur's role, noting in particular that it should include increased collaboration with UNHCR.[153] Viljoen criticizes Special Rapporteur mandates more generally, arguing that as the Commission's special mechanisms have proliferated, it has 'gradually started to neglect its core protective function by finalizing fewer and fewer communications at its sessions.... Time, energy, and resources devoted to these mechanisms have detracted from the Commission's core protective function'.[154] Despite these critiques—and perhaps not surprisingly given his previous role—former Commissioner Nyanduga maintains that 'the continued use of the African Commission as a forum for discussion of refugee rights issues is an important protection mechanism for refugees'.[155] The current Special Rapporteur echoed this view, stressing that much important discussion about refugee rights happens on the sidelines of Commission sessions further to state reports, and during her missions to states.[156] Her descriptions of this informal diplomatic work and of her role more generally gave the impression of an impassioned advocate doing her utmost for refugees in a difficult context: a continent in which states have difficulty securing human rights for even their own citizens. Much of this engagement is by its very nature invisible to outsiders, however, this should not be taken to imply that the mandate is of no or limited effect. Certainly, the presence within the African Commission of a committed Commissioner with a mandate dedicated to refugees and related issues must have some impact. Of late, however, it seems that the focus is on those related issues, such as IDPs and nationality and statelessness, at the expense of issues falling squarely within the refugee domain.

(b) Refugees within the protective mandate

Refugee cases declared admissible[157] can be classified as flowing from expulsion or deportation on the one hand and repatriation or return on the other. First among

[152] African Commission (n 150) 7–10. [153] Naldi and D'Orsi (n 88) 40.

[154] Viljoen (n 15) 296–97.

[155] Bahame Tom Mukirya Nyanduga, 'Refugee Protection Under the 1969 OAU Convention Governing the Specific Aspects of Refugee Problems in Africa' (2004) 47 German YB Intl L 85, 103.

[156] Fadel interview (n 90).

[157] A number of cases brought by or on behalf of refugees have been found inadmissible: *Mouvement des réfugiés mauritaniens au Sénégal v Sénégal* comm no 162/97, 22nd Ordinary Session of the Af Cm

the expulsion and deportation line of cases was *OMT*, which concerned the expulsion of four Burundian refugees from Rwanda on ostensible security grounds.[158] This was found to have violated the rights to non-discrimination (article 2), liberty and security of the person (article 6), the right to have one's cause heard (article 7), including the right to asylum (article 12(3)), and the protection from expulsion without due process of law (article 12(4)), as well as the prohibition against the collective expulsion of non-nationals (article 12(5)).[159] Similarly, *Rencontre Africaine pour la défence des droits de l'homme (RADDHO) v Zambia* (*RADDHO*) related to the deportation of 517 West Africans (who were not all necessarily refugees) from Zambia, following a period of detention. The African Commission found violations of the rights to non-discrimination (article 2), the right to have one's cause heard (article 7), and the prohibition of the mass expulsion of non-nationals (article 12(5)).[160] *Union interafricaine des droits de l'homme and others v Angola* concerned the mass expulsion of West Africans (not all of whom were necessarily refugees) from Angola, which the African Commission found violated the rights to non-discrimination (article 2), the right to have one's cause heard (article 7), the prohibitions against the expulsion (article 12(4)), and mass expulsion (article 12(5)) of non-nationals and the rights to property (article 14) and family life (article 18).[161] *African Institute* concerned the Guinean President's proclamation over the radio that Sierra Leonean refugees should be arrested, searched, and detained. This led to massive violations of their rights by civilians and by the military; many of the refugees were forced to flee for a second time. The African Commission found violations of the rights to non-discrimination (article 2), to life and integrity of the person (article 4), to freedom from torture cruel, inhuman or degrading punishment and treatment (CIDT) (article 5), and to property (article 14); the African Commission also held that the prohibition against mass expulsion (article 12(5)) had been violated.[162] As mentioned earlier in this section, the African Commission also found the 1969 Convention's article IV non-discrimination provision to have been violated.[163]

In addition to holding host states responsible for expulsion and deportation, the Commission has held a country of origin responsible for violations that led to refugee flight, as well as for further violations that resulted from such flight. *John D Ouko v Kenya* concerned a Kenyan student leader who was arrested because of his political activity and detained in inhumane conditions in Nairobi. He fled to Uganda, where he was denied asylum. He moved on to the DRC, where he resided at the time of the complaint. The Commission found that Ouko's arrest for his activism violated

HPR (1997); *Institute for Human Rights and Development in Africa (on behalf of Jean Simbarakiye) v the Democratic Republic of Congo* comm no 247/02, 33rd Ordinary Session of the Af Cm HPR (2003); *Mouvement des réfugiés mauritaniens au Séneégal v Sénégal* comm no 254/02, 33rd Ordinary Session of the Af Cm HPR (2003).

158 *OMT* (n 61). 159 ibid.

160 *Rencontre Africaine pour la défence des droits de l'homme (RADDHO) v Zambia* comm no 71/92, 10th Annual Activity Report of the Af Cm HPR (2000).

161 *Union interafricaine des droits de l'homme and others v Angola* comm no 159/96, 11th Annual Activity Report of the Af Cm HPR (1997).

162 *African Institute* (n 51) para 74. 163 ibid.

article 9 protecting freedom of expression, his imprisonment in Nairobi offended article 6 on the right to liberty, and the conditions in detention violated the CIDT aspect of article 5. The Commission found further that flight itself deprived Ouko of his article 10 right to associate, his article 12(1) freedom of movement and residence within Kenya and his article 12(2) right to return to Kenya.[164]

Curtis Francis Doebbler v Sudan related to the repatriation and return of 14,000 Ethiopian refugees in Sudan.[165] They fled the Mengistu regime prior to 1991; in September 1999 Sudan invoked the 1951 Convention's article 1C(5) cessation clause and concluded an agreement with UNHCR for the refugees' repatriation. The complainant, a lawyer for the affected refugees, alleged their continuing need for international protection and characterized the repatriation as refoulement. He alleged that the repatriation and the treatment of the refugees in relation to it violated article 4 on the right to life, article 5 prohibiting torture and CIDT, article 6 on the right to liberty and the prohibition of arbitrary arrest, article 12(3) on the right to seek and obtain asylum, article 12(4) prohibiting the arbitrary expulsion of non-nationals, and article 12(5) prohibiting the mass expulsion of non-nationals. The decision considered the 1969 Convention—as well as the 1951 Convention—but unlike *African Institute*, this consideration had the limited purpose of exploring and explaining cessation and non-refoulement; the African Commission did not consider whether the provisions underlying these issues had themselves been violated. Ultimately, the African Commission ruled in favour of the respondent state. It did so largely on the facts, holding that 'the Communication was filed in anticipation of a violation, which did not happen in actual fact after the implementation of the cessation clause [was] set in motion'.[166]

Next in the repatriation and return line of cases came *Malawi African Association and Others v Mauritania*,[167] which joined several communications related to the treatment by Mauritania of its black population between 1986 and 1992, and in particular after April 1989 when it expelled about 50,000 black Mauritanians to Senegal and Mali. *Sudan Human Rights Organisation & Centre on Housing Rights and Evictions (COHRE) v Sudan* also addressed state obligations to returning refugees, among other things.[168] Together these cases demonstrate the Commission's willingness to hold refugee-producing states accountable for returnees' Charter rights.

The Commission's refugee jurisprudence has done little to elaborate upon the African Charter provisions of particular significance to refugees (which are discussed in Chapter 5).[169] The Commission's refugee-related jurisprudence does not feature much sophisticated reasoning, a criticism that has been made of the Commission's

[164] *John D Ouko v Kenya* comm no 232/99, 14th Annual Activity Report of the Af Cm HPR (2000) paras 20–31.

[165] *Curtis Francis Doebbler v Sudan* comm no 235/00, 27th Annual Activity Report of the Af Cm HPR (2009).

[166] ibid para 167.

[167] Comm nos 54/91, 61/91, 98/93, 164/97 to 196/97, 210/98, 13th Annual Activity Report of the Af Cm HPR (2000).

[168] Comm nos 279/03 to 296/05, 28th Annual Activity Report of the Af Cm HPR (2009).

[169] See section C.2.

case law more generally.[170] The holdings in early African Commission decisions were articulated in no more than two lines. Since then, the Commission's findings have become longer and its reasoning more elaborate, due largely to 'Commissioners who were prepared to articulate reasons more clearly, ... better secretarial support, ... the improved contribution of pleadings by the parties ... [and] greater and increasingly critical engagement of states'.[171] Yet, despite these improvements, Viljoen continues to characterize Commission jurisprudence as sometimes 'incoherent'.[172] While none of the Commission's refugee decisions can be characterized as such, they do fail to elucidate the relevant provisions in the refugee context. If the above discussion of African Commission cases advanced by or on behalf of refugees was largely limited to an enumeration of the provisions found to have been violated, this is an unfortunate reflection of the decisions themselves.

The above-mentioned cases brought by or on behalf of refugees (and in some cases, other non-nationals) demonstrate that, jurisprudential deficiencies notwithstanding, the African Commission is a viable forum for the enforcement of refugee rights. This is important because refugees, by definition, lack redress in their own countries, and as outsiders may face obstacles to accessing justice in host states. Moreover, while there is no body with meaningful oversight of the 1969 Convention, *African Institute* demonstrates that its provisions can nevertheless be enforced on a case-by-case basis by the African Commission.

The reality, however, is that very few refugees in Africa will have the awareness, funds, and/or connections required to bring a communication to the African Commission. Indeed, compared with other regional human rights systems, the African Commission attracts only a 'minute number of cases',[173] and just a tiny fraction of this minute number comes from refugees. Moreover, while useful for those few refugees who can access it, the case-by-case enforcement of refugee rights by the African Commission yields at best only patchwork protection. It is therefore likely that among the African Commission's refugee-related tools, its promotional mandate holds the most promise for refugees. It is imperative that the African Commission ensure that its efforts in this regard are not diluted by emerging concerns, such as with IDPs and statelessness, and that it work with the African Court and, if it is ever established, the New Merged Court, which also have a role to play in relation to refugees.

C. The African Court on Human and Peoples' Rights

Calls for the creation of an African human rights court originated at a 1961 Lagos meeting of African jurists.[174] Conditions were not, however, conducive to the

[170] For a summary of this criticism, see Rachel Murray, 'International Human Rights: Neglect of Perspective from African Institutions' (2006) 55 Intl & Comp LQ 193. See also Frans Viljoen, 'From a Cat into a Lion? An Overview of the Progress and Challenges of the African Human Rights System at the African Commission's 25 Year Mark' (2013) 17 Law, Democracy & Development 298, 310–11.

[171] Viljoen (n 15) 336. [172] ibid 296.

[173] Christof Heyns, 'Some Thoughts on Challenges Facing the International Protection of Human Rights in Africa' (2009) 27 NQHR 447, 447.

[174] Philip Amoah, 'The African Charter on Human and Peoples' Rights: An Effective Weapon for Human Rights?' (1992) 4 Afr J Intl Comp L 226, 238.

establishment of such a court until the early nineties, when the Cold War ended and waves of democratization swept states in Africa.[175] The latter led to greater reliance on national constitutional courts, while the former gave human rights increased prominence worldwide.[176] These developments, together with pressure from NGOs,[177] made human rights 'accepted widely enough in Africa ... for the decision to be made to give more "teeth" to the African human rights system in the form of a Court'.[178]

In 1994 the OAHG adopted a resolution requesting that the OAU Secretary General 'convene a meeting of government experts to ponder in conjunction with the African Commission ... over the means to enhance the efficiency of the Commission in considering particularly the establishment of an African Court on Human and Peoples' Rights'.[179] This commenced the process of drafting the African Court Protocol,[180] which was ultimately adopted in 1998 and entered into force in January 2004, creating a court aimed at complementing the African Commission's protective mandate.[181] The African Court's first eleven judges were elected by the AU Assembly in January 2006 and were sworn in during June of the same year. In August 2007 the Court concluded a host agreement with Tanzania. Interim Rules of Procedure were adopted in June 2008 and were replaced two years later with Rules of Court adopted further to harmonization discussions with the African Commission.[182]

The African Court has jurisdiction to hear contentious cases concerning the African Charter, its own establishing protocol and 'any other relevant human rights instrument ratified by the States concerned'.[183] The African Court's sources of law are, accordingly, 'the Charter and any other relevant human rights instruments ratified by the States concerned'.[184] The African Court can therefore undoubtedly hear cases concerning, and apply, the 1969 Convention.[185] The absence of the word 'African' from article 3 on jurisdiction and article 7 on sources of law suggests that the African Court may even adjudicate and apply international human rights treaties ratified by the state in question.[186]

The African Court can also issue advisory opinions 'on any legal matter relating to the Charter or any other relevant human rights instrument'.[187] Advisory opinions may be requested by AU member states, the AU or any of its organs and 'any African organization recognized by' the AU.[188] Viljoen argues that

[175] Heyns (n 25) 686.

[176] Andre Mbata B Mangu, 'The Changing Human Rights Landscape in Africa: Organisation of African Unity, African Union, New Partnership for Africa's Development and the African Court' (2005) 23 NQHR 379, 397.

[177] Viljoen (n 15) 412.

[178] Heyns (n 25) 686.

[179] OAU (OAHG), 'Resolution on the African Commission on Human and Peoples' Rights' (OAU Tunis 13–15 June 1994) AHG/Res.230 (XXX) para 4.

[180] For a brief account of the drafting process, see Viljoen (n 15) 412–13.

[181] African Court Protocol (n 2) art 2.

[182] Rules of Court (adopted 2 June 2010, entered into force 2 June 2010) <http://www.african-court.org/pt/images/documents/Court/African%20Rules%20of%20Court/Final_Rules_of_Court_for_Publication_after_Harmonization_-_Final__English_7_sept_1_.pdf> accessed 30 April 2015.

[183] African Court Protocol (n 2) art 3(1).

[184] ibid art 7.

[185] Viljoen (n 15) 435–36.

[186] ibid 437.

[187] African Court Protocol (n 2) art 4.

[188] ibid.

this latter category should include 'all African NGOs that enjoy observer status with the African Commission, … civil society organizations represented on the AU Economic, Social and Cultural Council, … regional economic arrangements … [and] [o]ther African organizations … in so far as they work in association with the AU or AEC'.[189] The African Court has clarified that the African Committee of Experts on the Rights and Welfare of the Child has standing to request advisory opinions.[190]

The African Court's expansive subject matter jurisdiction, coupled with its definitively binding judgments, represented great promise for human rights in Africa. This promise was undermined, however, by the rules governing access.[191] These prohibit individual and NGO access to the Court unless the defendant state has filed a declaration in this regard.[192] Only eight states have made article 34(6) declarations permitting individual and organizational standing.[193] Automatic standing in contentious cases is accorded to the African Commission and to states parties to the African Court Protocol, provided the state has lodged a complaint before the African Commission, is the subject of such an African Commission complaint, or is acting further to the violation of the rights of one of its citizens.[194] African intergovernmental organizations also enjoy automatic standing in contentious cases;[195] the African Court recently held that the African Committee of Experts on the Rights and Welfare of the Child is not an 'African intergovernmental organization'.[196]

This approach to access prevents the African Court from becoming a forum for the vindication of individual rights, leaving this role to the African Commission. Generally speaking, however, human rights commissions tend to be most effective at addressing widespread and massive patterns of human rights violations, while courts are best suited to individual cases. The architecture of the African human rights system either reverses this pattern or saddles the African Commission with the burden of addressing both systemic and individual violations. The opportunity to correct this arose in July 2004—just six months after the African Court Protocol's entry into force—when the AHG decided to create the Merged Court by merging the African Court with the non-existent African Court of Justice. The Merged Court Protocol, however, features the same access rules as those governing the African Court.[197]

[189] (n 15) 447.

[190] *Request for Advisory Opinion by the African Committee of Experts on the Rights and Welfare of the Child on the Standing of the African Committee of Experts on the Rights and Welfare of the Child before the African Court on Human and Peoples' Rights*, request no 002/2013 Af Ct HPR (December 2014).

[191] See, generally, Dan Juma, 'Access to the African Court on Human and Peoples' Rights: A Case of the Poacher Turned Gamekeeper' (2007) 4 Essex Hum Rts Rev 1; regarding individuals, see Frans Viljoen, 'A Human Rights Court for Africa, and Africans' (2004–05) 30 Brooklyn J Intl L 1.

[192] African Court Protocol (n 2) arts 5(3) and 34(6).

[193] Benin, Burkina Faso, Côte d'Ivoire, Ghana, Malawi, Mali, Tanzania, and Tunisia. Rwanda withdrew its article 34(6) declaration in March 2016.

[194] African Court Protocol (n 2) art 5(1). [195] ibid. [196] (n 190).

[197] Merged Court Protocol (n 7) art 8(3); Annex to the Merged Court Protocol (n 7) art 30(f); see section D.

1. Engagement with refugee issues

The African Court's access rules certainly limit its refugee protection role. Of the over forty cases finalized by the Court since its establishment, only *Michelot Yogogombaye v Senegal* (*Yogogombaye*) raised a refugee issue,[198] though the Chadian applicant Yogogombaye was not himself a refugee and the purported refugee law issue was poorly articulated. The application concerned efforts by Senegal to prosecute Hissene Habré—who had been living in Senegal as a refugee since 1990—for international crimes committed while he was the President of Chad; Habré was ultimately convicted of crimes against humanity, war crimes, and torture on 30 May 2016. The applicant alleged, among other things, that the prosecution violated the 1969 Convention, though no particular provisions were specified. The African Court ruled that the case fell outside of its jurisdiction, because Senegal has not filed an article 34(6) declaration permitting direct access by individual plaintiffs.[199] *Yogogombaye* provides a lone example of the chilling effect of the African Court's access rules on its engagement with refugee protection. It is surprising that *Yogogombaye* even reached the Court; potential plaintiffs aware of the African Court's access rules would not bother instituting proceedings.

That is not to say, however, that there is no scope for the African Court to engage with refugee issues. As mentioned above, the African Court has subject-matter jurisdiction over the 1969 Convention. Thus, those entities with direct access to the Court—the African Commission, states and African intergovernmental organizations—can bring contentious cases regarding the 1969 Convention, as can individuals and NGOs whose grievance is against a state that has filed an article 34(6) declaration. Moreover, as demonstrated in Chapter 5 and in section B above, the 1969 Convention is far from the only treaty relevant to refugee protection; the African Charter also has a role to play, and it is beyond a doubt that this instrument is within the Court's jurisdiction. As discussed earlier in this section, the African Court may even have jurisdiction over international instruments bearing on refugee protection, such as the 1951 Convention and the international human rights covenants, though it could be problematic if the Court were to exercise jurisdiction in this regard.[200]

Among the entities with direct access to the Court, the one most likely to bring refugee cases to the African Court is probably the African Commission. It has yet to do so, however the African Commission did bring a case against Libya, in which it alleged serious and widespread human rights violations.[201] It has also brought a case against Kenya regarding its eviction of the Ogiek minority ethnic group from the Mau forest.[202] The African Commission can also request advisory opinions 'on any legal matter relating to the Charter or any other relevant human rights instrument',[203]

198 App no 001/08 Af Ct HPR (2008). 199 ibid para 46.

200 See Viljoen (n 15) 437.

201 *African Commission on Human and Peoples' Rights v Great Socialist People's Libyan Arab Jamahiriya* app no 004/2011 Af Ct HPR (2011).

202 *African Commission on Human and Peoples' Rights v The Republic of Kenya* app no 006/2012 Af Ct HPR (2012).

203 African Court Protocol (n 2) art 4.

which includes refugee protection instruments such as the 1969 Convention. NGOs are also likely to advocate on behalf of refugees. While NGOs do not have direct access to the African Court in contentious cases, as discussed earlier in this section they do arguably have standing to request advisory opinions.

D. A New African Human Rights Court?

The African Court of Justice was to adjudicate matters relating to the AU Constitutive Act. However, it was never—and never will be—established, because before its establishing protocol entered into force, the AU Assembly decided to merge it with the African Court, in order to avoid 'the danger of not having enough funds to do what we should do and just proliferating organs'.[204] As mentioned in section A above, this decision led to the adoption in 2008 of the Merged Court Protocol, creating the Merged Court. The Merged Court Protocol was superseded in 2014 by the Malabo Protocol, which created the New Merged Court. The New Merged Court is almost identical to the Merged Court, with the addition of jurisdiction over international criminal matters.[205] The Malabo Protocol will enter into force 30 days after it receives its fifteenth ratification,[206] at which time the New Merged Court's jurisdiction will automatically supersede that of the African Court, as well as the theoretical jurisdiction of the Merged Court and that of the African Court of Justice,[207] neither of which will ever be established. As mentioned in section A, the Malabo Protocol currently has ten signatures but no ratifications.

The New Merged Court's human rights jurisdiction is largely the same as that of the African Court. While the African Court has jurisdiction over 'the interpretation and application of the Charter, ... [the African Court Protocol] and any other relevant Human Rights instrument ratified by the States concerned',[208] the New Merged Court has jurisdiction over matters relating to 'the interpretation and the application of the African Charter, the Charter on the Rights and Welfare of the Child, the Protocol to the African Charter ... on the Rights of Women in Africa, or any other legal instrument relating to human rights, ratified by the States Parties concerned'.[209] Like the African Court, the New Merged Court also has jurisdiction to adjudicate the 1969 Convention, though in the new court's case this is on the basis of its jurisdiction relating to 'the interpretation, application or validity of ... Union treaties and all subsidiary legal instruments adopted within the framework of the Union' or the OAU.[210]

[204] Nigerian President Obasanjo, cited in Viljoen (n 15) 449.

[205] Malabo Protocol (n 10) Annex, arts 13 and ff. This jurisdiction covers the international crimes of genocide, crimes against humanity, war crimes, unconstitutional change of government, piracy, terrorism, mercenarism, corruption, money laundering, trafficking in persons, trafficking in drugs, trafficking in hazardous wastes, illicit exploitation of natural resources, and aggression.

[206] ibid art 11(1).

[207] ibid art 6 *bis*.

[208] African Court Protocol (n 2) art 3.

[209] Merged Court Protocol (n 7) art 28(c).

[210] ibid art 28(b).

1. Refugee issues

While the New Merged Court's jurisdiction over human rights and the 1969 Convention largely mirrors that of the African Court, other aspects of the New Merged Court's jurisdiction broaden its capacity to address refugee issues. The New Merged Court has jurisdiction over legal disputes relating to 'any question of international law',[211] 'all acts, decisions, regulations and directives of the organs of the Union',[212] and 'the existence of any fact which, if established, would constitute a breach of an obligation owed to a State Party or to the Union'.[213] The New Merged Court's international law jurisdiction—as well as its broad international criminal jurisdiction—could allow it to address causes of displacement, including acts of aggression, occupation, foreign domination or events seriously disturbing public order. The New Merged Court's jurisdiction over AU organs means it can adjudicate any issues that may arise from the AU's refugee activities described in Chapter 6. Finally, the Court's incredibly broad jurisdiction over breaches of obligations owed to the AU or its member states mean the New Merged Court could be seized of matters related to the causes of displacement or stemming from a state's breach of its refugee protection obligations.

The exercise of this theoretically broad jurisdiction of course depends on the willingness of entities with standing to bring refugee matters before the New Merged Court. As with the African Court, standing to submit cases to the New Merged Court is accorded to states parties, the AU Assembly, and AU organs,[214] as well as to the Office of the Prosecutor, which will be established within the AU to try international criminal matters.[215] The list of entities with standing in matters stemming from the New Merged Court's article 28(c) human rights jurisdiction is longer, also including the African Commission, the African Committee of Experts on the Rights and Welfare of the Child, African intergovernmental organizations, and African national human rights institutions;[216] 'African individuals' and 'African Non-Governmental Organizations' with AU observer status also have standing if the state in question has filed an article 9(3) declaration permitting this.[217]

The Malabo Protocol makes it possible for the new continental court to assume a broad role in relation to refugees, extending beyond the adjudication of individual rights to include state responsibility for causing displacement and for states breaches of refugee protection obligations. At the moment, however, this jurisdiction is entirely theoretical: the Malabo Protocol has yet to receive a single ratification; moreover, if it ever receives the fifteen required for entry into force, the new court's role in relation to refugees will depend almost entirely on the willingness of entities with standing to involve the Court in refugee matters.

[211] ibid art 28(d). [212] ibid art 28(e). [213] ibid art 28(g).

[214] Merged Court Protocol (n 7) arts 29(a) and (b); AU staff members may also appeal disputes under the AU Staff Rules and Regulations to the New Merged Court (Merged Court Protocol (n 7) art 29(c)).

[215] Malabo Protocol (n 10) art 15. [216] Merged Court Protocol (n 7) art 30.

[217] Malabo Protocol (n 10) art 16.

E. Conclusions

It is too early to make a summary assessment of the record of judicial engagement with refugee issues in Africa. While the African Commission has involved itself in refugee matters for almost thirty years, the African Court has never adjudicated a refugee case on its merits, and the New Merged Court has yet to be established. The system's architecture, however, holds promise. The African Commission's promotional mandate creates space to address prevention and systemic issues. Violations in individual cases can be addressed within the African Commission's protective mandate or, given the poor record of compliance with the African Commission's arguably quasi-judicial findings, by the African Court and, eventually, by the New Merged Court. The latter institution's broad subject matter jurisdiction, including its international criminal jurisdiction, creates a forum to address state responsibility for producing refugees as well as responsibility for breaches of refugee protection obligations.

Unfortunately, however, the African Commission's record in relation to refugees suggests a disconnect between the system's potential and what might be achieved in practice. The African Commission's record of involvement with refugees spanning almost three decades has not produced systemic success. Its promotional initiatives have produced poor or, at the very best, mixed results. Little has come of the ambitious memorandum of understanding concluded between the African Commission and UNHCR, and there has been only limited cooperation between the African Commission and the AU in refugee matters. In the fifteen years since the expert report produced in connection with the AU's First Ministerial Meeting on Human Rights identified the African Commission as having supervisory authority over the 1969 Convention, the Commission has not undertaken any activity in this regard. The effectiveness of the Special Rapporteur has been limited, and resolutions and concluding observations adopted in the refugee arena have done little to improve protection. The African Commission has addressed several refugee communications in its protective role, but due to the difficulty of accessing the Commission, these represent only a tiny fraction of the refugee rights violations occurring in Africa. Moreover, refugee cases are not immune from the poor record of compliance with African Commission decisions more generally.

Overall, the African Commission 'cannot be said to have developed a coherent policy on human rights and refugees'.[218] In a sense, however, the African Commission is halfway there. Mubangizi argues that 'Although there has been criticism regarding the lack of clear mechanisms to deal with the issue of refugees as a whole, it is clear that the African [human rights] system has paid reasonable attention to the rights of refugees'.[219] The African Commission has indeed recognized the importance of addressing refugee issues; the challenge now is to address them

[218] Murray (n 62) 61.

[219] John Mubangizi, 'Some Reflections on Recent and Current Trends in the Promotion and Protection of Human Rights in Africa: The Pains and the Gains' (2006) 6 Afr Hum Rts LJ 146, 158.

coherently and effectively, which cannot be divorced from the challenges facing the African Commission more generally.[220]

If the African Commission can achieve this, the African Court's binding human rights jurisdiction and the New Merged Court's eventual public international and international criminal law jurisdiction would be effective complements. The African Commission could focus on systemic issues within its promotional mandate while the African Court or the New Merged Court could address individual and discrete matters. The architecture of a system featuring institutions with complementary mandates is in place. The challenge now is to realize their potential. Indeed, this gulf between potential and reality imbues all aspects of the regional refugee apparatus; it is addressed in the concluding chapter that follows.

220 See Viljoen (n 15) 295 and ff.

8
Conclusion

This book has articulated the regional legal regime for refugee protection in Africa, incorporating both refugee and human rights law elements as well as treaty and institutional components. It analysed the relationships of interpretation and the relationships of conflict arising within this regime, following the International Law Commission approach outlined in Chapter 1. The book also included history essential to understanding the contemporary legal framework, beginning in Chapter 2 with the drafting history of the Organization of African Unity Convention Governing the Specific Aspects of Refugee Problems in Africa (1969 Convention).

This revealed the common understanding of the impetus for a regional refugee instrument—that the international regime was incapable of addressing African realities—to be incorrect. Rather, the process of drafting the 1969 Convention commenced with a view to making international refugee law applicable in Africa, as well as to addressing concerns relating to subversion. Only when the 1967 entry into force of the Protocol relating to the Status of Refugees resolved the former issue did drafting an Africa-specific regime come to the fore of the agenda, resulting in the adoption of an instrument devoted exclusively to refugee issues particular to Africa. This instrument was the subject of Chapter 3.

Chapter 3 covered the 1969 Convention in depth, beginning with the article I(2) regional refugee definition's global influence. The chapter then interpreted key elements of the definition, covering the 'every person' language, which extends the ambit of article I(2) to all refugees in Africa, and the four 1969 Events. Among these, 'events seriously disturbing public order' was examined at length, in part because it is today the most relevant ground of refugee status under article I(2). It was determined that the term has no international requirement and that it may extend to provide refugee status to individuals fleeing environmental events. Ultimately, because 'events seriously disturbing public order' is inherently imprecise, the term's meaning is best illustrated through practical examples, which related for the most part to non-international armed conflict.

The remaining key elements of article I(2) were interpreted in terms of the test for refugee status under the regional definition, which requires geographic proximity between the relevant 1969 Event and the individual's former home. Finally, the interpretation of article I(2) concluded that internal relocation is not a relevant consideration in refugee status determination (RSD), and that article I(2) permits sur place claims.

It is hoped that this interpretation of article I(2) will contribute to it being applied more often in RSD in African states; the discussion revealed that in Kenya and South

Africa at least, the regional definition is only rarely invoked in practice, other than in prima facie status determination. This form of RSD, which is often incorrectly conflated with the erroneous concept of 'group' RSD, involves recognizing refugee status based on readily apparent circumstances in the country of origin. The use of prima facie procedures has no effect on post-recognition rights.

Chapter 3 then moved on from article I(2) to consider other novel features of the 1969 Convention, beginning with its progressive development of an individual right to asylum. This was followed by discussions of non-refoulement; the formalization of responsibility sharing, a form of temporary protection, and voluntary repatriation; and, finally, the article III prohibition of subversive activities.

Chapter 4 analysed the nature of the relationship between the 1969 Convention and its international counterpart, the 1951 Convention relating to the Status of Refugees (1951 Convention), in procedural as well as substantive terms. In adopting a treaty that addresses only refugee issues particular to Africa, the Organization of African Unity (OAU) created a legal regime in which two distinct instruments work together, in particular regarding refugee status and its associated rights. Arguments based on the law of treaties, general international law, equality, and *lex specialis* led to the conclusion that article I(2) of the 1969 Convention expands the class of individuals who may qualify for refugee status, while the rights framework applicable to such individuals is derived from the 1951 Convention.

In addition to this systemic relationship issue, the concurrent applicability of the 1951 and 1969 Conventions also gives rise to several more isolated relationships of interpretation and of conflict. The 1951 Convention's 'compelling reasons' proviso was analysed in the former category. In the conflict category were the freedoms of movement and association, as well as state obligations regarding the provision of travel documents. Each of these apparently conflicting relationships was resolved through harmonizing treaty interpretation.

In addition to rights derived from the 1951 and 1969 Conventions, refugees in Africa also enjoy human rights guaranteed under international and regional law. Chapter 5 addressed regional human rights law in refugee protection. It began with a general discussion of the role of human rights in refugee protection, and then moved on to address the core instruments of the African regional human rights regime, beginning with the African Charter on Human and Peoples' Rights (African Charter). Its contributions to non-refoulement and asylum, and to rights during exile, were canvassed. This was followed by a discussion of the Protocol to the African Charter on Human and Peoples' Rights on the Rights of Women in Africa and the African Charter on the Rights and Welfare of the Child.

The literature is as silent on the relationship between regional human rights law and the 1969 Convention as it is regarding the latter instrument and the 1951 Convention. The simultaneous applicability of regional refugee and human rights law to the same population gives rise to relationships of interpretation and to relationships of conflict. Asylum and return were analysed in the former category. Relationships of conflict arise between the 1969 Convention's prohibition of subversive activities and political rights under the African Charter, as well as regarding freedom of movement. The analysis argued that the prohibition of subversive activities should yield to political rights in respect of activities that are not truly 'subversive'. Speech or acts that rise to the level of subversion should be permitted unless such speech or acts are caught by permissible limitations on political rights. The apparent conflict regarding freedom of movement was resolved through a harmonizing treaty interpretation: the default position is that refugees have freedom of movement; however, organized settlements may be permitted in truly exceptional circumstances.

Chapter 5 was the final instalment in Part I on the treaty framework. Part II on the institutional architecture supportive of this legal framework began with Chapter 6's survey of the OAU's historic role and the African Union's (AU) contemporary role in relation to refugees in Africa. This discussion revealed that the AU, and the OAU before it, have created bodies with refugee-focused mandates, staged a surfeit of refugee-focused events, and authored innumerable soft law documents on refugees. The scale and scope of engagement has not, however, produced commensurate results for refugees. Moreover, recent AU focus on humanitarianism generally and on continental freedom of movement may compromise refugee protection. The latter, however, may also bolster protection under the 1951 Convention, by improving the treatment of groups of foreigners on whose treatment the standards owed to refugees depend.

The African Commission on Human and Peoples' Rights (African Commission), discussed in Chapter 7, has been similarly ineffectual. It is not clear that its promotional work on refugees has enhanced protection. Only a tiny fraction of the decisions issued within its protective mandate have related to refugees and these, like all African Commission decisions, have an inconsistent record of implementation and enforcement. It is too early to assess the refugee record of the African Court on Human and Peoples' Rights, however it and the human rights court that may replace it hold promise for refugees.

Together these seven chapters have outlined and analysed the regional legal regime for refugee protection in Africa. The picture that has emerged is of a largely robust framework, on paper. The regional and international refugee treaties together address the particular situation of exiled individuals, while regional and international human rights law supplement these refugee-specific provisions with protections that benefit all human beings. A steadily evolving and expanding network of institutions and series of initiatives complement these legal instruments. Bodies with refugee mandates were, and continue to be, created, and events and initiatives aimed at progressively developing the law proliferate. However, gaps in the system remain, most notably regarding supervision of the 1969 Convention.

When it adopted the regional instrument in 1969, the OAU did not create any body to supervise its implementation. Article IX of the 1969 Convention provides that any dispute between contracting states relating to the treaty's interpretation or application shall be referred to the OAU's Commission for Mediation, Conciliation and Arbitration. Under the AU, the authority to settle such disputes now rests with the African Court, as discussed in Chapter 2. Such dispute-resolution authority is not the same as supervision. This is illustrated well by the 1951 Convention example. The authority to settle disputes relating to the interpretation or application of that instrument rests with the International Court of Justice

(ICJ),[1] however, the authority to supervise the 1951 Convention clearly rests not with the ICJ but with Office of the United Nations High Commissioner for Refugees (UNHCR).[2]

Similarly, no supervisory treaty body was created when the AU supplanted the OAU in 2001. As discussed in Chapter 7, the conclusions of a March 2003 meeting between the African Commission and UNHCR recommended that the Commission monitor the implementation of the 1969 Convention. Two months later, an expert report prepared for the AU's First Ministerial Meeting on Human Rights identified the African Commission as having oversight of the 1969 Convention. While several authors have accepted this designation,[3] its legal basis is unclear. Typically, supervisory authority flows from the treaty under supervision and/or from the legal instrument establishing the supervisory body. For example, to continue the 1951 Convention analogy, UNHCR's supervisory authority flows from both the 1951 Convention's article 35 and from UNHCR's statute.[4] Neither the 1969 Convention nor the African Charter, which establishes the African Commission, vest the authority to supervise the 1969 Convention with the African Commission. Moreover, the African Commission has never actually exercised any supervisory function. While the African Commission may apply the 1969 Convention in communications before it further to the African Charter's articles 56(2) and 60, its ability to invoke the 1969 Convention is no substitute for treaty supervision. Scholarly statements about the African Commission's supervisory authority over the 1969 Convention provide cover for what is actually a significant lacuna.

Supervision of the 1969 Convention is essential to elaborate African regional refugee law and ensure that it keeps pace with evolving practical realities. The AU should seize the opportunities presented by Rwandan President Paul Kagame's ongoing reform initiative and the upcoming fiftieth anniversary of the 1969 Convention's adoption in 2019 to address supervision.

The 1969 Convention's article VII is an important starting point in any discussion of supervision. It exhorts states to provide the OAU Secretariat (now the AU Commission) with information on '(a) the condition of refugees; (b) the implementation of this Convention, and (c) laws, regulations and decrees which are, or may hereafter be, in force relating to refugees'. With states already obliged to report on these critical matters, the AU must determine how such information should be used to ensure that the 1969 Convention is effectively implemented and evolves as a living instrument capable of responding to the changing realities of forced external displacement in Africa.

This supervision lacuna aside, the legal regime for refugee protection is, as mentioned above, relatively robust. This is not, however, reflected in the practical situation for refugees on the continent. Almost one-third of the world's refugees reside

[1] Convention relating to the Status of Refugees (adopted 28 July 1951, entered into force 22 April 1954) 189 UNTS 137, art 38.

[2] ibid art 35. [3] See Chapter 7, notes 92 and 93.

[4] UNGA Res 428 (V) (14 December 1950) art 8.

in Africa, and to say that their circumstances do not reflect the promise of regional refugee and human rights law is understatement. As is the case in many human rights contexts, the issue is not the law, but rather its implementation. To borrow Heyns and Viljoen's terminology, the regional refugee protection framework pairs a high level of 'norm recognition' with a low level of 'norm enforcement'.[5]

Effective supervision is but one aspect of addressing this challenge. The implementation of the overall legal framework must also be improved at the regional level, by improving the effectiveness of the institutions and initiatives discussed in Chapters 6 and 7, and implementation must be improved at the national level. Indeed, 'the domestic level is the most important level on which human rights could potentially be protected by law in Africa' because if 'the legal system of a particular country protects the human rights of everyone within its jurisdiction, there will be no need for higher levels of protection'.[6] A critical component of improved national-level implementation of the 1969 Convention is for states to begin reporting their refugee decisions. This would improve due process and the quality of future decisions as well as contribute to the progressive development of regional refugee law.

There is an important role for the international community in implementation. The Syrian refugee crisis that captured the world's attention beginning in 2015 vividly demonstrates that responsibility for hosting refugees is often arbitrarily allocated based on geography, resulting in a highly inequitable distribution of what should be a shared global responsibility. This inequity is amplified in Africa, where developing countries host many more refugees than richer states in the Global North, sometimes on better terms. Hasan provides a stark example. He invites a comparison of Uganda and Denmark: the 'latter's GDP per capita is about 77 times larger than the former's. Yet in January [2016], the enlightened Danes passed a law allowing the authorities to seize the jewellery of refugees, supposedly . . . to cover the costs of hosting them. Uganda's 2006 Refugee Act, however, allows refugees in that country to work, travel and even start their own business'.[7] According to the Norwegian Refugee Council, Uganda welcomed more refugees each day in 2016 than many European states received during the entire year.[8] Northern states not doing their share contributes to protection fatigue and hence failures in Africa. For example, some observers viewed Kenya's 6 May 2016 announcement of its intention to close Dadaab as a reaction to Europe's dismal response to the influx of refugees from Syria.[9]

[5] Christof Heyns and Frans Viljoen, 'An Overview of International Human Rights Protection in Africa' (1999) 15 S Afr J Hum Rts 421, 424.

[6] ibid.

[7] Mehdi Hasan, 'Obsessing over Europe's Refugee Crisis while Ignoring Africa's is White Privilege at Work' *The Washington Post* (Washington DC, 3 November 2016) <https://www.washingtonpost.com/news/global-opinions/wp/2016/11/03/obsessing-over-europes-refugee-crisis-while-ignoring-africas-is-white-privilege-at-work/?utm_term=.7ead402fc3c1> accessed 25 April 2017.

[8] Reuters, 'Uganda Welcomes More Refugees Daily Than Some in Europe Annually, Charity Says' (25 January 2017) <http://www.voanews.com/a/uganda-more-refugees-daily-then-some-in-europe-annually-charity-says/3692807.html> accessed 25 April 2017.

[9] See, for example, Lucy Hovil, 'Why is the Cost of Hosting Refugees Falling on the World's Poorest States' *The Guardian* (13 May 2016) <https://www.theguardian.com/global-development/2016/may/13/why-is-the-cost-of-hosting-refugees-falling-on-poorest-states-kenya-dadaab-closing> accessed 25

Resource scarcity in Africa also contributes to the adoption of refugee policies, such as encampment, that violate refugee rights, and is a factor preventing the AU and African states from effectively implementing the regional legal framework. Developed nations must provide material, technical, and, most importantly, financial assistance to support African states and the AU in delivering upon the promise of the regional legal regime. States have recognized the importance of this form of responsibility sharing. UNHCR's Executive Committee (ExCom), for example, issued a statement on 'Enhancing International Cooperation, Solidarity, Local Capacities and Humanitarian Action for Refugees in Africa'. In the statement, ExCom member states reaffirmed their 'collective commitment, through enhanced regional and international solidarity, burden-sharing and partnership, to support host countries and communities in building their capacity to better address and resolve the multi-faceted challenges of forced displacement and, in particular, to strengthen protection, improve the situation of refugees, IDPs and stateless persons, and facilitate durable solutions'.[10] Moreover, the AU's Executive Council has repeatedly and recently called on the international community to provide 'financial and material assistance ... in the spirit of solidarity and burden sharing'.[11]

The process of converting commitments such as ExCom's into concerted action began in earnest in 2016, when the United Nations (UN) convened the Summit for Refugees and Migrants on 19 September. It was aimed at generating state support for a more humane and coordinated approach to migration and refugee protection. It resulted in the New York Declaration for Refugees and Migrants, which commits states to achieving more equitable responsibility sharing by adopting global compacts on refugees and migration in 2018.[12] The Summit for Refugees and Migrants was followed by the Leaders' Summit on Refugees, co-convened by the UN Secretary-General and seven UN member states. The Leaders' Summit generated pledges from both Northern and Southern states, including nine African states,[13] demonstrating how responsibility sharing can catalyse refugee protection. Unfortunately, however, political will for the global compacts has waned since the 2016 Summit, constituting a significant challenge to their elaboration.[14]

Such positive international responsibility sharing initiatives unfortunately exist alongside less constructive partnerships, notably the European Union's (EU) new

April 2017; Ben Rawlence, *City of Thorns: Nine Lives in the World's Largest Refugee Camp* (Vintage Canada 2016) 363–64.

[10] UNHCR ExCom, 'Statement of the Executive Committee on Enhancing International Cooperation, Solidarity, Local Capacities and Humanitarian Action for Refugees in Africa', on the occasion of the high-level segments of the 65th session of the Executive Committee of the High Commissioner's Program (30 September 2014).

[11] AU (Executive Council), 'Decision on the Reports of the PRC Sub-Committees' (AU Johannesburg 7–12 June 2015) EX.CL/Dec.877 (XXVII) para 29.

[12] UNGA, 'New York Declaration for Refugees and Migrants' (13 September 2016) UN Doc A/71/L.1, Annex I.

[13] Cameroon, Chad, Djibouti, Ethiopia, Kenya, Rwanda, Tanzania, Uganda, and Zambia.

[14] Tania Karas, 'UN Bid to Improve Migrant, Refugee Response Flounders as Political Will Evaporates' (IRIN, 30 November 2017) <https://www.irinnews.org/analysis/2017/11/30/un-bid-improve-migrant-refugee-response-flounders-political-will-evaporates> accessed 2 December 2017.

Migration Partnership Framework (MPF), which was endorsed by the European Council in June 2016. The MPF is but one outcome of a long line of migration policy dialogues between Europe and Africa—including the 2017 EU–AU summit in Côte d'Ivoire that focused in part on migration, 2015 Valletta Summit on Migration,[15] the 2014 EU–Horn of African Migration Route Initiative (known as the Khartoum Process),[16] and the 2006 Euro-African Dialogue on Migration and Development (known as the Rabat Process)[17]—through which the EU has effectively externalized its control over migration.[18] According to the European Commission, in the short term, the MPF aims to save lives at sea and in the desert, combat trafficking and smuggling networks, and open legal pathways to Europe while at the same time increasing opportunities for asylum within Africa. In the longer term, it apparently addresses root causes of forced and irregular migration by supporting development in countries of origin.[19] In reality, however, the objective of the MPF and other similar initiatives is containment.[20]

The MPF is implemented through agreements with source countries, initially Ethiopia, Mali, Niger, Nigeria, and Senegal. Niger has already been the site of significant EU efforts, as Agadez represents a major transit point between countries of origin in West Africa and Algeria and Libya, from where refugees embark on the perilous central Mediterranean route to Europe.[21] EU efforts in Niger have pushed people onto ever more circuitous routes, resulting in more deaths in the desert.[22] Not surprisingly then, the MPF has been heavily criticized, including in a joint statement signed by 104 non-governmental organizations. The statement characterizes

[15] European Council, 'Valletta Summit Political Declaration' (11–15 November 2015) <http://www.consilium.europa.eu/media/21841/political_decl_en.pdf> accessed 27 January 2018.

[16] See Tuesday Reitano, 'The Khartoum Process: A Sustainable Response to Human Smuggling and Trafficking?' (Institute for Security Studies, 30 November 2016) <https://issafrica.org/research/policy-brief/the-khartoum-process-a-sustainable-response-to-human-smuggling-and-trafficking> accessed 12 March 2017.

[17] See, in this connection, The Rabat Process, 'Rome Declaration' (adopted 27 November 2014) <https://www.rabat-process.org/images/RabatProcess/Documents/declaration-programme-rome-ministerial-conference-rome-2014-rabat-process.pdf> accessed 27 December 2017.

[18] See generally, Lorenzo Gabrielli, 'Multilevel Inter-Regional Governance of Mobility Between Africa and Europe' (2016) Interdisciplinary Research Group on Immigration Working Paper Series <https://www.upf.edu/documents/3329791/0/L.+Gabrielli+-+GRITIM+WP+30+2016.pdf/4a034bb9-882d-9721-2cd6-20b133d63945> accessed 3 April 2017.

[19] European Commission, 'Communication from the Commission to the European Parliament, the European Council, the Council and the European Investment Bank on Establishing a New Partnership Framework with Third Countries Under the European Agenda on Migration' (7 June 2016) COM(2016) 385 <https://ec.europa.eu/transparency/regdoc/rep/1/2016/EN/1-2016-385-EN-F1-1.PDF> accessed 15 March 2017.

[20] See, generally, the joint *Der Spiegel, El Pais, The Guardian, La Stampa, Le Monde,* and *Politiken* investigation into how the EU's new exclusionary approach has affected refugees and migrants in North Africa. All English-language articles are available at: <https://www.theguardian.com/world/series/migration-crisis-the-new-routes-to-europe> accessed 2 January 2018.

[21] See Somini Sengupta, 'Heat, Hunger and War Force Africans onto a "Road of Fire"' *The New York Times* (15 December 2016) <https://www.nytimes.com/interactive/2016/12/15/world/africa/agadez-climate-change.html> accessed 15 April 2017.

[22] Ibrahim Manzo Diallo, 'EU Strategy Stems Migrant Flow from Niger, But at What Cost?' IRIN (2 February 2017) <https://www.irinnews.org/special-report/2017/02/02/eu-strategy-stems-migrant-flow-niger-what-cost> accessed 11 April 2017.

the MPF as 'making deterrence and return the main objective of the [European] Union's relationship with third countries' and notes that it 'risks cementing a shift towards a foreign policy that serves one single objective, to curb migration, at the expense of European credibility and leverage in defence of fundamental values and human rights'. The statement goes on to question 'how Europe can ask partner countries to keep their doors open ... while at the same time Member States refuse to shoulder their fair share of responsibility for protecting people who flee'.[23]

A significant portion of any resources generated through constructive international responsibility sharing initiatives must be directed not at deportation, deterrence, and external control but at what is arguably the most pressing protection concern in Africa: the implementation of local integration as the most realistic durable solution for refugees in protracted situations. Encampment and labour market restrictions are the principal barriers to local integration. Rawlence portrays this vividly in the context of Dadaab. To leave the camp,

> residents require a 'movement pass,' just like under apartheid. Acquiring one usually involves a bribe. Thus, members of the third generation that is now beginning life in Dadaab may well spend their whole life in the camp. If they win one of the fiercely contested slots at secondary school, they could gain diplomas and degrees online or through the mail, but when there's no viable path to a free future elsewhere, education in the closed camp is a cruel trick: There are no jobs except volunteer positions with the aid agencies that run the hospitals, schools and social programs, and these pay a fraction of what Kenyan staff members receive for doing the same job.[24]

Host countries must allow refugees to exercise their rights under regional refugee law, in particular the rights to work under the 1951 Convention[25] and to freedom of movement and residence under this instrument and under the African Charter.[26]

While a significant proportion of the economic resources that would enable African states to attenuate their restrictive movement and work policies can come from the Global North, political leadership in this regard must come from within the continent. Chapters 6 and 7 demonstrated that the AU and the African Commission have separately produced a plethora of refugee-related norms, but many have never been implemented. The two should now work together and focus their efforts in favour of refugees on providing leadership on the most pressing issues. Fostering the local integration of refugees in protracted situations would be a sound initial priority. The AU and the African Commission should together encourage states to realize their international and regional obligations regarding employment and freedom of movement. While the AU's Executive Council has taken steps in this

[23] Human Rights Watch and others, 'Joint NGO Statement Ahead of the European Council of 28–29 June 2016: NGOs Strongly Condemn new EU Policies to Contain Migration' (2016) <https://www.hrw.org/news/2016/06/27/joint-ngo-statement-ahead-european-council-28-29-june-2016-ngos-strongly-condemn-new> accessed 25 April 2017.

[24] Ben Rawlence, 'The Other Refugee Crisis' *The New York Times* (9 October 2015) <https://www.nytimes.com/2015/10/10/opinion/the-other-refugee-crisis.html> accessed 25 April 2017.

[25] (n 1) arts 17–19.

[26] ibid art 26; (Adopted 27 June 1981, entered into force 21 October 1986) 21 ILM 58, art 12(1).

regard[27] and the AU's freedom of movement initiative may incidentally impact refugees' work rights, it seems unbalanced for the AU to focus on humanitarian affairs generally and for the African Commission to focus on nationality and statelessness while refugees' rights are still systemically and fundamentally violated across the continent. The AU's general humanitarian work and Agenda 2063, and the African Commission's new priorities—and indeed moral and legal failures in the EU and beyond—must not leave the individuals who are among the most vulnerable in Africa and the world behind.

[27] See Chapter 6, text attached to notes 172 and 173.

ANNEX 1

Organization of African Unity Convention Governing the Specific Aspects of Refugee Problems in Africa

Adopted 10 September 1969, Entered into force 20 June 1974, 1001 UNTS 45

PREAMBLE We, the Heads of State and Government, assembled in the city of Addis Ababa,

1. Noting with concern the constantly increasing numbers of refugees in Africa and desirous of finding ways and means of alleviating their misery and suffering as well as providing them with a better life and future,
2. Recognising the need for an essentially humanitarian approach towards solving the problems of refugees,
3. Aware, however, that refugee problems are a source of friction among many Member States, and desirous of eliminating the source of such discord,
4. Anxious to make a distinction between a refugee who seeks a peaceful and normal life and a person fleeing his country for the sole purpose of fomenting subversion from outside,
5. Determined that the activities of such subversive elements should be discouraged, in accordance with the Declaration on the Problems of Subversion and Resolution on the Problem of Refugees adopted at Accra in 1965,
6. Bearing in mind that the Charter of the United Nations and the Universal Declaration of Human Rights have affirmed the principle that human beings shall enjoy fundamental rights and freedoms without discrimination,
7. Recalling Resolution 2312 (XXII) of 14 December 1967 of the United Nations General Assembly, relating to the Declaration on Territorial Asylum,
8. Convinced that all the problems of our continent must be solved in the spirit of the Charter of the Organization of African Unity and in the African context,
9. Recognising that the United Nations Convention of 28 July 1951, as modified by the Protocol of 31 January 1967, constitutes the basic and universal instrument relating to the status of refugees and reflects the deep concern of States for refugees and their desire to establish common standards for their treatment,
10. Recalling Resolutions 26 and 104 of the OAU Assemblies of Heads of State and Government, calling upon Member States of the Organization who had not already done so to accede to the United Nations Convention of 1951 and to the Protocol of 1967 relating to the Status of Refugees, and meanwhile to apply their provisions to refugees in Africa,
11. Convinced that the efficiency of the measures recommended by the present Convention to solve the problem of refugees in Africa necessitates close and continuous collaboration between the Organization of African Unity and the Office of the United Nations High Commissioner for Refugees,

HAVE AGREED as follows:

Article I
Definition of the Term 'Refugee'

1. For the purposes of this Convention, the term 'refugee' shall mean every person who, owing to well-founded fear of being persecuted for reasons of race, religion, nationality, membership of a particular social group or political opinion, is outside the country of his nationality and is unable or, owing to such fear, is unwilling to avail himself of the protection of that country, or who, not having a nationality and being outside the country of his former habitual residence as a result of such events, is unable or, owing to such fear, is unwilling to return to it.
2. The term 'refugee' shall also apply to every person who, owing to external aggression, occupation, foreign domination or events seriously disturbing public order in either part or the whole of his country of origin or nationality, is compelled to leave his place of habitual residence in order to seek refuge in another place outside his country of origin or nationality.
3. In the case of a person who has several nationalities, the term 'a country of which he is a national' shall mean each of the countries of which he is a national, and a person shall not be deemed to be lacking the protection of the country of which he is a national if, without any valid reason based on well-founded fear, he has not availed himself of the protection of one of the countries of which he is a national.
4. This Convention shall cease to apply to any refugee if:

   (a) he has voluntarily re-availed himself of the protection of the country of his nationality, or
   (b) having lost his nationality, he has voluntarily reacquired it, or
   (c) he has acquired a new nationality, and enjoys the protection of the country of his new nationality, or
   (d) he has voluntarily re-established himself in the country which he left or outside which he remained owing to fear of persecution, or
   (e) he can no longer, because the circumstances in connection with which he was recognised as a refugee have ceased to exist, continue to refuse to avail himself of the protection of the country of his nationality, or
   (f) he has committed a serious non-political crime outside his country of refuge after his admission to that country as a refugee, or
   (g) he has seriously infringed the purposes and objectives of this Convention.

5. The provisions of this Convention shall not apply to any person with respect to whom the country of asylum has serious reasons for considering that:
   (a) he has committed a crime against peace, a war crime, or a crime against humanity, as defined in the international instruments drawn up to make provision in respect of such crimes,
   (b) he committed a serious non-political crime outside the country of refuge prior to his admission to that country as a refugee,
   (c) he has been guilty of acts contrary to the purposes and principles of the Organization of African Unity,
   (d) he has been guilty of acts contrary to the purposes and principles of the United Nations.
6. For the purposes of this Convention, the Contracting State of asylum shall determine whether an applicant is a refugee.

Article II
Asylum

1. Member States of the OAU shall use their best endeavours consistent with their respective legislation to receive refugees and to secure the settlement of those refugees who, for well-founded reasons, are unable or unwilling to return to their country of origin or nationality.
2. The granting of asylum to refugees is a peaceful and humanitarian act and shall not be regarded as an unfriendly act by any Member State.
3. No person shall be subjected by a Member State to measures such as rejection at the frontier, return or expulsion, which would compel him to return to or remain in a territory where his life, physical integrity or liberty would be threatened for the reasons set out in Article I, paragraphs 1 and 2.
4. Where a Member State finds difficulty in continuing to grant asylum to refugees, such Member State may appeal directly to other Member States and through the OAU, and such other Member States shall in the spirit of African solidarity and international co-operation take appropriate measures to lighten the burden of the Member State granting asylum.
5. Where a refugee has not received the right to reside in any country of asylum, he may be granted temporary residence in any country of asylum in which he first presented himself as a refugee pending arrangement for his re-settlement in accordance with the preceding paragraph. 6. For reasons of security, countries of asylum shall, as far as possible, settle refugees at a reasonable distance from the frontier of their country of origin.

Article III
Prohibition of Subversive Activities

1. Every refugee has duties to the country in which he finds himself, which require in particular that he conforms with its laws and regulations as well as with measures taken for the maintenance of public order. He shall also abstain from any subversive activities against any Member State of the OAU.
2. Signatory States undertake to prohibit refugees residing in their respective territories from attacking any State Member of the OAU, by any activity likely to cause tension between Member States, and in particular by use of arms, through the press, or by radio.

Article IV
Non-discrimination

Member States undertake to apply the provisions of this Convention to all refugees without discrimination as to race, religion, nationality, membership of a particular social group or political opinions.

Article V
Voluntary Repatriation

1. The essentially voluntary character of repatriation shall be respected in all cases and no refugee shall be repatriated against his will.
2. The country of asylum, in collaboration with the country of origin, shall make adequate arrangements for the safe return of refugees who request repatriation.

3. The country of origin, on receiving back refugees, shall facilitate their re-settlement and grant them the full rights and privileges of nationals of the country, and subject them to the same obligations.
4. Refugees who voluntarily return to their country shall in no way be penalised for having left it for any of the reasons giving rise to refugee situations. Whenever necessary, an appeal shall be made through national information media and through the Administrative Secretary-General of the OAU, inviting refugees to return home and giving assurance that the new circumstances prevailing in their country of origin will enable them to return without risk and to take up a normal and peaceful life without fear of being disturbed or punished, and that the text of such appeal should be given to refugees and clearly explained to them by their country of asylum.
5. Refugees who freely decide to return to their homeland, as a result of such assurances or on their own initiative, shall be given every possible assistance by the country of asylum, the country of origin, voluntary agencies and international and intergovernmental organisations, to facilitate their return.

Article VI
Travel Documents

1. Subject to Article III, Member States shall issue to refugees lawfully staying in their territories travel documents in accordance with the United Nations Convention relating to the Status of Refugees and the Schedule and Annex thereto, for the purpose of travel outside their territory, unless compelling reasons of national security or public order otherwise require. Member States may issue such a travel document to any other refugee in their territory.
2. Where an African country of second asylum accepts a refugee from a country of first asylum, the country of first asylum may be dispensed from issuing a document with a return clause.
3. Travel documents issued to refugees under previous international agreements by State Parties thereto shall be recognised and treated by Member States in the same way as if they had been issued to refugees pursuant to this Article.

Article VII
Co-operation of the National Authorities with the Organization of African Unity

In order to enable the Administrative Secretary-General of the Organization of African Unity to make reports to the competent organs of the Organization of African Unity, Member States undertake to provide the Secretariat in the appropriate form with information and statistical data requested concerning:

(a) the condition of refugees,

(b) the implementation of this Convention, and

(c) laws, regulations and decrees which are, or may hereafter in force relating to refugees.

Article VIII
Co-operation with the Office of the United Nations High Commissioner for Refugees

1. Member States shall co-operate with the Office of the United Nations High Commissioner for Refugees.

2. The Present Convention shall be the effective regional complement in Africa of the 1951 United Nations Convention on the Status of Refugees.

Article IX
Settlement of Disputes

Any dispute between States signatories to this Convention relating to its interpretation or application, which cannot be settled by other means, shall be referred to the Commission for Mediation, Conciliation and Arbitration of the Organization of African Unity, at the request of any one of the Parties to the dispute.

Article X
Signature and Ratification

1. This Convention is open for signature and accession by all Member States of the Organization of African Unity and shall be ratified by signatory States in accordance with their respective constitutional processes. The instruments of ratification shall be deposited with the Administrative Secretary-General of the Organization of African Unity.
2. The original instrument, done if possible in African languages, and in English and French, all texts being equally authentic, shall be deposited with the Administrative Secretary-General of the Organization of African Unity.
3. Any independent African State, Member of the Organization of African Unity, may at any time notify the Administrative Secretary-General of the Organization of African Unity of its accession to this Convention.

Article XI
Entry into Force

This Convention shall come into force upon deposit of instruments of ratification by one-third of the Member States of the Organization of African Unity.

Article XII
Amendment

This Convention may be amended or revised if any Member State makes a written request to the Administrative Secretary-General to that effect, provided, however, that the proposed amendment shall not be submitted to the Assembly of Heads of State and Government for consideration until all Member States have been duly notified of it and a period of one year has elapsed. Such an amendment shall not be effective unless approved by at least two-thirds of the Member States Parties to the present Convention.

Article XIII
Denunciation

1. Any Member State Party to this Convention may denounce its provisions by a written notification to the Administrative Secretary-General.
2. At the end of one year from the date of such notification, if not withdrawn, the Convention shall cease to apply with respect to the denouncing State.

Article XIV
Registration with the United Nations

Upon entry into force of this Convention, the Administrative Secretary-General of the OAU shall register it with the Secretary-General of the United Nations, in accordance with Article 102 of the Charter of the United Nations.

Article XV
Notifications by the Administrative Secretary-General of the Organization of African Unity

The Administrative Secretary-General of the Organization of African Unity shall inform all Members of the Organisation:

(a) of signatures, ratifications and accessions in accordance with Article X;

(b) of entry into force, in accordance with Article XI;

(c) of requests for amendments submitted under the terms of Article XII;

(d) of denunciations, in accordance with Article XIII.

DONE in the City of Addis Ababa this 10th day of September 1969.

ANNEX 2

African Charter on Human and Peoples' Rights

Adopted 27 June 1981, Entered into force 21 October 1986, 21 ILM 58

Preamble

The African States members of the Organization of African Unity, parties to the present convention entitled 'African Charter on Human and Peoples' Rights',

Recalling Decision 115 (XVI) of the Assembly of Heads of State and Government at its Sixteenth Ordinary Session held in Monrovia, Liberia, from 17 to 20 July 1979 on the preparation of a 'preliminary draft on an African Charter on Human and Peoples' Rights providing inter alia for the establishment of bodies to promote and protect human and peoples' rights';

Considering the Charter of the Organization of African Unity, which stipulates that 'freedom, equality, justice and dignity are essential objectives for the achievement of the legitimate aspirations of the African peoples';

Reaffirming the pledge they solemnly made in Article 2 of the said Charter to eradicate all forms of colonialism from Africa, to coordinate and intensify their cooperation and efforts to achieve a better life for the peoples of Africa and to promote international cooperation having due regard to the Charter of the United Nations. and the Universal Declaration of Human Rights;

Taking into consideration the virtues of their historical tradition and the values of African civilization which should inspire and characterize their reflection on the concept of human and peoples' rights;

Recognizing on the one hand, that fundamental human rights stem from the attributes of human beings which justifies their national and international protection and on the other hand that the reality and respect of peoples' rights should necessarily guarantee human rights;

Considering that the enjoyment of rights and freedoms also implies the performance of duties on the part of everyone;

Convinced that it is henceforth essential to pay a particular attention to the right to development and that civil and political rights cannot be dissociated from economic, social and cultural rights in their conception as well as universality and that the satisfaction of economic, social and cultural rights ia a guarantee for the enjoyment of civil and political rights;

Conscious of their duty to achieve the total liberation of Africa, the peoples of which are still struggling for their dignity and genuine independence, and undertaking to eliminate colonialism, neo-colonialism, apartheid, zionism and to dismantle aggressive foreign military bases and all forms of discrimination, particularly those based on race, ethnic group, color, sex. language, religion or political opinions;

Reaffirming their adherence to the principles of human and peoples' rights and freedoms contained in the declarations, conventions and other instrument adopted by the Organization of African Unity, the Movement of Non-Aligned Countries and the United Nations;

Firmly convinced of their duty to promote and protect human and peoples' rights and freedoms taking into account the importance traditionally attached to these rights and freedoms in Africa;

Have agreed as follows:

Part I: Rights and Duties

CHAPTER I: HUMAN AND PEOPLES' RIGHTS

Article 1

The Member States of the Organization of African Unity parties to the present Charter shall recognize the rights, duties and freedoms enshrined in this Chapter and shall undertake to adopt legislative or other measures to give effect to them.

Article 2

Every individual shall be entitled to the enjoyment of the rights and freedoms recognized and guaranteed in the present Charter without distinction of any kind such as race, ethnic group, color, sex, language, religion, political or any other opinion, national and social origin, fortune, birth or other status.

Article 3

1. Every individual shall be equal before the law.
2. Every individual shall be entitled to equal protection of the law.

Article 4

Human beings are inviolable. Every human being shall be entitled to respect for his life and the integrity of his person. No one may be arbitrarily deprived of this right.

Article 5

Every individual shall have the right to the respect of the dignity inherent in a human being and to the recognition of his legal status. All forms of exploitation and degradation of man particularly slavery, slave trade, torture, cruel, inhuman or degrading punishment and treatment shall be prohibited.

Article 6

Every individual shall have the right to liberty and to the security of his person. No one may be deprived of his freedom except for reasons and conditions previously laid down by law. In particular, no one may be arbitrarily arrested or detained.

Article 7

1. Every individual shall have the right to have his cause heard. This comprises:
   (a) the right to an appeal to competent national organs against acts of violating his fundamental rights as recognized and guaranteed by conventions, laws, regulations and customs in force;
   (b) the right to be presumed innocent until proved guilty by a competent court or tribunal;
   (c) the right to defense, including the right to be defended by counsel of his choice;
   (d) the right to be tried within a reasonable time by an impartial court or tribunal.

2. No one may be condemned for an act or omission which did not constitute a legally punishable offence at the time it was committed. No penalty may be inflicted for an offence for which no provision was made at the time it was committed. Punishment is personal and can be imposed only on the offender.

Article 8

Freedom of conscience, the profession and free practice of religion shall be guaranteed. No one may, subject to law and order, be submitted to measures restricting the exercise of these freedoms.

Article 9

1. Every individual shall have the right to receive information.
2. Every individual shall have the right to express and disseminate his opinions within the law.

Article 10

1. Every individual shall have the right to free association provided that he abides by the law.
2. Subject to the obligation of solidarity provided for in Article 29 no one may be compelled to join an association.

Article 11

Every individual shall have the right to assemble freely with others. The exercise of this right shall be subject only to necessary restrictions provided for by law in particular those enacted in the interest of national security, the safety, health, ethics and rights and freedoms of others.

Article 12

1. Every individual shall have the right to freedom of movement and residence within the borders of a State provided he abides by the law.
2. Every individual shall have the right to leave any country including his own, and to return to his country. This right may only be subject to restrictions, provided for by law for the protection of national security, law and order, public health or morality.
3. Every individual shall have the right, when persecuted, to seek and obtain asylum in other countries in accordance with laws of those countries and international conventions.
4. A non-national legally admitted in a territory of a State Party to the present Charter, may only be expelled from it by virtue of a decision taken in accordance with the law.
5. The mass expulsion of non-nationals shall be prohibited. Mass expulsion shall be that which is aimed at national, racial, ethnic or religious groups.

Article 13

1. Every citizen shall have the right to participate freely in the government of his country, either directly or through freely chosen representatives in accordance with the provisions of the law.
2. Every citizen shall have the right of equal access to the public service of his country.

3. Every individual shall have the right of access to public property and services in strict equality of all persons before the law.

Article 14

The right to property shall be guaranteed. It may only be encroached upon in the interest of public need or in the general interest of the community and in accordance with the provisions of appropriate laws.

Article 15

Every individual shall have the right to work under equitable and satisfactory conditions, and shall receive equal pay for equal work.

Article 16

1. Every individual shall have the right to enjoy the best attainable state of physical and mental health.
2. States parties to the present Charter shall take the necessary measures to protect the health of their people and to ensure that they receive medical attention when they are sick.

Article 17

1. Every individual shall have the right to education.
2. Every individual may freely take part in the cultural life of his community.
3. The promotion and protection of morals and traditional values recognized by the community shall be the duty of the State.

Article 18

1. The family shall be the natural unit and basis of society. It shall be protected by the State which shall take care of its physical health and moral.
2. The State shall have the duty to assist the family which is the custodian of morals and traditional values recognized by the community.
3. The State shall ensure the elimination of every discrimination against women and also ensure the protection of the rights of the woman and the child as stipulated in international declarations and conventions.
4. The aged and the disabled shall also have the right to special measures of protection in keeping with their physical or moral needs.

Article 19

All peoples shall be equal; they shall enjoy the same respect and shall have the same rights. Nothing shall justify the domination of a people by another.

Article 20

1. All peoples shall have the right to existence. They shall have the unquestionable and inalienable right to self- determination. They shall freely determine their political status and shall pursue their economic and social development according to the policy they have freely chosen.
2. Colonized or oppressed peoples shall have the right to free themselves from the bonds of domination by resorting to any means recognized by the international community.
3. All peoples shall have the right to the assistance of the States parties to the present Charter in their liberation struggle against foreign domination, be it political, economic or cultural.

Article 21

1. All peoples shall freely dispose of their wealth and natural resources. This right shall be exercised in the exclusive interest of the people. In no case shall a people be deprived of it.
2. In case of spoliation the dispossessed people shall have the right to the lawful recovery of its property as well as to an adequate compensation.
3. The free disposal of wealth and natural resources shall be exercised without prejudice to the obligation of promoting international economic cooperation based on mutual respect, equitable exchange and the principles of international law.
4. States parties to the present Charter shall individually and collectively exercise the right to free disposal of their wealth and natural resources with a view to strengthening African unity and solidarity.
5. States parties to the present Charter shall undertake to eliminate all forms of foreign economic exploitation particularly that practiced by international monopolies so as to enable their peoples to fully benefit from the advantages derived from their national resources.

Article 22

1. All peoples shall have the right to their economic, social and cultural development with due regard to their freedom and identity and in the equal enjoyment of the common heritage of mankind.
2. States shall have the duty, individually or collectively, to ensure the exercise of the right to development.

Article 23

1. All peoples shall have the right to national and international peace and security. The principles of solidarity and friendly relations implicitly affirmed by the Charter of the United Nations and reaffirmed by that of the Organization of African Unity shall govern relations between States.
2. For the purpose of strengthening peace, solidarity and friendly relations, States parties to the present Charter shall ensure that:

   (a) any individual enjoying the right of asylum under Article 12 of the present Charter shall not engage in subversive activities against his country of origin or any other State party to the present Charter;

   (b) their territories shall not be used as bases for subversive or terrorist activities against the people of any other State party to the present Charter.

Article 24

All peoples shall have the right to a general satisfactory environment favorable to their development.

Article 25

States parties to the present Charter shall have the duty to promote and ensure through teaching, education and publication, the respect of the rights and freedoms contained in the present Charter and to see to it that these freedoms and rights as well as corresponding obligations and duties are understood.

Article 26

States parties to the present Charter shall have the duty to guarantee the independence of the Courts and shall allow the establishment and improvement of appropriate national institutions entrusted with the promotion and protection of the rights and freedoms guaranteed by the present Charter.

CHAPTER II: DUTIES

Article 27

1. Every individual shall have duties towards his family and society, the State and other legally recognized communities and the international community.
2. The rights and freedoms of each individual shall be exercised with due regard to the rights of others, collective security, morality and common interest.

Article 28

Every individual shall have the duty to respect and consider his fellow beings without discrimination, and to maintain relations aimed at promoting, safeguarding and reinforcing mutual respect and tolerance.

Article 29

The individual shall also have the duty:

1. To preserve the harmonious development of the family and to work for the cohesion and respect of the family; to respect his parents at all times, to maintain them in case of need;
2. To serve his national community by placing his physical and intellectual abilities at its service;
3. Not to compromise the security of the State whose national or resident he is;
4. To preserve and strengthen social and national solidarity, particularly when the latter is threatened;
5. To preserve and strengthen the national independence and the territorial integrity of his country and to contribute to its defense in accordance with the law;
6. To work to the best of his abilities and competence, and to pay taxes imposed by law in the interest of the society;
7. To preserve and strengthen positive African cultural values in his relations with other members of the society, in the spirit of tolerance, dialogue and consultation and, in general, to contribute to the promotion of the moral well being of society;
8. To contribute to the best of his abilities, at all times and at all levels, to the promotion and achievement of African unity.

Part II: Measures of Safeguard

CHAPTER I: ESTABLISHMENT AND ORGANIZATION OF THE AFRICAN COMMISSION ON HUMAN AND PEOPLES' RIGHTS

Article 30

An African Commission on Human and Peoples' Rights, hereinafter called 'the Commission', shall be established within the Organization of African Unity to promote human and peoples' rights and ensure their protection in Africa.

Article 31

1. The Commission shall consist of eleven members chosen from amongst African personalities of the highest reputation, known for their high morality, integrity, impartiality and competence in matters of human and peoples' rights; particular consideration being given to persons having legal experience.
2. The members of the Commission shall serve in their personal capacity.

Article 32

The Commission shall not include more than one national of the same state.

Article 33

The members of the Commission shall be elected by secret ballot by the Assembly of Heads of State and Government, from a list of persons nominated by the States parties to the present Charter.

Article 34

Each State party to the present Charter may not nominate more than two candidates. The candidates must have the nationality of one of the States party to the present Charter. When two candidates are nominated by a State, one of them may not be a national of that State.

Article 35

1. The Secretary General of the Organization of African Unity shall invite States parties to the present Charter at least four months before the elections to nominate candidates;
2. The Secretary General of the Organization of African Unity shall make an alphabetical list of the persons thus nominated and communicate it to the Heads of State and Government at least one month before the elections.

Article 36

The members of the Commission shall be elected for a six year period and shall be eligible for re-election. However, the term of office of four of the members elected at the first election shall terminate after two years and the term of office of three others, at the end of four years.

Article 37

Immediately after the first election, the Chairman of the Assembly of Heads of State and Government of the Organization of African Unity shall draw lots to decide the names of those members referred to in Article 36.

Article 38

After their election, the members of the Commission shall make a solemn declaration to discharge their duties impartially and faithfully.

Article 39

1. In case of death or resignation of a member of the Commission the Chairman of the Commission shall immediately inform the Secretary General of the Organization of African Unity, who shall declare the seat vacant from the date of death or from the date on which the resignation takes effect.
2. If, in the unanimous opinion of other members of the Commission, a member has stopped discharging his duties for any reason other than a temporary absence, the

Chairman of the Commission shall inform the Secretary General of the Organization of African Unity, who shall then declare the seat vacant.

3. In each of the cases anticipated above, the Assembly of Heads of State and Government shall replace the member whose seat became vacant for the remaining period of his term unless the period is less than six months.

Article 40

Every member of the Commission shall be in office until the date his successor assumes office.

Article 41

The Secretary General of the Organization of African Unity shall appoint the Secretary of the Commission. He shall also provide the staff and services necessary for the effective discharge of the duties of the Commission. The Organization of African Unity shall bear the costs of the staff and services.

Article 42

1. The Commission shall elect its Chairman and Vice Chairman for a two-year period. They shall be eligible for re-election.
2. The Commission shall lay down its rules of procedure.
3. Seven members shall form the quorum.
4. In case of an equality of votes, the Chairman shall have a casting vote.
5. The Secretary General may attend the meetings of the Commission. He shall not participate in deliberations nor shall he be entitled to vote. The Chairman of the Commission may, however, invite him to speak.

Article 43

In discharging their duties, members of the Commission shall enjoy diplomatic privileges and immunities provided for in the General Convention on the Privileges and Immunities of the Organization of African Unity.

Article 44

Provision shall be made for the emoluments and allowances of the members of the Commission in the Regular Budget of the Organization of African Unity.

CHAPTER II: MANDATE OF THE COMMISSION

Article 45

The functions of the Commission shall be:

1. To promote Human and Peoples' Rights and in particular:
   (a) To collect documents, undertake studies and researches on African problems in the field of human and peoples' rights, organize seminars, symposia and conferences, disseminate information, encourage national and local institutions concerned with human and peoples' rights, and should the case arise, give its views or make recommendations to Governments.
   (b) To formulate and lay down, principles and rules aimed at solving legal problems relating to human and peoples' rights and fundamental freedoms upon which African Governments may base their legislations.

(c) Co-operate with other African and international institutions concerned with the promotion and protection of human and peoples' rights.

2. Ensure the protection of human and peoples' rights under conditions laid down by the present Charter.
3. Interpret all the provisions of the present Charter at the request of a State party, an institution of the OAU or an African Organization recognized by the OAU.
4. Perform any other tasks which may be entrusted to it by the Assembly of Heads of State and Government.

CHAPTER III: PROCEDURE OF THE COMMISSION

Article 46

The Commission may resort to any appropriate method of investigation; it may hear from the Secretary General of the Organization of African Unity or any other person capable of enlightening it.

COMMUNICATION FROM STATES

Article 47

If a State party to the present Charter has good reasons to believe that another State party to this Charter has violated the provisions of the Charter, it may draw, by written communication, the attention of that State to the matter. This communication shall also be addressed to the Secretary General of the OAU and to the Chairman of the Commission. Within three months of the receipt of the communication, the State to which the communication is addressed shall give the enquiring State, written explanation or statement elucidating the matter. This should include as much as possible relevant information relating to the laws and rules of procedure applied and applicable, and the redress already given or course of action available.

Article 48

If within three months from the date on which the original communication is received by the State to which it is addressed, the issue is not settled to the satisfaction of the two States involved through bilateral negotiation or by any other peaceful procedure, either State shall have the right to submit the matter to the Commission through the Chairman and shall notify the other States involved.

Article 49

Notwithstanding the provisions of Article 47, if a State party to the present Charter considers that another State party has violated the provisions of the Charter, it may refer the matter directly to the Commission by addressing a communication to the Chairman, to the Secretary General of the Organization of African Unity and the State concerned.

Article 50

The Commission can only deal with a matter submitted to it after making sure that all local remedies, if they exist, have been exhausted, unless it is obvious to the Commission that the procedure of achieving these remedies would be unduly prolonged.

Article 51

1. The Commission may ask the States concerned to provide it with all relevant information.
2. When the Commission is considering the matter, States concerned may be represented before it and submit written or oral representation.

Article 52

After having obtained from the States concerned and from other sources all the information it deems necessary and after having tried all appropriate means to reach an amicable solution based on the respect of Human and Peoples' Rights, the Commission shall prepare, within a reasonable period of time from the notification referred to in Article 48, a report stating the facts and its findings. This report shall be sent to the States concerned and communicated to the Assembly of Heads of State and Government.

Article 53

While transmitting its report, the Commission may make to the Assembly of Heads of State and Government such recommendations as it deems useful.

Article 54

The Commission shall submit to each ordinary Session of the Assembly of Heads of State and Government a report on its activities.

OTHER COMMUNICATIONS

Article 55

1. Before each Session, the Secretary of the Commission shall make a list of the communications other than those of States parties to the present Charter and transmit them to the members of the Commission, who shall indicate which communications should be considered by the Commission.
2. A communication shall be considered by the Commission if a simple majority of its members so decide.

Article 56

Communications relating to human and peoples' rights referred to in Article 55 received by the Commission, shall be considered if they:

1. Indicate their authors even if the latter request anonymity,
2. Are compatible with the Charter of the Organization of African Unity or with the present Charter,
3. Are not written in disparaging or insulting language directed against the State concerned and its institutions or to the Organization of African Unity,
4. Are not based exclusively on news discriminated through the mass media,
5. Are sent after exhausting local remedies, if any, unless it is obvious that this procedure is unduly prolonged,
6. Are submitted within a reasonable period from the time local remedies are exhausted or from the date the Commission is seized of the matter, and
7. Do not deal with cases which have been settled by these States involved in accordance with the principles of the Charter of the United Nations, or the Charter of the Organization of African Unity or the provisions of the present Charter.

Article 57

Prior to any substantive consideration, all communications shall be brought to the knowledge of the State concerned by the Chairman of the Commission.

Article 58

1. When it appears after deliberations of the Commission that one or more communications apparently relate to special cases which reveal the existence of a series of serious or massive violations of human and peoples' rights, the Commission shall draw the attention of the Assembly of Heads of State and Government to these special cases.
2. The Assembly of Heads of State and Government may then request the Commission to undertake an in-depth study of these cases and make a factual report, accompanied by its findings and recommendations.
3. A case of emergency duly noticed by the Commission shall be submitted by the latter to the Chairman of the Assembly of Heads of State and Government who may request an in-depth study.

Article 59

1. All measures taken within the provisions of the present Charter shall remain confidential until such a time as the Assembly of Heads of State and Government shall otherwise decide.
2. However, the report shall be published by the Chairman of the Commission upon the decision of the Assembly of Heads of State and Government.
3. The report on the activities of the Commission shall be published by its Chairman after it has been considered by the Assembly of Heads of State and Government.

CHAPTER IV: APPLICABLE PRINCIPLES

Article 60

The Commission shall draw inspiration from international law on human and peoples' rights, particularly from the provisions of various African instruments on human and peoples' rights, the Charter of the United Nations, the Charter of the Organization of African Unity, the Universal Declaration of Human Rights, other instruments adopted by the United Nations and by African countries in the field of human and peoples' rights as well as from the provisions of various instruments adopted within the Specialized Agencies of the United Nations of which the parties to the present Charter are members.

Article 61

The Commission shall also take into consideration, as subsidiary measures to determine the principles of law, other general or special international conventions, laying down rules expressly recognized by member states of the Organization of African Unity, African practices consistent with international norms on human and people's rights, customs generally accepted as law, general principles of law recognized by African states as well as legal precedents and doctrine.

Article 62

Each state party shall undertake to submit every two years, from the date the present Charter comes into force, a report on the legislative or other measures taken with a view to giving effect to the rights and freedoms recognized and guaranteed by the present Charter.

Article 63

1. The present Charter shall be open to signature, ratification or adherence of the member states of the Organization of African Unity.
2. The instruments of ratification or adherence to the present Charter shall be deposited with the Secretary General of the Organization of African Unity.
3. The present Charter shall come into force three months after the reception by the Secretary General of the instruments of ratification or adherence of a simple majority of the member states of the Organization of African Unity.

Part III: General Provisions

Article 64

1. After the coming into force of the present Charter, members of the Commission shall be elected in accordance with the relevant Articles of the present Charter.
2. The Secretary General of the Organization of African Unity shall convene the first meeting of the Commission at the Headquarters of the Organization within three months of the constitution of the Commission. Thereafter, the Commission shall be convened by its Chairman whenever necessary but at least once a year.

Article 65

For each of the States that will ratify or adhere to the present Charter after its coming into force, the Charter shall take effect three months after the date of the deposit by that State of its instrument of ratification or adherence.

Article 66

Special protocols or agreements may, if necessary, supplement the provisions of the present Charter.

Article 67

The Secretary General of the Organization of African Unity shall inform member states of the Organization of the deposit of each instrument of ratification or adherence.

Article 68

The present Charter may be amended if a State party makes a written request to that effect to the Secretary General of the Organization of African Unity. The Assembly of Heads of State and Government may only consider the draft amendment after all the States parties have been duly informed of it and the Commission has given its opinion on it at the request of the sponsoring State. The amendment shall be approved by a simple majority of the States parties. It shall come into force for each State which has accepted it in accordance with its constitutional procedure three months after the Secretary General has received notice of the acceptance.

Adopted by the eighteenth Assembly of Heads of State and Government June 1981, Nairobi, Kenya.

Select Bibliography

BOOKS AND MONOGRAPHS

Andenas M and Bjorge E (eds), *A Farewell to Fragmentation: Reassertion and Convergence in International Law* (CUP 2015)

Aust A, *Modern Treaty Law and Practice* (2nd edn, CUP 2007)

Beyani C, *Protection of the Right to Seek and Obtain Asylum Under the African Human Rights System* (Martinus Nijhoff 2013)

Brownlie I, *Principles of Public International Law* (6th edn, OUP 2003)

Cantor DJ and Durieux J (eds), *Refuge from Inhumanity? War Refugees and International Humanitarian Law* (Brill 2014)

D'Orsi C, *Asylum-Seeker and Refugee Protection in Sub-Saharan Africa: The Peregrination of a Persecuted Human Being in Search of a Safe Haven* (Routledge 2015)

Eggli AV, *Mass Refugee Influx and the Limits of Public International Law* (Martinus Nijhoff 2002)

Eriksson L, Melander G, and Nobel P, *An Analysing Account of the Conference on the African Refugee Problem, Arusha, May 1979* (Scandinavian Institute of African Studies 1981)

Ferguson O, *The Common European Asylum System: Background, Current State of Affairs, Future Direction* (TMC Asser 2007)

Fitzpatrick J (ed), *Human Rights Protection for Refugees, Asylum-Seekers and Internally Displaced Persons: A Guide to International Mechanisms and Procedures* (Transnational 2002)

Foster M, *International Refugee Law and Socio-Economic Rights: Refuge from Deprivation* (CUP 2007)

Gardiner R, *Treaty Interpretation* (2nd edn, OUP 2010)

Goodwin-Gill GS and Lambert H (eds), *The Limits of Transnational Law: Refugee Law, Policy Harmonization and Judicial Dialogue in the European Union* (CUP 2010)

Goodwin-Gill GS and McAdam J, *The Refugee in International Law* (3rd edn, OUP 2007)

Grahl-Madsen A, *Commentary on the Refugee Convention* (UNHCR 1963)

Grahl-Madsen A, *The Status of Refugees in International Law*, vols 1 and 2 (Sijthoff 1966)

Guild E, *The First Decade of European Union Migration and Asylum Law* (Martinus Nijhoff 2012)

Handmaker J, de la Hunt L, and Klaaren J (eds), *Advancing Refugee Protection in South Africa* (Berghahn Books 2008)

Harrell-Bond B, *Imposing Aid: Emergency Assistance to Refugees* (OUP 1986)

Hathaway JC, *The Law of Refugee Status* (Butterworths 1991)

Hathaway JC, *The Rights of Refugees Under International Law* (CUP 2005)

Hathaway JC and Foster M, *The Law of Refugee Status* (2nd edn, CUP 2014)

Heyns C, *Human Rights Law in Africa*, vol 1 (Brill 1996)

Heyns C, *Human Rights Law in Africa*, vol 3 (Brill 1998)

Holborn LW, *Refugees: A Problem of our Time—The Work of the United Nations High Commissioner for Refugees, 1951–1972*, vols I and II (Scarecrow Press 1974)

Hurwitz A, *The Collective Responsibility of States to Protect Refugees* (OUP 2009)

Jackson IC, *The Refugee Concept in Group Situations* (Martinus Nijhoff 1999)

Khan F and Schreier T (eds), *Refugee Law in South Africa* (Juta & Co 2014)

Lambert H, McAdam J, and Fullerton M (eds), *The Global Reach of European Refugee Law* (CUP 2013)
Lawyers Committee for Human Rights, *African Exodus: Refugee Crisis, Human Rights and the 1969 OAU Convention* (Lawyers Committee for Human Rights 1995)
McAdam J, *Complementary Protection in International Refugee Law* (OUP 2007)
McNair L, *The Law of Treaties* (OUP 1961)
Milner J, *Refugees, the State and the Politics of Asylum in Africa* (Palgrave Macmillan 2009)
Moreno-Lax V, *Accessing Asylum in Europe: Extraterritorial Border Controls and Refugee Rights under EU Law* (OUP 2017)
Murray R, *Human Rights in Africa: From the OAU to the African Union* (CUP 2004)
Murray R and Evans M (eds), *Documents of the African Commission on Human and Peoples' Rights*, vol 1 (Hart 2001)
Murray R and Long D, *The Implementation of the Findings of the African Commission on Human and Peoples' Rights* (CUP 2015)
Naldi G, *The Organization of African Unity: An Analysis of its Role* (2nd edn, Mansell 1999)
Pobjoy J, *The Child in International Refugee Law* (CUP 2017)
Prunier G, *From Genocide to Continental War: The 'Congolese' Conflict and the Crisis of Contemporary Africa* (Hurst 2009)
Rawlence B, *City of Thorns: Nine Lives in the World's Largest Refugee Camp* (Vintage Canada 2016)
Sadat-Akhavi SA, *Methods of Resolving Conflicts Between Treaties* (Nijhoff 2003)
Sen A, *Poverty and Famines: An Essay on Entitlement and Deprivation* (OUP 1981)
Sinclair I, *The Vienna Convention on the Law of Treaties* (2nd edn, Manchester University Press 1984)
Verdirame G and Harrell-Bond B, *Rights in Exile: Janus Faced Humanitarianism* (Berghahn Books 2005)
Viljoen F, *International Human Rights Law in Africa* (2nd edn, OUP 2012)
Villiger ME, *Commentary on the 1969 Vienna Convention on the Law of Treaties* (Martinus Nijhoff 2009)
Zieck M, *UNHCR and Voluntary Repatriation of Refugees: A Legal Analysis* (Martinus Nijhoff 1997)
Zimmermann A (ed), *The 1951 Convention Relating to the Status of Refugees and its 1967 Protocol: A Commentary* (OUP 2011)

ARTICLES, CHAPTERS, REPORTS AND OCCASIONAL PAPERS

Abass A and Mystris D, 'The African Union Legal Framework for Protecting Asylum Seekers' in Ademola Abass and Francesca Ippolito (eds), *Regional Approaches to the Protection of Asylum Seekers: An International Legal Perspective* (Ashgate 2014)
Abi-Saab G, 'The Admission and Expulsion of Refugees with Special Reference to Africa' (2000) 8 Afr YB Intl L 71
Abuya EO, 'United Nations High Commissioner for Refugees and Status Determination Imtaxaan in Kenya: An Empirical Survey' (2004) 48 J Afr L 193
Abuya EO, 'From Here to Where? Refugees Living in Protracted Situations in Africa' in Alice Edwards and Carla Ferstman (eds), *Human Security and Non-Citizens: Law, Policy and International Affairs* (CUP 2010)
Adepoju A, Boulton A, and Levin M, 'Promoting Integration Through Mobility: Free Movement under ECOWAS' (2010) 10 RSQ 120

Albert M, 'Governance and Prima Facie Refugee Status Determination: Clarifying the Boundaries of Temporary Protection, Group Determination, and Mass Influx' (2010) 29 RSQ 61

Amit R, 'No Refuge: Flawed Status Determination and the Failures of South Africa's Refugee System to Provide Protection' (2011) 23 IJRL 458

Amit R, 'All Roads Lead to Rejection: Persistent Bias and Incapacity in South African Refugee Status Determination' (2012) African Centre for Migration & Society Research Report <http://www.migration.org.za/publication/all-roads-lead-rejection-persistent-bias-and-incapacity-south-african-refugee-status-det> accessed 27 July 2012

Amoah P, 'The African Charter on Human and Peoples' Rights: An Effective Weapon for Human Rights?' (1992) 4 Afr J Intl Comp L 226

Ando N, 'The Evolution and Problems of the Jurisprudence of the Human Rights Committee's Views Concerning Article 26' in Nisuke Ando (ed), *Towards Implementing Universal Human Rights: Festschrift for the Twenty-Fifth Anniversary of the Human Rights Committee* (Brill 2004)

Andrysek O, 'Gaps in International Protection and the Potential for Redress through Individual Complaints Procedures' (1997) 9 IJRL 392

Arboleda E, 'Refugee Definition in Africa and Latin America: The Lessons of Pragmatism' (1991) 3 IJRL 185

Atak I and Simeon J, 'Human Trafficking: Mapping the Legal Boundaries of International Refugee Law and Criminal Justice' (2014) 12 J Intl Crim Justice 1019

Awuku EO, 'Refugee Movements in Africa and the OAU Convention on Refugees' (1995) 39 J Afr L 79

Bakwesegha CJ, 'The OAU and African Refugees' in Yassin El-Ayouty (ed), *The Organization of African Unity after Thirty Years* (Greenwood Publishing Group 1994)

Bakwesegha CJ, 'The Role of the Organization of African Unity in Conflict Prevention, Management and Resolution' (1995) 7 IJRL 207

Barutciski M, 'The Development of Refugee Law and Policy in South Africa: a Commentary on the 1997 Green Paper and 1998 White Paper/Draft Bill' (1998) 10 IJRL 700

Bekker G, 'Mass Expulsion of Foriegn Nationals: A 'Special Violation of Human Rights' – Communication 292/2004 Institute for Human Rights and Development in Africa v Republic of Angola' (2009) 9 Afr Hum Rts LJ 262

Bekker G, 'The Protection of Asylum Seekers and Refugees within the African Regional Human Rights System' (2013) 12 Afr Hum Rts LJ 1

Bewes WA, 'Public Order (Ordre Public)' (1921) 37 L Q Rev 315

Beyani C, 'The Role of Human Rights Bodies in Protecting Refugees' in Anne Bayefsky (ed), *Human Rights and Refugees, Internally Displaced Persons and Migrant Workers: Essays in Memory of Joan Fitzpatrick and Arthur Helton* (Martinus Nijhoff 2005)

Beyani C, 'Recent Developments in the African Human Rights System 2004–2006' (2007) 7 Hum Rts L Rev 582

Borgen CJ, 'Resolving Treaty Conflicts' (2005) 37 Geo Wash Intl LR 573

Brown N, Riordan S, and Sharpe M, 'The Insecurity of Eritreans and Ethiopians in Cairo' (2004) 16 IJRL 661

Carciotto S and D'Orsi C, 'Access to Socio-Economic Rights for Refugees: A Comparison Across Six African Countries' (March 2017) The Scalabrini Institute for Human Mobility in Africa <http://sihma.org.za/wp-content/uploads/2017/03/Access-to-socio-economic-rights_refugees.pdf> accessed 28 March 2017

Centre for Refugee Studies Refugee Research Unit, York University, 'The Temporary Protection of Refugees: A Solution-Oriented and Rights Regarding Approach' (1996)

Discussion Paper prepared under the auspices of the research project 'Toward the Reformulation of International Refugee Law'

Chartrand PE, 'The Organization of African Unity and African Refugees: A Progress Report' (1975) 137 World Aff 265

Chaulia SS, 'The Politics of Refugee Hosting in Tanzania: From Open Door to Unsustainability, Insecurity and Receding Receptivity' (2003) 3 JRS 147

Chetail V, 'Are Refugee Rights Human Rights? An Unorthodox Questioning of the Relations between Refugee Law and Human Rights Law' in R Rubio-Marin (ed), *Human Rights and Immigration, Collected Courses of the Academy of European Law* (OUP 2014)

Clark T, 'Rights Based Refuge, the Potential of the 1951 Convention and the Need for Authoritative Interpretation' (2004) 16 IJRL 584

Clark T and Crépeau F, 'Mainstreaming Refugee Rights: The 1951 Refugee Convention and International Human Rights Law' (1999) 17 NQHR 389

Corliss S, 'Asylum State Responsibility for the Hostile Acts of Foreign Exiles' (1990) 2 IJRL 181

Costello C and Foster M, 'Non-refoulement as Custom and Jus Cogens? Putting the Prohibition to the Test' (2016) 46 NYIL 2015 273

Crisp J, 'Africa's Refugees: Patterns, Problems and Policy Challenges' (2000) 8 Afr YB Intl L 93

Crisp J, 'No Solution in Sight: The Problem of Protracted Refugee Situations in Africa' in Itaru Ohta and Yntiso D Gebre (eds), *Displacement Risks in Africa: Refugees, Resettlers and Their Host Population* (Kyoto University Press 2005)

Crisp J, 'Forced Displacement in Africa: Dimensions, Difficulties, and Policy Directions' (2010) 29 RSQ 1

Crush J and Chikanda A, 'Forced Migration in Southern Africa' in Elena Fiddian-Qasmiyeh and others (eds), *The Oxford Handbook of Refugee and Forced Migration Studies* (OUP 2014)

Davies SE, 'Redundant or Essential? How Politics Shaped the Outcome of the 1967 Protocol' (2007) 19 IJRL 703

de Groot G, 'Children, Their Right to a Nationality and Child Statelessness' in Alice Edwards and Laura van Waas (eds), *Nationality and Statelessness Under International Law* (CUP 2014)

de la Hunt L, 'Refugee Law in South Africa: Making the Road of the Refugee Longer' in Legal Resources Foundation, *A Reference Guide to Refugee Law and Issues in Southern Africa* (Legal Resources Foundation, 2002)

Doebbler C, 'Complex Ambiguity: The Relationship between the African Comission on Human and Peoples' Rights and Other African Union Initiatives Affecting Respect for Human Rights' (2003) 13 Transnat'l L & Contemp Probs 7

D'Orsi C, 'Sub-Saharan Africa: Is a New Special Regional Refugee Law Regime Emerging?' (2008) 68 Heidelberg J Intl L 1057

D'Sa R, 'The African Refugee Problem, Relevant International Conventions and Recent Activities of the Organization of African Unity' (1984) 31 NILR 378

D'Sa R, 'Human and Peoples Rights: Distinctive Features of the African Charter' (1985) 29 J Afr L 72

Durieux J, 'The Many Faces of "Prima Facie": Group-Based Evidence in Refugee Status Determination' (2008) 25 Refuge 151

Durieux J and Hurwitz A, 'How Many Is Too Many? African and European Legal Responses to Mass Influx of Refugees' (2004) 47 German YB Intl L 105

Durieux J and McAdam J, 'Non-Refoulement through Time: The Case for a Derogation Clause to the Refugee Convention in Mass Influx Emergencies' (2004) 16 IJRL 4

Edwards A, 'Human Rights, Refugees, and the Right "To Enjoy" Asylum' (2005) 17 IJRL 293

Edwards A, 'Refugee Status Determination in Africa' (2006) 14 Afr J Intl Comp L 204

Farrell T and Schmitt O, 'The Causes, Character and Conduct of Internal Armed Conflict and the Effects on Civilian Populations, 1990–2010' in Volker Türk, Alice Edwards, and Cornelis Wouters (eds), *In Flight from Conflict and Violence: UNHCR's Consultations on Refugee Status and Other Forms of International Protection* (CUP 2017)

Fischer-Lescano A and Teubner G, 'Regime-Collisions: The Vain Search for Legal Unity in the Fragmentation of Global Law' (2004) 25 Mich J Intl L 999

Fitzpatrick J, 'Temporary Protection of Refugees: Elements of a Formalized Regime' (2000) 94 AJIL 279

Fitzpatrick J, 'Current Issues in Cessation of Protection Under Article 1C of the 1951 Refugee Convention and Article I.4 of the 1969 OAU Convention' (2001) UNHCR <http://eee.refworld.org/docid/3bf925ef4.html> accessed 13 January 2015

Fresia M, 'Forced Migration in West Africa' in Elena Fiddian-Qasmiyeh and others (eds), *The Oxford Handbook of Refugee and Forced Migration Studies* (OUP 2014)

Gabrielli L, 'Multilevel Inter-Regional Governance of Mobility Between Africa and Europe' (2016) Interdisciplinary Research Group on Immigration Working Paper Series <https://www.upf.edu/documents/3329791/0/L.+Gabrielli+-+GRITIM+WP+30+2016.pdf/4a034bb9-882d-9721-2cd6-20b133d63945> accessed 3 April 2017

Garlick M, Guild E, Procter C, and Salomons M, 'Building on the Foundation: Formative Evaluation of the Refugee Status Determination Transition Process in Kenya' (UNHCR 2015)

Gilbert G, 'Rights, Legitimate Expectations, Needs and Responsibilities: UNHCR and the New World Order' (1998) 10 IJRL 349

Gittleman R, 'African Charter on Human and Peoples' Rights: A Legal Analysis' (1981–1982) 22 Va J Intl L 667

Goodwin-Gill GS, 'Non-refoulement and the New Asylum Seekers' (1986) 26 Va J Intl L 897

Goodwin-Gill GS, 'International Law and Human Rights: Trends Concerning International Migrants and Refugees' (1989) 23 Intl Migr Rev 526

Goodwin-Gill GS, 'Non-refoulement, Temporary Refuge, and the "New" Asylum Seekers' in Cantor DJ and Durieux J-F (eds), *Refuge from Inhumanity? War Refugees and International Humanitarian Law* (Brill Nijhoff 2014)

Goundiam O, 'African Refugee Convention' [1970] Migr News 3

Grahl-Madsen A, 'Political Rights and Freedoms of Refugees' in Goran Melander and Peter Nobel (eds), *African Refugees and the Law* (The Scandinavian Institute of African Studies 1978)

Grahl-Madsen A, 'Commentary on the Refugee Convention 1951: Articles 2–11, 13–37' (1997) UNHCR <http://www.refworld.org/pdfid/4785ee9d2.pdf> accessed 13 January 2017

Greenfield R, 'The OAU and Africa's Refugees' in Yassin El-Ayouty and I William Zartman (eds), *The OAU After Twenty Years* (Praeger 1984)

Hailbronner M, 'Laws in Conflict: The Relationship Between Human Rights and International Humanitarian Law under the African Charter on Human and Peoples' Rights' (2016) 16 Afr Hum Rts LJ 339

Hanafi S, 'Forced Migration in the Middle East and North Africa' in Elena Fiddian-Qasmiyeh and others (eds), *The Oxford Handbook of Refugee and Forced Migration Studies* (OUP 2014)

Harrington J, 'Special Rapporteurs of the African Commission on Human and Peoples' Rights' (2001) 1 Afr Hum Rts LJ 247

Harvey C, 'Time for Reform? Refugees, Asylum-seekers, and Protection Under International Human Rights Law' (2015) 34 RSQ 43

Hathaway JC, 'Reconceiving Refugee Law as Human Rights Protection' (1991) 4 JRS 113

Hathaway JC, 'Fear of Persecution and the Law of Human Rights' (1992) 91 Bull Hum Rts 98

Hathaway JC, 'Leveraging Asylum' (2009) 45 Texas Intl LJ 503

Hathaway OA, 'Do Human Rights Treaties Make a Difference?' (2002) 111 Yale LJ 1935

Helmersen ST, 'Evolutive Treaty Interpretation: Legality, Semantics and Distinctions' (2013) 6 Euro J Leg Stud 127

Herlitz GN, 'The Meaning of the Term "Prima Facie"' (1994–1995) 55 Louisiana L Rev 391

Heyns C, 'The African Regional Human Rights System: The African Charter' (2003–04) 108 Penn State L Rev 679

Heyns C, 'Some Thoughts on Challenges Facing the International Protection of Human Rights in Africa' (2009) 27 NQHR 447

Heyns C and Viljoen F, 'An Overview of International Human Rights Protection in Africa' (1999) 15 S Afr J Hum Rts 421

Hofmann R, 'Refugee Law in the African Context' (1992) 52 Heidelberg J Intl L 318

Hovil L and Okello MC, 'The Right to Freedom of Movement for Refugees in Uganda' in David Hollenbach (ed), *Refugee Rights: Ethics, Advocacy and Africa* (Georgetown University Press 2008)

Hyndman J and Nylund BV, 'UNHCR and the Status of Prima Facie Refugees in Kenya' (1998) 10 IJRL 21

International Law Commission, 'Fragmentation of International Law: Difficulties Arising from the Diversification and Expansion of International Law—Report of the Study Group of the International Law Commission' (13 April 2006) A/CN4/L682

Jahn E, 'Development in Refugee Law in the Framework of Regional Organizations Outside Europe' (1966) 4 Association for the Study of the World Refugee Problem Bulletin 77

Jahn E, 'The Work of the Asian-African Legal Consultative Committee on the Legal Status of Refugees' (1967) 27 Heidelberg J Intl L 122

Jenks CW, 'The Conflict of Law-Making Treaties' (1953) 30 B YB Intl L 401

Juma D, 'Access to the African Court on Human and Peoples' Rights: A Case of the Poacher Turned Gamekeeper' (2007) 4 Essex Hum Rts Rev 1

Kagan M, 'Legal Refugee Recognition in the Urban South: Formal v. De Facto Refugee Status' (2007) 24 Refuge 11

Kaime T, 'From Lofty Jargon to Durable Solutions: Unaccompanied Refugee Children and the African Charter on the Rights and Welfare of the Child' (2004) 16 IJRL 336

Kälin W, 'Refugees and Civil Wars: Only a Matter of Interpretation?' (1991) 3 IJRL 435

Kamanga K, 'The (Tanzania) Refugees Act of 1998: Some Legal and Policy Implications' (2005) 18 JRS 100

Kibreab G, 'Forced Migration in the Great Lakes and Horn of Africa' in Elena Fiddian-Qasmiyeh and others (eds), *The Oxford Handbook of Refugee and Forced Migration Studies* (OUP 2014)

Kioko B, 'The Right of Intervention Under the African Union's Constitutive Act: From Non-interference to Non-intervention' (2003) 85 IRRC 807

Kolmannskog V, '"We Are in Between": Case Studies of the Protection of Somalis Displaced to Kenya and Egypt During the 2011 and 2012 Drought' (2014) 2 Intl J Soc Sci Stud 83

Koskenniemi M and Leino P, 'Fragmentation of International Law: Postmodern Anxieties?' (2002) 15 Leiden J Intl L 553

Kuch A, 'Naturalization of Burundian Refugees in Tanzania: The Debates on Local Integration and the Meaning of Citizenship Revisited' (2017) 30 JRS 468

Kuruk P, 'Asylum and the Non-Refoulement of Refugees: The Case of the Missing Shipload of Liberian Refugees' (1999) 35 Stanford J Intl L 313

Lauterpacht E and Bethlehem D, 'The Scope and Content of the Principle of Non-refoulement: Opinion' in Erika Feller, Volker Türk, and Frances Nicholson (eds), *Refugee Protection in International Law: UNHCR's Global Consultations on International Protection* (CUP 2003)

Levitt J, 'Conflict Prevention, Management, and Resolution: Africa—Regional Strategies for the Prevention of Displacement and Protection of Displaced Persons: The Cases of the OAU, ECOWAS, SADC and IGAD' (2001) 11 Duke J Comp Intl L 39

Levitt J, 'The Peace and Security Council of the African Union: The Known Unknowns' (2003) 13 Transnat'l L & Contemp Probs 109

Lloyd A and Murray R, 'Institutions with Responsibility for Human Rights Protection under the African Union' (2004) 48 J Afr L 165

Lomo ZA, 'The Struggle for the Protection of the Rights of Refugees and IDPs in Africa: Making the Existing International Legal Regime Work' (2000) 18 Berk J Intl L 268

Macharia-Mokobi E and Pfumorodze J, 'Advancing Refugee Protection in Botswana Through Improved Refugee Status Determination' (2013) 13 Afr Hum Rts LJ 152

Maluwa T, 'International Law Making in the Organization of African Unity: An Overview' (2000) 12 Afr J Intl Comp L 201

Mandal R, 'Political Rights of Refugees' (2003) UNHCR Legal and Protection Policy Research Series <http://www.refworld.org/pdfid/3fe820794.pdf> accessed 12 January 2015

Mandal R, 'Protection Mechanisms Outside the 1951 Convention ("Complementary Protection")' (2005) UNHCR Legal and Protection Policy Research Series <http://www.unhcr.org/435df0aa2.pdf> accessed 8 December 2010

Mangu AMB, 'The Changing Human Rights Landscape in Africa: Organisation of African Unity, African Union, New Partnership for Africa's Development and the African Court' (2005) 23 NQHR 379

Maple N, 'Rights at Risk: A Thematic Investigation into how States Restrict the Freedom of Movement of Refugees on the African Continent' (2016) UNHCR New Issues in Refugee Research Paper No 281 <http://www.unhcr.org/57ee60d57.pdf> accessed 11 January 2018

Matas D, 'A History of the Politics of Refugee Protection' in Kathleen Mahoney and Paul Mahoney (eds), *Human Rights in the Twenty-first Century: A Global Challenge* (Martinus Nijhoff 1993)

Mbaya E, 'Political Asylum in the Charter of the OAU: Pretensions and Reality' (1987) 35 L & State 63

McAdam J, 'Status Anxiety: Complementary Protection and the Rights of Non-Convention Refugees' (2010) University of New South Wales Faculty of Law Research Series <http://law.bepress.com/unswwps/flrps10/art1/> accessed 13 October 2011

McCrudden C, 'Equality and Discrimination' in David Feldman (ed), *English Public Law*, vol XI (OUP 2004)

McLachlan C, 'The Principle of Systemic Integration and Article 31(3)(c) of the Vienna Convention' (2005) 54 Intl & Comp LQ 279

Mendel TD, 'Refugee Law and Practice in Tanzania' (1995) 9 IJRL 35

Milanovic M, 'Norm Conflicts, International Humanitarian Law and Human Rights Law' in Orna Ben-Naftali (ed), *Human Rights and International Humanitarian Law, Collected Courses of the Academy of European Law*, vol XIX/1 (OUP 2010)

Moreno-Lax V, 'Seeking Asylum in the Mediterranean: Against a Fragmentary Reading of EU Member States' Obligations Accruing at Sea' (2011) 23 IJRL 174

Moreno-Lax V, 'Systematising Systemic Integration: "War Refugees", Regime Relations, and a Proposal for a Cumulative Approach to International Commitments' (2014) 12 J Intl Crim Justice 907

Mubangizi J, 'Some Reflections on Recent and Current Trends in the Promotion and Protection of Human Rights in Africa: The Pains and the Gains' (2006) 6 Afr Hum Rts LJ 146

Mujuzi JD, 'The African Commission on Human and Peoples' Rights and the Promotion and Protection of Refugees' Rights' (2009) 9 Afr Hum Rts LJ 160

Murray R, 'The African Charter on Human and Peoples' Rights 1987–2000: An Overview of its Progress and Problems' (2001) 1 Afr Hum Rts LJ 1

Murray R, 'Refugees and Internally Displaced Persons and Human Rights: the African System' (2005) 24 RSQ 56

Murray R, 'International Human Rights: Neglect of Perspective from African Institutions' (2006) 55 Intl & Comp LQ 193

Naldi GJ, 'Limitation of Rights Under the African Charter on Human and Peoples' Rights: The Contribution of the African Commission on Human and Peoples' Rights' (2001) 17 S Afr J Hum Rts 109

Naldi GJ and D'Orsi C, 'The Role of the African Human Rights System with Reference to Asylum Seekers' in Ademola Abass and Francesca Ippolito (eds), *Regional Approaches to the Protection of Asylum Seekers: An International Legal Perspective* (Ashgate 2014)

Naldi GJ and D'Orsi C, 'The Multi-faceted Aspects of Asylum-Law Applicable to Africa: Analysis for Reflection' (2014) 36 Loy LA Intl & Comp L Rev 115

Ngung EM, 'The Role of Regional and Sub-Regional Organizations in Situations of Conflict and Displacement' (1999) 18 RSQ 97

Nkhoma TS, 'The Institution of Asylum in Malawi and International Refugee Law: A Review of the 1989 Refugee Act' (2010) 4 Malawi LJ 97

Nobel P, 'Refugees, Law, and Development in Africa' (1982) 3 Mich YB Intl L Stud 255

Nyanduga BTM, 'Refugee Protection Under the 1969 OAU Convention Governing the Specific Aspects of Refugee Problems in Africa' (2004) 47 German YB Intl L 85

Odinkalu C, 'From Architecture to Geometry: The Relationship Between the African Commission on Human and Peoples' Rights and Organs of the African Union' (2013) 35 Hum Rts Q 850

Okogbule NS, 'The Legal Dimensions of the Refugee Problem in Africa' (2004) 10 E Afr J Peace & Hum Rts 176

Okoth-Obbo G, 'The OAU/UNHCR Symposium on Refugees and Forced Population Displacements in Africa-A Review Article' [Special Issue Summer 1995] IJRL 274

Okoth-Obbo G, 'Thirty Years On: A Legal Review of the 1969 OAU Convention Governing the Specific Aspects of Refugee Problems in Africa' (2001) 20 RSQ 79

Oloka-Onyango J, 'Human Rights, the OAU Convention and the Refugee Crisis in Africa: Forty Years After Geneva' (1991) 3 IJRL 453

Oloka-Onyango J, 'The Place and Role of the OAU Bureau for Refugees in the African Refugee Crisis' (1994) 6 IJRL 344

Oosterveld V, 'Gender at the Intersection of International Refugee Law and International Criminal Law' (2014) 12 J Intl Crim Justice 953

Perluss D and Fitzpatrick Hartman J, 'Temporary Refuge: Emergence of a Customary Norm' (1986) 26 Va J Intl L 551

Peters A, 'The Refinement of International Law: From Fragmentation to Regime Interaction and Politicization' (2016) Max Planck Institute for Comparative Public Law & International Law Research Paper No 2016–19

Plender R and Mole N, 'Beyond the Geneva Convention: Constructing a De Facto Right of Asylum from International Human Rights Instruments' in Frances Nicholson and Patrick Twomey (eds), *Refugee Rights and Realities: Evolving International Concepts and Regimes* (CUP 1999)

Pobjoy J, 'Treating Like Alike: The Principle of Non-Discrimination as a Tool to Mandate the Equal Treatment of Refugees and Beneficiaries of Complementary Protection' (2010) 34 MULR 181

Ramcharan R, 'The African Refugee Crisis: Contemporary Challenges to the Protection of Refugees and Displaced Persons in Africa' (2000) 8 Afr YB Intl L 119

Rankin MB, 'Extending the Limits or Narrowing the Scope? Deconstructing the OAU Refugee Definition Thirty Years On' (2005) 21 S Afr J Hum Rts 406

Reitano T, 'The Khartoum Process: A Sustainable Response to Human Smuggling and Trafficking?' Institute for Security Studies (30 November 2016) <https://issafrica.org/research/policy-brief/the-khartoum-process-a-sustainable-response-to-human-smuggling-and-trafficking> accessed 12 March 2017

Rutinwa B, 'Prima Facie Status and Refugee Protection' (2002) UNHCR New Issues in Refugee Research Working Paper No 69 <http://www.unhcr.org/3db9636c4.pdf> accessed 8 December 2010

Rutinwa B, 'The End of Asylum? The Changing Nature of Refugee Policies in Africa' (2002) 21 RSQ 12

Rutinwa B, 'Relationship Between the 1951 Refugee Convetion and the 1969 OAU Convention on Refugees' in Volker Türk, Alice Edwards, and Cornelis Wouters (eds), *In Flight from Conflict and Violence: UNHCR's Consultations on Refugee Status and Other Forms of International Protection* (CUP 2017)

Rwelamira MRK, 'Some Reflections on the OAU Convention on Refugees: Some Pending Issues' (1983) 16 Comp & Intl LJ S Afr 155

Rwelamira MRK, 'Two Decades of the 1969 OAU Convention Governing the Specific Aspects of the Refugee Problem in Africa' (1989) 1 IJRL 557

Sandvik K, 'A Legal History: The Emergence of the African Resettlement Candidate in International Refugee Management' (2010) 22 IJRL 20

Sceats S, 'Africa's New Human Rights Court: Whistling in the Wind?' (2009) Chatham House <https://www.chathamhouse.org/publications/papers/view/109010> Accessed 18 April 2018

Schachter O, 'Legal Aspects of the Refugee Problem' in HC Brooks and Y El-Ayouty (eds), *Refugees South of the Sahara: An African Dilemma* (Negro University Press 1970)

Schreier TH, 'An Evaluation of South Africa's Application of the OAU Refugee Definition' (2008) 25 Refuge 53

Schreier TH, 'The Expanded Refugee Definition' in Fatima Khan and Tal Schreier (eds), *Refugee Law in South Africa* (Juta 2014)

Sharpe M, 'The 1969 African Refugee Convention: Innovations, Misconceptions, and Omissions' (2012) 58 McGill LJ 95

Sharpe M, 'Organization of African Unity and African Union Engagement with Refugee Protection: 1963–2011' (2013) 21 Afr J Intl Comp L 50

Sharpe M, 'The 1951 Refugee Convention's Contingent Rights Framework and Article 26 of the ICCPR: A Fundamental Incompatibility?' (2014) 30 Refuge 5

Sharpe M, 'The 1969 OAU Refugee Convention in the Context of Individual Refugee Status Determination' in Volker Türk, Alice Edwards, and Cornelis Wouters (eds), *In Flight from Conflict and Violence: UNHCR's Consultations on Refugee Status and Other Forms of International Protection* (CUP 2017)

Sharpe M and Namusobya S, 'Refugee Status Determination and the Rights of Recognized Refugees under Uganda's Refugees Act 2006' (2012) 24 IJRL 561

Sperl S and Bradisteanu I, 'Refugee Resettlement in Developing Countries: The Experience of Benin and Burkina Faso, 1997–2003' UNHCR Evaluation and Policy Analysis Unit and Resettlement and Special Cases Section (2004) <http://www.refworld.org/docid/546467964.html> accessed 18 April 2017

Takahashi S, 'Recourse to Human Rights Treaty Bodies for Monitoring of the Refugee Convention' (2002) 20 NQHR 53

Tigere P and Amukhobu R, 'The African Union's Institutional Framework for Responding to Forced Displacement in Africa' [2005] Conflict Trends 48

Tuepker A, 'On the Threshold of Africa: OAU and UN Definitions in South African Asylum Practice' (2002) 15 JRS 409

Turner JL, 'Liberian Refugees: a Test of the 1969 OAU Convention Governing the Specific Aspects of Refugee Problems in Africa' (1994) 8 Geo Immigr LJ 281

Vadachalam A, 'Does the 1969 OAU Convention Governight the Specific Aspects of Refugee Problems in Africa Article III Provision Prohibiting "Subversive Activities" Unjustifiably Limit the Freedom of Expression of a Refugee?: A South African Answer' (2014) University of Cape Town Refugee Rights Unit Working Paper No 1 <http://www.refugeerights.uct.ac.za/usr/refugee/Working_papers/Working_Paper_1_of_2014.pdf> accessed 12 January 2015

Van Aaken A, 'Defragmentation of Public International Law Through Interpretation: A Methodological Proposal' (2009) 16 Indiana J Global Leg Stud 483

Van Garderen J and Ebenstein J, 'Regional Developments: Africa' in Andreas Zimmermann (ed), *The 1951 Convention Relating to the Status of Refugees and its 1967 Protocol* (OUP 2011)

Van Hövell tot Westerflier WJEM, 'Africa and Refugees: the OAU Refugee Convention in Theory and Practice' (1989) 7 NQHR 172

Viljoen F, 'The Realization of Human Rights in Africa Through Sub-regional Institutions' (1999) 7 Afr YB Intl L 186

Viljoen F, 'A Human Rights Court for Africa, and Africans' (2004–05) 30 Brooklyn J Intl L 1

Viljoen F, 'From a Cat into a Lion? An Overview of the Progress and Challenges of the African Human Rights System at the African Commission's 25 Year Mark' (2013) 17 L, Dem & Devel 298

Viljoen F and Louw L, 'The Status of the Findings of the African Commission: From Moral Persuasion to Legal Obligation' (2004) 48 J Afr L 1

Viljoen F and Louw L, 'State Compliance with the Recommendations of the African Commission on Human and Peoples' Rights 1994–2004' (2007) 101 AJIL 1

Weis P, 'Legal Aspects of the Convention of 25 July 1951 relating to the Status of Refugees' (1953) 30 B YB Intl L 478

Weis P, 'The United Nations Declaration on Territorial Asylum' (1969) 7 Can YB Intl L 92

Weis P, 'The Convention of the Organization of African Unity Governing the Specific Aspects of Refugee Problems in Africa' (1970) 3 Rev des droits de l'homme 449

Wilkinson R, 'Thirty Years After … The OAU Refugee Convention was a Model of Generosity, but Times Have Changed' [1999] Refugees 4

Wood T, 'The African War Refugee: Using IHL to Interpret the 1969 African Refugee Convention's Expanded Refugee Definition' in David James Cantor and Jean-Francois

Durieux (eds), *Refuge from Inhumanity? Refugee Protection and the Laws of War* (Martinus Nijhoff 2014)

Wood T, 'Expanding Protection in Africa? Case Studies of the Implementation of the 1969 African Refugee Convention's Expanded Refugee Definition' (2015) 26 IJRL 555

Wood T, 'Protection and Disasters in the Horn of Africa: Norms and Practice for Addressing Cross-Border Displacement in Disaster Contexts' (2015) The Nansen Initiative <https://www2.nanseninitiative.org/wp-content/uploads/2015/03/190215_Technical_Paper_Tamara_Wood.pdf> accessed 18 April 2018

Zard M, 'African Union' in Matthew Gibney and Randall Hansen (eds), *Immigration and Asylum From 1900 to the Present* (ABC-CLIO 2005)

Index

The manufacturer's authorised representative in the EU for product safety is Oxford University Press España S.A. of el Parque Empresarial San Fernando de Henares, Avenida de Castilla, 2 – 28830 Madrid (www.oup.es/en or product.safety@oup.com). OUP España S.A. also acts as importer into Spain of products made by the manufacturer.

www.ingramcontent.com/pod-product-compliance
Lightning Source LLC
LaVergne TN
LVHW011748200926
848484LV00003B/652
9780198826224